Ivan Bunin
Russian Requiem, 1885–1920

IVAN BUNIN
RUSSIAN REQUIEM
1885–1920

* * *

A Portrait from
Letters, Diaries, and Fiction

*

EDITED WITH AN INTRODUCTION AND NOTES BY

Thomas Gaiton Marullo

IVAN R. DEE
Chicago · 1993

IVAN BUNIN: RUSSIAN REQUIEM, 1885–1920. Copyright ©
1993 by Thomas Gaiton Marullo. All rights reserved, including
the right to reproduce this book or portions thereof in any form.
For information, address: Ivan R. Dee, Inc., 1332 North Halsted
Street, Chicago 60622. Manufactured in the United States of
America and printed on acid-free paper.

Grateful acknowledgment is made to Possev-Verlag for permission
to use excerpts from *Ustami Buninykh*, and to Zaria Publishers for
permission to use excerpts from *Okaiannye dni*.

Library of Congress Cataloging-in-Publication Data:
Ivan Bunin : Russian requiem, 1885–1920 : a portrait from
   letters, diaries, and fiction / edited with an introduction
   and notes by Thomas Gaiton Marullo.
        p.   cm.
   Includes bibliographical references and index.
   ISBN 1-56663-012-6 (alk. paper)
      1. Bunin, Ivan Alekseevich, 1870–1953. 2. Authors,
   Russian—20th century—Biography.   I. Marullo, Thomas
   Gaiton.
   PG3453.B9Z72   1993
   891.78'309—dc20
   [B]   92-44233

To my mother, Elizabeth Marullo,
and
to the memory of my father, Thomas Marullo,
my first educators

PREFACE

IN MAY 1942 Ivan Bunin wrote in his Last Will and Testament, "There exist all kinds of letters to me in Russia. If these have been saved, then destroy them all *without reading them*, except for those that were written by more or less well-known writers, editors, public figures, and the like (and only if these letters are more or less interesting). Also, do not print or publish any of *my* letters.... This I ask of all my correspondents. Circumstances almost always forced me to write hastily, and in a bad and careless frame of mind; these letters rarely reflect my actual feelings at the time."[1]

Bunin was seventy-two years old when he wrote this and would live for eleven more years; but he had known enough chaos to fill several lifetimes and had learned to be wary. He was, in 1942, in his twenty-second year of exile from Russia. He had endured three revolutions and two world wars, the second of which still raged about his emigré home in Grasse, France. As was the case many times in his life, both in Russia and abroad, Bunin was in fact sick, poor, and despairing.

Bunin's Last Will and Testament leaves investigators of his life and work in a dilemma. On one hand they feel drawn, however grudgingly, to respect the wishes of the dead and to pass over many of Bunin's personal writings in silence. On the other hand they yearn to open new perspectives on Bunin's life and art.

There is ample evidence, despite his 1942 Testament, to show that Bunin would eventually allow researchers—"literary gravediggers,"[2] he called them—to have their way. Probably he would have delighted in having his life story told in the first person, and from a highly engaging, if selective, point of view. But making sense of Bunin's personal writings

[1]P. Viacheslavov, "Literaturnoe zaveshchanie I. A. Bunina," *Moskva*, no. 4 (1962), 222.
[2]*Ibid.*

vii

is difficult, for they reflect a singularly complex individual amidst complex times. Bunin and his Russia were like two lovers from Dostoevsky: passionate, doomed, and unable to live with or without each other.

Bunin valued personal writing as much as he did artistic literature. He particularly loved diaries, his own and others, and he often regretted that many of the masters of Russian fiction had not left behind personal journals. "The diary is one of the most splendid literary forms," Bunin wrote in his own journal on February 23, 1916. "I think this form will force out all others in the not so distant future."[3] Reaffirming the value of diaries to Galina Kuznetsova years later as an emigré, Bunin claimed, "Here life is as it is: Everything is all stuffed in.... All the rest is nonsense!"[4] Diaries, he thought, should be seen by readers not as esoteric incunabula of archives and museums but as viable pieces of literature in their own right, perhaps even as valuable as the writer's works. "We know almost nothing about Pushkin's life," Bunin lamented to Nikolai Pusheshnikov. "If only Pushkin had written down what he saw and did, simply and without thinking about literature, what a book he would have written!"[5]

To Bunin, diaries were fertile seedbeds for a writer's images and ideals, telling commentaries on his inner and outer worlds. They could also be models of good fictional writing. In diaries, he suggested, writers could propose their ideas and images boldly, without the niceties of plot and other literary stratagems. They might enter into genuine "dialogue"[6] with their readers, affirming the moments and minutiae of life. Most important for Bunin, diaries helped him overcome a gnawing fear that his name and work would be lost forever. From his earliest years Bunin brooded over what lay beyond the grave, but the thought that he would be merely a footnote in the history of Russian literature, rather than a chapter, was even more terrifying.

"My life is doomed to decay and oblivion.... The consciousness... of this horror has haunted me almost since infancy.... I lived not only to write. I wanted glory, praise, even immortality.... I have always shuddered at the thought that after my death my books would wither

[3]M. Grin, ed., *Ustami Buninykh. Dnevniki Ivana Alekseevicha i Very Nikolaevny i drugie arkhivnye materialy*, vol. 1 (Frankfurt/Main, 1977), 149.

[4]G. Kuznetsova, *Grasskii dnevnik* (Washington, D.C., 1967), 91, 92.

[5]A. Baboreko, "I. A. Bunin na Kapri (Po neopublikovannym materialam)," *V bol'shoi sem'e* (Smolensk, 1960), 248.

[6]The principle of "dialog" or "dialogism" in literature, is, of course, recognized as a key idea of the Russian critic Mikhail Bakhtin (1895–1975). For more on literary "dialogism," see M. Holquist, *Dialogism: Bakhtin and His World* (New York, 1990); G. Morson and C. Emerson, *Mikhail Bakhtin: Creation of a Prosaics* (Stanford, 1990); T. Todorov, *The Dialogical Principle* (Minneapolis, 1984); and M. Bakhtin, *The Dialogic Imagination: Four Essays* (Austin, Tex., 1981).

away on library shelves . . . that thin-legged, petty bourgeois children would run around and scream idiotically about my bust in some cemetery or square . . . and that my tombstone would read: 'to so-and-so,' and who would care?"[7] This fear of oblivion, more than anything else, would have led Bunin to agree that excerpts from his personal writings be published.

In this book I consider a Bunin diary in the largest sense of this word. That is, I see it as a journal which Bunin could willingly embrace as his, a poignant and personal commentary on the first fifty years of his life and the "dark night" between the twilight of imperial Russia and the dawn of the new Soviet state. I have used selections from Bunin's diaries, letters, critical articles, and fictional works from the years between 1885 and 1920, that is, from Bunin's adolescence and early adulthood to his leaving Russia forever; and interpolations from the memoirs of Bunin's wife, Vera Muromtseva-Bunina, and from the writings of family, friends, colleagues, and critics in the same period. My focus is on Bunin and his world, specifically the political, social, and cultural aspects of a homeland in revolution and war. My hope is to present Bunin in a new light to the English-speaking world, so that readers will take up his other works and accord him the respect and admiration he deserves.

With the exception of Bunin's fictional works and the memoirs of Valentin Kataev, most of the materials in this study are here translated into English for the first time. All the translations are my own with the exception of Olga Shartse's translations of "Antonov Apples" and *Dry Valley*, as found in Ivan Bunin, *Shadowed Paths* (Moscow, 195-), which I have edited. Excerpts from Bunin's fiction have been selected to eluci-date his stance toward his world, to give the flavor of his prose, and to show instances in which he incorporated experiences from real life directly into his art. Given the overall focus of the work, Bunin's inter-national pieces—for example, "The Brothers" and *The Gentleman from San Francisco*—have not been included. Dates for all excerpts have been rendered according to the New Style calendar whenever this could be ascertained; dates for fictional works and essays are the dates of publi-cation.

For their help I wish to thank the following people: Professors Gary Hamburg, Klaus Lanzinger, and David Gasperetti at the University of Notre Dame, and Professor Gary Saul Morson of Northwestern Univer-

---

[7]V. Shcherbina, et al., eds., *Literaturnoe nasledstvo. Ivan Bunin. Kniga pervaia* (Moscow, 1973), 383; and I. Bunin, "Zapisi," *Sobranie sochinenii v deviati tomakh*, vol. 9 (1965), 365.

sity, for their support and advice; Ms. Linda Gregory, Barbara Snyder, Shelly Pershing, Carol Szambelan, and the staffs of the Departments of Reference, Interlibrary Loan, and Microtexts of the Theodore M. Hesburgh Library at Notre Dame for obtaining many of the materials for this study, for researching footnotes, and for photocopying texts; and Ms. Margaret Jasiewicz, Nancy Kegler, and Sherry Reichold for preparing the manuscript.

Several individuals deserve a special note of gratitude: Sister Mary Colleen Dillon, S.N.D., of the Sisters of Notre Dame of Covington, Kentucky, who edited the entire manuscript and who made valuable comments on the introductory essay; Ms. Helen Sullivan and the staff of the Slavic Department at the Library of the University of Illinois, Urbana, for finding sources and for researching additional footnotes; and my publisher, Ivan Dee, who helped me to define the focus of this work and who also edited the manuscript.

Most important, I thank my wife Gloria who supported me in this endeavor from the beginning, and my three cats, Ignatius, Augustine, and Margaret Mary, who helped keep things in perspective—that they, not Bunin, were the center of the universe.

T. G. M.

Notre Dame, Indiana
October 1992

CONTENTS

INTRODUCTION
Ivan Bunin: A Man for Modern Times

THE LAST OF the great gentry writers, the first Russian writer to receive the Nobel Prize, the cultural leader of the Russian emigrés in France—Ivan Bunin is a major figure in Russian literature. Yet he remains, like Winston Churchill's characterization of his homeland, a riddle wrapped in an enigma. Throughout much of his eighty-three years Bunin stood apart from literary schools, preferring to seek out his own vision of life. His noble origins, his stories of lords and peasants, and his hatred of modernity, political as well as cultural, earned him a reputation as the last of Russia's gentry writers, someone who did what so many other writers had already done so brilliantly, so many times before. Bunin seemed almost superfluous, yet another—if muffled—beat of a literary heart that was old, tired, and no longer able to move the blood of the people.

This popular estimate of Bunin does not, however, tell the whole story. Bunin was a highly talented writer who has as much to say to readers today as he did in his own time. He lived on the cusp of old and new; he was overwhelmed by change; he sought meaning and purpose in a world that often seemed to be coming to an end.

Ivan Alexeevich Bunin was born October 22, 1870, near Orel, Russia, in the fertile heartland south of Moscow which had nurtured such Russian gentry writers as Mikhail Lermontov, Ivan Turgenev, and Leo Tolstoy. The Bunins were aristocrats who traced their beginnings to the rise of Moscow in the fifteenth century but who, like so many of their class—as immortalized in Anton Chekhov's *The Cherry Orchard* (1904)—fell on hard times after the emancipation of

I

the serfs in 1861 and again in the 1890s after the rapid industrialization of Russia and the rise of a new middle class.

The Bunins differed greatly from the fictional estate-families of Alexander Pushkin's *Eugene Onegin* (1823–1831), Turgenev's *Fathers and Sons* (1862), and Tolstoy's *War and Peace* (1865–1869) and *Anna Karenina* (1875–1877). Unlike the Larins, Rostovs, or Levins, the Bunins more closely resembled the Nozdrevs, Plyushkins, and Sobakevichs of Gogol's *Dead Souls* (1842), or, nearer to Bunin's time, the characters in Saltykov-Shchedrin's *The Golovlyov Family* (1875–1880). That is, they were "larger than life" but also spoiled, perverse, and ill equipped to handle the changes of their time.

Members of Bunin's family often served as prototypes for the depraved gentry heroes and heroines of his fiction. In *Dry Valley*, for instance, Bunin recalled traits of his great aunt Olga Dmitrievna Bunina, a religious fanatic with a vow of virginity, who would run about at night and scream that "the snake of Adam" had entered her and was driving her to frenzy; and of his aunt Varvara Nikolaevna Bunina, who lived alone, wore no clothes except for an overcoat and cap, and was "hunchbacked, with a waxen oval face, a hooked nose, and a sharp chin."[1] Combined, these colorful characters from real life became the bizarre Aunt Tonya of *Dry Valley*.

Bunin's parents and siblings were similarly engaging and tragic. His father, Alexei Nikolaevich Bunin (1824–1906), was a hot-tempered but kindhearted man who helped defend Sevastopol in the Crimean War but who ended his days squandering both his and his wife's inheritances on wine, hunting, and cards. Bunin's mother, Lyudmilla Alexandrovna Bunina (*née* Chubarova) (1835?–1910), suffered greatly from her husband's profligacy as well as from her own strict religiosity. She bore nine children of whom Ivan was the seventh and only four of whom survived to adulthood. Of Bunin's siblings, Yuly Alexeevich (1857–1921) was the most important. Thirteen years older than his famous brother, Yuly became a well-known journalist and social figure who was linked to the terrorist group "The People's Will" that assassinated Tsar Alexander II in 1881. Arrested in 1884 for his political activities, Yuly spent a year in prison and then lived under police supervision with his family at their estate until 1888.

Ivan Bunin spent his childhood and adolescence first at the

---

[1] V. Muromtseva-Bunina, *Zhizn' Bunina* (Paris, 1958), 122.

family estate of Butyrka, then at the gymnasium in the town of Elets (1882–1886), and finally at Ozerka, another family estate where he completed his education privately, under the tutelage of his brother Yuly. Literary pursuits began early. At Yuly's urging, Bunin sent a poem, "Over the Grave of Nadson," to the magazine *Homeland*, which published it in February 1887. At the age of sixteen Bunin thus initiated a literary career of almost seventy years, surpassing in length even the creative life of Tolstoy.[2]

Encouraged by this success, Bunin continued to write. A collection of poems was published in Orel in 1891, followed by two anthologies of prose, *To the Edge of the World* in 1897 and *Under the Open Sky* in 1898. Bunin's stories about rural estate life quickly attracted public attention. Meanwhile, his poetry collection, *Falling Leaves* (1901), and his translation into Russian of Longfellow's "The Song of Hiawatha" (1898) earned him the Pushkin Prize for literature in 1903, an award he would receive twice more. (Bunin also translated Tennyson's "Lady Godiva" and Byron's "Cain," "Manfred," and "Heaven and Earth.")

These honors were singular bright spots in otherwise dark and troubled years. After Bunin left home in 1889 he encountered more than two decades of struggle and suffering. Wandering about Russia, he held sporadic jobs as proofreader, barrel-maker, statistician, librarian, and newspaper reporter. A tempestuous love affair with Varvara Vladimirova Pashchenko almost ended in his suicide. During a brief span as a spiritual disciple of Tolstoy (1893–1894) he was sentenced to three months in prison for distributing literature without a license from the publishing house Mediator[3] (the sentence was commuted, however, in the general amnesty proclaimed by Tsar Nicholas II in 1894). A marriage to Anna Nikolaevna Tsakni in 1898 failed in eighteen months. His only son, Kolya, died at the age of five. Bunin lived through the Revolution of 1905 and its aftermath in the provinces. And, perhaps most wrenching of all for him, readers and

---

[2]Writers were not new to the Bunin family. The poetess Anna Petrovna Bunina (1774–1828) was an important figure in the time of Catherine the Great; the great Romantic poet Vasily Alexeevich Zhukovsky (1783–1852) was the son of a Bunin and a captive Turkish woman.

[3]The publishing house Mediator (1834–1935) was founded by Leo Tolstoy and Vladimir Grigorievich Chertkov (1854–1936) to print inexpensive books and distribute them to the masses. Mediator was a highly successful venture, distributing more than three million copies of its publications to Russian readers each year. For more on Mediator, see J. Brooks, *When Russia Learned to Read* (Princeton, 1985), 337–340.

reviewers continued to misconstrue the meaning of his life and art.

During these tumultuous decades, Bunin's close ties to Chekhov and Gorky, as well as his acquaintance with Tolstoy, gave him sorely needed confidence and strength. In 1907 Vera Nikolaevna Muromtseva (1881–1961) became his devoted companion for life. (The two legalized their common-law marriage only in 1922 in France.) Bunin's frequent trips to Europe and to the Near and Far East allowed him respite from the troubles of his homeland and introduced him to the cultural and spiritual legacies of other lands. In 1909 he received another major award: the Academy of Sciences in Saint Petersburg elected him to its membership of twelve with the title "honored academician."

Bunin also took heart in his growing fame—if at times also his notoriety—as a writer. *The Village*, a novel published in 1910, was a major triumph. It was quickly followed by other successes: *Dry Valley* (1911), "The Brothers" (1914), *The Gentleman from San Francisco* (1915), "Nooselike Ears" (1916), and "Chang's Dreams" (1916), among others. Yet it was a bitter paradox that Bunin was gaining fame in a country he could no longer call his own. "Patriarchal" Russia was in the throes of revolution and war. Together with Vera Muromtseva, Bunin left Moscow in May 1918 to live in Odessa, which was still outside Bolshevik control. There he led a relatively quiet life, confining his "counterrevolutionary" activities to editing a local newspaper, *Our Word*, and to cursing the Bolsheviks, publicly and privately, at every turn. He dared not take many chances, though, for Soviet newspapers were attacking him openly, and he had had several near fatal run-ins with the mob. Despite his bravado, Bunin knew he was a marked man. With Vera he left Odessa in February 1920 to begin what became a thirty-three-year exile in France. There he became the cultural and spiritual leader of Russian emigré intellectuals. He continued to write and was awarded the Nobel Prize for literature on November 9, 1933, the first Russian ever to receive that award. When he died on November 8, 1953, he was buried in the Russian Orthodox cemetery in Sainte-Genevieve-des-Bois near Paris.

The many sad facts of Bunin's life are even more painful when measured against his reflections upon himself, Russia, and the world. Between 1885 and 1920 he was constantly haunted by a sense of closure in life. The Russia he had known was passing into oblivion; a modern existence brought him only to impasse. Bunin was, to borrow the title of Lermontov's novel, "a hero of his time":[4] he struggled desperately to find a place in a world characterized by change, violence, and death.

As the initial point of contention, Bunin bitterly regretted his childhood and youth, cursing his fate as a victim of the emancipation of the serfs by Tsar Alexander II. His was not the lock-step system to happiness and success, the rights and privileges of young gentry in "estate" Russia. He knew neither a close-knit family, idyllic friendship, advanced education, or an assured career. Rather, he encountered a life that was capricious and cold, offering him a painful past, a bitter present, and a grim future. At age thirty Bunin had yet to take hold. He declared to brother Yuly in 1910 that his life was a "joke"[5] and that existence meant only sadness and pain. The list of his grievances was long: he had no place to call his own; he lacked direction and goals; he was without mentors and patrons; he felt abandoned by God; he had to take whatever job was at hand because he lacked time and education, money and energy to develop his talent. In short, Bunin saw himself as a vagabond, compelled to wage a daily and desperate struggle for survival.

Bunin hated his wandering, especially the fact that he was lonely and detached from life. Years later as an emigré he recalled, "I grew up a solitary soul. Everyone else was preparing for something, and at a well-appointed time each stepped forth and took his place in the general enterprise. But where was I heading? I grew up without people my own age. . . . Everyone was studying somewhere; each had his own circle. . . . But I did not study anywhere; I had no circle."[6] The fledgling Bunin traversed the world "outside of any society"; he "lived *internally* . . . looking at everybody and everything from the sidelines."[7]

Gripped by a gnawing sense of failure, Bunin came to view existence as a Darwinian struggle, doubting his fitness for life. His sense of rootlessness and alienation made him physically and spiritually ill. He complained to his family and friends of fatigue and pain, convinced he was a candidate for cholera and consumption. In his correspondence, details of his maladies and treatments, fears that the

---

[4]Lermontov's *A Hero of Our Time* was published in 1840.

[5]See Bunin's letter to Yuly Bunin, written in February 1900, as quoted in A. Baboreko, *I. A. Bunin. Materialy dlia biografii (s 1870 po 1917)* (Moscow, 1967), 68.

[6]I. Bunin, "Iz zapisei," *Sobranie sochinenii v deviati tomakh,* vol. 9 (1965), 345.

[7]*Ibid.,* 352, 361.

plague was everywhere, prayers that humankind be spared all that he suffered, and pleas that his illnesses be taken seriously were typical flourishes. Spiritually Bunin was akin to Dostoevsky's Underground Man,[8] advancing from a hapless "little man" to a rebel-demon who reportedly loved humanity and dreamed of happiness but who also profoundly hated most of the people in his life. Like the Underground Man, he was "offended by everything and everybody."[9] The pillars of society were "garbage," his colleagues "the most vicious bastards."[1] He suffered regular periods of hysteria, paranoia, and morbidity, hoping that an early death would solve his problems. At twenty-six, Bunin had had his fill of wandering. He saw himself as a "hanged man";[2] suicide was an attractive option.

His sense of loss and drift nonetheless continued unabated. As Bunin grew older, a series of personal and political catastrophes underscored the fragility of his private world. In rapid succession he endured the loss of his friend Chekhov in 1904, his son in 1905, his father in 1906, and both his mother and Tolstoy in 1910. Again he fell victim to prolonged periods of sickness, depression, and thoughts of suicide. Wandering became intolerable, coldness and closure became enduring facts of life. "I am sick to death of the road," Bunin wrote Gorky in 1913. "I am literally crazy from loss of blood; I go with the doggedness of a drunkard. I keep looking for a place where I could find some warmth but find only hellish weather instead."[3] More searing, he confronted what he had long suspected but had stubbornly refused to admit: the impending collapse of patriarchal Russia in revolution and war.

The pogroms in Odessa in 1905 and the unrest at his family estate in 1906 exacerbated Bunin's feelings of transience, his estrangement from his homeland. He spurned the truisms that had sustained his country for centuries, denying that Russia had traveled

---

[8]Dostoevsky published *Notes from the Underground* in 1864.

[9]See Bunin's letter to Yuly Bunin dated July 8, 1892, as quoted in A. Baboreko, "Iunosheskii roman I. A. Bunina (Po neopublikovannym pis'mam)," *Literaturnyi Smolensk. Al'manakh* (Smolensk, 1956), 280.

[1]See Bunin's letters to Pashchenko, written in March–October 1891 and on November 12, 1891, as quoted in A. Baboreko, "Iz perepiski I. A. Bunina," *Novyi mir*, no. 10 (1956), 206; and "Neopublikovannye pis'ma I. A. Bunina," *Vesna prishla* (Smolensk, 1959), 219.

[2]See Bunin's letter to a friend dated October 10, 1896, as quoted in Baboreko, "Neopublikovannye pis'ma I. A. Bunina," 232.

[3]As quoted in B. Mikhailovskii, ed., *Gor'kovskie chteniia, 1958–1959* (Moscow, 1961), 71–72.

an original path or that its people were a chosen race. Unlike Turgenev and Tolstoy, he refused to champion peasants as spiritual masters or noblemen as eager disciples of the folk. For Bunin, Russia was a country lost in darkness, wracked by the elements, smelling of death and decay. The cities and villages of his homeland were "native Palestines":[4] places that had promised milk and honey to tribes of faith in the nineteenth century but that now offered sand and heat to godless nomads in the twentieth.

Russia's rapid industrialization especially worried him. His writings reflected dismay at the rape of the land, the rise of capitalism in his country, the escape of urbanites to the villages as well as the migration of peasants to the cities. Russia, too, was wandering, in flux. It had climbed back into Gogol's famed troika, from his novel *Dead Souls*, and was again hurtling toward an abyss. In Bunin's images, Russian sunsets burned with fiery streaks; Russian clouds shone with purple brilliance; Russian factories belched forth blood-red smoke; Russian trains were dragons, breathing fire and smoke. Both gentry and folk were wrong, Bunin thought, for abandoning traditional values of soul and soil, for bringing their country to ruin. He saw "masters" and "men" as brothers united in blood and soul; both groups had been mainstays of patriarchal Russia, but now their situation mirrored his own. They, too, were vagrants who moved steadily toward execution and death.

Bunin's focus on the gentry and the folk, his fascination with the "psyche of the Slav,"[5] was a key theme in his diaries and fiction. He sought to dissolve the worship of lord and peasant that had dominated Russian "estate" fiction in the nineteenth century, and that Russian readers stubbornly clung to in the twentieth. In Bunin's *The Village*, for instance, the peasant Tikhon Krasov is a material success but a spiritual failure. As a *kulak*-entrepreneur he roams the countryside buying and selling at will, but he lacks a key point of stability: he is deeply troubled that he is childless. So he squanders his days defending his possessions, dreading the onset of old age, and traveling anew. Tikhon's brother Kuzma is no less tragic. A self-styled philosopher, Kuzma tramps about Russia, castigating his country for its failings but doing nothing to reverse its precipitous

[4]I. Bunin, "Antonovskie iabloki," *Sobranie sochinenii*, vol. 2 (1965), 507.
[5]See Bunin's interview with *Moscow News* on September 12, 1911, as quoted in A. Ninov, "K avtobiografii I. Bunina," *Novyi mir*, no. 10 (1965), 225.

decline. Both brothers end their days as outcasts, in sickness and despair.

In *Dry Valley* Bunin expanded his focus to include a gentry family, the Khrushchevs, who struggle desperately to keep the old ways. Unable to negotiate change, however, the clan meets with disaster. Grandfather Pyotr Kirillovich, the nominal head of the family, is murdered by the servant, a bastard son Gervaska; Uncle Pyotr Petrovich is killed mysteriously, by either a peasant or a horse; Aunt Tonya goes mad from an unhappy love affair; and the servant Natalya is raped by the peasant Yushka. The Khrushchev clan is thrust into oblivion, even the graves of its members lost. Beyond their own troubles, both the Krasovs of *The Village* and the Khrushchevs of *Dry Valley* are host to entire classes of derelicts in transit. Beggars, cripples, and tramps; mad monks, wizards, and shamans; deformed and diseased people of all ages, sizes, and nationalities exacerbate the mood of despair and decline. They pass in somber procession through the estate and, in their very grotesqueness, celebrate a solemn requiem for their land.

The years of revolution and war offered Bunin a certain grim satisfaction that his prophesies of chaos for Russia had come true. His country and its citizens were not moving forward, as Lenin had proclaimed, but progressively backward, to premodern, pre-European, pre-Christian, and prehistoric times. He bemoaned the reversion of man to beast, the replacement of the New Testament with the Old. In his personal and artistic writings he compared Russia with the world before Genesis, using citations from Jeremiah and images of biblical famine and pestilence as frequent motifs. Everywhere he sensed destruction. Cities like Moscow, Saint Petersburg, and Odessa had become cold and dark wastelands; villages, fiery infernos and hells. To Bunin's horror, the folk of *The Village* and of *Dry Valley* had wandered off the pages of his novels, taken independent life, and seized control of Russia. Thus Bunin could not accept World War I and the Revolution of 1917 either as redeeming struggles or as turning points in history. Instead he perceived both events, variously, as triumphs of the devil, as God's punishment for sins, as the latest episodes in the blood-soaked history of the human race, and, in a more national focus, as the final round in the many cataclysmic cycles that had reduced his country to tragedy and farce. Loudly and clearly he sounded a death knell for his land. "I stood for a long time in a state of shock," he recorded in his diary on May 6, 1919. "The entire endless universe of Russia was becoming unraveled before my very eyes. . . . An immense grave yawned in the world. Death . . . the final kiss."[6]

Having strayed from the time-honored parameters of nationality, autocracy, and orthodoxy, Russians had once again reverted to "self-destruction and atavism," destroying "science, art, technology, and all kinds of human, working, or creative life."[7] If earlier Bunin had seen Russia as a land of ruined estates, now he saw how it resembled Asia, the home of Tatars and Scythians. If earlier he had captured the folk in Tikhon and Kuzma Krasov, now he epitomized them in Adam Sokolovich, the protagonist of "Nooselike Ears," a sailor and "son of man"[8] who condemns the atrocities of history but who challenges Dostoevsky's notion of crime and punishment by murdering the prostitute Korolkova without remorse.

Every facet of the new revolutionary order of the Bolsheviks Bunin found repulsive. He confided to a friend that he had gone grey from "freedom, equality, and brotherhood."[9] The violence and cruelty, vulgarity and hypocrisy of the "new masters" sickened him no less than garish May Day celebrations, untimely house searches, and increasing censorship. The growing lawlessness and lists of executions and arrests appalled him. "With uplifted fist"[1] he challenged the pervasive hate and lying, the subtle disparagement of religion, the sudden disempowerment of his class.

While Bunin resided in postrevolutionary Russia it was his daily fate to worry about food, money, prices, loved ones, the future, and the near inevitability that he would be condemned to perpetual wandering, divorced from his homeland forever. "What if I will not be buried next to my loved ones?"[2] he asked prophetically in May 1919. Rumors drove him to hope; reality drove him to despair. Valentin Kataev, a young writer and close acquaintance, relates that in the years immediately after 1917 Bunin was a man of extremes: he was as paralyzed as if he were condemned, yet he was also like an

[6]See Bunin's diary entry of May 6, 1919, in Ivan Bunin, *Okaiannye dni* (London, Canada, 1982), 89.
[7]See Bunin's diary excerpts dated May 23 and June 23, 1919, in M. Grin, ed., *Ustami Buninykh. Dnevniki Ivana Alekseevicha i Very Nikolaevny i drugie arkhivnye materialy*, vol. 1 (Frankfurt/Main, 1977), 156, 160.
[8]I. Bunin, "Petlistye ushi," *Sobranie sochinenii*, vol. 4 (1965), 388.
[9]See Bunin's letter to A. N. Tikhonov dated December 28, 1917, in V. Shcherbina, et al., eds., *Literaturnoe nasledstvo. Ivan Bunin. Kniga vtoraia* (Moscow, 1973), 57.
[1]See Muromtseva-Bunina's diary entry of May 28, 1919, in Grin, 257.
[2]See Bunin's diary entry of May 29, 1919, in Bunin, *Okaiannye dni*, 140.

animal, ready to gnaw the throats of the enemy. Either way he was a "modern." Believing that the dead were more blessed than the living, he again saw suicide as an attractive option. "To hang ourselves has long been overdue," he wrote in 1919.[3] Beyond a doubt, Bunin was already in spiritual exile from Russia, and from life.

He blamed everyone, including himself, for the collapse of patriarchal Russia. From the past he censured his immediate ancestors, such writers as Herzen and Dostoevsky, such literary heroes as Onegin, Pechorin, and Bazarov. He was no less harsh with Russians of the present. Estate owners who avoided work and study but who criticized everyone and everything; intellectuals who championed the folk in public but mocked them in private; writers who spoke of angels and resurrection by day but championed devils and orgies by night; teachers who proclaimed a new society but only destroyed the old one; leaders who heralded freedom for all but grasped power for themselves; citizens who craved freedom but yearned for an iron hand—each group bore a share of responsibility for cutting Russia loose from its moorings, for moving it out into the turbulent sea.

In his condemnations of those he judged guilty for Russia's collapse, Bunin was harshest with himself. Globe-trotting, he believed he had undervalued his homeland, its history and culture, and had thereby abandoned the sacred trust of his ancestors. He bitterly regretted remarks like the one he made in "The Shadow of a Bird" in 1907: "With joy, I recall that Russia is three hundred miles behind me. . . . I have never felt any love for my country. . . . And if the Russian revolution disturbs me more than a Persian one, I can only regret this."[4] Worse, he now felt he lacked the strength and stature to be a prophet, crying out in the post-Revolutionary wilderness. Although his forefathers had defeated the Tatars at Kazan in the sixteenth century, he had allowed modern barbarians to invade and conquer his land in the twentieth. It was thus more than dramatic gesture when in 1919 he bowed down before the tombs of the tsars in the Peter-Paul Cathedral in Saint Petersburg and begged their forgiveness.

The dynamics of revolution and the makeup of revolutionaries especially distressed him. He considered the French and Russian revolutions as sharing several features. Both had promised bright futures but had engendered only swirling gloom. They had generated

[3]See Bunin's diary excerpt of May 4, 1919, in Bunin, 74.
[4]I. Bunin, 'Ten' ptitsy," *Sobranie sochinenii*, vol. 3 (1965), 414, 428.

not reformers and saviors but thugs, despots, and technicians of the human soul. Instead of community and freedom the people had been repressed with legalism. Chaos and hunger had been camouflaged with pageantry and celebration. Spectacles sated the souls of the mob while "carnivallike indulgence"[5] filled their bellies. The new Soviet fiction extolled the future and buried the past while parades and processions only stylized a nation in exodus and fed the "ravenous hunger for play, dissembling, posturing, and puppet show."[6] "Russia is such a surprising country!" a German officer noted in Bunin's presence in July 1919. "Everyone is so eager to have a good time!"[7]

The Russian insurgents he indicted as "born criminals,"[8] hominids, and exemplars of "Mongolian atavism."[9] Russia, Bunin charged, was now ruled by hangmen and pirates, hottentots and gorillas, profligates and underground men. They were genuine "moderns," subjects for Chagall and Kandinsky, squares and circles replacing faces and torsos and dramatizing their passage to lower forms of life.

Dismayed by Russia's political and social chaos between 1885 and 1920, Bunin was also deeply concerned over the state of Russian culture. His quarrel with the arts was often a personal one, a battle for recognition amid the changing fortunes of the Russian literary world. The success of *The Village* and *Dry Valley* earned him only momentary attention, overshadowed by critics' confusion over his work, a lukewarm public response, and the success of both Modernist and proletarian writers.

Publishers and critics were Bunin's antagonists—the power brokers of Russian culture who, he believed, pandered to the customer mob and to tastes that meandered as erratically as readers' lives. Reviewers received his works according to their own values and needs, using Bunin as a foil to discuss their own twentieth-century anguish and their attitudes toward modern life. Thus they misrepresented his works to the public, seeing him neither as an innovator nor as a synthesizer of new and old, but merely as someone who roamed aimlessly in art. Like the blind men and the elephant, they seized an ear, trunk, or tail of Bunin's writing and pronounced confidently that it stood for the whole. They labeled him a classicist,

[5]See Bunin's diary excerpt of June 24, 1919, in Bunin, 175.
[6]See Bunin's diary excerpt of June 24, 1919, in Bunin, 172.
[7]See Bunin's diary excerpt of June 30, 1919, in Bunin, 179.
[8]See Bunin's diary excerpt of June 24, 1919, in Bunin, 174.
[9]See Bunin's diary excerpt of June 24, 1919, in Bunin, 172.

realist, Decadent, Symbolist, and, most hurtfully, a misanthrope who
hated Russia and its people. Thus the tepid reception of his works by
Russian readers and the fact that he seemed little known either in his
homeland or abroad. Bunin's response was to vacillate between
self-doubt and self-flagellation. As he confessed to family and friends,
writing could bring him the "torments of Tantallus";[1] it could make
his head dull, his body, weak; occasionally it could even spur in him
the wish to get a "real job."[2]

A favorable reception eluded Bunin also because he was awkward
in public. He flaunted his patrician ways and was stiff and formal
with strangers. (His associates called him "Mephistopheles" and
"Ivan the Terrible."[3]) Uncomfortable with formal readings and large
audiences, he could scarcely tolerate fools. Opponents he skewered
with raised eyebrows, lingering smirks, and looks of boredom and
contempt. Novice writers, young turk modernists, members of the
newly empowered déclassé, carping intellectuals, and even intimates
and friends all felt the lash of Bunin's tongue.

His lack of success with Russian readers he attributed largely to
the fashionability of modernist and proletarian writers. Bunin objected strenuously to the so-called Silver Age of Russian literature, a
period of intense cultural experimentation in the first two decades of
the twentieth century. His attacks on Modernism were often superficial, unfair, even wrong, but his remarks are important because of
what they reveal about his views on national culture and art, and
because they led many segments of Russian society to regard him as a
standard-bearer of tradition in both literature and life.

For Bunin the Modernists were the source of evil in contemporary aesthetics. Like everyone else in Russia, they were vagabonds and
Mongols but also despoilers of national fiction, Russia's greatest
claim to cultural fame. They had robbed indigenous literature of its
soul, turning their backs on almost a century of Russian literary
development. Idols and "isms" had infected Russian fiction with the
fin de siècle corruption of Europe. National writing, Bunin claimed,
had strayed "from people, from nature, and from the sun."[4] It had

---

[1]See Pusheshnikov's diary excerpt of February 1912, in A. Baboreko, "I. A. Bunin
na Kapri (Po neopublikovannym materialam)," V bol'shoi sem'e (Smolensk, 1960), 247.
   [2]Ibid.
   [3]V. Kataev, Sviatoi kolodets. Trava zabven'ia (Moscow, 1969), 160; and E. Viktorova,
"Gor'kii na Kapri," O Gor'kom—Sovremenniki. Sbornik vospominanii i statei (Moscow,
1928), 172.
   [4]See Bunin's article "Pamiati sil'nogo cheloveka" in Bunin, Sobranie sochinenii, vol.
9, 506.

abandoned "depth, seriousness, simplicity, spontaneity, nobility, and directness"; it had embraced "stylization," "trans-sense," and an "obscene arch-Russianness impossible to read."[5] Nervous and self-seeking, cerebral and confused, it was the product of overcharged minds and dead hearts.

It pained Bunin that the Modernists departed from the values and ideals of the "Golden Age" of Russian literature, the fiction of Pushkin, Turgenev, and Tolstoy. The Modernists, he charged, resembled Dostoevsky's men-gods, believing, like Smerdyakov in *The Brothers Karamazov*, that "all is permitted." They championed unlimited individualism, praised debauchery, erased social consciousness, preached mystical vagaries, relished depravity and scandal, and glorified suicide and death. It grieved Bunin more deeply that the Modernists not only welcomed the Revolution but infused its violence and chaos directly into their works. "Blok hears the 'revolution' like the wind," Bunin noted ironically of the Modernist poet in 1919. "Rivers of blood, a sea of tears, these do not phase him."[6]

He had still less respect for proletarian art. Like Pasternak's Zhivago, Bunin was a poet, not a politician. He detested the ideas of *Agit-Prop* and of the *Proletkult* that art should serve the state, or that the party should set aesthetic standards, or that the simplest worker could be taught to write poetry. Politics, economics, literature—"masters" should enlighten "men," not the reverse. "It would be a thousand times better to die from hunger," he affirmed, "than to teach iambic verse to an idiot so that he can sing while his colleagues rob, beat, and rape!"[7]

Living amidst the political, social, and cultural storms that battered Russia between 1885 and 1920, Bunin believed that Russia was racing headlong to universal destruction, to apocalypse. Not surprisingly, his journals and correspondence as well as his literary writings of this period often have a dark, morbid cast. Death alone, it seemed, was the only constant in the vortex of his life. "Be prepared," the narrator in his story "The Lord's Spear" (1913) warns. "Death is above you, in front of you, and around you; beyond the

[5]See Bunin's speech on the anniversary of *Russian News*, delivered on October 8, 1913, in V. Shcherbina, et al., eds., *Literaturnoe nasledstvo. Ivan Bunin. Kniga pervaia* (Moscow, 1973), 319. Also see Bunin's diary excerpt for May 22, 1919, in Bunin, *Okaiannye dni*, 129; and his interview with *Odessa News* on October 24, 1912, in Bunin, *Sobranie sochinenii*, vol. 9, 542. See also Kataev, 128.
[6]See Bunin's diary excerpt of April 29, 1919, in Bunin, *Okaiannye dni*, 54.
[7]See Bunin's diary excerpt of May 7, 1919, in Bunin, 94.

water, on the hot sandy shores of the sea, and amidst the wretchedness and dirt in which almost all humankind lives."[8]

Even as a youth he had been haunted by visions of funerals,
coffins, and ghosts. *The Village* and *Dry Valley* abound with corpses
and graveyards, fires and floods; they flare with light and rumble
with thunder before the onset of permanent silence and darkness.
Bunin's characters try to be merry but they know they will soon die.
When they stare at a yellow moon with rings of pale mist, they sense
"something apocalyptic" in their surroundings, that "*death* is looking
them squarely in the face."[9] Like Kapiton Ivanovich in the story "On
the Farm" (1901), Bunin's heroes are bitter that they have only one
life, after which they will be lost to oblivion. "How can it be?"
Kapiton Ivanovich says aloud to himself. "Everything will be as
before. The sun will set, the peasants will return from the fields with
their plows . . . and I will not see any of this because I will no longer
exist! And though a thousand years will pass by, I will never again
appear on this earth; I will never come and sit on this hill! Just where
will I be?"[1]

Given his frequently expressed hatred of life, one might ask if
Bunin knew any happiness or hope in the first half-century of his life.
The answer is that he did, and, surprisingly, in almost equal measure
to his despair. Upon first glance Bunin seems to have been a manic
depressive. Wallowings in self-pity could be immediately, if inexpli-
cably, juxtaposed with rushes of joy. "I feel like dying," he wrote to
his brother Yuly *circa* 1892, "but then I become hale and hearty in
my soul, the devil knows how."[2] His writings reveal that Bunin
wanted desperately to believe in life and, despite abundant evidence
to the contrary, often demonstrated his faith in it.

Whenever he was so inclined, and often without rhyme, reason,
or warning, Bunin set a positive course to his wandering. Instead of a
vagabond he could see himself as a pilgrim, an amalgam of seeker,
elder, and priest who, as he wrote to Chekhov's sister Maria, loved
the "hard-working and ascetic way of life."[3] The change of heart was
invariably his salvation. As a pilgrim he could affirm a breadth of
personality and a wealth of experience. He could willingly embrace

---

[8]I. Bunin, "Kop'e gospodne," *Sobranie sochinenii*, vol. 4, 121.

[9]I. Bunin, "Tuman," in Bunin, vol. 2, 234.

[1]I. Bunin, "Na khutore," 34.

[2]See Bunin's letter to Yuly Bunin *circa* 1892 in Baboreko, "Neopublikovannye pis'ma I. A. Bunina," 223.

[3]M. Chekhova, *Iz dalekogo proshlogo* (Moscow, 1960), 235.

the *anima* of modern man: restless, rootless, scornful of his immediate surroundings but intrigued with the rest of the world. He could be a "citizen of the universe" and an "eternal pilgrim, the happiest of all men, who sees everything, knows everything, and will know everything."[4]

As a pilgrim, too, he could overturn critical misconceptions about him (a misanthrope, a singer of gentry nests) and prove to readers and reviewers that he was more open, flexible, and adventuresome than most of them knew. "My life journey has been rather unusual," Bunin observed in his defense in 1915. "I have long been falsely represented.... I was very far from any kind of definition... for I was living a hundred times more keenly and more complexly than anything I had... written."[5] Deliberately, therefore, he filled his memoirs, letters, and interviews with accounts of cities visited, items accomplished, pilgrims met. He vaunted his need to live "like a bird all his life" and "to roam the world and observe the human tribe."[6] His journeys were often exhilarating—and exhausting. "We have been in Tsargrad, Athens, Alexandria, Haifa, Jerusalem, Jericho, Kherson, and near the Dead Sea," Bunin wrote to Teleshov in 1907. "And now I am writing to you from Syria, from Beirut. Tomorrow we are going to Damascus, then to Nazareth, Port Said, Cairo, and after we have seen the Pyramids we will come home by way of Athens."[7]

Whenever Bunin saw his life as pilgrimage he attained a measure of fulfillment and peace. He was free to be a man of thought and action despite cruel and trying times. He could break from the coldness and closure of existence, from the stranglehold that modernity seemed to have on him. He could search for values and delight in all he had found and learned: "the beauty of nature, the profound tie between art and the artist, the charm in learning about people and... the poetry of freedom."[8] Most important, he could identify with great seekers in history—Christ, the Buddha, Francis of Assisi, Leo Tolstoy[9]—who, like him, had turned their back on their surroundings and become pilgrims to expand their consciousness, pon-

[4]I. Bunin, "Ten' ptistsy," in Bunin, *Sobranie sochinenii,* vol. 3, 428; and his interview with *Vechernye izvestiia* on May 4, 1913, in Bunin, vol. 9, 546–547.

[5]I. Bunin, "Avtobiograficheskaia zametka," vol. 9, 262, 264.

[6]I. Bunin, "Avtobiograficheskaia zametka" and his diary excerpt dated June 3, 1893, in Bunin, 262, 348.

[7]See A. Dubovikova, "Perepiska s N. D. Teleshovym," in Shcherbina, 560.

[8]See Bunin's article "Na chaike," written in early 1888, in T. Bonami, *Khudozhestvennaia proza Ivana Bunina (1887–1904)* (Vladimir, 1962), 24.

[9]I. Bunin, *Osvobozhdenie Tolstogo,* in Bunin, 9, 8, 15, 49, 100–101.

der experience, and embrace the cultures, histories, and religions of the world. He, too, sought a suprapersonal meaning to life.

Bunin's means to pilgrimage were as revealing as his ends. Sojourns in mountains or deserts, sea voyages, trips to Europe, and journeys to the Near and Far East all thrilled him. So did shorter visits to Russian villages, to the Ukraine, and to Chekhov's study in Yalta. His trips activated a highly sensitive and prodigious memory which transported him psychically to many points in the past, and which periodically healed the cold, closed present with a spirit of warmth, forgiveness, and peace.

His recollections of "times gone by" were not, as many of his critics claimed, the saccharine or hallucinatory ramblings of an aristocrat yearning for Old World estates, serfs, and the like. For Bunin the past often assumed a mythopoetic function. It endowed him with psychosensory awareness, allowing him to live in "joyous union with the eternal and temporal, with the near and far, with all times and countries, with all the past and present."[1] Such powers of transcendence he articulated in *The Liberation of Tolstoy* (1937): "Certain people can sense not only their own time strongly but also another time, the past. They can sense not only their own country and tribe but also others alien to them. . . . They can 'reincarnate themselves' by means of a lively, visual, and sensitive 'memory.' "[2] Bunin's memory was the strength and power of the human psyche. It was the chief guide in his quest, a loving mentor, a Sophia-like feminine that transcended spatial, temporal, and biological confines, that stirred his intuition and creativity and served as a source of love, wisdom, and reconciliation in the world. "There is neither separation nor loss," he wrote in his story "The Rose of Jericho" (1925), "so long as there live my soul, my Love, my Memory."[3]

He cared little for remembering the historical facts of Russia before the emancipation of the serfs; in his view that era was only a prelude to his own troubled times. Rather, Bunin's "past" was a highly selective, personal affair beginning with a mythos of the ancestral estate and ending with a cosmology, his own vision of the world. If the ancestral estate had often been the bane of his early life, it could also be a blessing. When he wandered exclusively in the present, he regarded his home as "dirty, cold, and *terribly lonely*." But

---

[1] See Bunin's diary excerpt of February 12, 1911, in Grin, 96.
[2] Bunin, *Osvobozhdenie Tolstogo*, in Bunin, 33.
[3] I. Bunin, "Roza Ierikhona," *Sobranie sochinenii*, vol. 5 (1965), 7.

after he had journeyed to the past he could regard his native roots as a place to "reclaim his senses" and to "restore purity and innocence to his soul."[4] At home the memory-filled Bunin saw that in fact he had a loving family, that he could be an Old World landowner, that the peasants could be his friends, that the estate could nurture his talent. Indeed, when he let himself be seduced by memory he found his native haunts to be so enchanting that he was moved to write the story "Antonov Apples" (1900), portraying the ancestral estate as a timeless memorial to patriarchal Russia, an indigenous Eden before the fall.

The "remembering" Bunin also reveled in the cultural monuments of history, especially the religious testaments of the ancient and medieval world. He meditated upon the pyramids of Egypt, the temples of Ceylon, the churches of Germany, the Kremlins of Moscow and Rostov. He cherished the Bible, the Koran, the Vegas, and the texts of Buddhism. By his own admission he became a "fanatic"[5] whenever he hard the "Dies Irae," the "Stabat Mater," or the chanting of a cantor in a Warsaw synagogue. Services in the churches and temples in Moscow and Odessa were islands of Old World culture and beauty for him, moments of respite from the storms of revolution and war. Restored amid churches and shrines, the pilgrim Bunin came to understand that humankind need not be condemned *en masse*; instead it could rise to new values and ideals, and even in modern times could affirm faith, love, and hope. Human evil, he discerned, was rarely enshrined. Human goodness, on the other hand, was given enduring forms that could speak to later ages.

The deepening peace and optimism he discovered in his personal and cultural memories led him to "remember" further back in time and actually to relive the myth of Genesis. A remote jungle, a deserted seashore, a mountain Shangri-la—these were the settings in which Bunin saw himself as a sole Adamic dweller, living in a pervasive silence broken only by the ancient rhythms of life. In his

[4]See Bunin's letter to Yuly Bunin, written between March and October 1891, in Baboreko, "Neopublikovannye pis'ma I. A. Bunina," 219, and his diary excerpt *circa* 1887, as quoted in S. Gol'din, "O literaturnoi deiatel'nosti I. A. Bunina kontsa vos'midesiatykh—nachala devianostykh godov," *Uchenye zapiski Orekhovo-Zuevskogo pedagogicheskogo instituta*, vol. 9, no. 3 (1958), 4. Also see his letter to Yuly Bunin dated October 25, 1896, in Baboreko, *I. A. Bunin. Materialy*, 59, and his diary excerpt *circa* 1887, in Gol'din, 4.
[5]See the diary excerpt of October 21, 1911, in the memoirs of Bunin's nephew, Nikolai Pusheshnikov, in Baboreko, "I. A. Bunin na Kapri," 241.

travels he often proclaimed the existence of Eden on earth. The sight of naked rowers in Djibouti, the seas near the equator, the lush beauty of Ceylon convinced him of the presence of "something primordial, warm, and paradisaical" in the world.[6]

Returning from the past to the present, he saw modern life with fresh insight. He continued on as a pilgrim, rising above the world and his own inner darkness. He was literally filled with the wisdom of the ages, a newfound awareness that gave him confidence and strength and punctured his periods of anger and despair. In this strength, this wisdom, this awareness was a staunch belief in divine providence. In mountains as well as in deserts and on seas, Bunin intuited God's presence, and he realized that despite modernity's flux and pain there was "something sacredly stable in this world."[7] So enlightened, he could see that he was not a pawn of fate, nor was it mere chance that had rescued him from the military draft and other unpleasantries of life. Rather, God was watching over him; he was part of a divine purpose, a divine plan.

God's abiding presence impressed him particularly in his visits to the Holy Land. There he experienced "salvation history" firsthand. He could walk in the steps of Christ, the Virgin Mary, and the Apostles; he could sense their own difficulties in life; he could recreate something of their struggles with belief. Indeed, it was only after journeys to the Holy Land (or to Ceylon and other places of faith) that Bunin could proclaim to his Creator, "My closeness to You is so terrible and sweet; my love for You is so endless; my faith in Your Fatherly bosom is so strong."[8]

Attended by memory, infused with the past, and assured of God's presence and love, the pilgrim Bunin looked to modern life with wisdom and faith. He came to understand some of the reasons for human unhappiness. He saw that his race moved toward "some promised land" but also that its members "huddled in a vale of tears," since most people consumed themselves in "weakness and pride, envy and spite."[9] He regularly indicted himself for his failings. To his brother Yuly he confessed he was a "great egoist" and the

---

[6]See Bunin's letter to Yuly Bunin of February 18, 1911, in Bunin, "Neopubliko-vannye pis'ma I. A. Bunina," 236.

[7]See Bunin's diary excerpt of February 13, 1911, in Grin, 96.

[8]See Bunin's diary excerpt of March 1, 1911, in Grin, 100.

[9]See Bunin's diary excerpt of February 13, 1911, in Grin, 96.

victim of a *"mania grandiosa"* that was shallow and false.[1] From personal experience he knew that modern existence could be short and brutish, but he also realized that he did not need abstract knowledge, social causes, or material well-being to enjoy a full and purposeful life. His strategy for happiness was simple and innate: to proceed quietly through life, to be thankful for its momentary favors, to sit quietly and absorb the beauty of the world. As a pilgrim he regularly sang his own ode to joy. "What a great happiness it is to exist!" Bunin exclaimed to his nephew, Pusheshnikov, "if only to see the smoke from a ship, its color. If I had no arms or legs, if I could only sit behind the gate at a shop and look at the setting sun, I would be happy."[2] Whenever he felt rapturous about life he found delight in the very things that had grieved him. For Bunin, memory was like a magic wand, transforming darkness to light, despair to hope, hatred to love. Earlier, locked in the present, he had seen his adolescence and young adulthood only in terms of struggle and pain; now, liberated by the past, he saw both of these as precious. They had been recast as marvelous and formative times, filled with the wisdom and strength he needed for the present. He could also forgive past hurts; in particular, he could cast aside his youthful rancor over the idea that his birth was a cruel twist of fate. Bunin now saw his early years as "enchanting"; childhood colors and smells gave him "almost physical delight"; and his time as a librarian in Poltava became "happy and fresh."[3]

Whenever he reconciled himself with modern life he could also be at peace with the future. In a world that threatened him day and night, he could be the supreme optimist. He could pray to God "until his body hurt"; he could hope that salvation was just at hand; he could assure himself that "the coming of dawn is inevitable."[4] Where he had dreaded the onset of sickness and old age, now he

---

[1]See Bunin's letter to Leo Tolstoy of March 21, 1896, in Baboreko, *I. A. Bunin. Materialy,* 56; and his letter to Yuly Bunin of August 10, 1891, in Baboreko, "Neopublikovannye pis'ma I. A. Bunina," 221.

[2]See Pusheshnikov's diary excerpt of October 21, 1911, in Baboreko, "I. A. Bunin na Kapri," 240.

[3]I. Bunin, "Avtobiografichskaia zametka," *Sobranie sochinenii,* vol. 9, 259. See also Pusheshnikov's diary excerpt written in February 1912, in Baboreko, "I. A. Bunin na Kapri," 247.

[4]See Bunin's diary entry of May 3, 1919, in Bunin, *Okaiannye dni,* 64; and his interview with the *Odessa News* on September 8, 1911, in Shcherbina, 369.

dismissed the body's relentless decline. Illness, for example, he saw as yet another opportunity—first to enter the past, then to rejoice and live forever in the present. "I have caught a cold and stay inside," Bunin wrote to a friend in 1896. "And . . . I enjoy my sickness very much. . . . I find it pleasant to feel the fever arrive. . . . The intense heat of midday wraps the head in something gossamered and soft, clouding vision. . . . And when you get better, your soul feels both good and bad, for you have recalled so much in your loneliness. You have dreamt so sweetly, so very, very quietly that you want to live well and long for you have enjoyed . . . your prolonged reflections."[5]

His forty-ninth birthday he greeted not as he might have done earlier, with sorrow for a misspent life or fear of the grave, but with the belief he was still the man of his youth, grateful he was alive and could travel another day. Bunin recalled of that milestone: "By accident . . . I awoke that day precisely at dawn. Today I was born, I thought, and now I am forty-nine. Oh, how terrible and great a number like that once seemed! . . . What kind of person had I become? . . . I sensed I was . . . almost the same person I was when I was ten and twenty. And suddenly, having looked at the dawn, and having caught in it the birth of a new day, I again encountered the inexpressible feeling I have always had throughout my life when I perchance awoke in the early morning dawn. . . ."[6] His happiness is all the more remarkable, for the year was 1919. In little more than three months the escalating violence of civil warfare forced him to leave Russia forever.

Having imaginatively reclaimed past, present, and future, Bunin could do one more thing as a pilgrim that had eluded him earlier as a vagabond. He could become a prophet, addressing the issues of his time with confidence and hope. His comments on Russian society shared a common theme: Russians were being ravaged by spiritual sickness, but they had ample native strength and opportunities for recovery and renewal.

From the onset of his literary career he charged that Russian society was "broken in spirit," and, in particular, that Russian youth were a "lost generation," crippled, confused, and corrupt.[7] Russians

[5]A. Baboreko, "Neopublikovannye pis'ma I. A. Bunina," *Russkaia literatura*, no. 2, (1963), 178.
[6]Shcherbina, 385–386.
[7]See Bunin's interview with the *Odessa News* on September 8, 1911, in Shcherbina, 369. See also Kataev, 214.

were at a crossroads, Bunin thought. They could take a low road and seek release in decadence, revolution, and war, or they could take a high road and attempt spiritual renewal. He worried that the people were choosing or being coerced to accept the low road. The evidence was compelling: Prime Minister Stolypin had been assassinated; the proletariat was on the rise; the gap between city and country was growing; intellectuals were betraying the homeland; and the villages, always a problem, were becoming openly restless and cruel.

He repeatedly urged his countrymen to adopt "other ideals, other models of courage."[8] As an important first step he urged Russians to rediscover the treasures of their national culture, especially the fiction of the great Russian masters. Turgenev, Chekhov, and Tolstoy had much to tell contemporary readers. They had lived in troubled times; they, too, had yearned for social change. But instead of championing violence they had channeled their energies into writing, offering answers to questions that tormented not only their society but every human enclave since the beginning of time.

With Chekhov's death in 1904 and Tolstoy's in 1910, Bunin believed he had one stable point of reference: he was sole heir to the Russian literary tradition. "I am the last," he wrote in 1919, "who feels his past, the time of our fathers and grandfathers."[9] He had been confirmed as Russia's literary heir by Chekhov himself, by Maxim Gorky, and by other contemporaries, but even as a child he had sensed his destiny. "It never occurred to me to be anything less than a Pushkin or a Lermontov," Bunin recalled of his early years, "not because I had that high an opinion of myself, but because I felt it could not be otherwise."[1] But to be spokesman-guardian of the Russian literary tradition was for him a mixed blessing. On one hand he saw himself as a martyr who, like Gogol, Goncharov, and Dostoevsky, was figuratively stoned by the mob because of his views. On the other hand he reveled in his joy as an artist, a creator, even a kind of man-god who could immortalize people and things. "Kamenka has disappeared from the face of the earth," Vera Muromtseva-Bunina wrote of the family estate to her husband on August 14–15, 1911, "only *Dry Valley* safeguards its memory."[2]

God had given him a sacred trust, Bunin believed—to define

[8]See Bunin's letter to Varvara Pashchenko of March 19, 1892, in Baboreko, "Iunosheskii roman I. A. Bunina," 282.

[9]See Bunin's diary excerpt of May 29, 1919, in Bunin, *Okaiannye dni*, 139.

[1]Bunin, "Avtobiograficheskaia zametka," in Bunin, *Sobranie sochinenii*, vol. 9, 259.

[2]A. Baboreko, "Tipy i prototipy," *Voprosy literatury*, no. 6, (1960), 254.

the tasks of national literature and to instruct the Russian public on their duties as writers and readers. In a time of iconoclasts and equivocators, he upheld tradition with conviction and aplomb. Cultivating an image both immaculate and precise, he was maestro:[3] elegant, urbane, living in a style that mocked proletarian and Modernist mores. He dressed impeccably, resided in gracious surroundings, and refused to participate in committees or gatherings that celebrated either Modernism or the new Soviet state. In his sense of himself he could be compared with the old prisoner Y-81 in Solzhenitsyn's *One Day in the Life of Ivan Denisovich* who, despite years in the *gulag*, "stood straight as a ramrod, ate his food slowly, used a clean rag for a napkin, and lived by one rule: Never give in."[4]

Russian fiction, Bunin believed, had several tasks. It should set standards for taste, refinement, and civilized behavior; facilitate formation of moral character, particularly in youth; awaken and strengthen national consciousness; be free from dogma and external pressures; expose wrongs and espouse ideals; and, finally, emphasize both content *and* form. Bunin also had specific dicta for Russian writers. They might be of "an unusual, most elevated order," but they were also "like everyone else."[5] They, too, should be pilgrims, entering fully into the joys and sorrows of life and serving as a voice for society.

In his concerns for national art he also demanded that writers form a united front. This included coming together as a family to help fledgling writers in their craft. Mindful of his own difficulties as a novice, Bunin became a model mentor. To Voloshin, Kataev, and others he proposed the highest standards, urging them to read, study, and observe; to work unceasingly; to see all things as subjects for art; to use images and words that came from life and the heart; and to write with precision, brevity, and substance. "Noun, verb, period," he told Kataev *circa* August 1919, "perhaps a subordinate clause when absolutely necessary, always childishly simple. Like a fable. A prayer. A fairy tale."[6] Mindful also of his own joyless youth, he took his charges to task for personal depression and lethargy; for yearnings for fame, money, and easy success; for recourse to hackneyed or

---

[3]Viktorova, 174.

[4]A. Solzhenitsyn, *One Day in the Life of Ivan Denisovich*, trans. by Max Hayward and Ronald Hingley (New York, 1963), 177, 178.

[5]I. Bunin, "Nedostatki sovremennoi poezii," in Bunin, *Sobranie sochinenii*, vol. 9, 489.

[6]Kataev, 218.

sensationalist plots and ideas; and for complaints that they had nothing to tell their readers. "Take yourself by the scruff of your neck," Bunin wrote to a friend on November 14, 1899, "delve into memories and books; enter the spheres of intellectual life and art. . . . And, perhaps, without knowing how, you will awaken."[7]

He took to heart his demands for writer families. In the years between 1885 and 1920 he belonged to several artist clans with whom he exchanged ideas and support. They included writers of diverse ages, outlooks, and social standings. Authors such as Zhemchuzhnikov, Mikhailovsky, and Ertel shepherded Bunin in his early years. Chekhov nurtured him at Yalta; Gorky fostered him at Capri. Writers and intellectuals in Odessa attended his readings and visited his home to debate issues of politics and art, though revolution and war lay just outside his doors. "It may seem strange, almost incredible," Kataev wrote in 1919, "that at a time when civil war raged all around . . . there continued in Bunin's house . . . a life in which a quite small circle of people discussed questions of literature, poetry, criticism, the reading of the Goncourt Brothers in the original . . . the eternal Moscow arguments about Tolstoy and Dostoevsky."[8]

His need for writer families also had this unexpected benefit: it caused him to record his recollections about Tolstoy, Chekhov, and Gorky, and to recall all three men as pilgrims and to do so with details that gave special meaning to the term "slice of life." Tolstoy, for instance, was many things to Bunin. On one level he was "a god" of whom Bunin could not speak "without agitation."[9] *War and Peace* sent Bunin into raptures; *Resurrection* he esteemed as one of fiction's most valuable works. It was not meant as mere hyperbole when Bunin suggested that after Tolstoy "everyone should quit writing."[1] On a more intimate level, Tolstoy was a father figure to help Bunin handle his doubts and fears, a spiritual confessor who could arouse in him the desire to live and write, and, later in life, a sage who, though lonely and sad, still championed courage and truth.

[7]I. Gazer, "Neopublikovannye pis'ma Bunina," *Problemy realizma khudozhestvennoi pravdy* (L'vov, 1961), 169.

[8]Kataev, 193.

[9]See Bunin's interview with the *Odessa News* on July 2, 1914, in Ninov, 228. See also Nikolai Leont'ev's letter to Leo Tolstoy dated January 30, 1894, in Tolstoi, *Polnoe sobranie sochinenii v devianosta tomakh*, vol. 67 (Moscow, 1955), 49.

[1]See the diary excerpt of Nikolai Pusheshnikov written in February 1912, in A. Baboreko, "Bunin o Tolstom," *Iasnopolianskii sbornik. Stat'i i materialy. God 1960-i* (Tula, 1960), 131.

If Tolstoy was a father figure to him, Chekhov was an older brother who opened his home and heart to Bunin. He loved Chekhov not only as a mentor and friend but because aspects of Chekhov's life and outlook were so like his own. Chekhov, too, had known great poverty and hardship, disliked the Modernists, worshiped Tolstoy, loved travel, and advocated simplicity in art. He, too, was seen by critics as cold, passive, and morbid, and he, too, feared obscurity after his death.

In his memoirs Bunin sought to set the record straight, noting that Chekhov was often warm, affectionate, even playful. Chekhov tending his garden; Chekhov letting loose a mouse; Chekhov worrying about what to wear for a visit to Tolstoy; Chekhov offering contradictory opinions on life after death; Chekhov fearing what people would say after his passing—these were images in which Bunin's jottings captured Chekhov as painfully human, a writer who indeed was "like everyone else" in his passage through life. As a writer Chekhov was not a "moaner and a groaner,"[2] Bunin wrote, but someone who loved life and humankind, and whose works were filled with fire and truth.

If Tolstoy and Chekhov were the bright stars in Bunin's horizon, Gorky was a mysterious planet. Bunin's relationship with Gorky turned out to be one of the most tragic episodes in his literary career. Both men had no illusions about their friendship. Bunin was an aristocrat, Gorky a proletarian. Each struggled heroically to overlook the other's failings but finally could not. Bunin's "gentry neurasthenia" and his refusal "to stick the knife where he should"[3] led Gorky to view Bunin with suspicion and doubt. By the same token, Gorky's indiscriminate championing of the folk as artist-writers aroused in Bunin similar feelings of mistrust and ill will.

They shared, however, several features that made for an intense but brief friendship. Both loved Russia and were horrified by the chaos in their land; both lived as pilgrim "exiles" at home and abroad; and both detested Modernism, espoused social concerns in art, and championed faithfulness to Russian literary tradition. Between 1909 and 1912 these strong similarities outweighed the

---

[2]I. Bunin, "Chekhov," *Polnoe sobranie sochinenii v piati tomakh*, vol. 5 (1915), 298.

[3]See Gorky's letter to Chekhov written in early September 1900, as quoted in A. Ninov, "Bunin i Gor'kii, 1899–1918 gg.)," in V. Shcherbina, et al., eds., *Literaturnoe nasledstvo. Ivan Bunin. Kniga vtoraia*, 12. See also his letter to Valery Bryusov dated February 5, 1901, in V. Desnitskii, ed., *M. Gor'kii. Materialy i issledovaniia*, vol. 2 (Moscow, 1936), 221.

differences between the two men. Gorky championed Bunin repeat-edly. He roused him to write, praised his works (*The Village* was a key example), and proclaimed him as a model to novice writers. Gorky could even value Bunin's aristocratic origins. "It is good when nature makes a man an aristocrat," he wrote to Bunin in November 1900.[4] "Pull Bunin out of Russian literature," Gorky pronounced seven years later, "and it will grow dull. It will lose its lively cheerful sheen and the celestial radiance of his lonely pilgrim soul. . . . Bunin can still tell us many things about himself, about . . . Russians, and about the world in which we live."[5]

Bunin also stood by Gorky. He was Gorky's liaison to Russia while Gorky was in exile at Capri. In interviews with the press Bunin informed his countrymen that Gorky was alive, well, and working, and further that he was deeply concerned about Russia, its people, and its art. Tragically, though, the Revolution and the rise of the new Soviet state brought into focus Bunin's and Gorky's radical differences in background, temperament, and world-view. Politics drove a deep wedge between the two men and eventually separated them. Warm correspondence gave way to cold notes. To Bunin, Gorky was the leader of the culture born of revolution, the future; to Gorky, Bunin was the leader of the culture born of tradition, the past. "There will come a day," Bunin said of his former friend in 1919, "when I will rise up against Gorky openly, not only as a man but also as an artist. It is time to tell the truth about Gorky. . . . He once had talent, but now he has drowned it in lies and falsehood."[6] Such sentiments only grew worse with time. Bunin never forgave what he considered Gorky's political and aesthetic treachery. "For such a person," he said, "there can be no pardon!"[7]

Bunin's tragic relationship with Gorky was painful evidence for Bunin that all good things must end. War, revolution, and other human perversities could turn positive moments sour and return him from pilgrim to wanderer. From personal experience Bunin knew that peace and joy were fleeting, that human life was destined forever to be perched precariously over an abyss. "I constantly think," Bunin wrote in his diary on February 20, 1911, "what a terrible and strange thing is our existence. Every minute hangs by a thread! Here I am

[4]Mikhailovskii, 16.
[5]A. Zolotarev, "Bunin i Gor'kii," *Nash sovremennik,* no. 7 (July 1965), 103–104.
[6]See Muromtseva-Bunina's diary excerpt of October 20, 1918, in Grin, 191.
[7]See Muromtseva-Bunina's diary excerpt of January 19, 1920, in Grin, 333.

alive and well, but in the next second who knows what will happen to my heart, which, like any human heart, is something without equal in all creation . . . ?"[8] He sensed, almost ten years before the fact, that he would lose almost everything he held dear and that he would leave Russia, never to see it again. "Can it really be," he wrote in his diary on February 16, 1911, "that someday all that is so close, customary, and dear will suddenly be taken away from me forever. . . ? How can I believe this? How can I become reconciled with this? How can I grasp the staggering cruelty and absurdity implicit in this? Hence the pain that continually haunts all our lives . . . that arises from each irretrievable day, hour, and minute."[9]

But Bunin consoled himself in his calling. Somehow he felt it would be his destiny to "carry Russia away from Russia."[1] He was convinced that, like Moses, he would be called upon to lead the emigrés abroad and to keep alive Russian "scripture" and "tradition" in his writings in the diaspora. Like Moses also, Bunin would never see the promised land, but he would long be hailed as the prophet who kept exiled Russians faithful to their ways. But he also knew he would not be alone in his travels. Memory was a constant companion that grew stronger and kinder with age and that, no matter what the trials of the present, could immediately return him to the past, to the riches and wisdom of the ages. The sight of a ruined estate, the smell of Antonov apples, the sound of a church choir—these were the stimuli that led Bunin to anticipate by almost ten years Proust's famed device of *intermittence du coeur*, the use of sensual impressions to "search for a lost time," to recall the forgotten memories of life, family, and self.[2]

Bunin also knew that, as regards happiness in life, the choice was always his: he could be a wanderer locked in the present, or he could be a pilgrim, transcending time and space. He often vacillated wildly between the two, but it was this dilemma, this maddening contradiction that gave his life and his fiction its drama, complexity, and richness as well as a searing credibility with which modern readers could identify in their own struggles with existence, their own response to the present and the past. Following his example, they, too, could periodically take stock of their pilgrimage on earth

[8]Grin, 98.
[9]*Ibid.*, 97–98.
[1]See Muromtseva-Bunina's diary entry of January 20, 1920, in Grin, 333.
[2]R. Poggioli, "The Art of Ivan Bunin," *The Phoenix and the Spider* (Cambridge, Mass., 1957), 155.

and affirm that life was worth living. "I have had many moments when everyone and everything seemed stupid and vulgar," Bunin wrote in the summer of 1891. "But I have also had moments when everyone and everything seemed good, joyous, and meaningful. . . . The most profound arguments tell me that life is nonsense, that there is no happiness. . . . But there are even more profound and powerful arguments that tell me there is good in life, and I agree with them with joy."[3] "Life is so wilful and capricious," he reiterated to Gorky on August 20, 1910, "but there exist moments . . . that one never forgets, that exist by themselves and outside of any time . . . a present that makes people feel alive and that gives them unforgettable happiness."[4]

Finally, Bunin took solace in the fact that he could tell his life story over and over again in his fiction. Like him, his heroes and heroines confront modern life and seek to make sense of existence. Some, like the Krasovs in *The Village* and the Khrushchevs in *Dry Valley*, choose to roam their time and place. Others, like the captain in "Chang's Dreams," travel to their sordid reality and proclaim, "But how magnificent life is, my God, how magnificent!"[5]

In the years between 1885 and 1920 Ivan Bunin weathered many crises. Often he surrendered, a wanderer, a victim of modernity; equally often, though, he continued undaunted, a pilgrim filled with faith and hope, bravely facing whatever life sent his way. "How many difficult and lonely crossings have there already been in my life!" exclaims the narrator in Bunin's story "The Crossing" (1901). "Sorrows, sufferings, sicknesses, the treachery of loved ones, the bitter insults of friends have come down upon me like the night. The time has come for me to part with everything that has been mine. And reluctantly I again took up my pilgrim's staff. The ascents to new happiness were high and difficult; the night, the fog, and the storm met me in the heights; a terrifying loneliness seized me at the crossings. . . . But we go on! we go on!"[6] If Bunin has become a chapter instead of a footnote in the annals of Russian and of world literature, it is because he sought to be a consummate pilgrim, a writer who used memory and hope to journey through past, present, and future, a man for modern times.

[3] Bonami, 13.
[4] As quoted in Desnitskii, 419.
[5] I. Bunin, "Sny Changa," *Sobranie sochinenii*, vol. 4, 377.
[6] I. Bunin, "Pereval," *Sobranie sochinenii*, vol. 2, 9.

Ivan Bunin
Russian Requiem, 1885–1920

PART ONE

Grey Dawn

1885–1900

BUNIN, 1891

In 1885 Ivan Bunin was fifteen years old. By the time he was thirty he had lived through the last nine years of the reign of Alexander III (1881–1894) and the first six of that of Nicholas II (1894–1917). It was a period of sustained reaction in which both tsars sought to undo the "great reforms" of Alexander II (1855–1881) and return Russia to the "Orthodoxy, Autocracy, and Nationality" of Nicholas I (1825–1855).

But what had worked in Russia in the 1830s and '40s was unsuitable for the 1880s and '90s. The spirit if not the letter of the emancipation of the serfs was entering its third and fourth decades, producing profound political, social, and cultural change. Russia was now a secular society of many faiths and nations. It was also increasingly industrial or "capitalistic." Foreign businessmen, particularly the French, had invested more than a billion gold rubles in Russian enterprises and would eventually own more than a third of the nation's industry. Outputs of cotton, steel, and coal doubled and then tripled within a decade. Railroad track grew by some 40 percent between 1881 and 1894 and doubled again between 1895 and 1905. New classes superseded old as professionals and bourgeoisie displaced gentry and peasants. The growth of the "proletariat" was notable—and traumatic. From 720,000 skilled workers under Alexander III, the number swelled to at least two million by 1900. Strikes were common.

Neither Alexander III nor Nicholas II understood the problems or changes enveloping their land. They were certain only that the 1881 assassination of Alexander II, the "Tsar Liberator," proved that reform entailed risk, not reward. They thus sought to revitalize autocracy and to restore the old "patriarchal" system. They crushed revolutionary movements, increased censorship, controlled education, limited local government, and "russified" the

33

nonnationals of the empire. The last measure was particularly tragic. Beginning a course of action that would continue through the early years of the Soviet state, thousands of Jews were murdered. As Konstantin Pobedonostsev, the Procurator of the Holy Synod, allegedly remarked, the Jewish problem could be solved only if one-third of Russian Jews converted to Orthodoxy, a second third emigrated, and the final third was put to death.

In their attempts to halt reform, both Alexander III and Nicholas II sought especially to buttress the gentry, the pillar of Russian society. In 1889, for instance, the institution of the office of Land Captain transferred power from locally elected councils (the *zemstva*) back to the landowners, giving them new control over the peasants. The gentry also figured prominently in the government, the bureaucracy, and the imperial court. It was precisely with the gentry, though, that these "counterreforms" failed. Many landowners were deeply in debt. Deprived of serf labor, they lacked the education, outlook, or experience to farm successfully. "Cherry orchards"—the decline of gentry estates, as portrayed in Chekhov's play—became a fact of Russian provincial life.

Russian peasants fared even worse. Although the "folk" made up 85 percent of the population, most of them were desperately poor. Even more than the gentry, they lacked the capital, education, and initiative for modernization. Between 1880 and 1900 almost a third of all peasant households did not own a horse; two-thirds of them were unable to support themselves entirely from the land. They were crushed by taxes, often paying ten times more than the gentry because of indirect levies on vodka, sugar, tea, tobacco, cotton, and iron. Most important, they were still tied to the commune which was responsible for revenues and recruits and thus helped to perpetuate the old ways, including the partitioning of the land into small strips so that each family might have land of equal quality. The peasants in the thickly populated provinces of central European Russia suffered most; the so-called "pauperization of the center" was an economic black hole that cast long shadows over the entire land. The famine of 1891, the cholera epidemic of 1892, and the economic depression of 1900 dramatized the mounting suffering and decay.

"Patriarchal" Russia was giving way. A corrupt imperial court, a lumbering bureaucracy, and overworked police were battered and often overwhelmed by frustrated liberals, dissatisfied bourgeois, and desperate workers and peasants. Radical parties rose. The Social Democrats came into being in 1898, giving a voice to the Marxism that many had embraced as the truth.

In the years between 1885 and 1900 Russian literature reflected this searing change. The stirring traditions of Russian realism were declining, its leading practitioners dead or in spiritual flux. Dostoevsky had died in 1881, Turgenev in 1883. Tolstoy had suffered a profound spiritual crisis in the early 1880s and had begun to write spiritual and ethical treatises that differed markedly from his earlier fiction. The "thick" journals of the nineteenth century had either disappeared or no longer served as focal points for literary discourse. Even the major proponents of realism in this period reflected the angst of the times. Chekhov was at the apex of his literary career but showing a dark existential bent in such stories as *The Duel* (1891) and *Ward No. 6* (1893). In this period appeared two of his most famous plays—*The Seagull* in 1896 and *Uncle Vanya* in 1899—targeting the gentry for their stuffiness, baseless idealism, and inability to change. Chekhov enjoyed even greater popularity once his plays were staged by the Moscow Art Theatre under the "realist" direction of Konstantin Stanislavsky and Vladimir Nemirovich-Danchenko. *The Seagull* played to rave reviews there in 1898, though it had failed in Saint Petersburg only two years earlier. Gorky was even more the rage, tapping into the new radicalism with graphic stories of tramps and other hero-proletarians. In 1898 two volumes of his writing quickly reached a circulation of more than 100,000, a figure previously attained only by Tolstoy. Crowds gathered about Gorky's portrait in galleries; beggars claimed to be his brother hoboes; young men imitated his dress: boots, walking sticks, and black blouses buttoned at the neck.

But the void left by dead or aging realists was filled by the Russian Modernists. Baudelaire, Verlaine, Mallarmé, and Rimbaud in France; Ruskin and Wilde in England; Wagner and Nietzsche in Germany; Ibsen in Norway—these were the teachers of the "first" generation of the Russian avant-garde: Balmont, Bryusov, and Gippius, among others. The Russians were quick learners. Like their European counterparts, they exalted beauty, extolled the individual, and defended art for art's sake. They attacked realism, "civic" art, and positivist and utilitarian philosophy. In their writing they chose the musical sound over the logical idea, the intuitive over the rational. Bold and brash, they championed visions, dreams, and exotic and perverse emotions. They relished vague or symbolic vocabulary, unconventional rhymes and meters, and texts that were fragmented, distorted, and difficult to understand. "Who equals my might in song?" Balmont proclaimed. "No one!"

Given the political, social, and cultural winds raging about him, it is easy to see why Bunin saw himself as a wanderer. Behind him was a family and home that exemplified the declining fortunes of the gentry; in front of him was a grim future, a consequence of limited education and few connections. (He was always extremely sensitive about his lack of formal schooling.) Leaving home in 1889, he wandered from city to city, job to job. For two years he worked as assistant to the editor of the newspaper *Orel Herald*, for three years as a librarian and statistician for the *zemstvo* in Poltava, during which time he traveled extensively throughout the Ukraine and witnessed the suffering of the peasants there. From 1895 to 1900 he moved constantly among Saint Petersburg, Moscow, the Ukraine, the Crimea, and the family estates of Ognevka and Vasilevskoe in the province of Orel.

While Bunin echoed the apathy and depression pervading Russian society, his mood was highly personal. Later he became outspokenly angry, but now the changes occurring in his land provoked in him only vague apprehension and foreboding. His scenes of Russia featured only ill-defined images of destruction: flaring sunsets, howling storms, roaring trains, children bearing torches and coffins. His main response to the Modernists was to warn them against straying from home and hearth. Between 1885 and 1900 Bunin was preoccupied almost exclusively with self. He struggled merely to survive, battling poverty and a cruel world from without, and sickness, depression, and deep insecurity from within. He lamented not the fall of Russia so much as his rudimentary education, his fragmentary existence, his hostile colleagues, his undeveloped talents. He was seized by unfathomable yearnings for death and by fears of what lay beyond the grave.

Yet Bunin was also learning how to cope with existence and to turn life to his advantage. Unlike many people his age, he knew in his soul what he wanted from life—to be a writer and

walk in the footsteps of Pushkin, Turgenev, and Tolstoy. He also
knew that he was making progress toward his goal. He had
published several collections of his short stories and poems. He
had given a literary reading in Saint Petersburg in 1895. He had
made the acquaintance of Russian *litterati* of all ages and ranks,
and had established ties with Chekhov, Gorky, and Tolstoy.

Bunin was also learning the benefits of being a pilgrim in
life, discovering the sublime peace and beauty of his world. In
1900 he complemented spring and summer sojourns to the village,
his home, and the Ukraine with the first of his many trips abroad.
He saw Berlin, Paris, Munich, Vienna, and the Swiss Alps. He
was also discovering that not always did he have to live in the
present but that he could find refuge in the past. At seventeen he
was learning happily how to surrender to Memory, to the bliss of
bygone times, to Russia before the Emancipation.

His writing was influenced accordingly. Bunin saw that his
fiction could be both a shield and a sword, that it might halt the
ravages of modernity while protecting and enshrining what he
loved about life. In "Antonov Apples" (1900), for instance, he
resurrected and celebrated the glories of the estate and its
momentary triumphs. He was also sufficiently confident to rouse
novice writers from their lethargy and to take unpopular stands in
print. In a time of license he upheld morals; in a time of despair
he posited a bright future; in a time of politics he disparaged
Marxists and Populists. In the face of Modernism he championed
realism, "civic" art, and the idea that the poet was a person, not a
god.

✳ 1885 ✳

December 29, 1885
Ivan Bunin, from his diary

I suddenly recalled things that happened long, long ago. I was
about five years old, and the night was moonlit and summery. . . .

I was in the garden. . . . Suddenly, old acquaintances came out
from behind the bushes. Liza stopped, looked at me, and laughed. . . .
Then Varya and Dunya. . . . Suddenly they all bent down and picked
up . . . a coffin. Torches appeared in their hands. I jumped up and
rushed to the house. Emily Vas. stood on the balcony, but now she
seemed . . . divine, wrapped in a veil, all in roses, bright and beautiful. . . . She beckoned me to her. I rushed into her arms and covered
her dear sweet face with passionate kisses. . . . But then Liza, Dunya,
and Varya came out from behind the bushes with the coffin. Emily
screamed and held on to me. . . .

[My brother] Yuly Alexeevich told me: "When I came home
from prison, you were completely unformed; but I saw your giftedness, which was like father's. Hardly a year had passed by . . . and I
could talk to you about many things, almost as an equal. . . . Even
then your views were so original . . . and always independent." . . .

✳ 1886 ✳

December 20, 1886
Ivan Bunin, from his diary

It is evening. Outside a relentless and terrible storm rages. . . .
A cold, sharp wind beats my face with snow. Even the buildings are

lost in the deep, swirling darkness. . . . The snow-covered garden can barely be seen; the cold is unbearable.

On the table, a lamp burns weakly, quietly. The icy, white patterns on the windows cast brilliant colored lights. It is quiet. Only the storm howls. [Sister] Masha hums a song. If you listen carefully to the music, you . . . fall under the sway of the long, winter evening. You do not want to stir or think.

✳ 1887 ✳

Circa *1887*
Ivan Bunin, from his diary
I remember when I was still a small child. . . . It was a spring morning. . . . I could hear only the quiet warbling of the birds. And my childlike soul responded to their song. I remember that I listened and listened, and that I was seized by a quiet, incomprehensible sadness. Tears rolled down my cheeks. Such moments I enjoy even now. When I focus on the moment, forget my wretched life, and surrender to the past. . . . [Such moments] restore purity and innocence to my soul. . . .

✳ 1888 ✳

June 12, 1888
Ivan Bunin, from a critical article
In societies in which literature has reached a significant level of development, it is unthinkable that writers should find themselves aloof from one another. The family of writers must be a solid and united family . . . a *conditio sine qua non* for their success. . . .

The writer who does not belong . . . to the intelligentsia or the privileged classes is completely helpless. He faces the possibility he will remain unknown, even if he possesses the beginnings of talent. . . . Such giftedness can be lost altogether; or it can become abnormal and corrupt. Exceptions are very rare. . . .

[People have demanded] that the intelligentsia help the people.

... This group would serve the people better if its representatives took to heart ... the intellectual interests of the people ... and facilitated their development. ...

No matter how remote a backwater may be ... there exist bright and talented people among the lowest and downtrodden of society. This does not mean that we should go looking for them; that ... could lead to comic Don-Quixotism. ... Life itself will bring these people to the fore. ...

Late July 1888
Ivan Bunin, from a critical article
Poetry can and must take in the most diverse subjects. The poet is like everyone else; he, too, is influenced by conditions and interests that are both universal as well as national, local and temporal. Like everyone else, the poet [must see] that *nihil humani alienum est.* ... He must respond to any movement of the soul, to any phenomenon of the moral and intellectual world. He must be at one with people and nature. ...

But even this is not enough. The poet must penetrate all the joys and sorrows of humankind. He must be a sincere spokesman for the needs and demands of society ... for that which is good and splendid.

This is the genuine calling of the poet ... to be a powerful impetus to civilization and to the moral formation of people. ...

The morbid, pessimistic tenor of today's poetry is truly ... abnormal. No matter how cheerless the conditions of social life, no matter that vice, egoism, and self-interest run rampant through it, today's poets must not ... paint everything in ... exclusively black colors. A society like ours has only recently set out on the path of civilization. ... There exist many opportunities for a bright future ... if only [its members] do not lose their energy and spirit. ...

[This does not mean that writers should] close their eyes to the joyless phenomena of life. ... But [they must also] put forth ideals and [breathe] life and energy into them!

December 26, 1888
Ivan Bunin, from a letter to Yuly Bunin
I am writing this letter almost on the verge of tears. My angst is so great that my heart is breaking. ... I cannot make myself do

anything; I just sat the whole evening yesterday. . . . Today it is the same thing.

"Lonely, lost,
I am like in a desert. . . ."

Dear one, I am not making this up! I even dream of things that are unusually dark and sad. . . . [Brother] Evgeny says it is bile; but . . . my face is not at all yellow. True, I have gotten very thin and colorless like a fish. . . . I feel terrible that you did not come for Christmas. We could have lain in bed . . . and talked and read. . . . It seems that everything is going much worse than last year.

✳ 1890 ✳

June 12, 1890
Ivan Bunin, from a letter to Leo Tolstoy
I am one of many who have followed your every word with great interest and respect, and who dare trouble you with my own doubts and thoughts about my own life. I know you are probably tired of listening to the same trite and monotonous questions. Thus it is doubly awkward for me to ask you if I can sometime come and visit you, and talk with you if only for a few minutes. . . . Your thoughts have affected me so very deeply. . . .

July 22, 1890
Ivan Bunin, from a letter to Yuly Bunin
I have become rather indifferent to everything. . . . But do not think I have become apathetic . . . to poetry, to beauty in love and nature. . . . I am reading *War and Peace*; and, in several places, I have gone into complete rapture. What mastery! I simply adore Tolstoy!

July 27, 1890
Ivan Bunin, from a letter to Yuly Bunin
Guess what I am doing? I am writing a drama! . . . No gain, no pain . . . as you often say. Perhaps it will be a pitiful thing; but what if I feel like writing?

✱ 1891 ✱

Circa *1891*
Ivan Bunin, from a letter to Yuly Bunin

If only I could get a job that was interesting and that would take care of my needs—in a word, if only my life would improve. But no one, no one will help me! Am I really such a little boy, am I really so stupid that no one will trust me with anything?... People say I am a ne'er-do-well, a charlatan.... If only someone would give me a hand and set me on the right path....

January 1891
Ivan Bunin, from a letter to Anton Chekhov

Beginning "writers" have the habit of plaguing editors, poets, and writers... with requests to read their work and to give them an "objective" opinion of it....

I am one of those people; and although I realize that such requests are sometimes tactless and rude... I am making it nonetheless....

Since you are my favorite contemporary writer, and since I have heard... that you are a simple and good man, I have "chosen" you....

If you have time to look at my work, if but only once, then I ask that you please do so. For God's sake, tell me if I can send you two or three of my (published) stories, and if you can read them when you have nothing else to do, and give me your comments. Forgive my impudence, deeply respected Anton Pavlovich, and look kindly upon my request.

January 17, 1891
Ivan Bunin, from a letter to Varvara Pashchenko

Things [in the editorial office at the *Orel Herald*] are still very quiet, although I am already overwhelmed with work. My head spins when I have to write an article on *flour-grinding* (!) about which I understand as much as I do pigs in orange trees. Then I have to write about "peasant credits," "popular readings," "horticulture," and the like.

January 30, 1891
Anton Chekhov, from a letter to Ivan Bunin

Excuse me that it has taken me so long to answer your letter. I was in Petersburg and have only returned to Moscow today.

I will be very happy to be of service to you; but I warn you that I am a poor critic and that I have often been wrong, especially in my judgments of beginning writers. Send me your stories, but not only your printed ones.

March–October 1891
Ivan Bunin, from a letter to Yuly Bunin

My life is all fouled up. . . . Where am I to live? Home? There it is poor, dirty, cold, and *terribly lonely.* . . . The place where I work is wretched, and my colleagues . . . are the most vicious bastards. . . . I feel so unhappy, so lost, that I cannot even moan.

May 14, 1891
Ivan Bunin, from a letter to Varvara Pashchenko

I am at peace only when I am at home [in the village]. There everything is good; there everything is green, fresh, and quiet. The windows of my room are open; the wind from the fields is warm; the air smells of lilac; bees buzz in the cherry trees . . . and the only sounds are the muffled chopping of a wood-felling.

May 29, 1891
Ivan Bunin, from a letter to Yuly Bunin

If only you knew how difficult my life has become! . . . I think about money all the time. I don't have a single kopeck. I cannot begin work or write something, nor do I really care to. . . . My trousers are old; my shoes are worn out.

I know that you will tell me these are trifles. I might have agreed with you earlier, but now I see how devilishly poor I have become, how low I have stooped, how *from necessity* I have had to replace my best thoughts with worries. . . .

I know I am writing incoherently, like a child. But I cannot do anything else. . . . I go about like a dog. My death is near!

Circa *Summer 1891*
Ivan Bunin, from a letter to a friend

Life is a strange, inexplicable thing. . . . We do not feel life while we live. . . . I think this is because we cannot value life. We are never satisfied with what we have; we want more than there is. . . . That is why we are unhappy; we wait only to be satisfied in the future. I have had many moments when everyone and everything seemed stupid and vulgar. . . . But I have also had moments when everyone and everything seemed good, joyous, and meaningful. . . . The most profound arguments tell me that life is nonsense, that there is no happiness. . . . But there are even more profound and powerful arguments that tell me there is good in life, and I joyously agree with them.

July 1, 1891
Ivan Bunin, from a letter to Varvara Pashchenko
   The outskirts of Poltava are not at all like those of Orel or Elets with their filthy hovels, garbage piles, and so forth. Here there are the purest white huts, thick gardens, and giant poplars.
   We . . . went out into the fields. The sun had burned itself out far off into the steppe. Golden lights flashed here and there. . . . The silence and the warmth of a Ukrainian night, the dreamy chirping of the grasshoppers, the peaceful light in the west made for quiet . . . and perhaps the best moments in my life. . . . I lay down and thought. . . .

August 10, 1891
Ivan Bunin, from a letter to Yuly Bunin
   My condition is extremely alarming. Thoughts about the [military] draft torment me incessantly. Then I think about life . . . [giving it] a "philosophical" character, so to speak. Why was I born? . . . My *mania grandiosa* seems so shallow and trivial.

August 14, 1891
Ivan Bunin, from a letter to Varvara Pashchenko
   Today . . . the garden smelled of Antonov apples. . . . You simply could not get your fill of them!
   You know, my dear one, how much I love fall! [In fall] I not only lose all hatred for serfdom, but I even begin to poeticize it. How nice it was to be . . . at grandfather's estate, with the old house, the old barn, and the big garden! . . . How nice it was to travel about the fields, to go along the forest paths, the half-bare alleys, and to feel the cold air! . . .
   Truly I would like to have lived like a landowner for a while!

August 15, 1891
Ivan Bunin, from a letter to Yuly Bunin
Need is positively driving me to the wall. It is killing all my hopes and dreams with its *implacable hopelessness*. . . . More than once I have almost taken to the noose because of money. . . .

October 31, 1891
Ivan Bunin, from a letter to Varvara Pashchenko
[Brother] Evgeny and I talked about the draft. He is convinced I will be taken, and he told me to fast and not to get any sleep. . . . I took his advice. I did not eat bread; I went without dinner. . . . I also did not sleep; and in the end I got a terrible headache. . . .

People tell me to get a doctor's excuse so I can postpone appearing at the induction. Hopefully the quota will be met, and I won't be drafted. What do you think? Do you think I should give it a try? I don't think I'll get away with it. I am only making myself sick in vain. Perhaps something will happen.

November 12, 1891
Ivan Bunin, from a letter to Varvara Pashchenko
Who are the judges [of our society]? The officer who . . . has the eyes of a calf? Or the landowner who . . . drinks huge amounts of seltzer water to show that he is civilized? . . . Or the gentleman who is all buttoned-up like Domby and whose new gloves and well-groomed beard make up his glory and substance? . . . Or the fashionable woman lawyer who is in good spirits only when she runs around with her new briefcase . . . and when her hair has been sculpted to look like the bronze staircase of the courthouse?

Or His Excellency, a human ruin with an Adam's apple, who seeks only to stand up as straight as possible in his "cast-iron" starched shirt? . . . Or the dandies, beginning with barbershop youths who wear wild ties and horseshoelike buttons, and ending up as full-blown idiots in their fashionable suits? . . .

They are all garbage; may the devil take them all! . . . But, my dear Varechka, there are other people, other strivings, other companions. . . .

November 17, 1891
Ivan Bunin, from a letter to Varvara Pashchenko
I am free [from the draft]! Not only for next year but *forever*! Sheer chance was on my side. . . . I had given up hope that I would be

declared unfit or that I would get a high number. I didn't even expect a postponement until next year. Suddenly it all happened beyond my wildest dreams! . . .

I was sick at heart the morning of the induction. . . . My heart sank . . . when I lined up with the noisy, drunk, crying, frantic, and foul-mouthed crowd. These, I thought, were going to be the people with whom I would share cramped quarters, the cold, and cigarette smoke. . . . With them I would set out, alone and lost . . . to some dark and boring hole . . . where I would have to obey some red-haired officer, sleep on plank-beds, eat rotten "conserves," . . . do rifle practice in the cold early morning, and stand night-watch in blizzards and storms. . . .

Dear God, what a bad, bad business, Varechka! . . . The draft weighed like a stone on my soul. . . . I had to wait in line until 7:30 that evening. Finally I heard my name called: "Bunin, Ivan Alexeevich!" I stepped forward to the fatal box and lowered my hand. I grabbed hold of a ticket. But I let it go for some reason and took the one next to it. My heart was pounding. . . . I had expected that I would get 65, 72, 20, or the like. . . . but the captain intoned in a priestly voice—"471!"

December 13, 1891
Ivan Bunin, from a letter to Yuly Bunin
I have to decide something about my fate. I cannot remain a "free artist."

✳ 1892 ✳

Circa *1892*
Ivan Bunin, from a letter to Yuly Bunin
My head is splitting from "thousands of thoughts"! My angst is senseless and broad, like music that is terribly beautiful and sad. I feel like dying . . . but then I become hale and hearty in my soul, the devil knows how. . . .

March 19, 1892
Ivan Bunin, from a letter to Varvara Pashchenko
To go off or to be drafted in a war of liberation, for national

interests, like the war of 1877,[1] this has a purpose; but to be part of an absurd slaughter, arising from diplomatic high jinks . . . this is base. . . .

The heart that is stirred by the sounds of marches and by the sight of blood, smoke, and shooting—this is the heart of a savage. . . . There was a time when duelists were considered *noble* and *courageous* men. But this time is passing; someday there will be other ideals, [other models] of courage. . . .

May 14, 1892
Ivan Bunin, from a letter to Yuly Bunin

Oh, how difficult I find it all! . . . I don't know whether to believe in someone, to wait for something, or to hang my head in despair. . . .

I cannot get used to life! . . . I live in a fog. Would you believe that sometimes I have calmly and quietly . . . thought of suicide?

Circa June 12, 1892
Ivan Bunin, from a letter to Yuly Bunin

My hands are shaking; my head feels like it is in a fog. . . . For the first time in a week I am sitting in a chair . . . after having been in bed with a fever that reached 104 degrees. . . .

Yes, brother, I have fallen ill, seriously ill. . . . The doctor . . . tells me I have pleurisy. . . . I had sharp pains in my chest. My left side felt as though it was weighted down with rocks; I had terrible pain with each breath.

I feel a little better now, but I am still coughing and wheezing terribly from the dampness. What haven't they done to me! Four times my side was painted black with iodine; then I was plastered all over with ointment that made my side swell up and break out into pimples. . . .

The doctor will not let me work; he wants to send me to the village as soon as possible. . . . He says my left lung has been affected a little. . . . And if that isn't bad enough . . . I don't have a kopeck to my name. . . .

---

[1]Russia declared war on Turkey on April 24, 1877, the reason being Turkey's brutal suppression of Slavic insurrections in the Balkan peninsula. In the war's aftermath the Ottomans were defeated, and Russia obtained important border areas in the Caucasus and in southern Bessarabia. The conflict was also important in that it gave political force to the idea of Pan-Slavism, i.e., that Russia was the protector of the Slavic peoples.

July 8, 1892
Ivan Bunin, from a letter to Yuly Bunin

Oh, if you could only imagine what I have in my heart! Yesterday I had a genuine attack of hysterics. I sobbed for two hours. . . . I quieted down, then I started up again! . . . How old I have become, how oppressed I am! I am offended by everything and everyone! The consumption, it seems, will not pass me by.

Yurinka! . . . Take pity on me! . . . I cannot continue like this. Give me if only the promise of your help.

✳ 1893 ✳

February 7, 1893
Ivan Bunin, from a letter to Leo Tolstoy

[I have been told] that you need people to organize your everyday affairs. I would very much like to be of service to you, if only for a short time, but I am tied down by my work.

[If you need me] then I ask that you . . . tell me how, when, and where I should come. . . . Also, I ask that you write to me as soon as possible. I am afraid that time will slip by and that I will miss the chance to put in for a vacation.

February 20, 1893
Leo Tolstoy, from a letter to Ivan Bunin

There is no point for you to quit work and to come here for such a short period of time. . . . I wish you all the best.

April 28, 1893
Alexei Zhemchuzhnikov, from a letter to Ivan Bunin

You can become a graceful and original writer if you do not surrender to indulgence. Write not in any old way but very well. This is extremely possible for you. I am convinced of it.

July 15, 1893
Ivan Bunin, from a letter to Leo Tolstoy

Do not be surprised that I have enclosed a pamphlet [of my verse]. Perhaps you will find it completely useless and boring. But I am sending it to you nonetheless . . . because your every word is dear to me, and because your every work rouses my soul and awakens in me a passionate desire to write (if I dare use this word about myself).

I have wanted to write to you many times about many things, and to come and see you. But I am afraid you will count me among those who besiege you from motives of vulgar curiosity and the like.

Do not take any of this for impudence or insincerity.

P.S. This spring I learned that you needed help with your affairs . . . and so I wrote to you. You answered me, but you confused me with another Bunin who showed up in Poltava in the fall. . . . He is now far from here, at his estate.

✳ 1894 ✳

January 30, 1894
Nikolai Leont'ev, from a letter to Leo Tolstoy
Bunin came here very upset because he spent so little time with you. . . . He loves you very much. . . . He cannot talk about you calmly, without agitation.

February 15, 1894
Ivan Bunin, from a letter to Leo Tolstoy
I have been in poor spirits since I returned from Moscow. . . . I cannot explain precisely [what is bothering me]; but, in any case, it was not your words to me.

Although our conversation was brief and our meeting was unsuccessful, your words made a clear and kind impression on me. Something bright and lively shone from them. . . .

But I cannot say I feel good in my soul. I do not know how my future will turn out or where and what I should do. The days go by so terribly fast, and life only drives me insane. I keep waiting for something to happen. . . .

February 23, 1894
Leo Tolstoy, from a letter to Ivan Bunin
Do not expect anything from existence. The best is what you have right now. The most important and serious moment in life is the

one you are living. . . . It alone is genuine and under your control. Do not think about another, more attractive existence; one is the same as another. The best in life demands intense spiritual effort. . . . Continue to move forward in Christian perfection and in service to God.

Mid-March 1894
Ivan Bunin, from a critical article
   Just think about today's literature: Its main feature is that it has already lost the special stamp and character of precisely *Russian* literature. Many of our latest works can be ascribed to any writer you like—a Frenchman, a German, an Englishman. And poets? They write triolets, sonnets, and rondos on medieval and decadent themes— and it all turns out poor, lifeless, and shallow. . . . Today's poets invent phenomenal rhythms; they hatch absurd images and expressions. . . . Yes, we are a small, weak, and poor people!
   Russian writers are consciously moving away from the people, from nature, and from the sun. But nature will take cruel revenge for this. One must firmly remember this!

May 19, 1894
Ivan Bunin, from his diary
   On the road to Poltava I looked at the sunset. The sun kept flaring up. Suddenly the buildings of the town on the mountain before me, the complex of factories, the smoke of their stacks, burned forth like red blood, and the clouds in the west shone with purple brilliance.

✳ 1895 ✳

Circa March 1895
Ivan Bunin, from his diary
   Old, huge, and crowded: that was the Moscow that met me for the first time . . . a complex, colorful, and unwieldy picture, like a dream. . . .
   The *beginning* of my new life was my darkest spiritual period. Internally it was the deadest time of my youth, though I lived very differently on the outside . . . so that I would not be alone.

April 3, 1895
Ivan Bunin, from a letter to Yuly Bunin

The time passes by so terribly monotonously. I feel like doing something, but I am lazy and sluggish. I am afraid to think of the future. . . . Moscow in the fall? . . . Petersburg? . . . May all big cities be cursed!

May 1895
Ivan Bunin, from his story "On the Farm"

Kapiton Ivanovich looked out onto the distant field for a long time; and for a long time he took in the silence of the evening.

"How can it be?" he said aloud. "Everything will be as before. The sun will set; the peasants will return from the fields with their plows . . . and I will not see any of this, because I will no longer exist! And though a thousand years will pass by, I will never again appear on this earth; I will never come and sit on this hill! Just where will I be?"

October 14, 1895
Ivan Bunin, from a letter to a friend

What is important is not that we realize an idea so much as we first seek it out, that we love it. Sadly, there will come a time . . . when our youth . . . and all that filled our souls with . . . happiness . . . the joy of life, and the pulses of art, beauty, and truth will seem only like a notebook of long familiar verse that does not express even a thousandth of all we have felt. But who cares! Be thankful if only for those moments when you think you are a creator, an artist!

November 18, 1895
Ivan Bunin, from a letter to a friend

I was born on October 10, 1870, in Voronezh, where my parents had moved for a time so that my two brothers could be educated. . . . (From age four on) I had to live in a backwater, in one of the small ancestral nests (the farm of Butyrki, in the Elets district, in the region of Orel).

To tell the truth, I do not remember when I learned to read. I began to study in earnest only when I had a tutor: one N. O. Romashkov, a student at Moscow University, who was strange, hot-tempered, and quarrelsome, but who was also very talented in literature, music, and art. Romashkov could speak many languages—

English, French, German; he even knew some Eastern tongues. . . .
He had seen a great deal in his lifetime. Very probably it was his
enchanting stories . . . and the books we read together—*English Poets*[2]
and Homer's *Odyssey*—that aroused in me a passion for poetry. . . .

I spent about ten years in school at Elets, which fortunately I
did not finish because of illness. I returned home in the winter of
1886 to the village (Ozerka, Elets district), where I studied for my
diploma with my elder brother, a student at the university, and where
I began to write systematically.

Winter 1895
Ivan Bunin, from his diary
My first public reading was in the . . . winter of '95 in the
famous hall of the Credit Society in Saint Petersburg.

Not long before . . . I had published "To the Edge of the
World,"[3] a story about migrants. The critics were so unanimous in
their praise that I was invited to participate in other journals, and the
"Society for the Care of Migrants" in Petersburg requested that I
come there for a benefit. So here am I in Petersburg—for the first
time in my life. . . .

I, of course, read "To the Edge of the World"; and again, thanks
to the unfortunate migrants . . . I was a great success. . . .

My impressions of my Petersburg meetings are varied and sharp.
What extremes! From Grigorovich and Zhemchuzhnikov to Sologub!

✳ 1896 ✳

January 21, 1896
Ivan Bunin, from a letter to a friend
I have caught a cold. . . . And as always, whenever it is not
dangerous, I am very content with my illness. . . . I find it pleasant to
feel the fever arrive. It seems that the sultry afternoon has wrapped
my head in something muffled and soft, and that my vision has
become dulled. . . . Hearing, too, seems less sharp; sounds, particularly the buzzing of flies, seem especially soothing.

[2]*English Poets* was published by Nikolai Gerbel in Saint Petersburg in 1875.
[3]Bunin published "To the Edge of the World" in 1894.

And when you get better your soul feels so good and sad, because you have recalled so much in your loneliness. You have dreamed so very quietly and sweetly, and you want to live a long and good life. . . .

I read your letter about your travels. . . . Yes, it is so good in the mountains where there is eternal spring, eternal young life! Do you know Bjørnson's[4] wonderful song: "When you go the mountains . . . do not take anything extra along! Do not take the cares of the valley, but sing your own . . . song from high and rocky cliffs. . . . The birds will greet you with branches; the worries of the village are far away; the air is purer and calmer. Breathe with a full and joyful chest, and sing! Your childhood memories will shine before you . . . and you will sing a great song of solitude. . . ." How much happiness and youth is there in this song: quiet, bright, mountainlike!

So it must be in life. Do not take the cares of the valley; do not pack anything extra. I must have the soul of a vagabond, though I am drawn to the valley, the peaceful valley. . . .

Spring is still in flower here. The air is damp; the forest is like velvet, turning black in the bluish, warm fog. From my windows I have a splendid view of the lowlands around Poltava. Spring makes me exceedingly glad, and for a while my soul is happy.

March 21, 1896
Ivan Bunin, from a letter to Leo Tolstoy

I am now a full-blown vagabond. . . . I have not lived in the same place for more than two months. When I will put an end to all this . . . I do not know. . . .

Perhaps I am a great egoist. I have often told myself it would be better to rid myself of such a burden. . . .

Everything is so incredibly fragmented in my life! I have the most rudimentary education; I torment myself to the point of psychosis. There is so much, so very much to learn; and all I know are the most pitiful bits and pieces of things. I so much want to know something: its very beginnings, its very essence! Perhaps my ideas are childish. . . .

As regards my dealings with people: again the same shattered sympathies, false friendships, and moments of love. . . . One cannot

---

[4]Bjørnstjerne Bjørnson (1832–1910) was a Norwegian writer and a proponent of national culture in art.

forget the past; the future . . . will also be fragmented and incomplete, even though I yearn for youth, friendship, to understand everything, and to have bright and quiet days. . . . But then, I ask myself: what right do I have to all this?

But I do know one thing: All these trifles, my thirst for life, the torments it brings, all this will someday come to an end. At best I will live for another twenty-five years, but I will go through ten of them as in a dream. A funny, spiteful thought!

I have often convinced myself that there is no death; but then I think death must exist. . . . and that in less than a century there will not remain on this earth a single living entity . . . not a single beast, not a single human being, who, like me, wants to live and *is living now*—all will be new!

What do I believe in? Not that I will be around, like a burned-out candle, or that I will roam the earth forever. . . . What about God? How can I think about God when I find it enough to ask: Who am I? Or just where is our small world amidst countless other worlds?

Let's suppose that the world is one thing, something like a sphere; but, then, what surrounds this sphere? Nothing? What precisely is this "nothing"? Where is the end to this "nothing"? What is there behind this "nothing"? When did everything begin? And what was there before the beginning? That's quite enough to think about! . . .

Perhaps I should make my peace with everything, hang my head passively, and follow the beckonings of my heart. . . . But I find it difficult . . . to think about my powerlessness and passivity! . . .

Dear Lev Nikolaevich. . . . You are one of the few whose words lift up my soul and bring me to tears. . . . Right now I feel like crying and kissing your hand passionately, as if you were my own father!

October 10, 1896
Ivan Bunin, from a letter to a friend
As you see, I am here in the village. . . . My mood, especially over the past few days, has been poor; for when I am in the village I feel sharply all the vanity and insignificance of my thoughts and strivings.

Time goes by; everything seems so overwhelming and confused. I have little strength for anything. . . . Today I reached my twenty-sixth year, but I go about like a hanged man.

October 25, 1896
Ivan Bunin, from a letter to Yuly Bunin

I cannot tell you how burdened I have become in my soul! . . . I am overwhelmingly tired of this wandering life, and I see only the same thing before me, without any goals at all. . . .

You can imagine how I feel here in Moscow amidst these damned six-storyed houses, alone, not knowing anyone, and with only fifty rubles in my pocket. . . . How I wanted to visit the village! . . . So I returned to Ognevka and reclaimed my senses!

* 1897 *

March 15, 1897
Ivan Bunin, from a letter to a friend

I haven't written anything for a while. I still don't feel well, especially today. *New Time* wrote a vile review about me. They said I . . . was drawn to the mud and murk of life!! Are they scoundrels or what? Dirty and repulsive books pour forth like a flood, but I . . . compose village idylls and elegies. Even more vile, *New Time* praises my "sincere" (?) talent . . . as if I were a notorious photographer of dirty scenes. I knew, of course, that *New Time* would rake me over the coals, but why did they have to lie?

Circa *April 1897*
Ivan Bunin, from a letter to Yuly Bunin

Again, brother, I have written almost nothing, but I study all the time—from books and from life. I roam the villages and fairs. . . . I have met blind men, fools, and beggars; I have listened to their songs.

* 1898 *

Early 1898
Ivan Bunin, from an article

I do not need a lot of science, book knowledge, or material well-being to have a full life. It is when I travel that I discover the beauty of nature, the profound tie between art and the artist, the charm in learning about people and about . . . freedom.

January 27, 1898
Alexander Ertel, from a letter to Ivan Bunin
Your stories have pleased me greatly. It is so nice to come across something that is young and fresh among the well-known and boring trifles that have made up our literature as of late.

I do not want to exaggerate the artistic importance of your work, but . . . I see precise observation, genuine poetic talent, and a sincere and humane view of the world. . . .

It seems to me, though, that you still have not found yourself. . . . Sharp lines and screaming tones burst forth upon soft and pensive pictures, vague contours, and fragile colors like those of an ancient tapestry. . . . A sad, gauzelike dreaminess often yields to unpleasantly noisy scenes, coarse tendentiousness, and theoretical outbursts. . . . The result is uneven and often irritating. . . .

✳ 1899 ✳

January 1899
Ivan Bunin, from a letter to Yuly Bunin
I would like to love people, I even have love for *humankind*, but you know how little I love individuals.

April 1899
Ivan Bunin, from his story "Without Kith or Kin"
I laughed at both Marxists and Populists; and I said I could become a social person only in exceptional cases, for instance, if it were a time of a genuine social upheaval, or if I could be the least bit happy personally. . . .

I do not even have a tie to the homeland, nor a corner or refuge to call my own. . . . I have grown old quickly; I have been cast adrift morally and physically. I am a vagabond . . . who wants only a piece of bread. In my free moments I reflect dolefully on life and death, and I dream avidly for some undefined happiness. . . .

I love life hopelessly. . . . But I have never known happiness. Funny, isn't it?

April 14, 1899
Ivan Bunin, from a letter to Yuly Bunin

When I was in the Crimea I saw Chekhov and Gorky (Gorky and I became fast friends—in many respects he is a remarkable and splendid individual).

April 26, 1899
Ivan Bunin, from a letter to a friend

The idea that, no matter what, I had to write something *good* [for the hundredth anniversary of Pushkin's birth] stifled any emotion in me. I became exhausted, and Pushkin seemed to be my enemy.

May 1899
Ivan Bunin, from a letter to Valery Bryusov

How terribly lonely and incomprehensible is life. . . . I am going to the village. . . . There I will think about graves in the steppe.

June 18, 1899
Ivan Bunin, from a letter to Nikolai Teleshov

I read your letter with delight; and with delight I learned that you are undergoing the same thing I am: You, too, chew up plots and spit them out. . . .

The devil with plots! Don't try so hard to make things up, but write about what you have seen and about what you find pleasant to remember.

August 7, 1899
Ivan Bunin, from a letter to Nikolai Teleshov

I read and think; I am reading old things: *Ecclesiastes*, the *Trebnik*.[5]

November 14, 1899
Ivan Bunin, from a letter to a friend

You express well those familiar vile feelings that keep us from writing. . . . For Christ's sake, take advantage of your mood and surrender to your spitefully sweet contempt for life. . . . Think over the reasons for your lack of action . . . and change the conditions of life that keep you from working. . . . I myself have fallen prey to this

[5]The *Trebnik* is a prayer book of the Russian Orthodox church that contains the liturgies of all ceremonies and rites except the Eucharist and the ordination of priests.

torment—the revulsion to writing something that is "trifling" or "dull." . . . I also tell myself that "I have nothing to tell people, for I myself know nothing." But . . . we are wrong when we say this, and what's more, we are pigs, lazy pigs. . . . Take yourself by the scruff of your neck; delve into memories and books; enter into the spheres of intellectual life and . . . art. . . . Perhaps, without knowing how, you will awaken. . . .

<h1>✳ 1 9 0 0 ✳</h1>

Circa *1900*
Nikolai Pusheshnikov, from his memoirs
When Ivan Alexeevich was in Ognevka, he would always walk down the same road every evening—to the west, to the railroad. He said he loved to walk to the railroad because it reminded him of his travels, the south, and the things he loved most of all in life.

Late January 1900
Valery Bryusov, from his memoirs
Bunin is much more profound than he seems. Some of his thoughts about humankind, about the ancient Egyptians, about the vulgarity of everything contemporary, and about the disgrace of our science—these are powerful and have made their impression. He seems very unhappy in life.

February 1900
Ivan Bunin, from a letter to Yuly Bunin
My situation is tragic. I think a trip to Constantinople would be my salvation, but how can I do this? I see only now that I have been dreaming like a child. . . . Where am I going to get the money? *For God's sake, can't you think of something?*
You've got to understand—I am perishing. Every night I howl from outrage and grief. During the days I run around and clench my teeth. . . . I don't have a penny to my name! I have become so tired of this joke called life. And only more of the same lies ahead.

March 1900
Ivan Bunin, from a critical article

Russian literature offers a wealth of educational material to its readers. Its best examples embrace a spirit of humanity and emotions that are bright, noble, and pure. Russian writers and poets are concerned not so much with the beauty . . . of their images but with the content of their works, their ethical value. . . .

The reasons for this are many . . . [but the key one is] that our literature has been, and continues to be, one of the few outlets for social expression in our country. . . .

People in Russia talk a great deal about the forming of religious morals. Unfortunately, though, they have focused their attention on external rite and ritual, on grand forms of piety, and not on the very core of faith . . . a reverence for the mysterious Force that governs the world . . . and an awareness that summons the individual to live and act . . . in the name of higher ideals and of the social good. . . .

In my opinion, teachers should take special care to protect youth from the filth, from the unclean thoughts and deeds which . . . arise when young people . . . yield to corrupt surroundings . . . and to life's temptations.

[When corrupted, youth] snuff our sparks of poetic feeling, so splendid and sublime; they put an end to bright daydreams and poetic impulses, since they are driven by a sensuality they cannot regulate or restrain. . . . Unbridled passion often brings a youth to dens of iniquity, in which a woman, a person (in her own right), is sacrificed to the lust of another and to the shame of contemporary civilization.

Admittedly, the task of teachers in this area is very difficult and complex. They must . . . counter the pernicious influence of their surroundings; one way to do this would be to introduce youth to the world of poetry and art. . . .

The people of the 1860s [in Russia] . . . strove for freedom, democracy, and equal rights; they believed firmly in a bright future, in a *joie de vivre*. In our day many people see such notions as "equal rights" or "the people" as abstractions and clichés. . . . They see the "repentant" period of the 1860s and the figure of the "repentant nobleman"[6] as . . . sentimental and absurd. . . .

---

[6]The so-called "repentant nobleman" included writers such as Alexei Pleshcheev, Nikolai Nekrasov, and Alexei Zhemchuzhnikov, whose works expressed guilt and remorse for the lot of the folk in Russia.

In reality, though, the "repentant noblemen" of the 1860s embodied social conscience. They were people with an elevated moral sense and with a conscious feeling of duty, one which cannot be the destiny of one historical epoch but . . . of all times. . . .

The idea that youth must be isolated from life is losing more and more ground. This idea is yielding to the completely opposite view: that young people must reflect upon the most stirring questions of life; that they must respond to social woe and misfortune; and that they must foster in themselves feelings of humanity, solidarity, and justice.

The best and most progressive figures among all civilized lands and peoples now support this idea; more and more, demands are being made of professional teachers.

True, very little that is practical is being done in this regard; but it is important to assert these new ideals. The path to their attainment is difficult, but it can be done!

April 18, 1900
Ivan Bunin, from a letter to Yuly Bunin
On the 14th, actors from the Moscow Art Theatre[7] came to Yalta. On the 15th we had dinner with Nemirovich and his wife. . . . I met Vishnevsky, Stanislavsky, Knipper, and Andreeva. I was at Chekhov's who, it seems, is marrying Knipper. I am paying court to [his sister] Maria Pavlovna Chekhova.

May 28, 1900
Ivan Bunin, from a letter to Nikolai Teleshov
In Yalta . . . I got acquainted with all the actors. Several of them are great people. I often went out with Gorky. . . . I was at Chekhov's several times at his own request . . . and I think we will become good friends.

June 1900
Ivan Bunin, from a critical article
It seems the time has come when aesthetics is gaining a solid foundation not only in practice but also . . . in theory. And it makes the fullest sense that the study of our fatherland's literature is getting first priority. This facet of knowledge cannot only formulate notions

[7]The Moscow Art Theatre was founded in 1898 by Konstantin Stanislavsky and Vladimir Nemirovich-Danchenko; it championed theatrical naturalism in Russia.

GREY DAWN # GREY DAWN 61

of grace and precise taste but can also... widen the psychological world-view and develop moral feelings.... The study of our fatherland's literature can also be the best means to awaken and strengthen national consciousness....

Without a doubt, literature can touch many strings in the youthful soul, especially when this soul begins to ponder the higher questions, when it thirsts for answers to the riddles of being, about the meaning of the individual on earth and about his role in the faceless mob. Who among us has not had such a period?...

Goethe said:

"Wer den Dichter will verstehen
Muss in Dichters Land gehen"—

and, in these few words, he expressed an idea which would eventually become an entire theory.... To understand a work of art... one must study the milieu... of the artist in question.... One must know the locale of the artist, the influence of nature on him, his place in society, the political and social conditions of the time, and, finally, the ideas, emotions, and moods of the epoch.

The study of a writer's milieu, though, even when it is understood in the broad sense of the word, is not enough. One must also study the individual qualities of a writer... his character, temperament, and intellectual propensities....

The human soul is a very complex thing and demands answers to the most diverse questions. If it does not receive these answers, it retreats into a narrow frame of mind and has no opportunity to develop its full potential. I am talking, of course, not only about the spiritual side of the soul... the moral point of view, but, without a doubt... also the psychological side which seeks to answer *the eternal questions of existence and the meaning of human life*, that is, those questions which our poet struggles to resolve.

True education... must not protect the individual from troublesome ideas. On the contrary, it must... acquaint individuals with *all aspects* of life... so that they will be able to grasp the ideas and emotions which are taking hold in society now, and which have taken hold in the generations who have created our contemporary culture. This includes the philosophy of pessimism. Leaders of today's youth must see to it that philosophical pessimism is given a prominent place in their studies, and that it is compared with other philosophical movements so as to create a synthesized world-view for their charges . . . and the opportunity for them to serve . . . society intelligently and sincerely.

July 16, 1900
Ivan Bunin, from a letter to Nikolai Teleshov
  As I see it, Gorky only pretends to be vulgar. He puts on an act. I am surprised that many do not feel this.

Early September 1900
Maxim Gorky, from a letter to Anton Chekhov
  You know—Bunin is a bright man. He has a precise sense for all that is beautiful, and when he is sincere, he is magnificent. It's a shame that his gentry neurasthenia ruins him.

October 1900
Ivan Bunin, from his story "Antonov Apples"
  I remember a fine, early autumn . . . a fresh, quiet morning . . . a big golden orchard, with dry and thinning leaves. I remember the walks lined with maples, the subtle fragrance of fallen leaves, and—the smell of Antonov apples. . . .
  A peasant . . . would eat one after another with a juicy crunch. . . . His employer would never stop him but would say, "Go ahead, eat up!" . . .
  In fair weather it grew very cold and damp. . . . And then there would be a new smell, that of a fire in the orchard . . . and the fragrant smoke of the burning cherry branches.
  The picture . . . was like a scene from a fairy tale: In the dark depths of the orchard the crimson flames . . . were like a corner of hell. . . . Monstrous shadows moved about the apple trees. . . . Suddenly they would slip down from the tree—and one would fall along the entire path, from the tent to the very gate. . . .
  We would listen attentively for a long time and make out a tremor running along the ground. . . . The tremor grew and grew until it seemed that wheels were beating time loudly and hurriedly just beyond the orchard. Knocking and clamoring, the train rushed on . . . closer and closer, louder and angrier. . . . And suddenly the sound grew fainter and muffled as though it was vanishing into the ground. . . .
  You would run and get the gun . . . and fire at random. A crimson spurt of flame would shoot up into the sky with a deafening

sound; it would blind you for a moment and snuff out the stars; and a grand echo would roar and roll like a ring about the horizon and fade in the pure and keen air, far, far away.

"Good for you!" the tradesman would say. "Scare the daylights out of 'em, young master, scare the daylights out of 'em! Otherwise we'll have nothing but trouble!" . . .

Our Viselki had always been known as a "prosperous place" from time immemorial, since Grandfather's time. Viselki people lived for a long time—the first sign of a prosperous village. . . . You would always hear. . . conversations like this:

"When are you going to die, Pankrat? You've got to be a hundred by now?"

"What's that you're saying, dear sir?"

"I'm asking how old you are?"

"I don't know, dear sir."

"Do you remember Platon Apollonich?"

"That I do. I remember him well."

"There, you see! That means you can't be less than a hundred."

The old man, standing erect before his master, would smile a humble and guilty smile. What could he do, after all? He was guilty, he had outlived his time. And probably he would have lived even longer if he had not eaten too many onions on Saint Peter's Day.

I also remember his wife. . . . She was a big woman, everything about her was dark. The shirt she wore was almost from the last century; her cloth slippers were like those they put on a dead body; her neck was yellow and scraggly; and her blouse . . . was always very, very white—"ready for the grave," they said. A large stone slab lay near the porch. She had bought it for her grave, just like she did her burial robe—a splendid shroud with angels, crosses, and a prayer printed about the edges. . . .

I remember times when I thought how tempting it would be to be a peasant. You would ride through the village on a sunny morning, thinking how good it would be to mow and thresh, to sleep in the haystacks in the barn, and on holidays to get up with the sun to the deep, melodious pealing of church bells. . . .

Until very recently, already in my time, the way of life of the average country squires had much in common with that of the wealthy peasants in their thriftiness and rustic old-world prosperity. Such was the estate of Aunt Anna Gerasimovna, for example. . . .

I had neither known nor seen serfdom, but I remember I could sense it at Aunt Anna Gerasimovna's. You rode through the gate and you felt right away that it was still alive and well. . . .

When you walked into the house you first noticed the fragrance of apples, then the smell of old mahogany furniture and of dried lime blossoms which had lain on the windowsills since June. . . . All the rooms were . . . cold and dark. . . . All was quiet and clean, though it seemed the armchairs, the inlaid tables, and the mirrors in their narrow, fluted gilt frames had never been moved from their places. And then you would hear a light cough, and out would come Aunt Anna. She was not a tall woman but, like everything about her, sturdy. . . . Refreshments would immediately appear: first pears and four kinds of apples, and then a splendid dinner: pink boiled ham with green peas, stuffed chicken, turkey, pickles, and red kvas, strong, and very, very sweet. . . .

In recent years the only thing that kept up the waning spirit of the landowners was hunting.

Estates such as our aunt's were no rarity in the old days. There were also those that were going to rack and ruin but that still lived in high style, with their vast properties and fifty-acre orchards. And though it is true that some of these estates have managed to survive to this day, there is no life in them. . . . There are no troikas, no Kirghiz horses, no hounds, no borzois, no serfs, even no owners. . . .

From the end of September our orchards and fields were bare, and the weather would change suddenly. The wind rushed through and tore at the trees for days on end; rain drenched them from morning to night. . . . The wind disturbed the garden . . . and drove clouds that were ominous, shaggy, and ashen colored. The clouds sailed low and fast and soon blocked out the sun in a smoky cloud. . . . Night would fall, long and uneasy. . . .

And now I remember the estate of Arseny Semyonich, the hall of his large house, filled with sunlight and the smoke of pipes and cigarettes. . . . The people there had just finished a huge dinner; they were flushed with excitement in their noisy talk of the coming hunt, but they had not forgotten to finish the vodka after dinner. . . . A black borzoi, Arseny Semyonich's favorite, climbed up to the table and began to gorge himself on the remains of the roast hare. Arseny Semyonich, coming out of his study with a hunting crop and a revolver, suddenly fired with a deafening sound and the dog, squealing horribly, bounded off the table, turning over plates and glasses.

The hall was filled with thickening clouds of smoke, but Arseny Semyonich just stood there laughing.

"Pity I missed," he said, his eyes flashing. . . . The bright, crowded house seemed very warm after a day out in the cold air. Everyone wandered from room to room with their coats open, eating and drinking any way they liked, discussing the day noisily over the body of the big wolf which lay in the middle of the hall, dyeing the floor with pale congealed blood, its teeth bared, its eyes rolled up, its fluffy tail hanging out. After the vodka and food you felt so deliciously tired, so sweetly drowsy. . . that if you closed your eyes the ground seemed to slip away from under your feet . . . and you did not remember that the room had once been the chapel of an old man whose name was the stuff of sinister estate legends, and who had died in that very room and probably in that very bed. . . .

You would settle down to the books of Grandfather's day, volumes bound in thick leather with golden stars on their morocco backs. There was a nice smell about those volumes which looked like prayer books with their rough, yellowed pages. A smell of old perfume clung to them, and a pleasant tang of mustiness. I liked the notes which had been made in the margins with a quill in a soft, rounded hand. I would open a book and read: "A thought worthy of ancient and modern philosophers, the light of reason and deep feeling." And you could not help becoming engrossed in the book itself. It was the *Nobleman-Philosopher*,[8] an allegory. . . the story of a "nobleman-philosopher" who, having the time and aptitude for reflection, to which the mind of man might be elevated, one day conceived the desire to write a plan for the world. Then you would come across "The Satirical and Philosophical Works of M. Voltaire." . . . After that, from the ancient times of Catherine the Great you would pass on to the age of romance, to almanacs, to novels—sentimentally pompous and long. . . . And beloved old worlds would flash before your eyes: rocks and groves, a pale moon and loneliness, ghosts, Cupid's darts, roses and lilies, "the playful pranks of naughty youths," lily-white hands, Lyudmillas and Alinas. . . . And then there were periodicals with the names of Zhukovsky, Batyushkov, and Pushkin, the young Lycée student. And you would wistfully recall

[8]The Nobleman-Philosopher was the pseudonym of Fyodor Ivanovich Dmitriev-Mamanov (1727–1805), a Russian writer and freethinker influenced by Voltaire.

Grandmama, the polonaises she played on the clavichord, the languid way she read verses from *Evgeny Onegin.* And the old dreamy world rose before you. . . . How lovely were the girls and women who once lived in these country homes! These beautiful, noble women with old-world coiffures looked down on me from their portraits on the wall and dropped their long eyelashes meekly and gracefully over their sad and gentle eyes. . . .

The fragrance of Antonov apples is disappearing from the country houses. Those days were such a short while ago, and yet it seems to me that a whole century has passed since then. The old people of Viselki are all dead; Anna Gerasimovna is dead, too, and Arseny Semyonich has shot himself. . . . The reign of the small estate owners, impoverished to the state of beggary, has now taken over. But even the beggarly life of the small estates is good. . . . The life of a small estate owner was good, too. . . .

In the old days the small estate owners would go visiting one another, drinking away the last of their money and spending all their days in the snow-clad fields. And at night, in the darkness of winter. . . in a room, filled with clouds of smoke, lighted with dimly burning tallow candles, a guitar would be tuned up . . .

> A blizzard fierce arose at night
> And threw my gates wide open,

a deep tenor would begin, and the others would join in discordantly with sad and hopeless bravado, pretending this was nothing but fun;

> It threw my gates wide open
> And buried roads in snowdrifts white. . . .

November 18, 1900
Ivan Bunin, from a letter to Yuly Bunin

Dear, sweet one! I left Paris on the 10th and arrived in Geneva that evening. . . . We went out early the next day; we marveled at the quiet warm morning. In the delicate fog . . . mountains and a lake, soft and azure green, appeared in the distance. . . . One could hear the pure ringing of bells, and the silence, the eternal silence of the lake and mountains.

I have thought about the quiet that reigns in the Alpine kingdom, where only the muffled sounds of waterfalls and eagles greet the afternoon. . . .

A Swiss man came out with a long wooden horn. . . . He soaked it in water, stood it like a giant pipe on the ground, blew into it, and made a sound. Hardly had the sound of the horn begun to die when it echoed in a thousand harmonies. . . . as if someone with a mighty hand had struck a crystal harp . . . and created a heavenly harmony. . . . that rose to the sky. . . . It was marvelous! . . .

In the mountains one could see . . . forests billowing in the fog . . . and the misted ravines filled with twilight. We stepped into the clouds; the lakes disappeared from sight. What silence! . . . We crossed a bridge over a terrible abyss . . . then we moved on into the snow . . . on a jagged road that seemed to head straight into the sky. . . . I remember standing on a precipice. . . . The deeper I looked, the darker it became . . . and I remembered Russia, the north. . . .

Circa *November 25, 1900*
Maxim Gorky, from a letter to Ivan Bunin
Thank you for your "Apples." It is good. Here Ivan Bunin has sung like a young god. It is beautiful, rich, and inspiring.

It is good when nature makes a man an aristocrat. . . . But my child, you should work and not travel all over the world.

PART TWO

Gathering Clouds

1901–1905

CHEKHOV, 1901   BUNIN, 1902

Between 1901 and 1905 Russian officials led a precarious existence. The minister of education was assassinated in 1901, the minister of the interior in 1902, another minister of the interior in 1904, and Grand Duke Sergius, governor general of Moscow, in 1905. It was business as usual in Russia: soldiers rebelled, students protested, peasants destroyed. Pogroms increased in number and fury, provoked by right-wing nationalists, wealthy peasants, and petty bourgeois who contended that the Jews and students were stirring up trouble while real Russians did not want change. Policies of repression clashed with the politics of reform. The government continued to centralize power, strengthen the bureaucracy, "russify" border peoples, and nurture corruption (Grigory Rasputin was introduced to the court in 1905). Opponents were crushed. On January 22, 1905—"Bloody Sunday," as it became known—some 150,000 workers in Saint Petersburg marched to the Winter Palace carrying icons, portraits of Nicholas II, and petitions for reform. They were met by mounted police who killed an estimated thousand people, including women and children, and wounded at least two thousand more.

The political and social problems of "patriarchal" Russia could no longer be denied—or endured. By 1905 Count Witte, minister of finance, had doubled Russia's foreign debt to three billion gold rubles, with the treasury paying out 130 million rubles yearly in interest. In the cities labor went on the offensive. Strikes and demonstrations multiplied and often turned into pitched battles with police. In 1905 alone more than fourteen thousand strikes involved several million workers. In the provinces the folk became restless because they still lacked sufficient land. Finally, Russia's stunning defeat in the Russo-Japanese War

(1904–1905), and the disaster of "Bloody Sunday," inflamed the populace.

Aristocrats and burghers called for freedom and a constitution; professionals advanced resolutions for reform; academics defiantly sang the "Marseillaise," though it had been banned by the police. Mutiny aboard the battleship *Potemkin* showed that even the army and navy could not be trusted. In October 1905 all of Russia was in revolt. A general, almost spontaneous strike began on October 20 and lasted ten days, paralyzing public and private life. Tsar Nicholas compromised reluctantly. In a manifesto of October 30, 1905, he declared Russia a constitutional monarchy and promised an elected legislative body (the duma) as well as freedom of speech, press, and assembly. Hope revived.

In these years insurgents in Russian art also took the offensive. Gorky was now the "stormy petrel" of the revolution. His appearance on the streets of Saint Petersburg caused traffic jams, and police often had to rescue him from his admirers. His play *The Lower Depths* (1902) enjoyed meteoric success, the audience calling for the author nineteen times on opening night in Moscow. The play was performed for fifty consecutive nights in Saint Petersburg but was banned in the provinces. The Modernists likewise gained in prominence, confidence, and nerve. A second generation of avant-garde writers (Blok and Bely, among others) had capitalized on the advances of the first wave and were now exploring uncharted philosophical and aesthetic frontiers. Impatient with worldly existence and anticipating the millennium, they moved boldly from Decadence to Symbolism, from rationalism to mysticism, from melancholy and passivity to arrogance and narcissism. *Building on Fire* and *Let Us Be Like the Sun* were common titles indicative of prevailing attitudes. But political and social events quickly returned the Modernists to dark and Decadent themes. In 1904, for instance, Blok published his *Verses on a Beautiful Lady*, in which his heroine was a blending of the Virgin Mary and Sophia, the representation of divine wisdom. At the same time despair and terror invaded his verse in poems about ghosts, demons, prostitutes, and gypsies.

For Bunin, the years between 1901 and 1905 were ones of triumph and tragedy. In 1901, to enthusiastic applause from readers and reviewers, he published a collection of poems, *Falling*

Leaves. In 1902 he began publishing collections of his stories with Gorky's publishing house, Knowledge *(Znanie)*, and would reach a total of five volumes by 1909. In 1903 he received his first Pushkin Prize for *Falling Leaves* and for his translation of Longfellow's *Hiawatha.* He was also traveling widely. In 1903 he made the first of thirteen visits to Constantinople; he also journeyed to France and Italy. His happiness and success, though, were marred by sadness and loss: Chekhov died in 1904, and Bunin's only son, Nikolai, in 1905.

Bunin's anguish in these years assumed a profoundly existential bent. He focused not so much on his physical illnesses as on his plight as a wanderer, estranged from Russia and the world. Having roamed the cities and villages of his homeland, he sensed that change was imminent and would soon destroy life as he knew it. Thus the image of the train in his fiction took on a new and menacing prominence—a dragon breathing fire and smoke, racing unopposed through dark and quiet forests. His stories featured people from the cities—urban heroes who, without remorse, gash the soil, trample the grass, and build factories and cities on the sites of abandoned churches, cemeteries, and crosses.

Bunin realized he could do little to prevent the destruction of his native land or to spare Russia its imminent chaos. Often he blamed his country for being godforsaken and cursed; just as often, though, he indicted himself for being an intellectual wanderer who paid too little attention to his country's distress.

Such deepening angst Bunin also projected onto the world. It seemed to him that the entire universe was moving toward apocalypse. In his story "The Fog" (1901), for instance, thick fogs, sad moons, and crimson suns surround people aboard a boat, celebrating a last supper before execution and death. Bunin was dreadfully accurate in his vision.

In these years Bunin was fortunate to have a friend, Anton Chekhov, who kept him from the abyss. During the last three years of his life Chekhov gave Bunin stability and strength. He provided him with a home, with people and surroundings that were totally unlike Bunin's own clan and haunts. The warmth of Chekhov and his sister, Maria Pavlovna, and the dazzling beauty of the Crimea, created an oasis for Bunin's dreams and writings, and helped to heal the wounds he had suffered early in life. For him Chekhov was also a mentor who epitomized the rewards and risks of writing. Chekhov had scored triumphs with *The Three Sisters* (1901) and *The Cherry Orchard* (1904), but he paid a high price for success in his earlier years of poverty and sickness, loneliness and doubt, capped by fears of oblivion and new misreadings by the critics. But Chekhov showed Bunin how to cope—to be brave, joyful, childlike, and, above all, committed to art. Bunin returned the confidence and support. He not only championed Chekhov after his death but challenged novice writers to meet the same high standards Chekhov had set for him: to write simply, to avoid fashion (read: Modernism), and to speak from life and the heart.

✳ 1901 ✳

January 13, 1901
Ivan Bunin, from a letter to Anton Chekhov

I am writing . . . to thank you for your hospitality. . . . The village where I had been living . . . was a veritable north pole . . . blizzards, snow, and a yellowish metallic sun that shone dimly in a wide frosty circle. I got bored quickly . . . and so, when I received the invitation from [your sister] Maria Pavlovna, I left for Yalta with the greatest of pleasure.

Yalta is very quiet. The weather is mild, and I have rested thoroughly in your home. . . . Mornings, my room is full of sunlight; your study . . . is even better: cheerful and spacious. The big, beautiful window casts green, blue, and red reflections on the wall and floor. I love colored windows, but at dusk they seem so sad. Your study is so empty and lonely when you are far away. . . .

I hear from Maria Pavlovna that you are working. I wish you good spirits and peace. I am also scribbling away and reading, and I am living peacefully and well.

February 5, 1901
Maxim Gorky, from a letter to Valery Bryusov

I love Bunin, but I do not understand him. His talent is like fine silver, but he does not sharpen it into a knife and stick it where he should.

February 15, 1901
Ivan Bunin, from his diary

One time, around twilight, I was reading to Chekhov his story "Gusev."[1] He said, "I want to get married."

[1]Chekhov wrote "Gusev" in 1890.

Mid-February 1901
Ivan Bunin, from a letter to a friend

My days here in Yalta pass by in a kind of poetic intoxication. . . .
We have sun, a joyous, turquoise sky, and the sea below. If only you
knew what a view I have from my windows! . . . In Anton Pavlovich's
study there is a very large window. . . with the top third made of
stained glass. Here on sunny days you can fancy all kinds of things!
Anton Pavlovich is well and working. His family is enchanting. . . .
His sister, Maria Pavlovna, is a rare girl! I am in town almost every
day; I have many acquaintances. I am writing a lot of poetry, and I
am beginning many, many stories. I am reading. . . . And I dream.

February 18, 1901
Ivan Bunin, from a letter to Maria Chekhova

I have been at your brother's . . . for days on end, of course, at
his invitation. . . . He has been very affectionate with me, and I have
found it very pleasant to be with him. . . . May God give him a
thousand healthy years.

February 22, 1901
Ivan Bunin, from a letter to Nikolai Teleshov

Chekhov has kept me here in Yalta. I have spent a marvelous
week with him. If only you knew what kind of person he was.

Spring 1901
Ivan Bunin, from a letter to Yuly Bunin

I am one of the family at the Chekhovs'.

March 8, 1901
Maria Chekhova, from a letter to Ivan Bunin

I am leaving for Yalta in two weeks. . . . and I cannot imagine
life there without you! Whom will I walk with on the embankment;
whom will I read with in the evening? . . .

Don't go to the north . . . where it is cold and wet. Come
straight to Yalta. . . . Antosha writes that the almond trees are already
blooming in the Crimea, and that it is so warm and nice there that
he doesn't feel like sitting in his room and writing.

"Uncle Vanya" and "The Three Sisters" have not been very
successful in Petersburg. The newspapers tear them to pieces, especially our Knipushcha. Everybody is dissatisfied; many of the actors

are crestfallen; Knipper even shed a few tears. . . . But Gorky is praising the plays, and he is respected.

I feel in my heart that my brother is not entirely well. . . . Your remark that he is "relatively well" worries me. . . .

April 1901
Ivan Bunin, from an early version of his story "The New Road"
All of Russia seems to me a solid desert of snows and forests, upon which a long and silent night slowly descends. . . .

To what country do I belong, a Russian intellectual-wanderer who roams his native land alone? What do I have in common with this forest backwater? Russia is so endlessly great; how can I understand its sorrows, how can I help it? I have spent my life in disarray, chasing after moments of happiness to which I also have a right; but where are they in this snowy desert? How terribly lonely are we who feebly seek beauty, truth, and the higher joys for ourselves and for others in this gigantic forest country? . . .

The train that I am on struggles on . . . with labored breathing it moves forth like a giant dragon. . . . Its head disgorges a red flame . . . which lights up the sullen alley of silent and still pines. The alley withdraws into the darkness, but the train moves on stubbornly. The smoke, like the tale of a comet, wafts over it in a long whitish arc, full of fiery sparks and tinged by the bloody flame below.

April 1901
Ivan Bunin, from his story "The Fog"
Oh, what a strange night it was! It was already very late, perhaps, early morning. We were singing, drinking, laughing, and telling each other all sorts of nonsense, here, in this alien world of sky, fog, and sea; the moon rose, lonely, gentle, and always sad. A deep night reigned . . . exactly like it did five, ten thousand years ago. . . . The fog embraced us tightly, in a terrifying sort of way. . . . There arose something like a bright mystic vision. The late-night yellow moon descended in the south; it froze in a pale curtain of mist and, as if alive, looked out from a huge wide ring. There was something apocalyptic in this circle . . . something unearthly and full of secret mystery. The moon stood in deathly silence . . . it was surprisingly close to the earth and looked at me with a sad and impassive expression. . . .

I do not understand the silent mysteries of this night, just as I do not understand anything about life. I am completely alone; I do not know why I exist. . . . I need no one, and no one needs me; and we are all alien to each other. . . .

For the first time it occurred to me that . . . this great thing we call *death* was looking me squarely in the face; and that for the first time I was looking at it squarely and understanding it as everyone must do. . . .

In the morning I opened my eyes . . . and jumped up from the berth, again full of an unconscious joy of life. . . . I felt a childlike gratitude for everything we must undergo. The night and the fog, it seemed to me, were there only so I could still love and value the morning more. . . .

April 30, 1901
Ivan Bunin, from a letter to Anton Chekhov

As you see, I am already in the village. It is awfully cold here; now it is raining cats and dogs—more cold. But the garden is green, and a nightingale is singing. . . . I live here as in a monastery. My soul is pure, and I am happy that I am writing so much poetry. God forbid someone put an evil eye on this.

June 1, 1901
Ivan Bunin, from a letter to a friend

We still have many old-fashioned tastes among readers in our country—just give us "happenings" and "events."

June 6, 1901
Maria Chekhova, from a letter to Ivan Bunin

I am in a murderous mood; all the time I feel that my existence is useless. The reason for this, in part, is my brother's marriage. It happened suddenly. I left him in Moscow in an absolutely sick condition. . . . Then on May 25 we get a telegram that he is getting married.[2]

I was upset for a long time. . . . but now it seems that everything has turned out well. . . . Of course, I am afraid that my relations with [his wife] Knipper have not changed. I even started thinking . . . that you could find me a fiancé who is rich and generous.

---

[2]Chekhov, in fact, married Knipper on May 25, 1901.

July 1901
Ivan Bunin, from his story "Silence"

What a great joy it is to live, to exist in the world, to breathe, and to see the sky, the water, the sun! But all the same we are unhappy! Why? Is it because our life is short, lonely, and chaotic?

August 1901
Ivan Bunin, from his story "The Crossing"

One night long ago I was roaming the mountains, heading for the crossing. I was going against the wind, in a cold fog, and in a hopeless state of mind. . . .

Toward dusk I rested at the edge of a pine forest, behind which rose a barren, deserted slope. I looked down at the immense depths beneath me, with the special emotions of power and pride with which one always looks down from great heights. One could still make out the lights in the darkening valley below, and the shore of a narrow gulf which became wider and wider toward the east, rising like a misty blue wall and embracing half the sky.

But night had already come to the mountains. . . . The mountains were rearing up ever darker and more majestic . . . a thick fog rolled in, chased by the storm from above. . . . The fog seemed to fill the forest with smoke and approached me, accompanied by the deep and inhuman sound of the pines. . . . For a long time I walked under the dark and droning vaults of the mountain forests, bending my head against the wind.

"The crossing will be soon," I told myself. "Soon I'll be where it is calm, beyond the mountains, in a bright house with people."

But half an hour passed by, then an hour. . . . Every minute it seemed to me the crossing was close by, but the bare and rocky slope did not end. I had long left the pine forests below; I had long passed the stunted, bent shrubs; and I began to get tired and shake. I recalled several graves amidst the pines not far from the crossing, where some woodcutters were buried after they had been hurled down from the mountains by a winter storm. I felt I was on some wild, uninhabited summit. I felt there were only fog and cliffs about me, and I thought . . . Do I have the strength to come down from the mountains when I have lost all sense of time and space?

Amidst the rushing fog, something turned dimly black in front of me . . . dark hills that looked like sleeping bears. . . . Suddenly I noticed that the road ahead again began to rise slowly up the hill! I stopped, seized by despair. I was shaking all over from tension and tiredness. My clothes were soaked through from snow; the wind was going right through them. Should I have screamed? But even the shepherds were huddled in their huts together with their sheep and goats. Who would have heard me? And I looked around with horror:

"Dear God! Surely I haven't gotten lost?"

It was late. The forest droned sleepily and thickly in the distance. Night was becoming more and more mysterious; I felt all of this, though I had lost track of time and space. The last light had now gone out in the deep valley, and a grey fog ruled over everything. The fog knew that its time had come, that long time when it seems that all has died on this earth; that morning will never come; that only the fogs will rise up and guard the stately mountains in a midnight watch; that the forests will drone dully through the mountains; and that the snow will fly more and more thickly on the deserted crossing.

Taking cover against the wind, I made my way over to my horse. He was the only living creature who remained with me! But the horse did not look at me. It was wet, frozen, and bent under the high saddle which hung clumsily on its back. It quietly lowered its head and pressed down its ears. Spitefully I pulled the rein; I again exposed my face to the wet snow and wind, and I went to meet them stubbornly. When I tried to make out my surroundings I saw only a grey mist filled with snow. When I listened attentively I made out only the whistle of the wind in my ears and a monotonous jingling behind me: the stirrups clanking against each other.

But it was strange. My despair began to strengthen me! I began to step forward more boldly; the malicious rebuke that I held against everyone for everything made me glad. It had already crossed over into that gloomy and steadfast submissiveness to everything that one must endure, and in which hopelessness becomes so sweet. . . .

Finally I came to the crossing. But I didn't care. I was going along the even, flat steppe; the wind was turning the fog into long strands and assailing me from head to foot; but I paid no attention to it. Each bit of fog, each whistle of the wind made me feel how deeply the late night had taken hold of the mountains. . . . I did not hurry. I went along, gritting my teeth; I muttered, turning to the horse:

"Come along, come along. We will wander until we drop. How many difficult and lonely crossings have there already been in my life! Sorrows, sufferings, sicknesses, the treachery of loved ones, and the bitter insults of friends have come down upon me like the night. The time has come for me to part with everything that has been mine.

And, reluctantly, I again took up my pilgrim's staff. The ascents to new happiness were high and difficult; the night, the fog, and the storm met me in the heights; a terrifying loneliness seized me at the crossings. . . . But, we go on! we go on!"

August 1901
Ivan Bunin, from his story "The Epitaph"

New people are appearing on the steppe. More and more, they are arriving from the city. . . . At night they light fires to chase away the darkness; shadows run from them along the roads. At dawn they go out to the fields and pierce the earth with long drills. All around there are black piles of dirt that look like grave mounds. Without remorse the new people trample down the sparse rye that still grows here and there . . . without remorse they cover it with earth, looking for a new happiness. . . .

Perhaps the smokestacks of factories will soon belch forth smoke; iron rails will replace the old road; and a city will rise over the wild village. The gray cross which once blessed the old life has fallen to earth and will soon be forgotten. . . . But how will the new people hallow their new life? How will they bless their brisk and noisy work?

Mid-October 1901
Maxim Gorky, from a letter to a friend

From a literary point of view—Bunin is an artist, and not a bad one at that. But whereas other artists have a face, Bunin has fog in its place.

Mid-November 1901
Maxim Gorky, from a letter to a friend

Bunin's "Antonov Apples" smells very good, but it is hardly democratic, don't you think so?

✳   1902   ✳

January 15, 1902
Anton Chekhov, from a letter to Ivan Bunin

Happy New Year! I wish that you become famous throughout the entire world, that you meet the very best woman around, and that you win two hundred thousand rubles. . . .

Your story "The Pines"[3] ... is very new, very fresh, and very good. Only it is way too dense, like thick broth. ...

July 2–3, 1902
Maxim Gorky, from a letter to a friend
We are going to put forth Bunin as a novelist, poet, and translator. The public is reading him, and there are blockheads who say he is better than Andreev.

August 2, 1902
Ivan Bunin, from a letter to Maria Chekhova
Again I am on my way, my endless way; and, like yesterday and today, I do not have a single person nearby whom I could call a close relative. I feel like crying from loneliness. Indeed, the people who are close to me number no more than ten in the entire world.

December 28, 1902
Ivan Bunin, from an interview with the Odessa News; *and also as told to Georgy Adamovich*
I do not like to visit Tolstoy. ... I find it terrifying to be with him. Tolstoy is so colossal, so demanding of the person. ... Every word he says bears the imprint of his character.

One terribly cold evening last year, I was walking along at the Arbat in Moscow. I saw Tolstoy in the darkness ... running along with his usual springlike gait. ... I stopped and took off my hat. He recognized me immediately:

"Oh, it's you. Hello, hello, Ivan Alexeevich," he said. "Put your hat back on, please. Well, where have you been, and what have you been doing. ... How come I have not seen you?"

I was as lost as a schoolboy. I simply didn't know what to do with my hat. "I'm afraid to visit you," I confessed to him frankly.

"People should never be afraid, never," Lev Nikolaevich repeated insistently and assuredly. ...

His old face was frozen; it had turned blue and had taken on a completely unhappy look. ... His big hand ... was like ice. He shook my hand firmly and affectionately, but his eyes were sad. ...

"Well, God be with you, God be with you," Tolstoy said. Then he disappeared quickly into the darkness, leaving me overwhelmed and shy.

[3]Bunin wrote "The Pines" in 1901.

December 29, 1902
Ivan Bunin, from an interview with the Odessa News
The idea that Chekhov is a cold writer, an observer who views life "from the side," is absolutely incorrect. Chekhov is a most sincere and open individual; he is alien to all falsehood and pretense, an artistically sensitive and perceptive being. . . . Last year when I visited him . . . all we did was laugh. . . . They say that when Anton Pavlovich was a schoolboy, there was not a kid who was happier and more carefree than he.

✳ 1903 ✳

Circa *1903*
Natalya Tolstaya-Krandievskaya, from her memoirs
I was fifteen years old . . . and writing verse; and . . . I was on my way to meet with the poet Ivan Bunin. . . .
"Come in. You will forgive my domestic look?" Bunin said.
Bunin was wearing a Bukhara robe. He was sitting in a chair in front of a box with cases; he was filling them up with tobacco, spilling it on the floor. His quiet, icy eyes looked at me attentively. He sat me down on a chair next to him and said, "Go ahead. I'm listening."
Shaking, I pulled out my notebook. Without stopping, I began to read about nightingales, lilies, the moon, grief, love, seagulls, fjords, reefs, and reeds. Finally Bunin stopped me:
"Why are you writing about seagulls? Have you ever seen a seagull up close?" he asked. "A voracious, clumsy bird, with a short trunk and smelling of raw fish. You write: 'the lonely, sad seagull.' And then you go and compare yourself to it."
"Ai, ai, ai," Bunin said, shaking his head, "this is not good; such nonsense comes from sitting in a room."
"But don't you remember Balmont's poem?" I said. " 'A seagull, a grey seagull, born aloft on sad cries . . .'."
"Balmont!" Bunin snorted and broke into soundless laughter. . . . "Look here, missy, let's agree on one thing once and for all. Don't rely on Balmont. . . . His kind are a dangerous lot; they have a chrysanthemum on their shoulders instead of a head. . . . Beware of Balmont!" . . .

I have made him angry, I thought. We were both silent for a while.

"I am telling you all this," Bunin said, "because you are young. . . . But tell me why seagulls? . . . Have you ever been in the village? No? Have you seen a rabbit's footprints in the snow? . . . Do you know that snow has a smell? Imagine what a storm would smell like."

"Like a watermelon," I suddenly blurted out.

"Aha!" Bunin cried. "Bravo, my colleague! A watermelon? That's not bad."

He smiled; I suddenly felt better. Things were getting easier between Bunin and me. . . .

"Now here you write," Bunin said, " 'Wait for me by the shore of the fjord.' What kind of fjord, only Allah knows. Neither you nor I have ever seen a fjord. That is why your poem is colorless, forced, and without a single living detail. And here you write: 'The yacht was smashed by the storm.' Pardon me, but I do not believe your storm because you have made it up. Keep reading."

I continued reading and thought how nice it would be if I hadn't written any of it. . . . Bunin laughed, and I was extremely offended. I started to get angry. I felt like a frog in a trap.

"I'll burn it all," I suddenly decided. "I'll burn all my notebooks. Just like Gogol did.[4] In the stove."

But Bunin continued on in a now serious, kind voice, just like that of a doctor:

"You have to live a bit. . . . What do you know? What are your poetic sources? Books, imagination, and books again. What is in your heart? Nothing for now. Just coolness and impatience. That's bad, bad. There is little spark in your poetry. Life will straighten this out—just wait. Life will stir up some fire in you. . . . Tell me now, are you an observing person?" Bunin suddenly asked.

I didn't know what to answer.

"Life!" continued Bunin, "is not so simple. It moves, shines, sounds, flowers, and smells. It changes minute by minute. One must observe and remember every detail. One must be curious. Can you do that? The reason why I am telling you this is because at your age, one lets life pass by. . . . I did it, too, when I was young. But if snow smells like a watermelon. . . ."

---

[4]A reference to Gogol's burning of a portion of the second part of his novel *Dead Souls* (1842).

In the foyer. . . Bunin said farewell:

"Let's make peace. Your poetry has strength. . . . That's why I am scolding you, my dear colleague. . . ."

I was upset. I didn't know if I should be offended or if I should laugh with him. But I changed my mind about burning my notebooks. Tying my hood, I ran down the stairs.

"Beware of Balmont!" Bunin cried after me.

Circa *March–April 1903*
Andrei Bely, from his book The Beginning of the Century

Bunin was a bilious, scrawny-looking individual. He looked like he had been on a bender, with dark green spots around his eyes and with a pointed and beaklike profile, making him look like a carrion crow. He had a lock of falling hair, a dark red Spanish beard, and lips that looked like they were perpetually wrapped around a lemon. Bunin would always grumble and look at you askance. . . . As a youth, I feared him greatly. . . . He would always throw me a sidelong glance, like a condor stealing up to something alone, supine, and wounded.

April 27, 1903
Ivan Bunin, from a letter to a friend

I love form, but I love the human soul, no matter what form it takes.

✳ 1904 ✳

January 1904
Ivan Bunin, from his story "The Golden Bottom"

The splendor of the night grows dim. The fields take on a blue melancholic cast; far off in the distance the sun sets . . . like a huge dully crimson sphere. There is something so anciently Russian in this sad scene, in this bluish distance with its dull crimson shield. The sun becomes more wan. Only a small part of it remains, and then a quivering fiery streak. . . . The meadows are cold like graves, the dewy verdure smells sharply. . . . Willow bushes flash in the twilight; ravens sleep in their branches. . . . The big head of a pale moon rises slowly in the east. . . .

Circa *July 1904*
Anton Chekhov, as recalled by contemporaries

Soon I will die; but as regards my place in Russian literature, I see a worthy successor in Bunin.

July 9, 1904
Ivan Bunin, from a letter to Maria Chekhova

The passing of your brother[5] has literally struck me like lightning. . . . I ask only that you know that I am sharing all your suffering . . . with indescribable pain.

September 1904
Ivan Bunin, from his memoirs

I met Chekhov in Moscow, in late 1895. . . .

"Do you write a lot?" he once asked me.

I answered that I wrote little.

"This is not good," Chekhov said almost gloomily, and in a low baritone voice. "You have to work . . . incessantly. . . your entire life."

After some silence . . . he added:

"As I see it, once you have written a story, you must cross out the beginning and the end. We writers lie more than anything else. . . . You must write more briefly, as briefly as possible." . . .

We did not see each other again until spring 1899. Having spent several days in Yalta, I met Chekhov on the quay.

"Why haven't you come to see me?" he said. "Come tomorrow without fail."

"When?" I asked.

"In the morning, around eight."

And, most likely, seeing the surprise on my face, he explained:

"We get up early. And you?"

"Me, too," I said.

"So then come when you get up. We will drink some coffee. Do you drink coffee?"

"I drink it now and then."

"Drink it every day. It is a splendid thing. When I work I limit myself only to coffee and broth until the evening. Coffee in the morning, broth at midday. Otherwise I don't work well."

I thanked him for his invitation. Then we walked along the quay and sat on a bench in the square.

---

[5]Chekhov died in Badenweiler, Germany, on July 2, 1904.

"Do you like the sea?" I once asked Chekhov.

"Yes," he answered. "Only it is so very empty."

"But that's good," I said.

"I'm not so sure," he said. . . . "I think it would be nice to be an officer or a young student. . . . And to sit somewhere in a place with people amidst cheerful music. . . ."

Then . . . Chekhov changed the topic:

"It is very difficult to describe the sea. Not long ago I read a description of the sea in a student's notebook. 'The sea was big,' the student wrote. That was it. Tremendous." . . .

Chekhov loved only that which was sincere, vital, and organic. . . . He could not stand phrasemongers, bookish types, and pharisees. . . . In his works he almost never talked about himself, his tastes, his views . . . and for a long time he was seen as an individual without principles or social concerns. In his life, too, Chekhov rarely spoke about his likes and dislikes. . . . But he had them, and sincerity was first among the things he prized. . . . Chekhov constantly yearned for utmost simplicity; he was repulsed by anything artificial or strained. . . . He loved life. . . .

People say Chekhov's death was hastened by *The Cherry Orchard*, and that on the night before its premiere Chekhov was so upset, and so afraid that no one would like his play, that he was delirious all night long. This is absolute garbage. . . .

In Moscow in 1895 I saw a middle-aged man with a pince-nez, rather tall, very well proportioned, simply and pleasantly dressed, and . . . very light in his movements. He was cordial but so simple in his manner—that I . . . took it for coldness. When I later met Chekhov in Yalta . . . he had changed a great deal. He had become thin; his face had gotten dark. . . . His elegance was not that of a young man but of one who had experienced much in life and who had become nobler for it. Even his voice was softer. . . . But, in general, Chekhov was almost the same as he was in Moscow: cordial but restrained. . . .

The morning after our meeting on the quay I went to his dacha. . . . From then I visited Chekhov's house more and more often; I became one of the fixtures. Needless to say . . . Chekhov became more animated and sincere in my presence. . . . But he was still reserved: not only with me but also with those who were closest to him. I convinced myself then that this reserve was not indifference but something far greater.

The white stone dacha . . . the southern sun, the blue sky; the small garden which Chekhov tended with such care (he loved flowers, trees, and animals); his study with its huge semicircular window... and its two or three paintings by Levitan; its view of the valley, gardens, the river, and the blue triangular sea; the hours, days, and sometimes even months I spent at this dacha; and the knowledge that I was close to someone who had captivated me not only with his mind and talent but also even with his quiet voice and childlike smile—these will always remain among the best memories of my life.

Chekhov was . . . friendly toward me; sometimes he was almost tender. But he did not abandon his reserve even in our most intimate conversations. . . . He loved to laugh, but he most often laughed his dear, infectious laugh only when someone told him something that was funny. He himself could say the funniest things without the slightest smile. He loved jokes, absurd nicknames, and hoaxes. In his last years, when he was feeling well if only for a short period of time, he could be full of the devil. . . . He would toss out two or three words, and his eyes would take on a wicked look. . . .

Chekhov could manifest his reserve in other, more important ways. . . . Who ever heard him complain? And he had many reasons to do so. He was from a large family; he was poor as a youth; he worked for pennies and in conditions that would have snuffed out the spark of inspiration. . . . He was in need long after that. But no one ever heard Chekhov complain about his fate—but not because his needs were few. He kept an extremely modest way of life; but he also hated his grey and sparse existence. . . . For fifteen years Chekhov was sick with a debilitating illness which eventually caused his death; but did the reader know this—the Russian reader who hears so many bitter wails from writers?

Sick people love their privileged position; often, almost with delight, they torment those around them with spiteful, bitter, and unending conversations about their illnesses; but the courage with which Chekhov met his sickness and death was truly astounding! Even during those days of his greatest pain, no one suspected how he was suffering.

"Aren't you feeling well, Antosha?" his mother or sister would ask when they saw that he had been sitting in his chair with his eyes closed.

"Me?" Chekhov would answer calmly, opening his eyes which were so big and gentle without his pince-nez. "No, it's nothing. It's just that my head hurts a little."

Chekhov loved literature passionately. . . and it was sheer delight for him to talk about Maupassant, Flaubert, or Tolstoy. . . . He
loved Lermontov's "Taman."[6]

"I cannot understand," he would say, "how Lermontov could
write such a thing when he was so young!. . ."

Chekhov's discussions about literature were not at all like the
usual professional discussions that are so distasteful, petty, and
narrow. . . . He would talk about literature only when he knew that
his companion loved writing as free and disinterested art.

"No one should read his own writings until they are in print,"
Chekhov would often say. "More important, one should never listen
to advice. If a writer makes a mistake, if he talks nonsense—then it
should stand. The mistake will belong to him alone. After the high
standards which Maupassant imposed on his work, it is very difficult
to write, but one must do so all the same, especially we Russians; one
must be daring in his work. . . . Little dogs must not fear big dogs:
Everyone should bark with the voice that God gave him."

Everything that happened in the literary world was close to
Chekhov's heart. He often became very upset at the stupidity,
falsehood, roguery, and affectation which flowered so luxuriously in
contemporary literature. . . . He truly rejoiced over any talent. . . . But
he regarded his own successes with hidden bitterness.

Chekhov worked for almost twenty-five years. How many trivial
and coarse reproofs did he hear about his writing in that time!. . .
Chekhov did not preach. So how could he enjoy the favor of critics in
Russia?. . .

"Anton Pavlovich, soon we'll be celebrating your anniversary as a
writer!"

"I know these anniversaries well. Critics tear you apart for
twenty-five years, then they give you a quill . . . and talk the most
solemn nonsense, and with tears and kisses to boot. . . ."

"Have you read what they wrote about you, Anton Pavlovich?"
you would say to him when there was an article about him. . . .

"This I need!. . . They always end: 'But, just the same, Chekhov
is a moaner and a groaner. . .' But am I a moaner and groaner? Am I
a 'gloomy individual'? Where is the 'cold blood' that the critics say I
have? What kind of 'pessimist' am I? After all, 'The Student'[7] is my
most favorite story. . . . And the word 'pessimist' is such a repulsive

---

[6]"Taman" is a key episode in Lermontov's novel *A Hero of Our Time* (1840).
[7]Chekhov's story "The Student" appeared in 1894.

word. . . . No, critics are worse than actors. And you know that actors lag a full seventy-five years behind the rest of Russian society."

Then Chekhov added:

"You must remember. . . that we writers live as if in a seminary; critics flog us for the slightest fault. One predicted I would die in the street: I imagined him to be a young man who had been expelled from school for drunkenness."

Chekhov became irritated rarely, but when he did he quickly took himself in hand. But he was never cold. As he himself confessed, he became cold only when he was working. He would never sit down to write until the thought and images of his piece were completely clear to him so that he could write almost without interruption.

"You should write only when you feel as cold as ice," he said. . . .

I remember one night in Yalta in early spring 1903. It was already late; suddenly the phone rang. . . .

"Dear one," Chekhov said, "grab a cab, and come by my place. Let's go for a ride."

"A ride? Now?" I said with surprise. "What's with you, Anton Pavlovich?"

"I'm in love."

"That's nice, but it's already after ten. . . . You might catch a cold."

"Dear boy, stop arguing!"

In ten minutes I was there. The home where Chekhov and his mother lived was, as always, deathly silent and dark. . . . As always, my heart clutched at the sight of Chekhov's quiet study where he spent so many lonely winter evenings, absorbed, perhaps, by bitter thoughts about his fate.

"What a night!" Chekhov said. . . . He was unusually tender, both joyful and sad. . . . "It's so boring here at home! The only joy I have is when the phone rings, and when someone asks me what I am doing. Catching mice, I say. Let's go. . . . Who cares if I catch a cold."

The night was warm and quiet. There was a clear moon, light white clouds, and a few bright stars in the deep blue sky. The carriage softly made its way along the white road. We were silent as we looked at the valley of the sea, shining like tarnished gold. . . . Forest shadows were like a spider web but already springlike: tender, beautiful, and pensive . . . a grove of darkening cypress trees rose up to the bright stars. We stopped the carriage and walked quietly. . . past the ruins of a palace that was bluish white in the moonlight. Chekhov suddenly said to me:

"Do you know how long people will continue to read me? Seven years."

"Why seven?" I asked.

"Then seven and a half."

"No," I said. "Your work will live on for a long time; the longer it lasts, the more powerful it becomes."

Chekhov didn't say anything; but when we sat down on a bench, and again with a view of the sea shining in the moonlight, he took off his pince-nez, and, looking at me with his kind and tired eyes, he said:

"People are considered poets, dear boy, only when they use such phrases as 'the purple distance,' 'musical chords,' or 'onward, forward, to battle the darkness!' "

"You are sad today, Anton Pavlovich," I said, looking at his simple, kind, and splendid face, slightly pale in the moonlight.

He lowered his eyes . . . but then he playfully looked askance at me.

"You're the one that's sad," he answered. "And the reason is that you have spent money on a cabby."

Then he added seriously:

"Nonetheless people will read me for only seven years, but I have less to live than that: six years. Not a word of this to the reporters."

But this time Chekhov was wrong . . . he died peacefully [a year later], without suffering, and amidst the quiet and beauty of a summer sunrise which he loved so much. When Chekhov died, "an expression of happiness appeared on his suddenly youthful face. . . ." I remembered the words of L. Delille:

Moi, je t'envie, au fond du tombeau calme et noir,
D'être affranchi de vivre et de ne plus savoir
La honte de penser et l'horreur d'être un homme.[8]

---

[8]Jacques Delille (1738–1813) was a French poet and translator who was popular in Russia in the beginning of the nineteenth century. The inscription reads: "As for me, I envy you, at the bottom of a tomb, calm and black/ To be freed from life and to know no more/ The shame of thinking and the horror of being a man."

✳ 1905 ✳

October 18, 1905
Ivan Bunin, from his diary, and later recollections

I was living in Yalta . . . in Chekhov's house, now [after his death] always quiet, empty, and sad. . . . The days were invariably grey and fall-like; life with Chekhov's sister and mother flowed by so steadily, so monotonously. . . . I found it very difficult: All around, in the garden, in his study, it was like he was there, even though he really wasn't.

It was not easy for me to leave, to tear myself away from this life. It was pitiful to leave these two genuinely lonely, deeply unhappy women. . . . I often saw how their silent tears overwhelmed them. The one indulgence they allowed themselves was to ask me to stay a little longer. "Do you remember," they said, "how Antosha loved when you visited and stayed with us!"

Yes, it was so difficult to leave this home which was almost like my own. I already felt I could no longer come back here. The study was exactly like it was when Chekhov was alive. His desk had all kinds of trifles on it—dear, elegant things which he brought back from Sakhalin and Colombo. It always surprised me that he could write with such clutter.

Chekhov's bedroom was narrow, white, tidy, like a girl's. . . . His study had a little recess with a couch on which he would love to sit and read something. There was a copy of Tolstoy's *Resurrection*;[9] I kept recalling how Chekhov would visit Tolstoy when Tolstoy was lying sick in the Crimea, and how, when he returned, he would tell me with great excitement:

"You know, there is something marvelous, unbelievable about Tolstoy. An old man lies in his bed; physically he is hardly alive, with one foot in the grave, but spiritually he is a genius, a super-genius!" . . .

Yesterday evening the phone in Anton Pavlovich's study rang. . . . I learned that Russia was in the throes of a revolution. . . . The trains had stopped running; the telegraphs and post office were closed. . . .

[9]Tolstoy published *Resurrection* in 1899.

I immediately went into the city. The night was terrifying; there was unrest everywhere. Small groups of people gathered in hushed yet animated conversations. . . . I was very much afraid I would get stuck in Yalta and be cut off from all that was going on. I went to the pier, and, thank God, a ship was leaving the next day for Odessa. I decided to go there.

Today I woke up in an excited frame of mind. . . . but also with heaviness and anxiety in my heart. The weather was grey and unpleasant. . . . The sun lit up the sky . . . with a rose and blue-grey hue. . . .

In Sevastopol . . . I heard a policeman . . . saying that a manifesto had been issued concerning freedom of speech, unions, all "freedoms" in general. I was so excited that my hands were shaking. . . . I finally read the manifesto! Such tremendous joy, the feeling of a major event.

Tonight (on my way to Odessa) I had a long conversation with an officer on ship, a thoroughly intellectual type of individual. . . . The conversation tended to extremely revolutionary themes: quiet, firm, threatening. The officer talked to me without turning around and looking at the dark surface of the sea that rushed up to meet us.

October 19, 1905
Ivan Bunin, from his diary

We put in at Odessa at about eight. The morning was grey and rainy, with a nasty wind. . . . I learned . . . that several Jews have been killed. It seems as if they were killed by disguised policemen for allegedly trampling on a picture of the tsar. . . .

I arrived at the hotel and caught sight of soldiers outside. I asked the doorman, "Why are there soldiers?" But he only grinned with a confused look on his face. . . . Everything was empty: the stores were closed; there were no cabbies. . . . The town governor appealed for calm. People clustered here and there.

Very much afraid, I went to the editorial office of the *Southern Review*. The premises were packed with Jews with sad, serious faces. A huge wreath with red ribbons leaned against the wall; on it was the inscription: "Fallen for the cause of freedom."

One of the Jews said, "Our last days have come."

"Why?" I asked.

"A parade of patriots is leaving the port and coming here. . . ."

Another asked, "Perhaps they'll crack my head open?"

"Perhaps. . . ."

Black flags hung all along the gates of the city garden. . . . The councilors of the local duma[1] met with the public; unanimously they decided to raise a red flag over the building . . . then there was a demand that those who had "fallen for freedom" be buried on Cathedral Square. Again the duma agreed.

An acquaintance warned me that . . . the patriots' parade was already in progress and that hoodlums were killing everyone who got in their way. People were running toward me in panic.

At three o'clock I learned that the market was being pillaged. The police were already there; hospital orderlies were everywhere. . . . I felt under siege. . . . The shooting went on throughout the night. Jewish stores and homes were ransacked everywhere. People say that the Jews were shooting from windows, and that the soldiers were firing volleys at them.

Toward evening, people were running past us on the street; "policemen" were running after them, shooting at them. Several of them were arrested. The wounded were carried away in a cab. . . . A student had all his clothes ripped off him and sat at the bottom of the cab. . . . His head was wrapped in bloody rags.

October 20, 1905
Ivan Bunin, from his diary

The early morning is grey and foggy. People . . . are saying that all is now quiet everywhere. . . .

A thick fog comes in from the sea. . . . A machine gun . . . rattles on all day along . . . first in scattered firing and then without interruption. It is dangerous to go out. In the evening the gunfire and the clattering of the machine gun have so intensified that it seems as if a genuine battle is going on.

By nightfall a deathlike stillness, an emptiness has fallen upon the city. The house where I am staying is a big, three-storyed building that stands on a bluff overlooking the port. This afternoon we went up into the attic; from there we could see a building being destroyed. . . . By evening we thought we should take cover, so we went into the big cave under the museum.

Later on we again went up to the attic, looked through the dormer window, and saw and heard: the fog, the wet silhouettes of dark roofs, the evening, the dampness of the sea, and . . . the firing that was beginning to quiet down.

[1]The duma was the locally elected government body.

October 22, 1905
Ivan Bunin, from his diary

This morning I went to the hotel. The cabby told me that . . . "Jews were being hacked to pieces." Shaking his head, he grieved that many of them were innocent. He was furious with the Cossacks and swore at them profusely. So it was the whole time I was there: People were furious at the "Cossack-beasts" and angry at the Jews. . . .

At noon . . . the town came back to life and took on its everyday character: the trams and cabs were moving.

At about three o'clock I ran into an acquaintance . . . who told me that . . . Ukrainian men and lads were going down the streets with scythes and daggers. . . . They had come from the farms to destroy the town and to kill not only the Jews but everyone else.

[One person] told me he saw . . . a whole caravan of soldiers with rifles. They had seen someone in a window alongside the hotel. So they stopped and sprayed the front of the building with gunfire. . . . "Just in case," they said.

Today the churches will have a special service—"for the softening of hearts."

[A second person told me:] "They were beating the Jews mercilessly, savagely on Moldavanka Street . . . and on Trinity a crowd had just marched by, waving national flags and a portrait of the tsar. The crowd stopped at the corner, yelled 'Hurrah,' and then began to destroy the stores. The Cossacks soon arrived, but they passed by the scene with smiles on their faces. Then a detachment of soldiers came, but they, too, passed by, smiling. . . . The offices of *Southern Review* have been smashed to smithereens, and there has been shooting from there. . . ."

[A third person told me:] "I was on the tram, and we came upon a crowd crying, 'Stand up and say hurrah for His Majesty the Emperor!' Everyone got up and said, 'Hurrah!'—and with a platoon of soldiers going peacefully by. Many policemen have been killed. The hospital orderlies are shooting at the Cossacks, and the Cossacks are shooting back at them." . . .

[A fourth told me] that . . . there are "hardly any Jews left on Romanov Square," and [a fifth] that about ten thousand people have been killed.

The trains are still not working. I will leave tomorrow on the first one out of town.

It is dusk. A nurse told me that on Romanov Square children's heads were being bashed against the wall, and that the soldiers and

Cossacks stood idly by, shooting their guns into the air. . . . In town the rumor is that the city governor has refused to accept a telegram from the duma in Petersburg with questions as to what is going on. . . .

Utochkin, a well-known athlete, is near death. He saw. . . hoods beating up an old Jew, and he rushed to help him. . . . "It was like a gust of wind hitting me in the gut," that's how he later described it. The hoods had chopped him up "right under his heart."

It is evening. A friend sighs with pity for the Jews. He says, "Everyone feels sorry for them. . . . Dear God, how sad they are . . . afraid and frozen from the cold. The Cossacks took pity on them; they brought them to a shelter and fed them. . . ."

Russia, O Russia!

PART THREE

First Blood

1906–1910

VERA MUROMTSEVA, 1906   BUNIN, 1906

In 1906 Russia's first revolution continued with riots, strikes, and mutinies. Much of the national revolt was chaotic and purposeless, an expression of fury rather than faith. As the country sank deeper into anarchy, its citizens yearned for law and order at any cost. The newly formed soviets, or "worker's councils," fought the duma, which in turn fought the tsar. Aided by traditionalists, the government quickly regained power. Nicholas II reasserted autocracy as a divine right. The First Duma lasted only a month in 1906; the second, four months in 1907. The Third Duma (1907–1912) was far more docile and yielding: 46 percent of its members were landowners.

Battered and shaken, the government heeded the motto of Prime Minister Stolypin: "Order first, reforms later." Huge numbers of people were tortured and jailed. Others were executed without trial, the recipients of "Stolypin's necktie," the noose that hung from more than seven thousand gallows. Still others were dispatched to Siberia, where exiles swelled to some twenty thousand. Publications of all kinds were censored, terminated, or seized. Between 1908 and 1909 more than a thousand newspapers and magazines were forced to suspend operations. In 1907 Tolstoy could no longer "remain silent," but his famous treatise against capital punishment led authorities to confiscate more than forty of his works.

In a series of reforms begun in 1906, Stolypin sought to dismantle the peasant *mir*, or commune, and create a class of independent farmers who, he hoped, would stimulate the economy and support the regime. The measure was a success. Between 1906 and 1914 two million peasant households claimed land from the *mir* and became private landowners. The "Stolypin reforms," though, had the unfortunate result of stratifying the folk into rich

99

and poor, with *kulaks* or entrepreneurial peasants advancing at the expense of their poorer and more egalitarian brothers. Hostilities between the two groups grew and added new instability to the countryside.

Between 1905 and 1910 the Symbolists reached the height of their leadership and popularity in Russian fiction, a position they would hold until the outbreak of World War I. Russian realism was at a nadir. Tolstoy, the leader of the "old" realists, died in 1910; Gorky, the leader of the "new" realists, was in exile abroad and, thanks to the government, the target of mounting hostility at home. The Symbolists knew precisely what their readers wanted: an escape from life into fantasy, exoticism, black magic, and sex. Debauchery and hedonism became the guiding principles of Russian life. Leagues of Free Love, Athenian Nights, Satanic cults, and suicide clubs were everyday fare. Such license quickly penetrated into literature. Publishing ventures such as *The Facts of Life* and *The Mysteries of Sex* took their place among erotic fiction, translations of Strindberg and Mirabeau, and homegrown works that were morbid and depraved.

Just as Bunin had witnessed the chaos in Odessa in 1905, so now he confronted the violence in the provinces the next year. Peasants had seized control of his brother's estate and had driven his family from the land. Bunin had had his fill of revolutionary Russia; he was also tired of being lonely. In the fall of 1906 he met Vera Nikolaevna Muromtseva (he was thirty-six, she was twenty-five), a university student, the daughter of a member of the Moscow city council, and a niece of Sergei Andreevich Muromtsev, president of the First Duma and one of the founders of the Constitutional Democratic party. The liberalism in Muromtseva's family was not confined to politics; six months after their meeting she became Bunin's common-law wife (Bunin's first spouse, Anna Tsakni, would not grant him a divorce), and together they traveled throughout Western Europe and the Near and Far East.

Muromtseva was Bunin's salvation. From the very beginning of their relationship she understood him as no one else did. Somehow she intuited that the fate of "gentry" literature was entrusted to her care, a challenge that would last for almost fifty years and that she met with admirable courage and aplomb. She was Bunin's helpmate, his confidante, his buffer, sometimes his protector from the outside world.

With Muromtseva, Bunin embarked on travels that grew more frequent, exotic, and prolonged: Turkey, Egypt, and Singapore, to name but a few of the places that the couple visited. Bunin's knowledge and experience with the outside world was almost unprecedented for a Russian writer of his time. His travels afforded him many benefits. They not only gave him periodic respite from his troubled homeland but exposed him to the cultural and spiritual legacies of other peoples and places. In Palestine, for instance, he experienced Christianity firsthand, walking in the footsteps of Christ. His annual visits to Capri (1909–1913) were undoubtedly the happiest periods of his life. Beyond the natural and historical riches of the isle, Capri was home to Gorky, in exile from Russia since 1907. Bunin had known Gorky since 1899, but his sojourns to Capri kindled an intense (if short-lived) friendship between the two men. Together they lamented the chaos at home, discussed ideas for works, and wondered about their place in the world.

Bunin's travels also allowed him to view life from fresh perspectives. Whenever he returned to Russia from abroad he could see that though his family estate was humble, it was home and thus unmatched. He could mentor novice writers (Kataev, for example) and attack the Modernists with new vigor and resolve. He could take heart in his stance as a roving reporter on the state of the world as well as in his growing fame and expertise as a writer.

In 1910 Bunin published *The Village*, his first full-length work, in which he entered a debate about Russian provincial life that had raged since 1905. On one side optimists praised the village, believing the folk had awakened from their centuries-old slumber and were revitalizing national life. Pessimists, though, dismissed this dream of a village renaissance. The folk, they said, were plagued by debt, dislocation, and disease; *kulaks* and railroads had destroyed old values and beliefs, and only nihilism and Marx had filled the void.

Bunin sided squarely with the pessimists. The heroes of *The Village*, Tikhon and Kuzma Krasnov, have abandoned the values of soul and soil and are adrift in a revolutionary sea. Tikhon is a *kulak*, materially rich but spiritually poor. Childless, he questions the worth of his accomplishments and quickly loses his grip on life. Kuzma has a similar fate. Too weak to be a writer, he blames everyone but himself for his ills. But it is the village itself that emerges as the true *dramatis personae* of the work. Unlike Tolstoy's Platon Karataev, the peasant-hero in *War and Peace*, the folk in *The Village* have no idea how to live other than to rave, riot, and await the apocalypse.

The Village enjoyed a *succès de scandale*, intensifying the doubts of Russians who feared for the very continuance of their land. While the work had its defenders (Gorky at their head), it was soundly condemned by critics who saw Bunin as an angst-ridden intellectual, a "child of the cherry orchard," and a casualty of 1905. To the uproar over *The Village* Bunin reacted publicly with outrage but privately with delight. Never again would one of his works galvanize attention and debate to such a degree. His sense of triumph, though, was always tinged with pain; for it was one of the supreme ironies in his life that the same readers and reviewers who condemned him for *The Village* in 1910 would hail him as a prophet a decade later.

✳ 1906 ✳

May 19, 1906
Ivan Bunin, from a letter to Maria Chekhova

I so want to see you that I almost left Moscow for the Crimea. But these are troubled times. The ships are not running, and, judging by the newspapers, it is heating up in Sevastopol. . . .

So I am going to the village where the night is wondrous and purely Russian. . . .

June 14, 1906
Yuly Bunin, from a letter to a friend

[Brother] Evgeny had a fire. Two kitchens were destroyed, along with a cattle barn. . . . The peasants . . . said it was an accident.

They then passed a resolution informing Evgeny . . . that from now on no one could work for him except the peasants of our village; that everyone else must be fired right away or they would be removed by force; and that there would be new pay scales. . . . The peasants also told Evgeny that if he did not agree to these conditions they . . . would not give the crop to him. . . . They did this as an assembly, and, though restrained, they were very defiant.

Evgeny, of course, would not agree to these conditions . . . but the nonvillage workers were quickly let go; conflict was unavoidable.

Mother, Masha, and everyone else became extremely frightened; they right away went to Efremov and rented an apartment there.

Meanwhile Evgeny went . . . to the police station. Many landowners were in the same predicament. The police chief told them the situation was becoming extremely difficult and that there were not enough troops. He assured them, though, that the peasants . . .

would not become violent if the landowners did not call for help.

We do not know what will happen next, but we can hardly return to the village. . . . The unrest is spreading like wildfire.

June 25, 1906
Yuly Bunin, from a letter to a friend

We are returning to the village. The business with the peasants has been settled peacefully. Evgeny had to raise the salaries by quite a bit and to give the peasants . . . that part of the land that was in arrears. The assembly gathered. . . . Evgeny concluded the agreement, and, as a sign of reconciliation, he treated them to huge servings of vodka.

August 19, 1906
Yuly Bunin, from a letter to a friend

Evgeny has surrendered the entire estate, except the house, to the peasants.

November 4, 1906
Vera Muromtseva-Bunina, from her diary

Bunin quickly took his place at the gathering [a literary reading], and I again heard his ample voice.

He read simply, but each line called forth a picture. . . .

Bunin had changed since October. . . . He had gotten thin: there were circles under his eyes. It was apparent that he had led an unhealthy life in Petersburg and that he was doing the same thing in Moscow.

I remembered when I met him for the first time, almost ten years ago. . . . his face was fresh and healthy. . . .

Bunin appeared at the door.

"How did you wind up here?" he asked.

I was angry, but I answered quietly:

"The same as you."

"Who are you?"

"A person."

"What are you studying?"

"Chemistry."

"What is your last name?"

"Muromtseva." . . .

We talked a little. . . . Then Bunin mentioned he was in Odessa last year, during the pogroms.

"When can I see you again?" he asked.

"Only at home. We receive guests on Saturdays. I am busy the rest of the time." . . .

On Sunday I was informed . . . that Bunin would be coming on the following Saturday. . . .

We began to see each other daily. First we would have breakfast, then we would go to exhibits . . . and concerts. Sometimes I had to rush over to meet him from the laboratory. . . . He liked it when my fingers were burned by acid.

✳ 1907 ✳

February 1907
Vera Muromtseva-Bunina, from her diary
I decided to call Bunin Ian: first, because no other woman called him that, and second, because his family were Lithuanians who came to Russia. He liked this name very much.

March 1907
Vera Muromtseva-Bunina, from her diary
In March I decided to talk to papa. . . . I said:

"You know that Bunin and I have decided to take a trip to the Holy Land."

He stood there quietly, turned his back toward me, and walked over . . . to a map. He showed me where Palestine was, but he did not say a word about my decision to tie my life to that of Ivan Alexeevich. . . .

Then the day arrived, April 10, 1907, when I radically changed my life: from a settled person to almost twenty years as a nomad.

Circa *March 1907*
Maxim Gorky, from a letter to a friend
Contemporary literature has made a strange impression on me. Only Bunin is true to himself; everyone else has gone off on a wild rampage. . . .

Circa *May 1907*
Ivan Bunin, from his sketch "The Shadow of a Bird"
   The second day on the Black Sea. . . . With joy I recall that Russia is three hundred miles behind me. . . .
   I have never felt any love for my country. . . . And if the Russian revolution disturbs me more than a Persian one, I can only regret this. Truly blessed is every moment when we feel ourselves to be citizens of the universe.

May 4, 1907
Ivan Bunin, from a letter to Nikolai Teleshov
   We have been in Tsargrad, Athens, Alexandria, Haifa, Jerusalem, Jericho, Hebron, and by the Dead Sea! I am now writing to you from Syria, from Beirut. Tomorrow we are going to Damascus and then to Nazareth, Port Said, Cairo; and, after we have seen the Pyramids, we are coming home, again through Athens.

May 5, 1907
Ivan and Vera Bunin, from a letter to the Muromtsevs
   Greetings from Syria, from Baalbek.[1] We have been to the ruins of the ancient Temple of the Sun! We are alive and well!

May 9, 1907
Vera Muromtseva-Bunina, from her diary
   Bunin talked about Christ:
   "In evenings such as these He taught. . . . One should always think of the present as coming from the past. . . . True, it was greener then, and the land was more settled. But the mountains were the same; the sun was setting in the very same place that it does now; and the sunsets were just as simple and charming. . . ."
   Bunin began to talk about the apostles. He particularly loves Peter for his passion. (I prefer John because he was the most gentle.)
   "Peter was the liveliest of all the apostles." Bunin said. "I can envision him best of all. . . . Peter renounced Christ and cried. Then he asked to be crucified upside down because he was not worthy to be crucified in the same way as the Teacher was. . . ."
   The apostle Thomas also very much interested Bunin. "It would

---

[1]Baalbek, or "City of the Sun," was an ancient city in Syria; its remains comprise three temples and the vestiges of the city walls.

be a good thing to write about Thomas," he said. "It is not at all as simple as it first seems: Thomas's wish to put his fingers into the wound of Christ. . . ."

May 10, 1907
Vera Muromtseva-Bunina, from her diary

At a fountain in Nazareth . . . women were filling clay pitchers with water and putting them on their shoulders. They then scattered, moving slowly and gracefully to their homes.

"Nothing has changed here," Ian said. "It is just the way it was when the Mother of God brought water home in the evenings."

We stopped near Joseph's home, where Jesus spent his childhood and youth: a dark hole with a door.

"Yes, yes," Ian said sadly. "Here She sat on this very threshold and mended His blue shirt, just like those they are wearing now. Legend says They were so poor They could not buy oil for the lamp, and fireflies flew into Their hut so the Baby would not be afraid and would fall asleep quietly."

Mid-May 1907
Vera Muromtseva-Bunina, from her diary

[In a zoo in Cairo] Bunin and I stood for a long time in front of a terrarium that had small and very poisonous African snakes. Ian grimaced. He has a mystical horror of snakes, but . . . he cannot tear himself away from them and follows their sinuous motions with great torment in his eyes.

Circa *May 17, 1907*
Vera Muromtseva-Bunina, from her diary

Ian suddenly said, "I am done for; I probably will not write anymore."

I looked at him with surprise.

"A poet must not be happy," he continued. "He must live alone. The better he feels, the worse his writing. . . ."

"Then I will try to be as bad as possible," I said laughing; but my heart contracted from pain.

June 6, 1907
Vera Muromtseva-Bunina, from her diary

Ian's room at [the family estate at] Vasilevskoe is a corner one, with huge old dark icons in silver frames. It is very bright because of the white wallpaper, and because a third window looks south onto a fruit garden: A spreading maple rises in the distance.

The furniture is simple but comfortable: a very wide wooden bed and a big desk covered with thick pieces of blotting paper. There is a potbellied lamp with a white lampshade, a large inkwell with ink, and several penholders with pens and pencils of various widths. ... A shelf with books hangs over the desk. ... Between the windows is a chest of drawers, filled with books, and, by the southern window, a comfortable, boldly colored couch.

A single door leads into a half-dark room. There was Ian's trunk, also filled with books, and a sink. ...

After several days of merrymaking, we got down to work. Ian will not start work without me, but he so wanted to get down to business, despite doubts about his giftedness. ...

Ian always read a great deal right before he wrote. ... He would write poetry for a long while. Then he would read it to me on walks outside. ...

The first thing I noticed about the Bunins was that the dinner table was very lively, with frequent bursts of laughter. ... and that Ian was the most lively of them all. ... The second thing I noticed— and which was very new to me—was the way the family treated the peasants. They did not look upon the folk idealistically, as I and others did. They did not feel guilty before them; rather... they treated them as equals, even as members of the family. By contrast, I and others looked upon the folk with condescension. ... We treated them like children; we wanted to teach them, to help them, to give them a moral foundation. No one here thought like this. Bunin's family did not talk to the peasants in the saccharine language that city dwellers use with them; rather, they talked in a language that was genuine, powerful, and folklike. ... The third thing I noticed about Bunin's family was that the masters loved the estate and their way of life not like a rich peasant would, but with a love that was poetic more than anything else.

Late June 1907
Vera Muromtseva-Bunina, from her diary

From Vasilevskoe ... we left for Efremov to visit Ian's mother. ...

I stopped at the door of the house and took a look at the living room, which was decorated with pictures, soft furniture, and big plants. Then I saw a thin, somewhat bent woman in a dark dress and with a black lace headdress about her still barely grey hair. She looked at her son with somewhat tired eyes. This was Ian's mother, Lyudmilla Alexandrovna.

I was surprised at her spriteliness. She was, after all, over seventy; she had suffered from asthma for many years. She couldn't lie down at night but would sleep in a chair.

We sat in the summer house; Lyudmilla was nice to me.

She asked about the Holy Land, about Jerusalem. She was a deeply religious woman. She expressed a desire to make a trip to Kiev to worship the relics. "Vanya [Ivan] will take me there," she said.

I began to ask her about Vanya. She said that from the very beginning he was very different from the other children, that she always knew "he would be special," that "no one has such a delicate and tender soul as he," and that "no one loved her as much as he did." . . .

She believed her son had inherited his lyricism and poetic nature from her; I think she was absolutely correct. From his father, Ian received his facility with language, his power of imagination, his artistic images.

She said Ian had it harder than his brothers, since he had received nothing from their former fortune; he had entered life with a "chip on his shoulder," and "Yuly had been his guide."

Lyudmilla lapsed into memories. . . . Ian loved nature more than anything else; as a child . . . he would quietly wake up [sister] Masha, and together they would silently crawl out the window to meet the morning . . . and when Masha couldn't fall asleep he would tell her fairy tales.

Late November 1907
Vera Muromtseva-Bunina, from her diary
The Ian of the village is not the Ian of the city. When he is in the village everything is different about him, beginning with his clothes and ending with his schedule. Truly he is a completely different person.

In the village Ian keeps a strict schedule. He gets up and goes to bed early, eats on time, does not drink wine, even on holidays. . . . In the village Ian is even-tempered.

✳ 1908 ✳

Circa *1908*
Alexander Kuprin, from a parody of Ivan Bunin

MUSHROOM PIES

I sit by the window and chew thoughtfully on a mop. A beautiful sadness shines forth from my nobleman's eyes. It is night. My legs are wrapped in an expensive English plaid. A cigarette gives off gentle smoke from the windowsill. Who knows, perhaps a thousand years ago someone else sat here, daydreamed, and chewed on a mop, perhaps a poet that I do not know? The rye, the oats, and cabbages run off into the endless distance. There, at the very edge of the winter field, over by a lonely haystack, a rook strolls by importantly. True, I cannot see him at night, but I need him for my setting. A gopher whistles softly on a tree under my window.

Why do I find it all so sour, so sad, so wet? The night wind rushes through my window and rustles the pages of the Sixth Book of Gentry Heraldry. Strange sounds wander through the old gentry home. Perhaps it is mice; perhaps it is the shadows of my ancestors? Who knows? The whole world is mysterious. I look at my finger and I am seized with mystical horror!

How good it would to be eat a mushroom pie now. But how can this be done? A sweet and tender sorrow presses upon my heart; my eyes are moist. Where are you, the splendid time of mushroom pies, borzoi dogs, distant fields, peasant souls, Antonov apples, and payment redemptions?

With languid sorrow in my soul, I walk out onto the porch and whistle to a violet, molting turkey. An old, blind, grey-muzzled hound . . . scratches his mangy back against the balcony. The gardener Ksenofont goes by, but he does not take off his hat to me. In earlier times I would have banished the boor to the stables!

I return to my sad room. The garden smells of angelica . . . and roosters. A sleepless bird cries out on the spinning wheels behind the barns. Why does my stomach hurt? Who knows? Some secret pity wafts its invisible wing over me.

The entire world is incomprehensible, mysterious! Bored, wan, and weak, like a fly from yesteryear, I approach the door. I open it and cry into the sinister darkness:

"Martha, come here! . . . Rub me down with bay oil!"

February 1908?
Vera Muromtseva-Bunina, from her diary
Ian does not write in the evenings. After dinner we go for an evening walk. If it is quiet we go through the alley of lime trees out into the field. We are fond of the stars. . . .

November 5, 1908
Ivan Bunin, from a letter to Konstantin Stanislavsky
The papers are writing a great deal about the fact that the Moscow Art Theatre is thinking about staging Shakespeare's *Hamlet.* If there is any truth to this, be so kind and let me translate it.

✳ 1909 ✳

Circa 1909
Valentin Kataev, from his memoirs
"Now take Bunin—there's a genuine poet for you. Have you ever read him?" my poet-friend asked me.

"No," I said.

"You've never read Bunin's verse?" my friend said in horror. . . .

"I suppose I have," I lied. "In a magazine somewhere. He's kind of long and tedious. . . ."

My friend looked at me with silent reproach. . . . He took a book from the shelf and began leafing through it. . . .

"'The sea is like a pearly mirror,'" my friend read . . . his voice trembling with genuine delight. "'The lilac is tinted milky gold. How warm it is before sunset, how sweet the smoke over the hut. . . . A seagull settles in a rocky cove . . . bobbing like a water float. . . .'"

I was stunned. I suddenly learned a very simple secret of poetry. . . .

That very evening I asked my father to buy me a book of

Bunin's poetry. My father looked at me . . . with eyes filled with joy.
At long last his blockhead of a son had come around. He had not
asked for skates or a football . . . but for a book. And not *Sherlock
Holmes* . . . but a splendid book by a Russian poet. It was, perhaps,
the one truly happy day of his life. . . .

March 16, 1909
Maxim Gorky, from a letter to Ekaterina Peshkova
    Bunin came with his young wife. . . . She is lovely. He is the
same as always . . . a bit older. . . a flirt, but alive in soul. He delights
me with his serious stance toward . . . the word.

March 26, 1909
Vera Muromtseva-Bunina, from her diary
    Ian has been in good form. . . . Gorky has roused him power-
fully. They look at many things differently, but the main thing is that
they love sincerely.

April 9, 1909
Vera Muromtseva-Bunina, from her diary
    Our last visit to Capri was quiet. We were at Gorky's almost
daily. Sometimes all three of us would go for a walk. Ian and Gorky
often talked about Tolstoy. They sometimes disagreed about him, but
they both admired him. I felt, though, that Gorky did not share the
deep . . . love that Ivan Alexeevich had for Tolstoy.
    Alexei Maximovich . . . remembered that he once saw Lev Niko-
laevich from afar, sitting alone on the shore.
    "Now there's a genuine master for you!" he repeated, "a genuine
master!"
    Gorky always cried when . . . he looked at someone dancing the
tarantella, or when he listened to Ian's verse.
    Gorky always drank out of a very tall glass; he did not stop until
he reached the bottom. But as much as he drank, he never got
drunk. Except for Asti during holidays, he drank only French wine at
the table, although the local wines . . . were excellent. He was tem-
perate in his eating habits; I never knew him to be greedy. He
dressed simply but somewhat like a dandy.

May 26, 1909
Ivan Bunin, from his diary
    [Brother] Evgeny told us about the peasants Donka Simanova

and her husband. Donka's husband was like a monkey: thin, strong, quiet and cruel. . . . He would so beat up his wife with a whip that she'd be all bandaged up like a mummy. . . . Like any peasant, he debauched his wife so coarsely and cruelly that they had a record number of children. "Of course, they did it every night," Evgeny said. "How else could they have had so many kids? The minute the light went out, he went straight for her." . . .

Evgeny told me another story about how a peasant tied his naked wife by her braid to his saddle and then beat her with the reins until she lost consciousness.

August 26, 1909
Ivan Bunin, from a letter to Maxim Gorky
When I read your letter I recalled Italy with great tenderness and hope—with tenderness because I only now understand how Italy has entered into my heart, and with hope that someday I will again make my way to you, to your casa, to your wine.

September 22, 1909
Ivan Bunin, from a letter to Maxim Gorky
I have returned to what you had advised me to do—to write a big story about the village. . . .

Oh, this Rus and its history!

✳ 1910 ✳

Circa *1910*
Valentin Kataev, from his memoirs
Before us stood a forty-year-old gentleman—pinched, bilious, dandified . . . with the aura of an Honored Academician. . . . Later I realized that Bunin was not so much bilious as he was hemorrhoidal, but that's besides the point.

Well-cut trousers. Yellow English shoes with thick soles. The ones that never wear out. A dark red, French, writer's goatee, but more pointed and groomed than Chekhov's. . . . A pince-nez also like Chekhov's, steel-rimmed . . . folded in two, and tucked into the side pocket of a sports jacket. . . .

A starched collar... high and firm, with corners folded flamboyantly over a proper purple necktie, like calling cards made from the very best Bristol board....

Bunin looked at us sternly, formally; though he stood at a distance from us, he held out his hands—one to me, the other to my friend—not to shake hands, but to take our poems....

Obeying Bunin's immobile stare, we placed our works in his outstretched hands. My friend gave him a book of decadent verse which he just had printed at his own expense... and which was entitled *The Faded Wreath*....

"I've read your verse," Bunin said sternly, like a doctor.... "What can I say? It's hard to say anything positive about it. I personally don't care for this kind of stuff."

My friend smiled a stupid and arrogant smile.

"You," Bunin continued, "should go to one of the decadents—Balmont, for example.... What you've given me is mannered, coy, imprecise, vague, and pretentious.... It's not even Russian in spots...."

"But don't you accept 'trans-sense' in poetry?"[2] My friend interrupted him bravely, licking his wet and shapeless little lips. "Lots of people do today."

"Perhaps. But I think that if something is trans-sense, if it defies reason, then it is stupid," Bunin said....

What did we have in common? Why did I love Bunin so passionately? I had heard of him only quite recently. I knew well the names of Kuprin, Andreev, Gorky... but I knew absolutely nothing about Bunin. But suddenly one fine day he became my idol....

There was absolutely no way I could tell if Bunin liked my poems or not.... I think he was searching for pieces of truth. He could care less about the rest.

In one poem... I had ventured... the thought that the poet was also an artist and that, by painting a still life—asters in a clay pitcher—he had... immortalized these flowers on canvas, or something like that.

I had written: "Fall flowers in a pitcher, rescued by the poet from early blight, remnants of beauty, dreams of lost delight."

Bunin winced as though he had a toothache.... He crossed out

---

[2] A reference to the "transrational language" of the Futurists and, in particular, of Alexei Kruchonykh (1886–1969) and Viktor Khlebnikov (1885–1922).

the last line . . . and wrote in the margin, "Autumn flowers on the table, rescued by the poet from early death."

He thought a bit more, then he wrote firmly: "Sketchboxes. Crumpled canvases. Someone's hat upon the easel."

I was struck by Bunin's precision, brevity, and substance. In only three strokes of his brush he had cut through my confused and vague lines and had captured my friend's studio. . . .

Bunin paused briefly over another of my poems. . . . He put a check at the top of the page . . . as if to say that the poem was not great but "true to life."

Only two poems . . . had checks. I despaired at the thought I had failed in Bunin's eyes and would never become a good poet, all the more since Bunin said nothing encouraging to me when we parted. . . . He seemed quite indifferent to what I had done: "Fair. Keep writing. Observe nature. Poetry is daily work."

[Bunin continued:] "One must write every day, just like a violinist or a pianist must practice for several hours each day without stopping. Otherwise your talent will stagnate and run dry, like a well from which no water has been drawn. . . . What should you write about? Anything you like. . . . If you have no subject or idea, then simply write about what you see. Say you see a dog running with its tongue hanging out," Bunin said. . . . "Then write about the dog. One or two stanzas. But accurately, authentically, so that it is precisely this dog and no other one. Write about a tree. The sea. A park bench. Describe those features which belong to them alone. Write about the sound of gravel under the sandals of a girl when she runs down to the sea. . . . What kind of sound is it? It's not a creak or a crunch, a sound, or a rustle, but something different—pebblylike— and demanding a single necessary and true word. Take this winding bush with its red flowers stretching over the wall as if wishing to look into the window . . . and see what you and I are doing there. . . .

"I know that there are times when you have despaired," Bunin said, "when you think that everything has been said . . . that there are no new subjects or emotions, that all rhymes have been used up and are worn out, that one can count all the meters on the fingers of one's hand, and that, in the end, it is quite impossible to become a poet. Thoughts like that drove me crazy when I was young. But that's nonsense, my dear fellow. Every object about you, every feeling you have is the subject for a poem. Listen carefully to your feelings, observe the world around you, and write. But write what you feel and see, and not what other poets, even the most brilliant, have felt and seen before you. Be independent in art. That you can learn. And then the endless world of genuine poetry will open before you. . . ."

Bunin advised me to read books about the history of peoples inhabiting the globe. A genuine poet, he said, must know well the history of world civilization. The life, the habits, the nature of various countries, their religions, beliefs, folk songs, legends, and sagas.

But in those days—alas!—none of this interested me in the least, though I pretended I was glad for such wise advice; with feigned emotion I wrote down the names of books Bunin had dictated. . . .

I would rather have read something that would teach me at once and without much effort how to write splendid verse and become a famous poet.

I was also disappointed by Bunin's insistent advice not to publish my work right away but to wait a bit . . . since all would come in its own time.

"I've no doubt," Bunin noted with a dry half smile, "that you won't take my advice, and that you'll send your poems to all the publishers if only to see them and your name in print. I did that, too. And now I very much regret that I published a lot of weak stuff. Please understand, dear boy, that it would cost me nothing to give you my calling card and that you would be published in any of the big journals . . . but it's better if I don't. Wait a bit."

Oh, how I wanted to rush to Bunin and beg: "Please, please, Ivan Alexeevich, recommend my poems, give me your card. . . . You yourself said it would cost you nothing."

But with false obedience I agreed with him.

"I understand. Yes, yes, of course, you're right. It's better to wait."

He looked at me sarcastically.

"I bet you'll run to the *Odessa Bulletin* with your poems today. I know you young poets! You can't fool me. I was just like you once."

Then Bunin changed the subject.

"You, of course, would like me to tell you all the secrets of writing as quickly as possible," Bunin said very seriously, with deep conviction. "I don't know if I can help you. But remember the following. First—and this is the main thing—you must overcome the revulsion for a clean piece of paper that nearly every genuine writer experiences. You must write every day, regularly, without waiting for inspiration, the mood, and so forth. You must write in the same way that you would go to work—or to school."

January 13, 1910
Ivan Bunin, from a letter to Yuly Bunin

We had a quiet crossing over the Black Sea.... The swells were big and even . . . but the ship was large and heavy....

On Christmas Eve . . . I suddenly felt an unbearable pain.... It was so great that I almost lost consciousness. I dragged myself over to my cabin; covered with icy sweat, I began to yell for help....

No one could understand that my pain was so great that *my pulse was actually stopping*. The doctors began applying poultices.... The pain subsided, although I was terribly weak the next day....

Today the pain started again; it has continued for almost the whole day. Doctor Rabinovich says that my kidney has moved and tells me to have it x-rayed.... I will think about it.

We are living in a villa on the outskirts of a small, clean, flat-roofed city.... From the north, south, and west we have a view of the Pyramids, of the entire Nile Valley.

January 17, 1910
Ivan Bunin, from his memoirs

The Moscow Art Theatre was celebrating the fiftieth anniversary of Chekhov's birth with a literary matinee in which I took part.... The theater was filled to overflowing. In a box on the right sat Chekhov's relatives: his mother, sister, and brothers....

My performance evoked genuine delight. When I read my conversations with Anton Pavlovich, I rendered his words in his own voice, with his own intonations. It affected his family profoundly; his mother and sister were crying.

After several days Stanislavsky and Nemirovich came up to me and suggested that I join their troupe.

February 5, 1910
Ivan Bunin, from a letter to a friend

So critics of my peasant stories will abuse me, will they? So what? I have never chased after their praises. The abuse of hacks and ignoramuses does not affect me. Who are they to talk about my portraits of the people? Why, they understand more about papooses than they do about the people, about Russia. . . .

The critics say my works are not objective. . . . But I understand the village in my own way. I consider the peasant fiction of Tolstoy, Gleb Uspensky, and Ertel to be the only ones of value; each has understood the folk in his own way.

I know the village. Perhaps like no one else who is writing now. . . .

February 11, 1910
Ivan Bunin, from a letter to Maxim Gorky
Generally speaking, and with one or two exceptions . . . literature is completely empty and boring. No one is saying anything about social causes and currents. It is terrible how much I really want to come to Capri and to talk to you and about your things.

March 1910
Ivan Bunin, from Part One of The Village[3]
The Krasovs' great-grandfather, nicknamed "Gypsy" by the household serfs, was hunted down by the borzois of Durnovo, his master. Gypsy had taken the master's mistress for his own. . . . One cannot run away from borzois.

The Krasovs' grandfather got his freedom. He moved to town with his family and . . . became a famous thief . . . who robbed churches in the region. When he was caught, he behaved in such a way that he became the talk of the district. . . . He stood before the judge dressed in a velvet kaftan and leather boots. Brazenly playing with his eyes and cheekbones, he admitted to the pettiest crimes in a most respectful tone:

"Exactly right, sir. That I did."

The Krasovs' father was a peddler. . . . He was about to start a small store, but then he went bankrupt, began drinking . . . and died. His sons, Tikhon and Kuzma . . . were also petty traders. They went about in a cart . . . crying out mournfully:

"Goods for sale, ladies! Goods for sale!"

The items—small mirrors, cakes of soap, rings, thread, ker-

[3]The three parts of Bunin's *The Village* were published serially, in March, October, and November 1910.

chiefs, needles, pretzels—the brothers kept in a bin. They put in the cart anything they got in exchange—dead cats, eggs, canvases, rags. . . .

By the time Tikhon reached forty his beard was streaked with silver. But he was as handsome, tall, and well built as ever; his face was stern, swarthy, and slightly pockmarked; his shoulders were broad and spare; his conversation was powerful and sharp; his movements were quick and lithe. . . . Only his eyes shone more sharply than before.

Tikhon chased after business without stopping. . . . He bought up crops from landlords for next to nothing; he leased land for pennies. . . . The peasants shone with pride when he purchased the master's estate. . . . They marveled that he could be so clever and not come apart at the seams: always to buy, sell . . . and watch everything like a hawk. . . .

The loss of hope of ever having children . . . was a major blow to Tikhon Ilyich. He aged noticeably when he knew for certain that he would not be a father. He joked about it at first:

"I ain't giving up," Tikhon told his friends. "Without children, a man is not a man. He's not much of anything. . . ."

When Tikhon Ilyich lost all hope for children, he thought more and more, "Who is all this backbreaking work for, damn it all?" . . . Tikhon still tried to look younger than he was. . . . But his beard had become thin, matted, and grey. . . .

During the fast for Saint Peter's Day, Tikhon Ilyich spent four days . . . at a fair; but he got more upset by his thoughts, the heat, and the sleepless nights. . . .

The fair . . . was, as always, noisy and confused. People blustered and brawled; horses neighed, children blew whistles, and calliopes . . . belted out marches and polkas. All day long, men and women . . . walked along the dusty and manured lanes between the carts and tents, the horses and cows, the booths and canteens, reeking of fumes and grease.

As always, also, the fair was full of racketeers. . . . blind men, beggars, paupers, and cripples who moved on crutches or in carts in endless processions. . . .

Dear God, what a land! The black soil here was over a yard deep . . . but five years did not pass without a famine! The town was famous throughout Russia for its grain trade, but only a hundred people ate their fill of bread! . . .

Halfway home was a large village. . . . Dry, hot winds whipped through the empty streets . . . scorched by the sun. . . . A wildly colored church stood out brazenly on the bare common. Behind it was a shallow, clayey pond. . . . A herd of cows stood in the thick yellow water, urinating continually; a naked peasant was lathering his head. He stood waist-deep in the water; a small copper cross glittered on his chest; his neck and face were black from the sun; his body was strikingly pale and white. . . . The horse made for the pond, but the water was so repulsive and warm that the animal turned away. . . .

"That's some water you got there. Can you really drink it?" Tikhon asked the peasant.

"And I suppose you've got sugar water where you live?" the peasant replied. "We've been drinking it for a thousand years. Water's one thing, it's bread we don't have. . . ."

The road continued through fields—thin, feeble, and choked with cornflowers. . . . Rooks with silvery beaks descended in a cloud on a gnarled and hollow willow. . . . All that remained of the village was its name and the charred frames of huts. . . . Milky smoke rose from the debris, the ashes gave off a sour smell. . . .

The war with Japan and the revolution . . . were the major events of the time. . . .

Tikhon took spiteful delight in the terrible routs the Russian army had suffered.

"Good for 'em! Serves the sons-of-bitches right!"

Tikhon reveled in the revolution and the assassinations.

"The Minister got it right in the gut," he exulted. . . .

But as soon as people started talking about seizing the land, Tikhon became angry. "The Jews are at it again! . . . The Jews and those ragged students!" . . . Everybody was saying, "Revolution, revolution!" . . .

"The people have become secretive . . . so secretive that it's scary!" Tikhon Ilyich would say.

And, forgetting all about the "Jews," he would add: "It's clear what the people want. But they keep their mouths shut. We've got to watch 'em and make sure they go on keeping their mouths shut. Don't give 'em a chance. Otherwise . . . they'll smash us to pieces!" . . .

Tikhon Ilyich heard rumors that the peasants were . . . planning to attack his estate. . . . He raced to Durnovka. . . . The sun was setting . . . into greyish red clouds, the trunks of the birches in the grove were crimson, the mud . . . had a sharp purple-black color. . . .

Tikhon Ilyich saw the peasants' herd grazing on his fallow land. So, it has begun, he thought. . . .

What happened next . . . was beyond words. . . . Tikhon Ilyich sat in his trap in a far-off field. His heart hammered, his hands shook, his face burned, and his hearing was as keen as a wild beast's. He listened to the cries coming from Durnovka, and he recalled how the crowd . . . had massed at the front porch, shouting, cursing, and pressing him to the door. He had only a whip in his hands. He swung it . . . and lunged desperately into the crowd. But a harness-maker, a mean, wiry man with a deep-sunk belly and a sharp nose, swung his stick even more widely and boldly. . . . He was yelling, in the name of the crowd, that orders had come to strike on the same day and hour throughout the region, to chase out the hired workers . . . and to replace them with local people for a ruble a day. Tikhon Ilyich shouted even more furiously to drown out the harness-maker:

"So that's what you want! Where'd you get that from, you bum, the agitators? Learned your lessons well, didn't you?"

The harness-maker answered: "It's you who's a bum, you grey-haired fool!" he yelled, the blood rushing to his face. "As if I didn't know how much land you've got? How much, you catflayer? Two hundred? What the hell do I have? A plot that's smaller than your porch! Why? Who the hell are you?" . . .

The land . . . was as black as an abyss. . . . Suddenly a dark red column of fire shot up into the sky: The peasants had set fire to the shed; a pistol . . . began firing all by itself. . . .

Young Lass was a slender girl with very white, soft skin, and a delicate blush. . . . Her lowered eyelashes excited Tikhon Ilyich terribly. . . . One evening, when Young Lass was sweeping in the dark threshing barn, Tikhon Ilyich . . . sneaked up on her and said quickly: "You'll have shoes, silk shawls. . . . I don't care what it costs. . . ."

But Young Lass was deathly quiet.

"Did you hear what I said?" Tikhon Ilyich shouted in a whisper.

But Young Lass became like a stone. . . . And Tikhon got nowhere with her. . . .

Around Saint Elijah's Day . . . Young Lass was washing the floors in the house. . . . Tikhon Ilyich entered the room, glanced at her figure bent over the floor, at her white legs, splashed with dirty water, at her entire ample body that had spread since her marriage to the peasant Rodka. . . . Suddenly Tikhon moved over to her. Young Lass straightened up quickly, raised her flushed, excited face to him, and clutching the wet washrag in her hand, she shouted in a strange voice: "I'll bash your face in, laddy."

The air smelled of dirty water, of a hot body, of sweat. . . . Tikhon Ilyich gripped Young Lass's hand, and crushed it savagely. . . . He pressed her so tightly to himself that her bones cracked. He carried her. . . into the bedroom. With her head thrown back and her eyes grown wide, Young Lass did not struggle. . . . A month passed, then another. . . . Young Lass had not conceived. . . .

Kuzma said to Tikhon, "I am an anarchist, you see. . . . a strange type of Russian."

"I'm Russian, too, don't forget," Tikhon Ilyich put in.

"But a different kind. . . . You're proud to be Russian . . . but, for God's sake, don't brag about it. We're a savage people!"

Frowning, Tikhon Ilyich drummed his fingers on the table.

"You're right there, perhaps," he said. "We are a savage lot. We're wild."

"Now you're talking sense. I've roamed the world—and you know what?—I've never seen duller and lazier types anywhere. And those who aren't lazy," Kuzma looked askance at his brother, "they're nothing to rave about either. They just rush off and stuff their own nest. And what's the use of that? . . ."

"Well, you know the old song," said Tikhon Ilyich, " 'Come and live in our village, try our watery soup, wear our bast shoes!' "

"Bast shoes!" Kuzma echoed bitterly. "We've been wearing them for over a thousand years, may they be thrice cursed! And whose fault is it? The Tatars for crushing us! We're a young nation, you see! As if the Mongols hadn't crushed Europe again and again. As if the Germans are older than us.". . .

Kuzma exclaimed, tapping his fingernail on the table: "Our favorite, most destructive trait is to preach one thing and do another! It's music to a Russian's ears, dear brother: to live poorly, like pigs, because we want to!" . . .

On the feast of Our Lady of Kazan, the townsmen gave a "party" in a cabin. They invited Nanny Goat and Young Lass. . . . But at daybreak they suddenly. . . threw the drunk Young Lass on the ground, tied her hands, raised up her skirts, twisted them up into a braid above her head, and began to tie the braid with a rope.

Frightened, Donka ran away. . . . Later she saw Young Lass, stripped to the waist, hanging from a tree. . . .

Kuzma said: "Now think: is there anyone more cruel than our people? If a child pinches a penny cake, the entire market will hunt him down . . . and make him eat soap. If there's a fire or a fight, everyone turns out, and how sorry they are if it all ends too soon! And don't we love it when someone beats his wife to death, or when a kid gets a flogging. . . ."

"And for fun, they teach poor fools to masturbate! . . . They set dogs on beggars! They knock pigeons off roofs with stones; but they think it's a great sin to eat them. . . . The Holy Spirit, you know. . . ."

"Our people are a fine lot! . . . Kind ones they are! When you read our history, your hair stands up on end: brother against brother . . . son against father, treachery and murder, murder and treachery. . . . The *bylinas*,[4] now they're also a joy to read: 'he ripped out his white chest,' 'he let his bowels drop to the ground.' . . . They 'stepped on her left foot and pulled her apart with her right.' And our songs? Always the same thing: The stepmother is 'evil and greedy' . . . the mother-in-law is . . . like a 'bitch on a chain' . . . the husband is 'either a fool or a drunkard'; his 'good father teaches him to beat his wife, to flay her good'; his wife makes her father-in-law 'soup from dishwater, and a pie from dirt off the floor.' And to her husband she says, 'Get up, you bum, here's some dishwater to wash your face, a rag to wipe it with, and a rope to hang yourself.' . . ."

A peasant told Kuzma: "The years of the famine, we apprentices would go out to Black Square. The prostitutes were everywhere. Boy, were they hungry! You'd give 'em half a pound of bread for the job and she'd *gobble into it while she was still under you.* . . . The good times we had!" . . .

Tikhon . . . returned indoors and looked into the large kitchen. The hut had a warm, repulsive smell; the cook was sleeping on a bare chest. Her face was covered with her apron, her hip stuck out, and her legs . . . were drawn up to her belly. Oska lay on the plank bed, in a sheepskin and bast shoes, his head buried in the heavy, greasy pillow.

"The devil and the lad!" Tikhon Ilyich looked at them with

[4]The *bylina* is a special type of epic folk song, often loosely connected with some historical movement or event, and embellished with fantasy or hyperbole.

disgust. "Just look, she whores all night, and dead asleep in the morning!"

And looking at the black walls, the tiny windows, the tub full of slops, and the huge broad-shouldered stove, Tikhon shouted in a loud, severe voice:

"Hey, my noble ones! Enough's enough!" . . .

Suddenly Tikhon heard the sound of loud and crude hymns. Opening his eyes in fright, he . . . saw two men: one was blind, with a pockmarked face, a small nose, a long upperlip, and a large, round skull; the other man was Makar Ivanovich himself!

This Makar was once simply called . . . "Makarka the Wanderer." . . . One day he stopped by Tikhon Ilyich's pub. . . . He wore bast shoes, a skullcap, and a greasy cassock; he carried a long verdigris-painted staff topped with a cross at one end and with a spear at the other; a knapsack and a soldier's mess tin hung from his back; his hair was long and yellow; his face was wide and the color of putty; his nostrils were like two rifle muzzles; his nose had been broken and looked like a saddle-bow; his eyes were pale, sharp, and bright. . . .

Tikhon Ilyich had hired Makar as his assistant. . . . He had turned out to be such a shameless thief, though, that Tikhon Ilyich had had to beat him up and throw him out. A year later Makarka became known throughout the region for his prophesies which were so ominous that his visits were dreaded like fire. Makarka would go up to someone's window, chant, "May he rest in peace," or sprinkle some incense—and someone would die in the house.

Now Makarka . . . was at Tikhon's door and singing. The blind man joined in, rolling his milky eyes upward. . . . He was a runaway convict, a terrible and ruthless beast. But even more terrible still was what the tramps were singing. The blind man . . . sang with a dreadful nasal tenor, Makarka droned in a ferocious base. . . . They sang something that was far too loud, crudely harmonious, anciently religious, powerful and threatening.

"Mother Earth shall weep and wail!" sang the blind man.

"Weep and wail!" Makarka echoed with conviction.

"Before the Savior, before his Icon," howled the blind man.

"Sinners shall repent!" threatened Makarka. . . .

"They will not escape divine punishment!"

"They will not escape eternal fire!" . . .

Tikhon Ilyich waited for something terrible to happen to him. After all, he was no longer a kid. How many men his age had already left the world? You can't escape death and old age.... Life was so short; people grew up, aged, and died so quickly; they knew each other so little and forgot everything they had lived through so quickly that you'd go crazy if you really thought about it! Tikhon had been wanting to tell the story of his life, but what was there to tell? Nothing.... He hardly remembered anything. For instance, he had quite forgotten his childhood....

If Tikhon's father, Ilya Mironov, were still alive he would have fed the old man out of charity, but Tikhon would not have known him or even noticed him.... If someone asked Tikhon if he remembered his mother, he'd answer, "I remember some bent old woman or other... who dried horse manure... drank on the quiet, and grumbled.... Nothing more."...

Friends who had been abroad... told Tikhon Ilyich what life was like there.... Take Russian Germans or the Jews. All of them behaved sensibly, prudently, all of them knew one another, all were friends... all helped one another; if they moved somewhere else, they corresponded; families exchanged portraits of fathers, mothers, and friends; they taught their children, loved them, took walks with them, and spoke to them as equals—something that the child would always remember. But Russians treated each other as enemies; they were envious, gossips. They visited each other once a year.... They begrudged a spoonful of jam... a second glass of tea!...

The peasant Deniska... pulled the booklets from his pocket. Tikhon Ilyich... read the titles... "'The Role of the ...'" The word stumped Tikhon Ilyich, and Deniska... prompted him quickly, shyly: "'The Role of the Proletariat in Russia.'"

Tikhon Ilyich shook his head.

"Now that's a new one! Nothing to eat, but buying books! And what books at that! No wonder they call you a troublemaker."...

Tikhon kept on drinking, clamping his jaws ever more tightly, and staring more and more fixedly... at the wick burning evenly in the lamp....

His mind was in a fog—first it seemed that everything was ahead of him: joy, freedom, and good times. Then his heart again began to ache hopelessly. He tried to cheer himself up: "So long as you've got money in your pocket, you're king of the jungle!"...

Tikhon Ilyich polished off the vodka; he had smoked so many cigarettes that the room had grown dark. Trying to keep his balance ... he went out onto the dark porch....

A dead silence hung over the land, darkening softly in the starlight. . . . The pale highway disappeared into the dusk. Far away, a hollow sound seemed to come from the earth; it grew louder until it burst into the open and could be heard all around: the southeastern express sped past into the distance . . . it flashed a chain of electrically lit windows and gave off strands of smoke, like the hair of a flying witch, redly illumined from below. . . .

Tikhon Ilyich wanted to sleep, but he sat for a long time, clenching his teeth and staring sleepily and glumly at the table.

March 2, 1910
Ivan Bunin, from an interview with the Odessa Leaflet

How the people of Capri love Gorky, how they greet him so enthusiastically when he appears on the square, in the street. . . .

In general, I love the East and its religions. . . . India interests me as a cradle of humanity and religion.

March 12, 1910
Ivan Bunin, from an interview with the Odessa Leaflet

Critics and those who write about authors in general are extremely conservative in the way they understand a writer. . . . In the beginning of a writer's literary career they tag his fiction with some epithet, and rest content forever. . . .

So it has been with me. . . . Critics have called my works the "Lyrics of Fading Away" and "The Sadness of Desolation" . . . old labels which, of course, are easier to use than to seek out new ones. . . .

March 21, 1910
Ivan Bunin, from an interview with the Odessa Leaflet

As readers know, I have never liked the fashionable writers of today, including L. Andreev. When I wrote that Andreev's works were chaotic, obscure, without content and form, readers reprimanded me sternly. . . . But the public cannot delude itself forever. Readers will soon sober up. . . .

May 16, 1910
Ivan Bunin, from an interview with the Odessa News

We were guests of Alexei Maximovich Gorky for two weeks on the island of Capri. Gorky looks good, hale and hearty, although he has grown a bit thin. His face is as tanned as any native on the island. At present Gorky gives all his time to writing. . . . He also follows the social, political, and literary life of Russia with attention and vigilance. He receives tons of journals, newspapers, and all the latest books. . . . Gorky is better informed of the social and literary life of this country than people who live in our capitals. Gorky regrets the overall situation in Russia and the state of contemporary Russian literature. He thinks that . . . both are in decline. . . . He sympathizes only with those representatives of today's literature . . . who have remained faithful to the good old literary traditions. But, generally speaking, he is doing very well.

June 10, 1910
Ivan Bunin, from his diary
　　Tolstoy's *Resurrection* is one of the most valuable books on earth.

June 15, 1910
Ivan Bunin, from a letter to Maxim Gorky
　　I will never forget, dear one, what you told me when we parted. . . . I remember so powerfully, so vividly . . . you, Naples, and all that is graceful and charming in the Italian people. . . . I find it such a terrible pity that I do not understand Italian; I dream again to visit Italy during the fall, an entire fall!
　　There is little sense to what I see here; I again feel tired, insane. I am drinking too much; I do not see any way out. . . . Icy rains and the cholera rage throughout Russia. And I cannot find peace and quiet anywhere!

July 7, 1910
Yuly Bunin, from a letter to a friend
　　Cholera has broken out in the village where I live; there have been several deaths. . . .
　　It was impossible to stay here, so Vanya, Vera Nikolaevna, and I . . . left today for Efremov. . . .
　　But the situation is extremely difficult even in Efremov.

August 1, 1910
Yuly Bunin, from a letter to a friend.
　　You are not correct when you say that all of the family's affairs have fallen on me. . . .

The only one who was absent at mother's passing was Vanya [Ivan] who left for Moscow. . . . He said he could not bear such goings-on; besides, he had to finish a story. . . .

August 3, 1910
Ivan Bunin, from his diary
"Art is best recognized when it is dressed in shabby clothes" (Nietzsche).
"Be a poet of nature—and you will be a poet of *people*" (Hugo).
"Art is to the individual what nature is to God" (Hugo).
"A snake lies next to any treasure" (Gulistan Saadi).[5]

August 20, 1910
Ivan Bunin, from a letter to Maxim Gorky
Life is so willful and capricious; but there exist moments in human relationships that one never forgets, that exist by themselves and outside of any time—like those moments when I am with you: a present that makes people feel alive and that gives unforgettable happiness.

October 1910
Ivan Bunin, from Part Two of The Village
All his life Kuzma wanted to study and write. . . . He wanted to write about how he was dying to describe, with an unheard-of mercilessness, his poverty and life, both so horribly ordinary, but which had crippled him and made him a "barren fig-tree." . . .
Kuzma's was the story of all Russia's self-taught men. He was born in a country in which over a hundred million people were illiterate. He grew up in the Black Suburb, where even now men killed each other in fistfights, amidst abysmal ignorance and cruelty. . . .
[Kuzma's teacher] Balashkin was a huge, old, scrawny individual. . . . He was almost frightening with . . . his deep, ancient, baselike voice; the silver bristles on his grey cheeks; his huge green eye that squinted and squinted. . . .
Balashkin let out a hollow roar: "Good Lord! Pushkin was killed! Lermontov was killed, Pisarev was drowned, Ryleev was strangled. . . . Dostoevsky was dragged to the scaffold, Gogol was

[5]Gulistan Saadi is one of the greatest figures in classical Persian literature.

driven insane. . . . The government is guilty, you say? Lord or peasant, you get what you deserve. Oh, is there another such country in the world, another such people, be they thrice cursed!"

But Kuzma . . . frowning and grinning in turns, replied: "Such a people! The greatest people, I say. . . . After all, these writers came from the people. Platon Karataev[6]—he's our national type!"

"Why Karataev . . . and not a Karamazov and Oblomov, a Khlestakov and Nozdrev,[7] or, closer to home, your own scoundrel brother?"

"But Platon Karataev. . . ."

"The lice have eaten up your Karataev! I see no ideal there! . . . We're rushing back, to Asia, as fast as we can go! . . . *All Russia is a village*, get that into your head this once and for all!" . . .

Kuzma saw . . . three Ukrainians. . . . The bandages on their heads had hardened with dried pus; their eyes were swollen; their faces were bloated, glasslike, covered with greenish yellow bruises and black, crusted wounds. The three had been bitten by a rabid wolf; they were sent to a hospital in Kiev but had been held up at almost every large station without money or food for days on end. . . .

Kuzma went on to Kiev . . . and for three whole days he walked about the town . . . in happy, heady excitement. At the morning service in the Cathedral of Saint Sophia,[8] many stared in surprise at the scrawny Muscovite who stood before the sarcophagus of Yaroslav the Wise.[9] Kuzma was a strange sight: the service was over, the congregation was leaving, the watchmen were putting out the candles, but he still stood there, his teeth clenched, his thin greying beard dropped on his chest, his deep-sunken eyes closed in a sweet agony as he listened to the melodious bells humming with a hollow sound above the cathedral.

That evening Kuzma was seen at the Lavra.[1] He was sitting beside a crippled boy who gazed with a vague and sad smile at the white walls and the small gold domes. The boy wore . . . filthy rags on his thin body. . . . With one hand he was holding a small wooden bowl with a kopeck at the bottom; with the other he kept shifting

[6]Platon Karataev is the peasant-hero of Tolstoy's *War and Peace*.

[7]The references, of course, are to Dostoevsky's novel *The Brothers Karamazov* (1879–1880), Goncharov's *Oblomov* (1859), and Gogol's *Dead Souls* (1842).

[8]The Church of Saint Sophia is an outstanding example of ancient Russian architecture. The foundation of the church was laid in 1037.

[9]Yaroslav the Wise ruled in Kiev from 1019 until his death in 1054. His reign is generally recognized as the high point of Kievan development and success.

[1]Also known as the Kiev-Pechersk Monastery.

his ugly right leg . . . which was pale, unnaturally thin . . . burnt black by the sun, and covered with golden hair. There was no one around, but the boy . . . taking no notice of the flies feeding on the drippings from his nose, droned on without pause:

> Look at us, mothers,
> Poor, suffering cripples!
> And God forbid that you, mothers,
> Should suffer like us! . . .

Kuzma . . . peeped into the semidarkness. . . . He saw . . . a small coffin in which lay a dead baby with a large, almost bald head and a bluish little face. . . . A fat, blind girl sat at the table, scooping up bread and milk with a big wooden spoon. The flies buzzed over her like bees in a hive; they crawled over the dead baby's head and then fell into the milk. But the blind girl, sitting upright like a graven image . . . ate and ate. Horrified, Kuzma turned away. . . .

Night suddenly descended. Bluish lightning flashed more boldly and unexpectedly now. . . . The figure of a wet, thin-necked horse shone sharply in the deathly blue light. . . . A pale, metallically green oat field flashed into view against the inky background . . . The horse raised its head, and Kuzma became terrified. . . . Terrible thoughts of a flood began to flash through his mind.

October 13, 1910
Ivan Bunin, from an interview with the Voice of Moscow
It is naive to see the artist as a being of a special realm, not of this world. . . .

The artist is, first of all, an individual with well-defined thoughts and sensations. . . . Being influenced by the word, working with a brush, or developing a musical talent—in all spheres of art—the artist must have a tie with people, with surrounding social conditions. Coming into contact with life, influencing it, and in turn coming under its influence, the artist must, in one way or another, become a social being.

I do not understand "pure" art, and I find talk about it tiresome and obsolete. . . .

Creative freedom must not be subject to infringement or force . . . for art is independent of external forms and dogmas.

November 1910
Ivan Bunin, from Part Three of The Village

Kuzma was only a child when . . . he lived in Durnovka, a long time ago. All he remembered was . . . one dark summer night: There was not a single light in the village . . . "nine virgins, nine wives, and one widow" passed by his hut. They were all barefoot, with uncovered heads and shirts that shone white in the darkness. They were carrying brooms, sticks, and pitchforks . . . striking oven doors and frying pans, and singing a savage song. . . .

> Cattle death, cattle death,
> Do not come to our village!

The choir drawled as in a sad funereal chant, singing with harsh, guttural voices:

> We are plowing
> with incense, with the cross. . . .

Old Ivanushka . . . was like something from the Old Testament. . . . He was once famous for being as strong as a bear; but now thickset, his spine bent into an arc, he never raised his shaggy head. . . . Ivanushka's entire huge family had perished in the cholera of '92. . . . He preferred to be a wanderer and live by begging. Pigeon-toed, he waddled through the yard, a sack in his right hand, a stick and hat in his left, his bare head whitened by snow; for some reason the dogs did not bark at him. Ivanushka entered the house, muttering, "Bless this house and the master in it." Then he sat down on the floor against the wall. . . .

When Kuzma and Young Lass asked Ivanushka questions, he talked as in a dream, as if from somewhere far, far away. In an ancient and awkward tongue he said the tsar was made of gold . . . that Elijah the Prophet had crashed through the sky and had fallen to earth because he was "too heavy," that John the Baptist was born as shaggy as a ram and that when he baptized someone he'd beat the convert over the head with an iron staff so he'd "come to his senses," and that any horse would try to kill a man on the feast of Saints Florus and Laurus. . . .

The snowstorm continued. . . . Neither the village nor the windmill could be seen in the grey swirling haze. . . . The garden had turned white; the droning of the trees merged with the sound of the

wind and the tinkling of distant church bells. . . . From the porch
Kuzma could barely make out the dark, shadowy figures of peasants,
horses, and sleighs. . . . Young Lass's blue skirt and overcoat were
pulled up over her head . . . so as not to crumple the dress. Her head
was adorned with a crown of paper flowers and bound up in kerchiefs
and shawls. Young Lass was so weak from crying that she saw the
dark figures in the storm and heard the sounds of wind, voices, and
merry sleighbells as if in a dream. . . . The wind . . . painted mous-
taches, beards, and hats white; people barely recognized each another
in the hazy dusk. . . .

In the church watchman's lodge . . . everyone got sick from the
fumes. The church also smelled of smoke; it was cold and gloomy
because of the snowstorm outside and the low ceilings and barred
windows inside. Only the bride and groom held candles. . . . The
priest glanced sternly . . . at the bride and groom, at their tense,
anxious figures, at their faces, frozen in meekness and obedience, and
shining goldenlike from the light of the candles below. From force of
habit he uttered some words with feeling . . . but he cared little about
what he was saying or the people he was praying for.

"O God most pure, the Creator of all things, . . ." the priest
spoke hurriedly. . . . "Thou who didst bless thy servant Abraham and
open the womb of Sarah . . . who gave Isaac to Rebecca . . . who joined
Jacob and Rachel. . . . show now your kindness to your servants. . . ."

"Names?" he whispered sternly without changing the expression
on his face . . . and having heard—"Denis, Evdokya"[2]—he went on
with feeling:

"Give your servants, Denis and Evdokia, peace, long life,
chastity. . . . May they see children's children. . . . Fill their houses
with wheat and wine and oil. . . . Exalt them like the cedars of
Lebanon." . . .

Deniska found it awkward and terrifying to hold . . . the huge
copper crown which was topped by a cross, and crammed down low
over his ears; he felt both uncomfortable and scared. Young Lass's
hand . . . trembled, causing the wax of her candle to drip on the trim
of her pale blue dress. . . .

The storm was becoming even more terrifying in the twilight.
. . . [A woman] danced like a shaman, waving a handkerchief and
shrieking into the wind, the raging dark haze, and the snow that
blew into her mouth, muffling her wolflike howl:

[2]That is, Deniska and Young Lass.

Ah, the dove, the young grey dove
Has a golden head!

November 9, 1910
Maxim Gorky, from a letter to Ivan Bunin

I have read *The Village*. . . . It is a "first-class" work. . . . severe, honest—and good. How many of its tormenting thoughts stick to the soul like black pitch. . . .

I see so many qualities in your story; you have touched me to the depths of my soul. Almost every page has something so close, so Russian, so native—that I cannot find words to express how I feel! The writer Ivan Bunin is of good blood—he must take care of himself.

If one has to talk of an inadequacy in your work . . . I find only one—it is dense! . . . There is a lot of material in it. Every phrase squeezes together three, four objects; every page is a museum! . . .

November 13, 1910
Ivan Bunin, from a letter to Maxim Gorky

Thank you very much, dear friend, for your praise of *The Village*. You arouse me to new and better work. Your comment that *The Village* is dense—is a holy truth. . . . When I wrote it I felt as though I were rammed in a vice.

November 26, 1910
Ivan Bunin, from a letter to Maxim Gorky

This morning [a friend] . . . came into the room and said about Tolstoy, "The end has come."[3] For several days afterward I went about as in a dream. . . . I could not read the newspaper because of my tears. . . . Even now I cannot think calmly about Tolstoy's passing.

Tolstoy's death was supposed to have disturbed the public, youth, but it seems to me that no one is really upset. The indifference of everyone to everything is unbelievable.

Mid-December 1910
Maxim Gorky, from a letter to Ivan Bunin

I have read the end of *The Village*—with excitement and happiness for you. . . . As far as I am concerned, no one has portrayed the village as profoundly, as historically as you have. One could talk

[3]Tolstoy died on November 20, 1910.

about Leo Tolstoy... but that is a different era. [Chekhov's] "The Peasants" and "In the Ravine"[4] are episodes—you will forgive me—from the life of a hypochondriac. I do not know with what I can compare your work; I have been touched so powerfully by it. Dear to me is its humble, hidden, and muffled wail for Russia... its noble sorrow, its tormenting fear for our homeland—all this is new. No one has written like this before....

You have written courageously, even heroically. Good Lord, Russian literature is such a great thing; what tormenting love it arouses.

Do not consider my remarks about *The Village* overblown or exaggerated.... I am almost certain that the Johnny-Know-Nothing critics, all the parties and groups in Moscow and Petersburg... will neither appreciate *The Village* nor understand its content and form. The threat hidden in it... is unacceptable to both the left and the right....

But I know that when the confusion and dismay pass, when we shake off our boorish dissoluteness—and we must do so or perish! —then serious people will say: "Beyond its first-rate artistry, Bunin's *The Village* was the push that forced a broken and tottering society to think long and hard not about the peasant or the people but about the burning question—will there be a Russia or not? We still have not thought about Russia—as a whole—and this work has shown us the need to think in terms of the entire country, and to think about it historically.

December 15, 1910
Ivan Bunin, from an interview with the Odessa News
The passing of Leo Nikolaevich Tolstoy made such an unusual impression on me... that truly I find it difficult to express it in several words.

I could not read the newspapers. My eyes would well up with tears. They were confused tears, tears of sorrow and joy. I was genuinely happy that... one of the greatest of the greats had taken a step that would call forth the admiration of the entire world. I was happy that neither old age nor broken health could keep this genius from taking this step....

But I cried when I thought how great Tolstoy's sufferings must have been, the contradictions that tormented him and that forced

[4]Chekhov wrote "The Peasants" in 1897 and "In the Ravine" in 1900.

him to leave his home in secret, in the dead of night, and to set out God knows where.... [5]

I imagined the night when the great pilgrim . . . left his home. The wind had torn off his hat; he went looking for it in the bushes; and when he found it he ran off into the great expanse.

Tolstoy's soul thirsted to embrace the whole world; but, alas, by the will of fate, this genius had to go to some obscure station to finish out his glorious days. . . .

Contemporary literature this winter has turned out to be extremely colorless. At the very least last year people spoke a good deal about pornography, but they now have even stopped talking about that. One thing has stood out with undoubtable and extreme clarity—the sharp turn . . . to realism. . . . A critic even demanded that Sologub remove all mysticism from his book *The Petty Demon*.[6] . . . the public has gotten tired of all this devil stuff. . . . I welcome this as a sign that readers are returning to a healthy state.

December 16, 1910
Ivan Bunin, from an interview with the Odessa News

All these rumors that Gorky's talent has declined are absurd and unfounded. . . . Alexei Maximovich has spent all his life in Russia; he has absorbed a wealth of impressions and knowledge about his homeland. It is wrong to link the growth or decline of talent to whether the artist is bound to his country or not.

Earlier Gorky was a writer of Russia; now . . . he is a writer for humankind. . . . It is unimportant whether such a writer lives in Russia, Italy, or some other country. . . . Alexei Maximovich is one of very few writers in contemporary Russian literature who is doing great and genuine things.

December 17, 1910
Ivan Bunin, from a letter to Maxim Gorky

Allow me to say that if I write anything sensible after *The Village*, I will be indebted to you, Alexei Maximovich. You cannot imagine how valuable your words are to me, how you have sprinkled me with living water.

[5]Tolstoy's difficulties with his wife, Sofia Andreevna; the struggle between Sofia and his disciples for control of his papers; and the writer's wish to become a pilgrim in life led Tolstoy to leave the family estate at Yasnaya Polyana on November 10, 1910, and to embark on a journey which ended in his death ten days later at the train station of Astapovo.
[6]Fyodor Sologub wrote *The Petty Demon* in 1907.

PART FOUR

False Hopes

1911–1913

BUNIN, 1913

Between 1911 and 1913 Russians breathed a sigh of relief. It appeared that the revolution was over and that prosperity lay just beyond the horizon. There was evidence that Russia was at last becoming a modern state. Cities now housed nearly 30 million people, or roughly 17 percent of the population. Industry was growing dramatically. Russians employed in manufacturing rose from 1.4 million in 1890 to 3.1 million in 1913. Between 1909 and 1913 the production of pig iron increased by 60 percent, copper by 50 percent, and coal by 40 percent. The provinces were also alive and well. Bountiful harvests were now annual events, the result of new credit and consumer cooperatives, additional laws supporting the Stolypin reforms, and increased cultivation. For many citizens life was good and getting better: national income in European Russia nearly doubled in the first thirteen years of the new century.

But in truth Russia was merely passing through the eye of a hurricane. Rapid change was producing severe dislocations. True, some transformations proceeded quietly. The landed nobility were leaving Russian society with a whimper. If the gentry owned almost 200 million acres of land in 1887, they held only 90 million in 1911. More ominously, Rasputin was becoming ascendant in the imperial court, helping to revive opposition to the throne even among the more moderate groups of the third and fourth dumas.

Other changes were loud and disruptive. In 1911 Stolypin was assassinated; his place was filled by a series of ineffective ministers. Russian labor was deeply restive. In April 1912—the same month that the Bolshevik newspaper *Pravda* was founded in Saint Petersburg—the police fired on protesting workers in the Lena gold fields, killing or wounding more than a hundred of them. Also in 1912, 725,000 workers went on strike, their numbers increasing to 887,000 the following year.

Russian literature mirrored these political and social events. A demand for "normalcy" in art was followed by new turmoil and revolt. Economic stability had given the middle class a sense of security, a feeling that soon penetrated into fiction. Readers were tired of Modernism and wanted a return to realism. They yearned for concreteness, not abstraction; accidents, not essence; the particular, not the universal. Such desires were not difficult to satisfy. Symbolism, the dominant aesthetic mode, had become stagnant and smug, a victim of its own success. While the movement remained popular throughout the decade, it faced problems from within and without. Amorphous and ill defined, Symbolism had become a receptacle for all the currents in Russian thought: religious quest, social awareness, moral inquiry, revolutionary dreams, messianic hopes, and an enduring fascination with Europe and its culture. Complicating matters, the Symbolists were careless about whom they admitted into their ranks. Hundreds of minor writers, intellectuals, and aesthete-snobs claimed affiliation with the Symbolists, thereby vulgarizing the school. On the eve of World War I almost everyone was trying to write in the "new style"; erstwhile rebels were now respectable academicians.

Symbolism also faced challenges from new literary movements which either championed a return to realism or extolled even more "revolutionary" approaches to art. The Acmeists, for instance, demanded plain colors, definite lines, and clear-cut images. "Art is solidity, firmness," they affirmed. "We are fighting for this world, for our earth; we want to admire a rose because it is beautiful, not because it is the symbol of poetry." Another group, the Neo-Realists, led by Gorky who had returned to Russia from exile in 1913, wanted a meld of old and new. Much like Bunin whom they sometimes counted as a member, the Neo-Realists recalled the old gentry masters in the way they depicted provincial life, portrayed characters from the people, stressed the national traits of their heroes, and dwelt on the minutiae of everyday life. They often did this, though, by using rhythmic prose, by shunning straightforward narratives, and by opting for the lyrical, the fantastic, and the grotesque.

The Futurists, a group of anarchically inclined artists and

poets, wanted nothing less than a radical reformation of the arts. In such manifestos as "A Slap in the Face of Public Taste" (1912) they attacked all culture and demanded a language of "trans-sense" that violated the rules of syntax, semantics—and propriety. Their first anthology, *The Moribund Moon* (1913), shocked readers with its relish for unprintable words. "The past is narrow," they maintained. "Pushkin and the Academy are less comprehensible than hieroglyphics; we must jettison Pushkin, Dostoevsky, Tolstoy, and all the others from the ship of modernity." The Futurists loved causing scandal not only in literature but also in life. They strutted about with painted faces in motley clothing; they outraged audiences with profanity and abuse; they broke up respectable literary meetings with catcalls. (Mayakovsky, one of their leaders, strolled the streets wearing a silk top hat, a bright orange jacket or a yellow-striped blazer, and no necktie.) In general the Futurists did everything they could to attract attention, shock the bourgeois, and arouse indignation. They were, in their view, the people of the future, and their art was the seedbed for new life.

Given the times, Bunin had to agree with the Symbolist poet Alexander Blok, who sensed that the "arm of the seismograph had already moved" and that a cataclysm would soon destroy the old life. Rather than accept the inevitable, Bunin assumed the difficult (and thankless) role of speaking for sense and sensibility in Russia. Increasingly combative, he sought to call Russia back to its senses. He chided the people for their debauchery and despair; censured intellectuals for their messianism and fashionable love of the folk; flayed the Modernists for their radicalism, their love of Dostoevsky, and their calls for "art for art's sake." Even his beloved gentry masters Bunin took to task for their idealized portraits of provincial life. In his second full-length work, *Dry Valley* (1911), he portrayed a noble family, the Khrushchevs, who cannot cope with change. Seen through the eyes of "my sister and I," the last survivors of the clan, and of the house servant Natalya, the Khrushchevs complete the fall of the house of Russia begun by the Krasovs in *The Village*. They struggle heroically to keep the old ways, but they end their days as "living dead," victims of modernity.

Bunin took on the "modern" world not because he was a "mean, old man," as his detractors kept insisting, but because he was moved by his convictions. Between 1911 and 1913 he became increasingly philosophical about existence. Questions of life, not death, now engaged his energies. Old devils surely continued to haunt him. He still lamented his youth, his loneliness, his sickness and pain; he still saw writing as tortuous; he still regarded his race as pitiful and wandering; he still hated peasants and proletarians; he still condemned existence as fickle and cruel. But now he was often able to get beyond his darkness and to conclude not only that life was worth living but that it offered "moments" of happiness and peace to those who had the courage and stamina to look for them. He saw that he was not a pawn in life but that he had the power, through his writing, to arrest time and space, to preserve gentry culture, and to uphold sacred scripture and tradition in life. For Bunin, heaven and earth might pass away, but his words would not.

❋ 1911 ❋

Circa *1911*
Nikolai Pusheshnikov, from his diary

[Bunin said:] "All this talk about how Russia travels down some original path that is distinct from that of Western Europe, all this talk about our primordial peasant beginnings, or about how the peasant will have some final word . . . all this is nonsense."

January 20, 1911
Ivan Bunin, from a letter to Maxim Gorky

That which I had been feeling from time to time in the summer and fall—a dull pain in the right part of the stomach, across from the kidney . . . suddenly got so bad that I doubled over in pain. I hobbled back to my cabin [aboard ship to Egypt]; there I fell, covered with an icy sweat. I began to yell at the top of my lungs. The pain in my kidney and elsewhere caused me to faint for a while; then it tormented me all night long. . . . The next day I was so exhausted I could barely drag myself out of the cabin; I lay motionless on deck, feeling, incidentally, a sweet joy of life that I have never known before. . . . I also have gout and splendid hemorrhoids. . . . Excuse the wretched details—I won't talk about them any more. . . .

I do not know the fate of *The Village*. That which I have read in Moscow and Odessa reviews is stupid to the point of indecency. . . . [Reading them] my eyes pop out of my head.

February 1911
Elena Koltonovskaya, from a review of The Village

There is neither future nor hope for the Russian people. There is only dullness and stupidity, dirt and poverty, barbarism and hardheartedness, the fullest degradation, a kingdom of hottentots and gorillas. So affirms Bunin in *The Village*.

February 12, 1911
Ivan Bunin, from his diary
I have always had in my possession a small Suzdalian icon[1] framed in dark silver: a sacred vessel that ties me . . . to my ancestors, my world, my cradle, my youth. . . .

"Your Ways are unknown to me . . . O Lord." But I thank you for this lamp, for this quiet, for the fact that I am alive, that I can travel, that I can love and be glad, and that I can bow down before You. . . .

My life is a trembling, joyous union with the eternal and temporal, with the near and far, with all times and countries, with all the past and present. . . . Extend my days, O God!

February 13, 1911
Ivan Bunin, from a letter to Nikolai Teleshov
Now that we have worn out our shoes roving the sands, the graves, the Pyramids, and the ruins of temples, we are waiting for a boat to Ceylon, to Colombo.

February 13, 1911
Ivan Bunin, from his diary
We were already far from Port Said and in a completely dead and long uninhabited kingdom. . . .

I felt God's closeness . . . His abiding dominion over the earth. I recalled His eternal words: "I am the Lord your God. . . . Remember the days of the Lord. . . . Honor your father and your mother. . . . Do not do evil to your neighbor. . . . Do not covet his goods. . . ."

I thought: There is something sacredly stable in this world. . . . For all its wanderings, humankind strives to move forward . . . to some promised land . . . even though its members . . . huddle in a vale of tears . . . amidst a shallow, everyday life made up of weakness and pride, of envy and spite.

---

[1]Suzdal is a city that lies directly northeast of Moscow. The so-called Vladimir-Suzdal school of medieval Russian iconography (twelfth and thirteenth centuries) emphasizes a patrician air, a fondness for decoration, and features that are heavy, asymmetrical, and linear.

God's chosen ones, his prophets and wise men, often shuddered at such vileness. In their despair they smashed the tablets . . . the covenant between man and God. But again and again they gathered up the broken pieces. Again and again they restored the commandments; for again and again they heard these terrible but comforting words roared out from the gloom . . . and showed the way to salvation.

February 15, 1911
Ivan Bunin, from his diary

Yesterday was a day of extremes; the weather changed almost hourly.

But then we came upon a timeless bright summer, a completely new world which spoke to me about some long forgotten, heavenly, and blissful life.

Late in the evening the captain congratulated us on our entry into the tropics. The cherished line I had dreamed about for so long was crossed.

February 16, 1911
Ivan Bunin, from his diary

At six o'clock, right after sunset, I saw . . . the silver constellation of Orion. Orion in the afternoon! How can I thank God for everything He has given me, for all this joy and novelty!

Can it really be that someday all that is so close, customary, and dear will suddenly be taken away from me forever . . . ? How can I believe this? How can I become reconciled with this? How can I grasp the staggering cruelty and absurdity implicit in this?

Hence the pain that continually haunts all our lives . . . that arises from each irretrievable day, hour, and minute.

February 18, 1911
Ivan Bunin, from a letter to Yuly Bunin

We have been in Djibouti. The rowers were naked; those who met us in their canoes were also naked. . . . Again I had a strong and lively feeling that here was something primordial, warm, and paradisiacal. . . .

At first I thought this primitiveness, this ancientness was terrible; but then I gave way to feelings that were altogether different, sublime, almost terrifying. This quasi-animal life has gone on for thousands of years. Its divine purpose is unknown to us. In this dirty human nest, amidst this primitive desert, births and deaths, joys, sorrows, and sufferings have gone on for thousands of years. . . . Why? There has to be a reason.

A great and absolute sorrow, a great hopelessness rules over this pitiful and confused human existence.

February 19, 1911
Ivan Bunin, from his diary

I am on the ocean. A very special feeling of endless freedom. . . .

I am on the upper deck. The new moon is very high and shines very brightly. . . . The constellation of Orion is at its zenith. The Southern Cross is to the south, lying in the huge expanse of an almost empty sky. Looking at it, I suddenly recalled Dante: "The Southern Cross shows the way to Paradise." On the left the Big Dipper lies low in the sky, spreading out like silver against the dark blue; beneath it, almost on the horizon, the Polar Star is sadly white. A huge, splendid star sails like the wind, like a red flame in the east, evenly and powerfully. And we are heading straight for it.

February 20, 1911
Ivan Bunin, from his diary

When I see a ship I cannot help but recall a grave. I constantly think: What a terrible and strange thing is our existence—every minute hangs by a thread! Here I am alive and well; but in the next second who knows what will happen to my heart, which, like any human heart, is something without equal in all creation . . . ?

How comical are those people who belong to the petty literary world, who exaggerate their worth in everyday life, and who live among people who know only the Bible, the Koran, and the Vedas!

February 20, 1911
Ivan Bunin, from a letter to Maria Chekhova

God knows where I am—in Africa, among the Somalians who go about absolutely naked and who are chocolate-colored from head to toe (with terrible manes and covered with lime, to boot). If they don't eat me up, I'll write from Ceylon.

February 25, 1911
Ivan Bunin, from his diary

The night is so unspeakably beautiful. . . . it shines over the oceans. . . . The stars play in semiprecious light. The wind is truly like the Breath of God keeping alive this entire charming and inscrutable world. It blows into our windows and doors, into our souls, which are so trustfully open to it, to this night, and to all the unearthly purity of the wind.

February 28, 1911
Ivan Bunin, from his diary

The moon is green! I looked out the window...yes, it was green! Tender green in the heliotropelike sky, amidst ashen clouds, over the green splendor of the ocean!...A moist wind comes pouring through the windows and penetrates the very depths of the soul.

March 1, 1911
Ivan Bunin, from his diary

Our last night on the ocean, tomorrow Ceylon, Colombo. "Your Way...and Your signs are unknown...." My closeness to You is so terrible and sweet; my love for You is so endless; my faith in Your fatherly Bosom is so strong!

March 19, 1911
Vera Muromtseva-Bunina, from her diary

Now we are in Kandy, in the mountain locality of Ceylon.... We have seen so many new things. They are unlike anything we have known before; they are so beautiful that I still cannot take them in as I should....

Legend has it that here was paradise. Here on Ceylon is Adam's peak: a bridge on which he and Eve fled to India after they were cast out of the garden. Yes, here truly is paradise.

I was astounded by a Buddhist service. We entered a temple for the first time in the evening. In the half dusk there were the din of tambourines, the pounding of the drums, the playing on flutes, many flowers with heavy scents, and Buddhist priests in yellow robes. I liked it all so much that I brought flowers to the service.

April 20, 1911
Ivan Bunin, from a letter to Maxim Gorky

I have read a review or two about *The Village*.... And both the damnation and praise seem so undistinguished and flat that I feel like crying.... Critics are writing about my "lacquered" shoes; they talk about my estates, my migraine headaches, and my fears of peasant writers to such an extent that I find it offensive. Migraines I have had and perhaps will always have; but estates, lands, drivers—hardly. . . . All my life I have had literally nothing except my suitcase. . . .

May 10, 1911
Maria Chekhova, from a letter to Pyotr Bykov
You asked me for someone who could write a biography of my deceased brother; if you recall, I recommended Iv. Al. Bunin. . . . Now I even ask you to do it. No one writes better than he; he knew and understood my deceased brother very well; he can go about this endeavor objectively. . . . I repeat, I would very much like this biography to correspond to reality and that it be written by I. A. Bunin.

May 20, 1911
Ivan Bunin, from his diary
A rather young peasant came through here. . . . He said he had spent fourteen years at the Lavra in Kiev. He bragged, "I got chased out on account of girls. . . . Guess that means I'm a bad monk." . . .
I said to him, "You mean to tell me you're just wandering about, without working?" "The devil couldn't make me work now!" he replied.
The peasant was wearing a cassock and beaten-up red shoes. He had a feminine face, long sparse hair, and a youthful appearance, the result of a shaven chin. . . . He was narrow-shouldered and . . . slightly hunchbacked. . . . I gave him a shirt; he was tickled to death. "Well, now," he said, "I'll be all right for some time."

June 5, 1911
Ivan Bunin, from his diary
The old peasant woman Lukovka. Her specialty is to wash dead bodies and to be at funerals. She has done this for a very long time, almost from her youth. A subject for a small story.

June 8, 1911
Ivan Bunin, from his diary
Vaska, the imbecile from Efremov, has died. The merchants there gave him a grand funeral. They made fun of him his entire life. . . . They died laughing whenever he "tried to do something." But his funeral was so grand that the entire town was amazed: a magnificent coffin and singing. . . . Another subject for a story.

July 3, 1911
Ivan Bunin, from his diary

We have just returned from seeing Taganok, a man who is 108 years old. . . . Taganok is a dear, sweet, childlike individual. . . . He sleeps on a sled in a dugout behind the hut. . . .

When I arrived, Taganok had difficulty pulling his cap off his bald head: He is pathetically thin, with sunken shoulders and a light white beard. His eyes are without expression. . . . His face and hands are dark. . . .

Taganok lives in another world. He vaguely remembers the French . . . that they begrudged him the smallest things.

He spoke with pauses; he did not answer questions right away.

"Well, what say, Taganok, would you like to live a bit longer?"

"God knows. . . . What can I do about it? You can't force one to die!"

"Well, say you could live for one more year or five more years, which would you choose?"

"Why should I invite death?" he said. He burst out laughing, but his eyes took on a pensive look. "Death won't get me. Let it take someone younger; it won't get me. No way."

"But tell us, one year or five years?"

He thought and then he said with hesitation:

"In five years the lice will be eating me. . . ."

Circa *Mid-July 1911*
Sergei Demkin,[2] from his memoirs

Ivan Alexeevich loved to hunt and fish with the peasant children. He would give away the fish he caught to those who sang songs to him. He loved to talk to my grandfather, Taganok. Grandfather was very talkative; he had a good memory; and he knew many songs. He would chase me away whenever he was talking to Ivan Alexeevich. But I remember a thing or two. When Ivan Alexeevich visited us he would always take a look at the garden and the hemp. He was interested in everything; he asked questions about everything. If he heard a local word or phrase he would invariably write it down in his notebook. The hero in his story "The Ancient Man"[3] is an exact copy of my grandfather.

[2]Sergei Demkin was Taganok's grandson. See the preceding entry.
[3]Bunin published the story "The Ancient Man" on July 8, 1911.

July 15, 1911
Ivan Bunin, from his diary

A feast day, a fair. . . . Two rows of ghastly looking beggars at the church gates. One cripple is especially striking. . . . He is lying in dreadful rags . . . with milk blue, almost white, inhuman eyes. His body is all crooked and broken; one leg is extremely thin, purple colored, and sticks out on purpose (as if to attract the compassion and attention of the crowd). . . .

Another one: thin . . . without buttocks . . . his legs spread out in rotting shoes. His shirt and bag are unbelievably foul, dirty, and caked with dried blood. His bag has some greasy uncooked meat, pieces of bread, raw lamb bones. A thin boy stands next to him, sharp-eared, pockmarked, with narrow eyes. He cries out happily, "Give me something, sirs!"

There were still others: a small one, about twenty-five, also pockmarked and happy . . . another whose legs had caked wounds and purple spots . . . "a leper." All the beggars made the rounds of the fair. The leper also moved about, dragging his rear on the ground.

July 20, 1911
Ivan Bunin, from a letter to a friend

We have been inundated by rain and overwhelmed by storms. You feel like screaming for help! I have so much to do, but I find it tormenting to write in the rain. . . .

July 29, 1911
Ivan Bunin, from his diary

Again [the old man] Taganok. . . . One could write a genuine tragedy about an individual who has lived such a long life. The longer a life, the more terrible death must seem. At eighty years old one can hope to live to one hundred. But at one hundred? Then one *becomes used* to living!

July 30, 1911
Ivan Bunin, from his diary

"If you do not know anything about life, how can you know anything about death?" (Confucius).

August 7, 1911
Elena Koltonovskaya, from a review of The Village

Our intellectual rarely comes into contact with the village; he knows little about it. In the abstract, and from afar, he has the best feelings and concerns for it. But let fate throw him into the village, have him come up against it head on, and the intellectual will immediately run away from it, in earnest fear, in squeamish disgust. The only prayer our intellectual will address to the heavens will be the prayer of Bunin's hero Kuzma Krasov in *The Village*: "Dear God, save me and have mercy! Get me out of here as fast as possible!" . . .

One of the sickest strains in the psychology of our intellectual is his helplessness before the primordial darkness of the village, his estrangement from it. Whom does the village not frighten and repulse? In whom does it not rouse vague sensations of guilt and thirst for repentance? But the village remains foreign, far off, and mysterious. . . . The village and the city are separated not only by poor and impassable roads but also by a genuine abyss in ideas, thoughts, and feelings! Russian life is full of contrasts, but . . . the contrast between the village and the city is the most glaring of them all.

August 12, 1911
Ivan Bunin, from a letter to the Gorkys

If I were a bit freer and richer, I would immediately set sail for Capri! Yesterday evening I looked for a long, long time at the lights of the ship that was leaving for Italy.

August 14–15, 1911
Vera Muromtseva-Bunina, from a letter to Ivan Bunin

[Your nephew] and I were in Kamenka;[4] we went all around recalling its at first peaceful but then turbulent life. . . . There is brownish purple grass and two or three apple trees where the famous garden used to be. . . . Everything has grown old; many people have died. . . . Yes, Kamenka has disappeared from the face of the earth; only *Dry Valley* safeguards its memory.

September 8, 1911
Ivan Bunin, from an interview with the Odessa News

The assassination of P. A. Stolypin[5] is, of course, a great, enormous event, but . . . it will hardly affect our politics. . . . One can

---

[4]Kamenka was one of the estates that belonged to the Bunin family.

[5]Pyotr Arkadievich Stolypin (1863–1911) was Russia's prime minister from 1906 to 1911, and sought to suppress the revolutionary movement by mass exiles and executions. His agrarian reforms created a landowning *kulak* class and freed labor for industry.

hope for a change of direction only after some time. . . . One hopes
this direction will be toward humanity. The alternative is simple
revenge.

Today's fears are the result of a society that is broken in spirit.
The past few years have plunged everyone into a terrible pessimism;
everything is now painted in dark colors. But logic dictates that life
cannot continue on this path and that the coming of dawn is
inevitable. . . .

As I see it, the working classes of Western Europe . . . have
become a powerful force that are more and more affirming their
rights. These classes . . . are like streams feeding an enormous current
that very soon—five to ten years—will overwhelm all of Western
Europe. . . .

One can see this force not only in protests against rising prices
but also . . . in the strikes in England and especially in the growing
conflict between Germany and France. . . . And if we have not had
catastrophes so far, it is only because the proletariat are against any
political adventures. . . . The ruling classes must take the proletariat
into account. . . .

The interests of the working classes in Western Europe and
Russia are the same. The only difference is that the Western European
proletariat is splendidly organized . . . and ready for battle. One
cannot say this about the Russian proletariat. . . .

September 12, 1911
Ivan Bunin, from an interview with the Moscow News

I am interested not in the peasants per se but in the soul of
Russian people in general . . . the psyche of the Slav. . . .

However strange it may sound, fiction about the Russian gentry
is far from complete. Investigation of this area is not finished. We
know the gentry of Turgenev and Tolstoy. But one cannot judge the
mass of Russian gentry from these, since Turgenev and Tolstoy
portrayed the upper strata: rare oases of culture.

The life of most of the gentry in Russia was much more
rudimentary, and their soul was much more typically Russian than
either Tolstoy or Turgenev depicted. After the works of Tolstoy and
Turgenev, there is a gap in fiction about the gentry. . . .

As I see it, the lives and souls of the Russian gentry are identical
to those of the peasants: the only difference is material. In no other
land are the lives of the gentry and the peasants so close, so tightly
bound, as in our country. . . .

To show the features of village peasant life as they exist at the estates of the gentry—this is the task I set for myself in my works. . . .

I am also interested in genuine folk language. . . . Examples of the folk speech of central Russia I find only in the works of Gleb Uspensky and Leo Tolstoy. As regards the contrivances and stylization that the Modernists pass off as folk language, these I consider the utmost vulgarity.

October 19, 1911
Nikolai Pusheshnikov, from his memoirs
Ivan Alexeevich said that he never feels so good as in those moments when a big road stands before him. . . .

He recalled Chekhov. . . saying that Chekhov was "such a great, such a gifted, such a remarkable individual, artist, and poet," and that he achieved such great perfection in his final writings. Bunin said that "The Archbishop"[6] is a splendidly written piece and that only those who engage in literature, and who themselves experience hellish torment in their writing, can grasp the beauty of this piece. . . .

Bunin also praised "In the Ravine"[7]. . . . as "one of the most splendid creations in Russian literature" and even as one of the best pieces in all of world literature. . . .

Ivan Alexeevich also said that "despite the fact that Saint Petersburg is a splendid city, it is impossible to live in it, and it is not surprising that Dostoevsky gave birth to such nightmares there." . . .

October 21, 1911
Nikolai Pusheshnikov, from his memoirs
Ivan Alexeevich said: ". . . What a great joy it is to exist! If only to see the smoke from a ship, its color. If I had no arms or legs, and if I could only sit behind the gate at a shop and look at the setting sun, this would not keep me from being happy. Only one thing is necessary: to sit and to breathe.

"I always say: Nothing gives as much pleasure as colors. I have grown accustomed *to see*; artists have taught me this art. When Goethe and Byron were alive, people only saw the *silver* shade of the moonlight; now there exists an endless number of shades. . . ."

[6]Chekhov wrote "The Archbishop" in 1902.
[7]Chekhov published "In the Ravine" in 1900.

We walked around Nuremberg. Bunin was enthralled by the ancient architecture of the medieval town and especially by the famous Lorenzokirche[8]. . . .

Ivan Alexeevich said that when he saw something splendid, he regretted that he had lived so many years so terribly and poorly, and that he had completely wasted the best and most tender years of his life. . . . He said: "I have wasted so much of my energy and youth— on what? It is terrible to recall how much time has gone by to no purpose, in vain! Surely I should have written; if only I had spent my youth in another way, if only I had studied more, if only I had developed myself more, if only I were not born in Butyrki . . . if only I had not been so poor in my youth. When I was eighteen I was literally the editor of the *Orel Herald*, where I wrote editorials on the decrees of the Holy Synod, about widows' homes and bull breeding, when I should have studied, studied for days on end! . . .

"I so love these Gothic cathedrals, with their portals, stained glass, and organs! . . . When I hear the 'Stabat Mater Dolorosa'[9] and the 'Dies Irae'[1] . . . my whole body shudders. I become a fanatic, a zeal- ot. It seems to me that I could burn heretics with my own hands. . . .

"How many wondrous things are there in this world about which we have not the slightest understanding. How many astonish- ing creations of literature and music are there, things which we have not heard or seen or do not recognize because we are busy reading vulgar stories and poems! . . . I feel like pulling out my hair from despair!

"I do not understand anything; I do not recognize anything; but I feel like living forever—for life is so interesting and poetic!"

October 26, 1911
Nikolai Pusheshnikov, from his memoirs
To examine ships in port—this is Ivan Alexeevich's favorite occupation.

November 21, 1911
Maxim Gorky, from a letter to his son
Bunin was here and told me very sad things about Russia. I

---

[8]The Gothic Church of Saint Lorenz in Nuremberg was begun in the 1270s and completed in the late fifteenth century.
[9]The "Stabat Mater Dolorosa" is a thirteenth-century Latin hymn describing the sorrows of the Virgin Mary at the Crucifixion.
[1]The "Dies Irae" is a twelfth-or thirteenth-century hymn about the Last Judgment.

listened to him, but for some reason I did not believe him. I find it very difficult to believe in that which is evil, even though I know it exists, and to a great degree.

November 25, 1911
Ivan Bunin, from a letter to Nikolai Teleshov
The weather here in Capri is splendid, not like where you are in Russia. And there are few writers here—that is also good.

December 1911
Maria Andreeva, from a letter to a friend
Right now we have a conference of writers going on. . . . Bunin has written such truly splendid things . . . but they are horrible to listen to. Your hair stands on end.

Circa *December 1911*
Nikolai Pusheshnikov, from his memoirs
At Capri Bunin visited Gorky daily, sometimes even twice a day. . . . On the gramaphone they played music of Chaliapin, Caruso, Titta Ruffo,[2] and, especially for Ivan Alexeevich, the singing of the cantor of the Warsaw synagogue, a remarkable performer of ancient Hebrew religious melodies. . . .
Dinner was very lively; there were many toasts. Gorky wished that Bunin would write two thousand stories like *The Village*. . . .
Ivan Alexeevich said, "When I experience a strong feeling of beauty, I always also feel . . . a sensation of the sweetest sadness, and in particular of a terrible languor, which reconciles me with death." . . .
Bunin said to Gorky, "I know, Alexei Maximovich, that you have long predicted that there will be no death, that life will be splendid, elevated, and so forth; but you and I will have rotted away by that time." . . .

December 8, 1911
Ivan Bunin, from a letter to Nikolai Teleshov
Gorky and I sit and swear at contemporary fiction and literary mores.

[2]Titta Ruffo (1877–1953) was an Italian baritone, most famous for his role of Figaro in Rossini's opera *The Barber of Seville*.

December 19, 1911
Ivan Bunin, from a letter to a friend

Truly the publishers are corrupt to the last man; now they are also corrupting writers—the weakest and least known of them, of course. Generally speaking, things have become so bad in the literary world that it is long, long overdue for writers to think a bit . . . about the purpose of their existence, their work, their life.

Circa December 28, 1911
Maxim Gorky, from a letter to a friend

Ivan Bunin is our contemporary writer. This will soon become clear for anyone who sincerely loves literature and the Russian language!

✱   1912   ✱

Circa 1912
Alexei Zolotarev, from his memoirs

Gorky said, "Pull Bunin out of Russian literature and it will grow dull. It will lose its lively cheerful sheen and the celestial radiance of his lonely wanderer-soul. We have to take care of people like Ivan Alexeevich. He can still tell us many things about himself, about . . . Russians, and about the world in which we live."

Circa 1912
Elena Viktorova, from her memoirs

Once . . . Alexei Maximovich [Gorky] received a whole stack of poems. He read them in his study and came to dinner disturbed and excited. . . . With delight he read the best of them to all who were present.

Ivan Alexeevich Bunin was at the dinner. This bilious individual despised everything; with a squeamish look on his face, he listened to what Alexei Maximovich was reading.

"I don't hear anything special," Bunin muttered through his teeth. "It is apparent that the writer is young and uneducated."

Alexei Maximovich raised his eyes from the page on which tears glistened.

"Uneducated, you say? No, Ivan Alexeevich, the issue here is not education but the force you feel from reading these writers . . . our native Russian force, our energy, our life. We will educate these writers. . . ."

Bunin began to show that the poet was completely ignorant of versification. Alexei Maximovich argued with him hotly. Soon after this, the poet was invited to Capri. . . .

There was a bell. . . . In the brightly lit corridor I saw a short man with a Semitic face. Alexei Maximovich, so tall and broad-shouldered, bent down and looked attentively at the big, prominent eyes of the poet.

Rubbing his cold, blue hands, the poet looked confusedly at everyone; then he stared at Gorky's face for a long time.

Bunin was drinking tea; with the smile of a Mephistopheles he watched the young poet. The questions which the highly cultured maestro Bunin asked both distracted and unnerved the young guest; he uttered some nonsense. Apparently he was quite shy.

Alexei Maximovich tried to reassure the poor man. . . . But Bunin stretched and yawned several times. Then he left . . . taking the other writers with him. Only the three of us remained. . . .

[Another time] Alexei Maximovich was sitting by the fire-place . . . alongside him was I. A. Bunin, greenish bilious, like a mummy. . . .

Gorky asked Bunin to begin the reading, but Bunin, looking at all of us, smiled ironically and said:

"Many people get upset, even frightened by what I write."

We all knew how highly Bunin regarded himself and how he despised our opinions, even if we dared to criticize him.

Alexei Maximovich chuckled and said jokingly:

"They don't frighten easily; you won't scare them." . . .

A brightly realistic tone; rich, figurative language; precise, sharpened words. We were carried away from a rainy day on Capri to a quiet Russian village, engulfed in the burning rays of a July sun. . . .

I stared at Bunin; then I shifted my eyes to Alexei Maximovich. An open face with prominent cheekbones and eyes that burned brightly with delight, clear, joyful, like the azure blue sky of the village in Bunin's story. When Bunin read how a bull had gored an old woman's stomach, big tears flowed down Gorky's face.

Bunin finished reading his story. We all sat there stunned.

Alexei Maximovich got up, went up to the diminutive Bunin, and seemingly wrapped his broad-shouldered body around him.

"Ivan Alexeevich! That was so good!" Gorky solemnly said, embracing him. "Now that's how you should write!" he turned to us. "Learn from him! Here let me read!"

And Gorky reread the best parts.

After that, Bunin folded the manuscript and stuck it in his pocket.

"Why the fuss?" Bunin said to Gorky with a sly, ambiguous smile. "After all, you have better things than that."

"Not like that," Gorky said. . . .

January 30, 1912
Maxim Gorky, from a letter to Ekaterina Peshkova
Bunin has matured. Everyone else has withered away.

February 1912
Nikolai Pusheshnikov, from his diary
Bunin said: "After Tolstoy, everyone should quit writing!. . . His *Cossacks*[3] . . . is a superhuman piece!. . . One should imitate Tolstoy in a most brazen and shameless way. If I were reproached for imitating Tolstoy, I would be only too glad. What the critics see as his supposed weaknesses are his greatest strengths. . . .

"Yesterday I read Tolstoy's story 'Father Vasily.'[4] . . . Two or three words, no more, about the landscape; two words about the peasant; two words about the priest—and the result is an absolutely exceptional piece of art.

"For 'Father Vasily,' I would give away all of contemporary literature with its Andreevs, Artsybashevs, and the like. Literature would only be the winner. There would be no vulgarity, nonsense, or tastelessness.

"I do not understand how critics and historians can put, say, Turgenev or Dostoevsky on the same level with Tolstoy; or how, as regards descriptions of love, women, and nature, they put Turgenev even higher. What a savage mistake. . . .

"If all writers should imitate Tolstoy. . . they would break themselves of nonsense."

Bunin said that as soon as he heard the name of Tolstoy, his soul

[3]Tolstoy wrote *The Cossacks* between 1853 and 1863.
[4]Tolstoy published "Father Vasily" in 1911.

caught fire, he felt like writing, and he had faith in literature. . . .

He added: "I was probably born to be a poet. . . . For me, the main thing is to find the sound. As soon as I have found the sound, all the rest follows; I know that the job is done.

"I have never written what I felt or how I felt. I did not dare. I want to write without any form, without literary devices. But what torment, what unbelievable suffering is art! I begin to write, to say the simplest phrase; but I suddenly remember that Lermontov or Turgenev said something similar. I turn the phrase around and say it in a different way, and the result is awful. . . .

"Sometimes I work all morning; after hellish torment I write only several lines. . . . In general, all literary devices should be sent to the devil! . . . Perhaps I will write something sensible when I'm old. . . .

"Literary craftsmanship has not moved forward since the time of Pushkin and Lermontov. New themes, new feelings, and the like have been introduced, but literary art itself has not advanced. Pushkin and Lermontov have not been surpassed. . . .

"All my life I have experienced the torments of Tantalus. All my life I have suffered because I could not express what I wanted to say. To tell the truth, I have taken up an impossible task. I am exhausted from the fact that I look at the world only with my eyes, and that I can look at it in no other way. . . . Take the present moment. How can one talk about all this beauty? . . . It is genuine torment! I despair when I cannot recall it. My head grows dull; my body grows heavy and weak. I write, and tears flow down my cheeks from exhaustion. What torment is our writing craft. I sometimes think it would be better for me to get a real job.

"I remember that when I worked for the *zemstvo*[5] in Poltava, and was taking care of the library, I felt I was a fresh and happy being. Or perhaps I felt so good then because I was young? In our line of work it is terrible when the mind is in a rut. . . . What torment it is to find the sound, the melody of the story. . . . When I do not find the sound I cannot write . . . especially when I live . . . amidst such foulness and vileness! . . .

"I do not understand why everyone thinks Dostoevsky's *The*

[5]The *zemstvo* was a provincial or district council established in 1864 by Alexander II. The *zemstvos* played an important part in the formation of a liberal Russian intelligentsia. They were abolished in 1917 by the Bolsheviks in favor of the "soviets" or workers' councils.

Double[6] is so profound. It is an obscene, stupid woodcut, a shameless imitation of Gogol. Dostoevsky so exaggerates the worst qualities of Gogol that I am literally astounded—a phenomenon which, incidentally, continues to our own time. . . ."

When Bunin read Bely he cried, bit his fists, and threw himself face down on the sofa. He said: "I am beside myself! I do not have the strength to express what I feel when I read . . . Andrei Bely. . . . All that is the most foul, the most hysterical, and the most frenzied is embodied in him! Bely cannot say a single simple human word! Everything he writes is forced, dead, and bookish. . . . And worse, no one cries out about this . . . as if there were nothing revealing or terrible in it all!"

March 1, 1912
Ivan Bunin, from an interview with the Odessa News
I have just finished a trip around Europe; at the end I stopped at Capri, where I spent winter, about four months.

You, of course, are interested in Gorky. As always, he is hale and hearty . . . and in love with work. He is not one to moan and groan. From the outside you cannot tell how he feels about his exile, but his longing for his country slips through. . . .

"Oh," Gorky will suddenly say, "how I would love to pass through Russia now, even in third class, to the very thick of Russian life!" . . .

All the petitions, the unpardonable action of several Moscow newspapers demanding leniency for Gorky, this, of course, he finds extremely unpleasant. . . . [7]

Although Gorky is far from his homeland, he follows the social and political life of Russia with constant interest. He is in contact with all the groups of Russia, not only with the intelligentsia but also with members of the working class.

Gorky is deeply distressed by the letters he receives. Moans and complaints about . . . life, its lack of purpose, these are recurring motifs. He is especially bothered by . . . letters which say that one should quit this life: a confession of suicide.

As a result, Gorky has written a lengthy article . . . in which he

---

[6]Dostoevsky wrote *The Double* in 1846.

[7]In the aftermath of the Revolution of 1905, Gorky left Russia in 1906 and was living as a political exile at Capri. Several newspapers had initiated a petition to Nicholas II asking that Gorky be allowed to return to Russia.

details the reasons for the current depression among youth. . . . He believes that . . . there have long been warnings of a rift between "fathers and sons." What have you given us, children rightly ask their parents, to prepare us for life, to make sense of it?

Gorky also takes up arms against contemporary Russian literature. . . . Russian fiction, he believes, has lost respect. It has little that is good and much that is egoism and lying. It cannot stimulate the reader or lead him to life. . . .

I repeat: One of the main culprits for the current mood among youth Gorky sees as contemporary Russian literature, which has not been able to teach our youth as it should.

April 1912
Ivan Bunin, from Dry Valley
We were always amazed by Natalya's attachment to Dry Valley.

Natalya was the daughter of Father's wet-nurse and grew up with him. She lived with us at Lunevo for eight years but like a member of the family, not like a servant at all. All those eight years, as she herself used to say, she was recovering from Dry Valley, from all the place had made her suffer. But evidently what is bred in the bone never leaves the flesh: when Natalya raised us to adolescence, she returned to Dry Valley once more. . . .

As we grew older, we listened more attentively to everything that was being said in our house about Dry Valley: and whatever we did not understand earlier became clearer now, and the strange peculiarities of life at Dry Valley stood out more sharply. Who if not we should feel that Natalya . . . was really one of us Khrushchevs, gentlefolk of ancient lineage! . . .

[From Natalya] we learned . . . that "there was no one kinder and simpler than the masters at Dry Valley"; but we also learned that no one was "hotter" than they. We learned that the old house had been dark and gloomy, that our insane Grandfather Pyotr Kirillich had been murdered there by his bastard son Gervaska . . . that our Aunt Tonya had gone mad a long time ago because of an unhappy love affair and that she was now living in one of the servants' huts . . . where she played solemn *écossaises* on the piano which droned and jingled from old age; we learned that Natalya had also gone out of her mind, that as a very young girl she had forever fallen in love with our late Uncle Pyotr Petrovich, but that he had banished her to the farmstead of Soshki. . . . For us Dry Valley was only a poetic

memorial to the past. But what was it for Natalya? It was she . . .
who once said with great bitterness:

"That's the way it was! At Dry Valley they sat down to dinner
with Tatar whips in their hands. I even shudder when I think about
it." . . .

"What for?" we asked.

"In case they quarreled."

"Did they all quarrel at Dry Valley?"

"Heaven save us! Never a day without a fight. They were all
hot-tempered—real gunpowder." . . .

Natalya was not the only one who suffered for her love for Dry
Valley. Good Lord, all the other members of Dry Valley were as
ardently devoted to it, as passionately fond of its memory.

Aunt Tonya was living in misery, in a hovel. Dry Valley had
deprived her of happiness, sanity, and human dignity. But she never
even thought of leaving the nest . . . no matter how much Father
persuaded her, or reasoned with her.

"Why, I'd rather break stones in a quarry," she'd say.

Father was a carefree man; he seemed to have no attachment to
anything. But his stories of Dry Valley also resounded with deep
sadness. He had left it a long time ago and had settled at our
great-aunt Olga Kirillovna's estate at Lunevo, yet he complained
almost to the day he died: "Only one, one Khrushchev left in the
world! And he's not at Dry Valley!"

And after saying this Father would grow thoughtful and stare
out the window at the fields, and then suddenly he would laugh and,
taking down his guitar from the wall, he would add as sincerely as he
had said a minute before: "But Dry Valley's a great place to be, damn
it!"

But then Father's soul belonged to Dry Valley—the soul over
which the power of memories is so immeasurably strong, the sway of
the steppe, its sluggish way of life, that ancient clannishness that
united the village, the servants' hall and the manor house. It is true
that we Khrushchevs hail from an ancient family; our name is written
in the Sixth Book of Noblemen, and many of our legendary ancestors
were noblemen of old Lithuanian stock and Tatar princelings. But
then, since time immemorial, the blood of the lords has mingled
with that of the peasants. Who fathered Pyotr Kirillich? History
differs on this point. Who was the father of Gervaska, [Pyotr
Kirillich's] murderer? Ever since we were little we always heard that

it was Pyotr Kirillich. What caused the characters of our father and our uncle to differ so sharply? History differs on this point also. Natalya and Father were suckled at the same breast, Father and Gervaska exchanged baptismal crosses. . . . It is high time for the Khrushchevs to see the servants and the villagers as part of the clan! . . .

The history of a family, a clan, is deep, complex, mysterious and often gruesome. But its very strength lies in its dark depths, its legends and its past. The written records and other memorials of Dry Valley are no richer than any other estate in the Bashkir steppe. In Russia, legend takes their place. But legends and songs are poison to the soul of a Slav. Our former serfs were desperate idlers and dreamers—where, if not in our house, could they have their soul? Father was the last master of Dry Valley. The first language we learned to speak was Dry Valley talk. The first stories, the first songs that moved us were also Dry Valley ones—Natalya's and Father's. Could anyone sing like father? . . . Could anyone tell stories like Natalya? Was anyone closer to us than the peasants of Dry Valley? . . .

The peasants of Dry Valley. . . saw our home as their own. They would bow low to Father, kiss his hand, and . . . thrice on the lips, then Natalya and the two of us. They brought us gifts of honey, eggs, and towels. And, reared as we were in the open, as conscious of scents as we were of songs and legends, we remembered forever that peculiar and pleasant hemplike smell when we kissed the Dry Valley peasants. We remembered, too, the smell that clung to their gifts, the smell of an old village in the steppes: the honey smelled of flowering buckwheat and rotting oak beehives; the towels of hempen sacking and the smoking huts of our grandfather's day. The Dry Valley peasants told us no stories. What did they have to tell? They had no legends. Their graves have no names. Their lives were so like one another's, so poor, without a trace. . . . Why then did all of us feel drawn to the barren common, to the huts and gullies, to the ruined Dry Valley estate? . . .

We were already in our late teens when we visited Dry Valley, the estate we had heard so much about, which had shaped Natalya's soul and ruled her entire life.

I remember it as if it were yesterday. Rain poured down in torrents, thunder crashed in deafening claps, and lightning flashed blindingly in swift fiery snakes. . . . A dark mauve cloud slumped heavily down toward the northwest, arrogantly blotting out half the sky. . . . The green wheat field looked flat, clear, and deathly pale; the short wet grass seemed bright and unusually lush. . . . The wet horses suddenly seemed to have grown lean; they sloshed through the blue mud, their horseshoes sparkling; the carriage made moist sounds with its swishing wheels. . . . Suddenly we saw a tall and very strange figure, either an old man or woman, in a dressing gown and hood, standing in the tall wet rye and whipping a hornless, skewbald cow with a switch. . . . Yelling something, the old woman made for the coach and, coming up close, strained with her pale face toward us. Staring, terrified, into her black, mad eyes, feeling the touch of her sharp cold nose, and shrinking from her strong musty smell, we exchanged kisses with her. Was this not Baba-Yaga[8] herself? But this Baba-Yaga wore a tall hood made from a dirty rag on her head; her naked body was wrapped in a torn dressing gown, wet to the waist, that left her withered breasts uncovered. She screamed as though we were deaf or as though she were trying to start a fight. And from her screams we knew: this was Aunt Tonya.[9]

Everything was dark with age, plain and crude, in these low empty rooms, arranged the way it was in Grandfather's day. . . . In the corner of the hall hung a large dark icon of Saint Mercury of Smolensk[1] in iron sandals and a helmet. . . . We heard it said that Saint Mercury had been a distinguished man whom the icon of the Virgin had summoned to rescue the lands of Smolensk from the Tatars. After he had defeated the Tatars the Saint fell asleep and was beheaded by his foes. Then, with his head in his hands, he came to the town gate to tell the people what had happened. . . . We found it terrifying to look at this ancient Suzdal painting of the decapitated man, holding his deathly livid, helmeted head in one hand, and the icon of the Holy Virgin in the other. This painting of Saint Mercury, cherished by Grandfather, so we were told, had gone through several terrible fires and had split in the flames; it was encased in heavy silver and bore he family tree of the Khrushchevs on the back. . . .

As though to match the icon, the heavy folding doors to the dining hall were secured with heavy iron bars at top and bottom. The floors were unusually broad, dark, and slippery; the windows had

---

[8]Baba-Yaga is the famous witch of Russian folklore.

[9]Tonya bears strong resemblance to Bunin's great-aunt, Olga Dmitrievna Bunina.

[1]The events about Saint Mercurius of Smolensk took place in the year 1237, three years before the fall of Kiev to the Mongols. See, for instance, *Zhitiia sviatykh rossiiskoi tserkvi. Mesiats noiabr'* (Saint Petersburg, 1860), 352–356.

small sashes. The dining hall, where the Khrushchevs had once sat down to dinner armed with hunting crops, was half the size. . . .

If legend is to be believed, our great-grandfather, a wealthy man, moved to Dry Valley. . . toward the end of his days: he did not like Dry Valley with its remoteness and its woods. . . . Everything was lost in the forests then—the River Kamenka, the country up river, the village, the estate, and the winding fields around it. But it was no longer the same in Grandfather's time: a rolling expanse, bare hills . . . sparse hollow willows . . . and nothing but white pebbles on the rise where the house now stands. . . .

Natalya said, "The masters were carefree, neither good managers nor greedy ones. Semyon Kirillich, your grandfather's brother, divided the property: he himself took the bigger and better part . . . we only got Soshki, Dry Valley, and four hundred souls. But almost half of them ran away. . . ."

Grandfather Pyotr Kirillich died when he was about forty-five. Father often said that Grandfather went crazy after a sudden burst of wind had hurled a torrent of apples down upon him as he lay sleeping. . . . In the servants' hall, Natalya said, Grandfather's insanity was explained differently. They said Pyotr Kirillich had gone crazy from grief after our beautiful grandmother died. . . . So Pyotr Kirillich—a dark, round-shouldered man with a tender, intent look in his black eyes, a little like Aunt Tonya—had ended his days in a state of mild insanity.

According to Natalya, they had more money than they could spend in those days, and Grandfather, wearing morocco leather boots and a florid housecoat, wandered anxiously and quietly through the house and, glancing about, thrust gold pieces into the cracks of the oak walls.

"It's for Tonya's dowry," he muttered when caught in the act. "It's safer, my friends, much safer . . . but it's up to you. I won't do it if you don't want me to. . . ."

But he did so just the same. Then Grandfather started moving the heavy furniture in the hall and in the drawing room; he was always expecting visitors, though neighbors almost never came to Dry Valley. Sometimes Grandfather complained that he was hungry and made some hash for himself, awkwardly chopping and mashing some green onions in a wooden bowl, throwing in some shredded bread, pouring thick bubbly flour-water over it, and sprinkling the whole thing with such a quantity of grey, coarse salt that it was bitter and quite inedible. . . . Pyotr Kirillich, who slept very little even at night, did not know where to turn in his loneliness. When he could stand it no longer, he went peeping into the bedrooms and living rooms and quietly calling those who were asleep:

"Are you asleep, Arkasha? Are you sleeping, Tonya dear?"

And, rewarded with an angry shout: "Oh, leave me alone, for heaven's sake, Papa!" he mumbled hastily and placatingly, "Well, sleep, my dear, sleep. I won't wake you. . . ."

And Grandfather continued on his way, passing only the servants' hall, for they were a very rude lot. Within ten minutes he would be back at the bedroom doors, calling upon those who were sleeping with more caution than ever, inventing news of someone driving through the village with jingling stagecoach bells—"Could Petenka be on leave from the army?"—or of great hailclouds gathering in the sky.

"They, bless him, were all so afraid of storms," Natalya told us. "I was only a little thing at the time, but I remember it, too. Our house was so black somehow. . . a cheerless place, so help me. And the summer days were so long. We had so many servants—we had five footmen alone. Well, the young masters would naturally go to sleep after dinner, and we, faithful servants, good serfs, would do the same. But then Pyotr Kirillich had better not come near us, especially Gervaska. 'I say, footmen, are you asleep?' he would ask. And Gervaska would raise his head from his chest and say: 'D'you want me to stuff your pants with nettles?' 'Who d'you think you're talking to, you rascal?' 'To the house goblin, sir, in my sleep. . . .' Well, then Pyotr Kirillich would go back to the dining hall and the drawing room again, he'd stare out of the windows and into the garden to see whether a thunderstorm was gathering. It's true, thunderstorms broke out ever so often in the old days. And what terrible storms they were! Soon after dinner an oriole would start crying, and clouds would creep up from behind the garden . . . the house would grow dark, the grass and tangled nettle would start rustling, the turkeys and their chicks would all go under the terrace . . . real creepy it was. And they, the masters, would sigh, cross themselves, climb up to light a candle before the icons, and hang up the sacred towel from your great-grandfather's funeral—I was scared to death of that towel. Or they'd throw a pair of scissors out the window. That's the first thing you do, scissors I mean, it's very good against a thunderstorm." . . .

Before Grandmother died Dry Valley had masters and owners, rule and obedience, state rooms and family rooms, holidays and weekdays. . . . While the children were small, Pyotr Kirillich remained the nominal head of the house. But what could he do? Who ruled whom? Did he rule the servants or did the servants rule him? The piano was closed, the tablecloth vanished from the oak table, they ate in a slapdash way, and the front hall was always full of borzois. There was no one to take care of the house, and the dark log walls, the dark floors and ceilings, the dark heavy doors and door frames, and the old icons with their Suzdalian faces . . . soon grew quite black. The house was frightening at night, especially if there was a thunderstorm when the garden thrashed about in the wind and rain, when lightning lit up the faces of the saints in the corner, when the sky burst apart and opened wide its tremulous rosy-gold heavens above the trees and the thunder crashed mightily in the blackness. But in the daytime it was sleepy, empty, and dreary. Pyotr Kirillich grew feebler and feebler with the years, more and more insignificant, while the house was run by old Darya Ustinovna, Grandfather's wet-nurse. But her power was almost equal to his own. The bailiff Demyan . . . would sometimes say with a lazy smile, "Why, I wouldn't wrong my masters!"

My father, a youngster then, could have cared less about Dry Valley: he was crazy about hunting, the balalaika, and about Gervaska who was supposed to be footman but who spent days on end with him duck shooting . . . or in the coach house learning tricks on the balalaika or the reed pipe.

"We all knew it," Natalya said. "They came home only to sleep. And if they didn't even do that, that meant they were in the village, the coach house, or out shooting. . . . Gervaska was always the ringleader, but he pretended it was the young master who dragged him into things. And Arkady Petrovich loved this enemy of his, truly, like a brother, but Gervaska treated him even more rudely than before. The master would say, 'Come on, Gervaska, let's play our balalaikas. . . .' But Gervaska would look at him, blow some smoke out through his nostrils, and say with a smirk, 'First you kiss my hand.' Arkady Petrovich would turn deathly white, jump up, and hit him on the cheek with all his might, but Gervaska would only jerk his head and turn blacker still, scowling like some brigand. 'Get up, you scoundrel!' He'd stand up, stretching like a wolfhound, his velveteen trousers hanging . . . and say nothing. 'Beg my pardon!' 'It's my fault, sir.' But the young master almost choked with rage, he wouldn't know what to say next. 'Sir is right!' he'd shout. 'I'm trying to treat you like an equal, you scoundrel; at times I think I'd give my soul for you . . . And what do you do? Get me mad on purpose?' " . . .

At Dry Valley they loved strangely. They hated strangely, too.

Grandfather, whose end was as ridiculous as that of his murderer or, for that matter, of anyone who met his end at Dry Valley, was killed that same year. . . .

Uncle Pyotr Petrovich had wanted to charm his guests with his hospitality, and to show them that he was indeed the master of the house. But Grandfather was a terrible nuisance. Grandfather was blissfully happy but he was tactless, garrulous, and pathetic in his little velvet cap—a sacred relic—and his new and much too wide blue coat, made by the family tailor. He also fancied himself a good host and fussed from early morning, making some stupid ceremony of receiving the guests. . . .

Gervaska had grown terribly. Huge, awkward, but the best looking and the most clever of all the servants, he, like the others, was dressed up in a blue coat, blue trousers, and soft kidskin top-boots with flat soles. A worsted mauve neckerchief was knotted round his thin dark neck. His thick, brittle black hair was parted on the side . . . and trimmed in a bob round his head. There was nothing for him to shave; he had only two or three coarse black hairs curling on his chin and at the corners of his big mouth, "a slit from ear to ear," they teased him in the servants' hall. Lanky, very broad in his flat, bony chest, with a small head and deep eye sockets, thin ash-blue lips, and large bluish teeth, this ancient Aryan, a Persian from Dry Valley, had already been nicknamed "borzoi." Looking at his grin, hearing his cough, many thought, "You'll soon croak, borzoi." But to his face they called this cheeky youngster Gervasy Afanasyevich, thereby setting him apart from the other servants.

His masters were afraid of him, too. The masters and the serfs had one thing in common: they could either rule or cringe. . . .

Grandfather. . . started tugging at the neck of his coat and suddenly cried to the marshal at the other end of the table:

"Your Excellency! Lend me a hand! I appeal to you like a father and lodge a complaint against this servant of mine! This one here, this one—Gervasy Afanasyevich Kulikov! He flouts me at every turn! He . . ."

They did not let him finish but comforted and pacified him.

Grandfather was reduced to tears, but they all began to console him with such feigned deference that he succumbed and felt childishly happy again. . . . Grandfather darted frightened and uneasy glances at Gervaska, but he nevertheless went on shouting gleefully to the guests:

"All right, I'll forgive him, but only if, dear friends, you stay with me for three whole days. I positively refuse to let you go. I beg you, don't leave me so late in the evening! When night falls, I'm not myself at all: it's so melancholy, so sinister! Clouds are gathering . . . they say that two of Bonaparte's Frenchmen were caught in Troshin Wood. . . . I'm sure to die at night, mark my words. . . . The book of dreams says so. . . ."

But Grandfather died early in the morning. . . .

Gervaska came into the room and said to Grandfather in a stern whisper, "Knock if off! Why do you poke your nose into other people's business?"

Grandfather raised his excited face and whispered with the same tenderness he had been feeling all the previous evening and night: "Look Gervasy! I forgave you last night, but instead of being grateful to your master, you . . ."

"I'm sick and tired of your sniveling," Gervaska interrupted him. "Let go of the table!"

Grandfather threw a frightened look at the back of Gervaska's head that now seemed to stick out more above his thin neck. . . .

"*You* let go!" he shouted after a moment's thought, but his voice was not loud. "It's you who should give in to the master. You'll drive me too far: I'll stick a knife in your ribs."

"Will you?" Gervaska said angrily, flashing his teeth—and struck Grandfather hard across the chest.

Grandfather slipped on the smooth oak floor . . . and struck his temple against the sharp corner of the table. . . . Then Gervaska left the drawing room soundlessly and swiftly, and vanished into thin air. . . .

Natalya had two frightful dreams. . . . In one she saw with perfect clarity . . . a hideous, big-headed old dwarf in battered boots, hatless, with his red straggly hair tousled by the wind and a fiery red unbelted shirt streaming behind him. "Is there a fire?" Natalya screamed, alarmed and frightened. The dwarf screamed, too, his voice muffled by the hot wind: "Ruin, ruin, all is lost! A storm of untold horror is coming! Think not of marriage!" The other dream was even more horrible. Natalya was standing in a hot, empty cottage at midday... waiting for something—when suddenly a huge grey goat jumped out from behind the stove, reared and made straight for her, obscenely excited, with eyes burning like coals, gleefully mad and beseeching. "I'm your mate!" he shouted in a human voice, trotting toward her quickly and clumsily, his small rear hoofs clattering rapidly; with all his might he brought his front ones down on her breast. . . .

Klavdiya Markovna delivered a boy. . . . The young Khrushchev blew bubbles from his mouth. He toppled over helplessly, weighted down by his heavy head; he howled angrily, since he could hardly focus his milky, senseless eyes. He was already being called the young master. From the nursery came the age-old warnings: "Here he comes, here he comes, the old man with the bag. . . . Go away, old man, go away! We won't let you take the young master, he won't cry, he's a good boy. . . ." . . .

In the spring a wizard was brought to Aunt Tonya... the famous Klim Yerokhin... a dignified and handsome man with a large grey beard and curly grey hair parted in the middle, a very competent farmer whose conversation was usually very reasonable and simple until he transformed himself into a sorcerer at the sickbed. The clothes he wore were exceptionally strong and neat—a coat of steel grey coarse woolen cloth, a red sash and boots. His small eyes were sly and keen; they piously sought the icons when he walked into the house. . . . He spoke first of the harvest, of rains and drought, after that he took a long time over his tea, drinking it very tidily, then he crossed himself again, and only after all this did he ask about the patient, instantly changing his tone.

"Twilight... night is falling... the time has come," he began mysteriously.

Aunt Tonya, shaking with fever, ready to collapse in convulsions on the floor, sat in her twilight bedroom and waited for Klim to appear at her door. Natalya, too, standing by her side, was terrified from head to toe. . . . No one dared to light a single candle, no one dared to raise a voice. The carefree Soloshka, standing on guard in the corridor in case she was called upon to carry out Klim's orders, felt everything grow dim before her eyes and her heart hammer in her throat. Klim walked past her, unwrapping a handkerchief with some magic bones in it. Then his loud, strange voice rent the funereal silence in the bedroom: "Arise, my daughter!"

Then he stuck his grey head out of the door. "The board," he uttered lifelessly.

And Aunt Tonya, cold as a corpse, her eyes bulging from terror, was stood on the board which lay on the floor. It was so dark by then that Natalya could hardly make out Klim's face. And suddenly he began to intone in a disembodied, faraway voice: "Filat is coming. . . . He'll cry and say: woe, woe!"

"Woe, woe!" he cried with sudden force and stern authority: "Be gone, woe, into the dark forests below, that's where you belong! Across the oceans and the sea," his muttering was rapid and ominous now, "the stormy Buyan Island rears, and on it lies a bitch with a thick grey fleece. . . ." . . .

Summer was sultry, dusty and windy, with thunderstorms breaking out every day. Rumors were rife, obscure and alarming, of some new war, of riots and fires. Some said that all the serfs would be set free any day now; others said that, on the contrary, all the peasants would be inducted into the army in the fall. And, as usual, an endless stream of vagabonds, half-wits, and monks made their appearance. And Miss Tonya all but fought with the mistress . . . to hand out bread and eggs to them. . . .

Yushka was a peasant by birth. But he . . . lived the life of a stray, earning his keep with stories of his complete idleness and "misbehavior."

"I'm a peasant, brother, but I'm smart and look like a hunch-back," he would say, "so why should I work?"

And, indeed, Yushka did look like a hunchback. His eyes were mocking and wise; his face was hairless; his shoulders were raised because of his rickety chest. . . . His fingers were slim and strong. He thought it "indecent and boring" to till the land, and so he went off to Lavra at Kiev, "grew up" there, but was banished for his "misbehavior." Then, realizing that pretending to be a holy pilgrim, a man saving his soul, was too old a trick and even unprofitable, he tried another ruse: without taking off his cassock he began to flaunt his idleness and lechery, to smoke and to drink as much as he could—he never got drunk—to mock the monastery, and to explain, with obscene gestures and movements, precisely why he had been banished.

"Of course," he told the peasants with a wink, "I got thrown out right away. And so I returned home to Russia. . . . I'd do all right, I thought."

And get along Yushka did. Russia welcomed the bawdy sinner with no less enthusiasm than those who were saving their souls. Russia fed him, sheltered him at night, and listened to him enraptured. . . .

"The devil couldn't make me work now," Yushka said. "I'm spoiled, pal. I'm as horny as a monastery goat. The girls . . . are scared to death of me, but they love me. And why not? I'm not bad myself—my feathers aren't pretty, but I've got what they want." . . .

Natalya knew quite well what would happen. . . . Yushka had already hissed at her: "I'll come. I'll come if you kill me. And if you start yelling, I'll burn the place to the ground." But what sapped her strength more than anything else was that she knew something *inevitable* was happening, that her horrible dream . . . about the goat was about to come true, and that it was preordained she should perish together with Aunt Tonya. Everyone understood now: the devil himself dwelt in the house at night. Everyone understood what . . . was driving Aunt Tonya crazy, what made her moan voluptuously and wildly in her sleep, and then jump up with screams so terrifying that they drowned out the most deafening thunderclaps. "The snake of Eden, of Jerusalem is strangling me!" she would shriek. . . . Was there anything more frightening in the world than Yushka's coming in the darkness, on rainy nights when thunder rumbled in incessant rolls and lightning flashed across the black icons? The passion, the lust with which he whispered to Natalya was also inhuman: so how could she struggle against it? Brooding on the fatal hour. . . peering into the darkness with beating heart, listening to the slightest rustle or creak in the slumbering house, Natalya already felt the first attacks of that grave illness which was to torment her for a long time to come: the sole of one of her feet would suddenly begin to itch, she'd feel a sharp piercing cramp, twisting and turning her toes inward, the spasm would run up her legs and contort her nerves cruelly and sweetly, right up to her throat, and in a moment she would want to shriek more madly and with more ecstasy and agony than Aunt Tonya ever shrieked.

And the inevitable happened. Yushka came—on that ghastly night at the end of the summer, on the eve of the feast of Saint Elijah, the ancient flamethrower. There was no thunder that night, nor sleep for Natalya. . . . It was the dead hour of the night. . . . She jumped up, looked down one end of the corridor, then the other. . . . The sky, silent and full of fire and mystery, was flaring up, blazing and quivering with blinding flashes of gold and pale blue. Minute by minute the corridor grew light as day. She started running—and froze to the spot: the aspen logs . . . looked blindingly white in the flashes. She tried the dining hall . . . it was darker there, but the lightning outside the windows was the brighter for it . . . the garden, with all its lacy treetops, its ghastly pale green birches and poplars, would flicker, swell, and tremble against the vast heavens of gold and pale violet.

"Across the oceans and the seas, on the stormy Buyan Island," she started whispering as she rushed back, aware that she was bringing on her ruin with this eerie incantation. . . .

And just as she pronounced these primitive-menacing words, she looked back and saw Yushka, his shoulders raised high, not two steps away from her. Lightning flashed across his face—pale with black hollows for eyes. He pounced on her soundlessly, grasped her with his long arms, and, crushing her, brought her down to her knees, then on her back, onto the cold floor. . . .

Yushka grew tired of Natalya, and of Dry Valley. He vanished as suddenly as he had appeared.

A month later Natalya was with child. . . .

The discord between the brothers grew stronger. Sometimes things went so far that they grabbed knives and guns. And no one knows how it would all have ended if another calamity had not befallen Dry Valley. One winter day . . . Uncle Pyotr Petrovich drove to Lunevo where he had a mistress. He spent two days there, drinking all the time, and was drunk when he started back home. . . . Pyotr Petrovich ordered . . . a spirited young mare, which sank belly-deep into the loose snow, to be unharnessed and tied to the rear of the sledge; he himself lay down to sleep with his head toward the animal, so they said. Evening descended, misty and blue. . . . And at midnight, when everyone was sleeping the sleep of the dead at Dry Valley, someone rapped quickly and alarmingly on the window of the corridor where Natalya slept. She jumped down from her bench and ran out on to the porch in her bare feet. She saw the dim dark silhouettes of the horses and the sleigh, and Yevsei standing with a whip in his hand.

"There's been trouble, lass," he started mumbling hollowly, strangely, as though in sleep. "Master's been killed by the horse. . . . She ran up, stumbled, and kicked him. . . . Crushed his face right in. . . . He's getting cold already. . . . It wasn't me, it wasn't me, I swear to God it wasn't!"

Without a word Natalya went down the porch steps, her bare

feet sinking in the snow; she went to the sleigh, crossed herself, fell on her knees, clutched the icy, blood-clotted head to her breast, began to kiss it, and screamed a wildly joyous scream, choking with sobs and laughter. . . .

Whenever we happened to take a rest from city life in the destitute remoteness of Dry Valley, Natalya would tell us again and again the story of her wretched life. And at times her eyes would darken and stare blankly, her voice would change to a stern, clear half whisper. I kept recalling the crude image of the saint which had hung in the corner of the hall in our old home. Decapitated, the saint had come to his people, bearing his dead head in his hands, to prove the truth of his story. . . .

Even those few material traces of the past which we had once found at Dry Valley had disappeared. Our fathers and grandfathers had left us neither their portraits nor their letters, nor even any of their ordinary household things. Whatever there was had perished in the fire. . . . And the past of Dry Valley became more and more legendary.

The people of Dry Valley lived a life that was remote and dark but also complex and with a semblance of stability and prosperity. Judging by the stagnancy of this life and the attachment of its people to it, one might have thought it would have gone on forever. . . . Just as the little mounds that top the underground channels and burrows of hamsters vanish one after the other when a field is plowed, so we witnessed the nests of the Dry Valley disappearing swiftly without a trace. And the people of Dry Valley perished and fled, too; those who somehow managed to survive ended their days in some manner or other. So what we found was not the world of Dry Valley . . . but only the memory of it, an existence that was half wild in its simplicity. As the years went by we visited our home in the steppe more and more rarely. And we grew more and more estranged from it; we felt less and less our tie to the world and the class from which we were descended. Many of our countrymen were, like us, descendants of an illustrious, ancient lineage. The chronicles recorded our names: our ancestors were courtiers and commanders and "eminent men," the closest associates and even relatives of tsars. And had they been called knights, had we been born in the West, how confidently we would have talked of them, how much longer we would have held on! A descendant of the knights could not have said that an entire class had almost vanished off the face of the earth in as little as half a century, that so many of us had become degenerate, insane, had committed suicide, become inveterate drunkards, had gone to seed, or had simply gotten lost somewhere. He could not have confessed as I am doing now that we do not have the slightest idea of the life of our great-grandfathers, to say nothing of our earlier ancestors, that with every day we find it more difficult to picture things that took place a mere fifty years ago!

The place where the house at Lunevo stood has been tilled and sown a long time ago, just like the lands of many of the other estates. Dry Valley has held on somehow. But the last of the birches in the garden have been cut down, and practically all the arable land has been sold piecemeal. The owner himself, the son of Pyotr Petrovich, abandoned it—to work as a railway conductor. And the old people of Dry Valley—Klavdiya Markovna, Aunt Tonya, and Natalya—dragged out the last years of their lives in wretchedness. Spring gave way to summer, summer waned into autumn, autumn turned to winter. . . . They lost count of the seasons. They lived in their memories and dreams, in wrangles and worries about their daily bread. . . . There were cold and hunger in the empty, crumbling house. Blizzards blew snow over it, icy winds pierced it through. And as for heating, they lighted the stoves very seldom. In the evenings a little tin lamp would shed its frugal light. . . . Natalya would doze on the cold stove ledge while Aunt Tonya, who looked like a Siberian shaman, sat in her cottage and smoked a pipe. . . . Her place was crowded with pieces of broken furniture, cluttered with bits of smashed crockery, and obstructed by the piano which had collapsed on its side. . . . It was so ice-clad that the chickens, to whose care Aunt Tonya gave her remaining strength, had frostbitten feet from sleeping on these broken bits and pieces.

But there is no one left at Dry Valley now. All those mentioned in this chronicle, all their neighbors and contemporaries are dead. And sometimes you wonder if they ever really lived at all.

You only feel that they did live in this world when you come to the graveyards, you even sense an eerie closeness to them. But even this requires an effort, to sit and think near the family grave—if only you can find it. We are ashamed to say it, but we have to: We do not know where the graves of our grandfather, our grandmother, or Pyotr Petrovich are. We only know they are by the altar of the old church in Cherkizovo. You can't get there in the winter: the snowdrifts are waist-deep there, with a few crosses . . . sticking out of the snow. In the summer... you walk through the gate and you see a whole grove of short spreading elms, ash, and lime trees beyond the white church with its rusty cupola, all shadow and coolness. You wander for a long time among the shrubs, mounds, and hollows, covered with thin graveyard grass, you tread on stone slabs which have become porous from rains, overgrown with black, crumbly moss, and almost completely sunken into the ground.... You see two or three iron monuments. But whose are they? They have become such a greenish gold that you can no longer read the inscriptions on them. Which of these mounds guards the bones of Grandmother, of Grandfather? God alone knows! All you know is that they are here somewhere close. And you sit there and think, trying to picture those Khrushchevs whom everyone has forgotten. And the world in which they lived seems infinitely far, but then, suddenly, it becomes so very close.

May 14, 1912
Elena Koltonovskaya, from a review of Dry Valley

The terrible *Dry Valley* is for Bunin a symbol of our Slavic-Russian good-for-nothingness, our uselessness... of our "genuine Slavic soul": sluggishness and instability; wisdom and foolishness; wealth, clarity, and even profundity of emotion; but together with this, an overall pallor and coldness of nature and temperament, an indistinct physiognomy.

May 19, 1912
Ivan Bunin, from his diary

A pilgrim came through the village, and without looking at anyone he began to bawl:

> The time will come
> When the sky and earth will shake
> And all the stones will fall,
> When all thrones will be destroyed,
> And the sun and the moon will grow dark,
> When the Lord will pass through a fiery river
> And will destroy us and all the earthly beasts,
> When Michael the Archangel will descend from the sky
> And will blow on horns,
> When he will wake up the dead from their graves,
> And will proclaim:
> Those of you who,

For whatever reason,
Did not go to church,
Have masses said later:
Here is your ready paradise!
Inextinguishable fire! . . .

The pilgrim . . . talked with us for a long time. . . . He was going "to keep a promise" . . . to worship the relics because he had been so sick. Truly the man was very weak. He kept coughing all the time; his beard was thin; the entire contour of his skull was visible.

At first the pilgrim spoke piously, but then more simply. He began to smoke. . . . Ivan (that was his name) told us why he used tobacco: The Mother of God was coming away from the Cross and crying. All the flowers had dried up from her tears; only tobacco remained. Then God said: Burn it. . . .

Ivan boasted that he could tell such amusing stories and that he knew so much about things that landowners would send their horses after him, and that he would spend weeks in their homes. . . . He told us how blind people beg for a piece of sackcloth. They say:

There once lived three sisters, three Marys of Egypt.
They divided everything in three parts, for they were rich.
One part, they bought clothes for their bodies.
Another part they gave to the dungeon-jails.
And the last part they gave to cathedrals and churches.
Do not cover your body with rich clothes,
But cover your soul with sincere charity,
For this charity will put you first
Like a candle before the image of God.
Do not feed others when you are ready to die,
But feed them when you are healthy.
For the salvation of your soul,
For prayers for your parents,
Do not turn away from our request!

Ivan also told us how blind people would curse those who would not help them:

May God give you two fields of nettles
And a third of a swan
And thirty-three troubles!
May your new hut catch fire,
And your old one collapse!

May 21, 1912
Ivan Bunin, from an interview with the Moscow News

The critics have indicted me for my thick colors in my pictures of the village. As they see it, the pessimistic character of my works about the peasant comes from that fact that I am a *barin*.

Once and for all, I would like to make it clear that I have never owned land or engaged in farming. . . . I never tried to acquire property.

I love the folk with no less empathy than those who fight for the people's rights, no less than those who throw the word *barin* in my face.

My opinion of the nobility one can see if only from my work *Dry Valley*, where the gentry are portrayed in far from optimistic or rosy colors.

I protest against the critics' distortions of my world-view. . . and all the more because such slander does not correspond to reality.

May 25, 1912
Nikolai Korobka, from a review of Dry Valley

There is not a single stratum of society. . . not a single corner, from the remote village hut to the very pinnacle of the social ladder, in which we do not observe overt and pathological manifestations of debauchery and decay. . . . Without a doubt, Russia is sick. . . . Its entire organism has been poisoned, and it will not recover from its illness. . . .

Of all the strata of Russian society, the gentry is, perhaps, the most rotten. . . . All that is alive is leaving it; all that is worn out, little cultured, or perverted remains. The gentry is incapable of creative work; it cannot live without its privileges, without its purely animal egotism. . . . Here is a genuine kingdom of stagnation, a swamp in which miasmas of rot have found most welcome soil.

May 28, 1912
Ivan Bunin, from his diary

Evgeny told me the story about Nikolka Mudry's father. . . . The man was always completely drunk. He ran about like someone possessed; he beat his wife every day until she was half dead. Finally she told him she was going to the police. . . . He sat on the threshold of his house. Then he got up . . . took a rope, kissed his small daughter, went to the chimney corner, and hanged himself.

When Nikolka came home that evening (he used to beat up his father every holiday), the man had been dead for a long time. Nikolka cut the rope . . . dragged his father from the corner, and threw the body on a pile of manure. . . .

May 30, 1912
Ivan Bunin, from a letter to a friend
I am intimidated by critics. There are gracious ones, but there are ruthless ones, too. They begin nicely enough. They say that my writing is "marvelous, colorful, powerful," and the like; but then they say that "I am still a *barin* who fears pogroms." . . .

[One] made an effort: He wrote . . . that I was "a head higher than Gorky," but that there was absolutely no *love* in my stories. Now if that doesn't beat all! So now I will have to write a bit about love, too.

May 31, 1912
Ivan Bunin, from his diary
Today, about five o'clock, a destitute soldier came through. He was drunk and crying. He cursed the gentry and the strikers. He also cursed the tsar, saying that the tsar sees nothing.

An hour later another tramp wandered through . . . saying in a voice that was clear, excited, and tragic, "God is good, love is good."

June 16, 1912
Ivan Bunin, from his diary
There are huge dogs in the yard. The rumor is that they have torn a man to pieces.

July 6, 1912
Ivan Bunin, from a letter to Maxim Gorky
The rain, my damned eternal enemy, raps on the trees outside my window. At Capri, no doubt, the stars are so bright and clear . . . and the sea so nightlike, summery, Italian! If only you would tell me something about the night sea and about your nightly mysteries there. I am very proud of the fact that I convinced you to write a story about the birth of man.[2] Do you remember when it was? We had gone to see the comet—it was very, very late on the road to Anacapri. . . .

[2]Gorky published "The Birth of Man" in 1912.

July 23, 1912
Ivan Bunin, from an interview with the Moscow News

The Russian intelligentsia knows astonishing little about its folk.

One cannot compare our situation with that of other intellectuals—French, German, Italian, and so forth—who speak to the folk in a similar language. The languages of the Russian intellectual and of the Russian peasant are completely different.

Our intelligentsia love to show off their "knowledge" of the people by using . . . such expressions as "so 'tis, your excellency," which they hear on stage or read in works about the peasant.

In no other country is there such a striking gap between the cultured and uncultured classes as in ours.

It could not be otherwise. For in Russia there has never been a sincere study of the people.

Take, for example, Grigorovich's "Anton Goremyka."[3] Even when it was published, people said it was not about the Russian people.

Turgenev likewise did not fully portray the life of the folk. For the most part he lived abroad; the goal of his writings was to show that the serf had a living soul.

The literature of Zlatovratsky had a patently embellished character: the idealization of the peasant.

The one who genuinely studied the folk was Gleb Uspensky. Gleb Uspensky was a tremendous talent, a tremendous artist, and an important person . . . but his writing was neither unified nor systematic. . . .

Tolstoy wrote about the peasant from a well-known point of view: a religious idea about an industrious people who held the entire world together. . . .

One cannot say, as people do now, that I do not love the people, that I have a cold and withered heart, and that I do not search my soul when I write.

August 12, 1912
Ivan Bunin, from a letter to Maxim Gorky

As you see, we have settled here in the village. The silence, I repeat, is astounding—it is a pity to part with it.

[3]Grigorovich wrote "Anton Goremyka" in 1847.

September 6, 1912
Ivan Bunin, from an interview with the Odessa News

I find it unpleasant that I will be honored on the occasion of my twenty-fifth year as a writer . . . for I am afraid I will be listed in the annals of old men. For God's sake, I have only turned forty, and suddenly I run the risk of being counted among the old folks.

September 9, 1912
Vera Muromtseva-Bunina, from a letter to Ivan Bunin

No one, except me, can bring you peace of mind.

October 22, 1912
Ivan Bunin, from an interview with the Moscow News

I do not accept the division between poetry and prose. . . . This seems to me old-fashioned and artificial. The poetic element is innate to prose and verse. Prose must also have tonality.

Many artistic pieces read like poetry even though they do not have measure or rhythm. Tolstoy's *War and Peace*, for instance, has poetic descriptions which rival masterpieces of verse. Prose, no less than poetry, must answer the demands for musicality, for language that is pliant.

I also deny aesthetic theories that assign to poetry only purely artistic tasks . . . for the subject of a poetic piece must be the variety of life itself.

The world of ideas and subjects is great!

Take Byron, Shakespeare, Goethe, Schiller. . . .

The poet "responds with his heart to everything that asks from his heart an answer."

I believe that Russian poetry stopped moving forward with Fet and Alexei Tolstoy, and that the last fifteen years have been an empty space in the Russian poetic tradition.

I am told that poetic form is now more complex, that rhythms are richer, and that poetic images are more daring. . . . All this is debatable to the highest degree . . . for if one compares Pushkin, "the sun of Russian poetry," with today's leading poets (I will not mention names), what kind of comparison can there be?

October 24, 1912
Ivan Bunin, from an interview with the Odessa News

I come from an old gentry family which has already given us

several Russian writers: V. A. Zhukovsky, the son of a Bunin landowner and a Turkish captive named Salomé; and Anna Petrovna Bunina, a well-known poetess in the time of Catherine the Great. . . .

I lived in Orel, Kharkov, and Poltava. I studied, worked for provincial newspapers, wandered the south of Russia, and served for two years in a district council in Poltava as a statistician and a librarian. I was often greatly in need.

I started to write very early. My first poem was published . . . when I was only sixteen years old. That is why at the age of forty-two I have come to be listed among the old boys: I have just celebrated my twenty-fifth anniversary as a writer—it somehow sounds so solid. . . .

I survived a very long period of Populism, then Tolstoyism. Now I am attracted to the Social Democrats[4] most of all, though I avoid all party affiliations.

At present, newspapers say much about me that is untrue. One has decided I am obsessed with "world sorrow." Perhaps the critics have been misled by the sadness that shows through some of my youthful things. My sadness is a demand for joy; it is not pessimism, and very far from world sorrow. On the contrary, I love life so much that I would live for two thousand years with pleasure.

Which of my works do I consider my most successful? That is a difficult question.

Of all the books I have written so far, I consider *The Village* and *Dry Valley* (a collection of stories 1911–1912) to be the most successful. Then there are several recent poems, and the prose poems of my wanderings: "The Shadow of a Bird," "Judea," and "The Desert of the Devil."[5] I even have a kind of philosophy about my wanderings; I do not know anything better than travel.

I had planned to go around the world this winter, but I did not feel up to it. . . . The past few winters I have had to spend in warm climates. I know Turkey well; I have been more than once in Sofia, Palestine, Egypt, Nubia, the Sahara, and Ceylon. I have skirted the northwest coastline of Africa; and, of course, I have been almost everywhere in Western Europe. Traveling has played a large role in my life.

---

[4]The Social Democrats were Marxists, and the creation of their party in 1898 was a landmark in the development of Marxism in Russia. The Social Democrats split into the Bolsheviks and Mensheviks in 1903.

[5]Bunin published "The Shadow of a Bird" in 1907, "Judea" in 1908, and "The Desert of the Devil" in 1909.

You ask my opinion on contemporary literature? I must confess that, with few exceptions, I am dissatisfied with today's fiction. Russian writing is now becoming Europeanized. I am not against this, of course, but I cannot help but notice that such Europeanization has yielded the most insignificant results to date. . . .

Right now we are chasing after fashion. I look upon this infamous stylization and schematization quite negatively; they are the handiwork of a dead heart. People talk about searching for form and hide behind stylization when they have nothing to say.

Russian literature . . . has become confused; it does not know what to say. It has given itself over to something nervous and self-seeking . . . a kind of illness. . . .

Modern fiction may entice the critics . . . but it does not influence the reader. . . . The emotional, organic feature of literature figures so little in the works of contemporary writers; more than is necessary, it has ceded to a cerebral element.

October 31, 1912
Maxim Gorky, from a letter to Ivan Bunin
Your great heart knows not only the sadness of Russian life but also the "sadness of all lands and of all times"—a great, creative sadness about that happiness which keeps moving the world forward.

Both your prose and your poetry have similar beauty and force; for Russians they have moved back the borders of their monotonous existence and have gifted them generously with the treasures of world literature . . . they have tied Russian literature to that which is universal on earth.

Your work over these twenty years is full of earnest love for our native tongue—the beauty of which you have always felt. Your writing is still not appreciated, but it gives us the joyful right to proclaim that you are the worthy heir of those poets who linked Russian literature to European writing and who have made it one of the most remarkable phenomena of the nineteenth century.

Fondly and respectfully we, your readers, convey our best wishes to a poet who has "given his life to creating"—long live "the blessedly sweet anguish of your labors."

Circa *November 1912*
Ivan Bunin, from an interview with Footlights and Life
I have grown away from the theatre. And it is true that I have passed it by in my writing. . . . Of course, there have been moments

when the theatre has affected me greatly. . . . But the trouble is, I know what goes on "behind the scenes." . . . The falseness, the theatrical conventions often jar me. Like the opera: I like to hear a great artist . . . but with closed eyes. . . .

I have often felt like writing something for the stage. The very form of the theatre attracts me. In the drama, in its swift, powerful, and condensed dialogue, one can say so many things in a few words. Writing a play, you have to concentrate your thought, compress it into exact forms. This is very appealing. That is why the sonnet is my favorite form.

How great it would be to write a tragedy. . . . In it there is room for the widest generalizations . . . for powerful emotions. People, history, philosophy, religion—all these can be captured in such a clear form. . . .

Everything that Tolstoy wrote is simple, powerful, and profound. Tolstoy was not afraid of details which might seem offensive. [In *War and Peace*] Natasha runs into the hut to the wounded Prince Andrei. . . . Someone's snoring can be heard. . . . Then there is that brilliant "piti-piti"; everything rises up in a symphony of human love and suffering. The "snoring" going on behind the wall does not disturb the scene at all.[6] Yes, one must be broad and bold in fiction.

✳ 1 9 1 3 ✳

Circa *1913*
Maxim Gorky, from a letter to a friend
I consider I. A. Bunin to be a writer who is no less talented than Chekhov and more cultured than the latter.

January 11, 1913
Pyotr Kogan, from an article in the Odessa News
Only a celebration honoring Tolstoy could rival the grandeur of the one that honored Bunin. The festivities made an unexpected statement. . . . The Academy, the university, scholarly and literary societies, the mass of institutions, and the public honored Bunin as a

---

[6]Book Eleven of *War and Peace*.

bearer of ideas opposing Modernism and as a guardian of the classical canons of our realism.

The absence of the Modernists at this event spoke volumes in this regard. Bryusov, who discovered Russian Decadence in his verse, found it necessary to leave for Moscow . . . and sent a cold and curt telegram.

All this tells us that we are returning to a social-realistic direction in literature and that the period of despair and dismay, of writers who sought oblivion in drunken fantasies and the irrational phenomena of the soul, is coming to an end.

Circa *February 1913*
Ivan Bunin, from his memoirs

After dinner Chaliapin was asked to sing. Again it was an absolutely marvelous evening. All the guests and many locals crowded into the dining room and the salons of the hotel, holding their breath and listening to him with burning eyes.

February 28, 1913
Vera Muromtseva-Bunina, from a letter to Yuly Bunin

We have wonderful accommodations at Capri. Ian and I have two nice rooms with splendid views. From several windows we can see Mount Soliaro with the Barbarossa castle; from others, a view of the bay, Vesuvius, Mount Tiberio, and so forth. . . .

Bunin said: "Here we see the sea, the cliffs, olive trees, myrtle, and laurel. Why then should we have works with fauns, satyrs, pans, naiads, and sylvans who waste away in the grottos. . . . All this is garbage and lies. None of our poets has ever felt or feel. . . . I affirm again and again that Tolstoy is the only one who has not lied in art."

March 1913
Rafael Grigor'ev, from a review of Dry Valley

It seems as if there are no values which our revolutionary literature will not reappraise, no idol which it will not profane and chase out of empty cathedrals. The peasantry are complete savages; the revolutionaries are genuine Smerdyakovs.[7] Russia is an absolute terror, a black pit. . . . Only one relic has seemed inviolate—the beauty and particular poetry of the old gentry.

[7]Smerdyakov is the bastard son in Dostoevsky's *The Brothers Karamazov* (1879–1880).

The Child Harolde cape of Onegin, the romantic demonism of Pechorin, the fiery enthusiasm of Rudin, the warring passions of Pierre Bezukhov. . . . The estates of the Larins, the Lavretskys. . . . The chaste but firm family life of the Rostovs.[8] . . . The perfume of lime trees. . . . The sun of a golden autumn. . . . The sounds of a waltz. . . . The sweet enchantment of a first love. . . . The tender and shy petals of a maiden's heart blossoming for the first time. . . .

Yes, our noble gentry has succeeded in immortalizing itself poetically! Gentlemen's nests and cherry orchards have become a symbol of all that is splendid and fragrant. They have been touched by decay, true; but they have not lost . . . beauty, their personal charm. . . .

And we, people of a new century who have grown up in different circumstances, and who have been nurtured by social groups alien and hostile to the gentry, we nonetheless cannot help but revere and be moved by the beauty of this immortal time . . . and to feel sadness for all that has been lost.

But the gentry of contemporary life, the gentry of councils and dumas, the gentry that exudes such corpselike smells, this gentry we see as a pitiful regression from the one of former genuine greatness.

And now here comes a writer-nobleman, a great and indubitable artist, who tells us that the estates of the Larins are myths, and that the perfume of lime trees and roses has ceded to gloomy and oppressive Dry Valley: terrifying, insane, and filled with bloody legends, cruelty, and nonsense. . . .

The old gentry nests which we saw as such poetic monuments of a dying culture, and which we gifted so generously with the beauty and nobility of a feudal knighthood, these are rendered by Bunin in an unusual and repulsively revolting view. . . . the nightmarish history of the Khrushchevs.

March 1, 1913
Nikolai Pusheshnikov, from his memoirs

Ivan Alexeevich read two of his new stories to Gorky. . . . One of them brought him to tears. During the reading . . . Gorky began to cry. He got up, walked about the room, and said: "Devil take him. . . . I'm jealous."

[8]Onegin and the Larins are characters from Pushkin's *Eugene Onegin* (1823–1831). Pechorin is the hero of Lermontov's *A Hero of Our Time* (1840); Rudin, the hero of Turgenev's *Rudin* (1856); the Lavretskys, the family in Turgenev's *A Nest of Gentlefolk* (1859); and the Rostovs, the family in Tolstoy's *War and Peace*.

March 10, 1913
Ivan Bunin, from his story "The Lord's Spear"

"Be prepared—death is above you, in front of you, and around you; beyond the water, on the hot sandy shores of the sea, and amidst the wretchedness and dirt in which almost all humankind lives."

March 27, 1913
Maxim Gorky, from a letter to a friend

I very much recommend that you study Russian literature. It will help you. Turgenev will teach you how to write about nature, the landscape. Chekhov will show you what a dialogue is, how people talk in real life . . . how to structure a phrase, a sentence—briefly and precisely. . . . Bunin's most recent stories . . . rise to the heights of Turgenev and Chekhov. Bunin will help you understand how to structure a story, how to dispose of material. He will teach you that one must merge word and image. . . . Bunin will force you to feel all the terrible sadness of Russian life.

April 14, 1913
Ivan Bunin, from a letter to Maxim Gorky

As you already know, I have fallen seriously ill on the road. I literally went crazy from the loss of blood. I went about with the persistence of a drunkard—all the time looking for a place, somewhere I could be warm, but meeting hellish cold everywhere. . . . One thing I beg of you—do not think I am exaggerating my illness, my weakness, the anemia in my brain and elsewhere.

May 4, 1913
Ivan Bunin, from an interview with the Evening Moscow

Alexei Maximovich [Gorky] was very irritable this year; the reason for this was the amnesty, which triggered many rumors abroad. People hoped and dreamed. . . . But once they found out the truth they were disillusioned—the amnesty, it turned out, covered only a few people.[9]

Alexei Maximovich was on the verge of coming home, but he changed his mind. . . . He would not have restrained himself. He would have let out a cry of pain for Mother Russia, and he would have had to flee again.[1]

[9]In connection with the three-hundredth anniversary of the founding of the Romanov dynasty, the Russian government announced an amnesty on February 21, 1913, for people who had committed "criminal acts *via* the press."
[1]Gorky did, in fact, return home later that year.

But nothing can stop Alexei Maximovich; this year he worked like never before. . . .

People have asked me to write something for film, but I do not plan to do so as yet. Do not think I am afraid of the mob or of vulgarity. No! The mob and vulgarity are everywhere, of that you can be sure! But I am still unclear as to the precise form I need; and to write before figuring out what is needed, this I cannot do. I consider literature for the film a very serious question. It is time, high time, for genuine writers to pay attention to this area and to stop the vulgarity that reigns without end. . . .

People live so sadly; they are bored. This seems strange, even surprising to me. How can one be bored! Life is so interesting. . . . If I could find a person who could grant me a life that would last tens of thousands of years, I would not hesitate to conclude a bargain with him, no matter what the circumstances.

[The Interviewer]: Ivan Alexeevich's eyes began to catch fire; his face became animated. . . . Somehow he had become completely transformed; he had grown younger.

May 14, 1913
Ivan Bunin, from a letter to Maxim Gorky

In Moscow I was distressed by the Futurists.[2] This is not all that terrible; but good God, how flat and vulgar it has all become—how vile, offensive, and empty is this new "literary army!". . . . Thank God, I missed the celebration honoring Balmont. It was arranged exclusively by psychopaths and clown-aesthetes. . . .

May 18, 1913
Ivan Bunin, from a letter to a friend

I am thinking of naming my new anthology with the title of the first piece: "The Crime." . . . The stories will be different: themes of love, "noblemen," even "philosophy." . . . But the focus will again be on the peasant—not the peasant in the narrow sense of the word but the peasant soul—Russian, Slavic. Remember. . . the advice of Gl. Uspensky: "Look at the peasant. . . . No matter what. . . . You must look at the peasant!"

[2]Futurism was a Modernist poetic movement founded by Viktor Khlebnikov in 1910. An offshoot of Filippo Marinetti's Italian Futurism, the Russian Futurists rejected the fiction of Pushkin and Tolstoy and affirmed "trans-sense language" and *épater les bourgeois*, to "shock the bourgeois" in literature and life.

July 26, 1913
Ivan Bunin, from his diary

I have finished [Herzen's] *My Past and Thoughts*.[3] It is astounding in its thought, the power of its language, its simplicity, its expressiveness. Its language is native to me; it is the language of our fathers . . . of a now almost vanished tribe.

October 8, 1913
Ivan Bunin, from a speech on the occasion of the fiftieth anniversary of the Russian News

Russian readers are uncultured. Most of them still think of a newspaper as a novelty. . . . But the demand for newspapers grows with each day, and their number rises commensurately.

But we are still far from being Europeans. Unlike them, we still do not know the difference between genuine literature and the gutter press. . . . All too often Russian journals and newspapers . . . devote as much space to a serious discussion of Tolstoy's "Khadzhi Murat"[4] as to such pulp fiction as "The Pirate Churkin."[5] . . .

Just think what a newspaper means in our time, when we are Europeanizing ourselves so quickly; when we are giving birth to a middle class; when the proletariat has already gone out onto the streets and is attempting a complex and diverse way of life; and when everyone is developing a taste for newspapers and coming under their influence!

The writer now confronts a twofold influence: the power of the press and the power of the mob. How many of them can oppose it, the desire to please the crowd, the thirst for their applause, even if it be the stuff of scandal?

Steadfast writers have always been few and far between; in Russia now they are especially few. It cannot be any other way. Our writers, after all, are also uncultured. They are no less unsettled by changing events and moods; they are as little prepared for our new, fractured life as their readers. . . .

Russian life has done everything possible to cripple us; it has given us such horrifying contrasts: the sixties and the seventies, the

[3]*My Past and Thoughts*, a brilliant picture of Russian intellectual life in the 1840s, was written in 1855.
[4]Tolstoy wrote "Khadzhi-Murat" in 1904.
[5]*The Pirate Churkin: A Folk Legend of an "Old Acquaintance"* was written by Nikolai Ivanovich Pastukhov (1822–1911) in 1883–1884.

eighties and the nineties—and now the beginning of the nineteen hundreds!

You, ladies and gentlemen, know too well what Russian life has been like for the past twenty years. You know too well all its joyous and its ugly and terrible aspects. What has Russian literature been like during those years?

My answer will be necessarily short, but . . . I staunchly affirm that the ugly, negative aspects of Russian literature have been a hundred times greater than its positive ones. Our literature is sick; it is in a state of decline, of spasms and convulsions, of flings from one side to another. Tolstoy was a thousand times right when he said, "Literature, taste, and the common sense of the reading public have declined significantly in my lifetime." The reason for this decline, Tolstoy believed . . . was the fact that writers and the printed word cater to . . . the greatest number of customers, to tastes that are "coarse and base." . . .

A new *déclassé* has arrived in our literature, a spiritual *déclassé* who is absolutely devoid of tradition and overwhelmed . . . by European influences. . . .

What is this writer like? He is little cultured; he is almost a child in many, many respects; he lives his life by excesses, extremes, imitation, and at the expense of others. This writer has barely touched the surface of culture and knowledge, but he is extremely proud of what he knows. He drinks from the stream of currents coming from the West, and, having gotten drunk on them, suddenly proclaims that he is a "decadent," a "symbolist." He demands a radical restructuring of art . . . the newest art forms (as if form is separate from content). . . .

This, ladies and gentlemen, was only the beginning. Need I remind you of later developments? This is neither the time nor the place to discuss this. I will only remind you of the incredible, improbable number of schools, movements, moods, slogans, stormy reputations, and reversals we have seen in the last few years! Listen to the writer of the new type! In his own vulgar jargon, with his own lips or with the lips of his critic . . . he will say that he has created a countless number of new values; that he has transformed the language of prose; that he has enriched verse and has raised it to the heights; that he has touched upon the most profound questions of the soul; that he has "uncovered" a new state of mind; that he has assigned himself great "tasks"; that he is striving for great "accomplishments" and "possibilities"; and that, unashamedly, he calls himself "wise," "many-sided," "daring," and "sunlike." . . .

But . . . just the reverse has occurred: the unbelievable impoverishment, distortion, and deadening of Russian literature. . . .

The most precious features of Russian literature have disappeared: depth, seriousness, simplicity, spontaneity, nobility, and directness. Like a sea, there has poured forth vulgarity, shiftiness, boasting, foppery, and a tone that is forced, foolish, pompous, and invariably false. . . .

You will recall, ladies and gentlemen, what we have not done to our literature over the past few years, what we have not imitated, what we have not mimicked, what styles and epochs we have not taken, what gods we have not worshiped!

Every winter literally beings us a new idol. We have lived through decadence, and symbolism, and neonaturalism, and pornography (the so-called solution to the "problem of sex"), and battles among the gods, and mythmaking, and mystical anarchism, and Dionysius, and Apollo, and "flights into eternity, and sadism, and snobbery," and "acceptance of the world," and "nonacceptance of the world," and pulp reworkings of the Russian style, and Adamism, and Acmeism. Finally we have descended to the most trivial hooliganism, bearing the foolish name of "Futurism"! Truly it has been a witches' sabbath! . . .

October 8, 1913
Ivan Bunin, from an article in the newspaper Speech
"Where do you live?" a police officer asked academician I. A. Bunin.

"At the present time, at the Loskutin Hotel in Moscow."

"No, I want to know where is your permanent place of residence?"

"I live where my soul feels like," Bunin answered, "first in Italy, then in India."

October 13, 1913
Selected writers, from an interview in Voice of Moscow
At the jubilee celebrating the anniversary of the *Russian News*, the writer-academician I. A. Bunin vented his anger on the state of

contemporary Russian literature. . . . Was such anger deserved? Is Russian literature really in a period of decline? We asked several writers for their opinions.

Konstantin Balmont: I consider Bunin a talented individual but not a great one. He is taken with his academic manner. . . which is undeserved. As regards his attacks on everyone in literature, I find these inappropriate; one should not give eulogies at weddings or wedding toasts at funerals. . . . In my opinion, contemporary literature is developing in an unusual manner, by leaps and bounds. It is undergoing a period of fermentation, not a decline.

Yuly Baltrushaitis: Bunin has censured extremely diverse phenomena . . . in one grand sweep. He has taken it into his head to lump together people who have nothing in common . . . and things that seem similar on the surface but are profoundly different beneath.

Bunin believes that . . . compared with the situation twenty years ago, literature has declined. I do not agree. . . . Our literature has not changed other than to assume greater inner significance. Whether contemporary writing is genuine art or not, this is the question for our time. . . . But as long as people keep writing, we cannot talk about decline. . . .

Valery Bryusov: Unfortunately, I did not hear Bunin's speech. . . . But the version of it that appeared in the newspapers was simply stupid and showed a complete ignorance of the tasks of literature in general and of the development of contemporary Russian fiction in particular. Bunin . . . believes that the flowering of our poetry (beginning with Pushkin's time) has been compromised by developments which are abnormal and random. . . . Bunin is a man of intelligence who watches over the course of literature. I thus cannot accept the version of his speech that appeared in the press and I decline to judge it.

Mikhail Artsybashev: I know Bunin's speech only by what was printed in the newspapers . . . but I must say that I was unpleasantly surprised.

No one will deny, of course, that contemporary literature does not have such talents as Pushkin, Tolstoy, Dostoevsky, Lermontov, Gogol, and Turgenev. . . . I also admit that the literature of our days has lost its ideological integrity, its inner tension, and that it has become a more professional, even businesslike undertaking, obeying the laws of supply and demand in the most narrow sense of these words. But to assert that this has happened because the *déclassé* have entered literature!... What outmoded, class-based prejudice do I hear here! What do the *déclassé* have to do with the decline of literature?... Talent, ideology, and intelligence... are not privileges of the gentry class any more than the lack of principle or talent is characteristic of other sections of society. It is wrong even to talk about this!...

As regards the decline of contemporary literature, I can only say this: the temporary absence of great talents in our writing is a phenomenon that is random but also completely expected.... After all, Russian literature put forth so many great names in the course of two or three decades that it would not be surprising if there were a lull lasting twice that time. No matter how talented a people may be, it cannot give birth to Pushkins and Tolstoys daily.

If the literature of our days has become businesslike, then guilty is not some mythological *déclassé* but the very character of the times in which we live. Generally speaking, Russian life has lost its integrity; it has wandered off and gotten lost in a fog of hard times, of stagnation, political and social. Writers who have the misfortune to live in our times also have wandered off and gotten lost. They have no significance now. No one listens to them, no one demands anything from them, no one allows them to say what is on their mind. Their spirits have thus grown cold; they write from inertia, as much as the market demands from them, trying only to guess the tastes of their customers.

This is very sad, of course, but it is no different from anything else in our life. Give us freedom of the printed word and the entire picture will change immediately. One cannot write with passion when he is threatened with silence, that his mouth will be snapped shut. In other times the Russian reader was accustomed to hearing a vibrant voice in literature; the writer could write what he thought. But now neither the reader nor the writer likes the boundaries in which literature has been placed. That is why writing is indifferent, mechanical, and businesslike. And those who bear the fault for this—everyone knows who they are.

What good can come from inhibiting the "great Russian tongue," especially when it has the freedom only to search for new forms, and I must add, completely unnecessary ones at that. I say this because the old forms are still good enough; they still have not expressed even a hundredth of what they can. New forms are needed only when the old ones cannot render new ideas and feelings. This is not yet the case, and all these searchings, including the affectations of the Futurists, are only the result of an energy that is misshapen, misdirected, and has no other outlet for its release.

But all this has nothing to do with the *déclassé* or the gentry or aristocrats or democrats. Although I have the happiness or misfortune to belong to the gentry class, I cannot forget the century I live in, nor can I speak in the language of the preceding age. Bunin, apparently, has forgotten this.

Boris Zaitsev: Despite my deep respect for I. A. Bunin, I simply cannot agree with his assessment of the literature (and culture) of our time. . . .

Much of our literature is vulgar, true. But we have always had garbage in our fiction, and we always will. But to say that the Symbolists are little-cultured is not true. . . . .Balmont, Bunin, Blok, Sologub, Andrei Bely, and others . . . are very far from the hooliganism of the street. . . .

Everything that is genuine art in our time is tied to the spiritual culture of Europe—and that has only resulted in good. Take, for example, Pushkin and Turgenev. Both men were Europeans in culture and Slavophiles. . . .

The French esteem our ballet and art—should we complain? No . . . and the individuals about whom Bunin speaks so ironically should not be disturbed by his appeal to the great Russian artists, philosophers, and poets of the past. Bryusov studied Pushkin; Merezhkovsky was among the first to understand much in Gogol, Tolstoy, and Dostoevsky. . . . Andrei Bely studied Pushkin's rhythms. Was this just for mischief, for fun? Was this immaturity and flightiness? One can assert what he wants. But it is more difficult to be correct in these assertions.

November 17, 1913
Ivan Bunin, from a letter to Maxim Gorky
    The news is the same. The writers are fighting among themselves, and the public is laughing at them.

PART FIVE

Toward the Abyss

1914–1916

BUNIN, 1914

In August 1914 Nicholas II mobilized troops along the
Austro-Hungarian border and helped to precipitate World
War I. Russia now entered its most cataclysmic cycle of
reaction, upheaval, and reform. The war ended a centuries-old
dynasty because Russia was not ready to fight. It lacked money,
transport, communications, ammunition, supplies, and, most
important, a plan to put the country on a wartime footing. Russia
had, for example, only 60 artillery batteries to Germany's 381;
some regiments had no rifles at all; heavy ammunition was
sometimes rationed to four shells a day. For a period of time in
1915, as many as a fourth of Russian troops were sent to the front
unarmed, instructed to pick up whatever they could from the
dead. Although the Russians fought tenaciously, their losses were
enormous. Almost four million men were killed or injured in the
first ten months of the war; by its end, the country suffered more
casualties than any other nation involved in the struggle.

Things were equally disastrous on the home front. The
patriotism and unity that greeted the outbreak of the war quickly
gave way to anger and revolt. The internal economy collapsed.
Despite the success of the Stolypin reforms, more than eleven
million peasants still had no land while six million others had
plots that were insufficient for survival. The folk withheld from
the market what little food and fuel they had, resulting in severe
shortages, rampant inflation, and mounting strikes, riots, and
rebellions. More than 1.25 million workers struck between January
and June 1914, a rise of 60 percent over the entire preceding year.
Nicholas II only exacerbated the situation. Despite the protests of
ten of his twelve ministers, he joined the front in 1915, leaving
supreme power to Rasputin and the Empress Alexandra. Ministers
came and went; plots thickened. Rasputin was murdered in

December 1916, but his departure proved too little and too late.

Bunin's comments that "stupidity" had invaded national fiction of the war years, or that the public cared little about art, were grossly inaccurate. True, Russian writing between 1914 and 1916 was awash with hackneyed themes extolling the glories of the homeland and the patriotism of the folk. Yet beneath this swell, many established writers were swimming with the tide and newer ones were testing the waters. Gorky was upholding Neo-realism with the first two volumes of his celebrated autobiographical trilogy, *Childhood* (1913–1914) and *In the World* (1915–1916). (He completed the third volume, *My Universities*, in 1923.) Decadent and Symbolist writers were also hard at work. Gippius wrote her famous dramatic piece *The Green Ring* in 1914, describing a spiritually lost generation. A year later Andreev published his best play, *He Who Gets Slapped*, and Bely began his quasi-autobiographical novel *Kotik Letaev*.

The Futurists accelerated their rampage through the arts. Another manifesto, "The Roaring Parnassus" (1914), fired new salvos at Bunin and other writers for their "traditionalism." Mayakovsky continued to shock the public with pieces such as his autobiographical tragedy, *Vladimir Mayakovsky* (1914), in which he systematically compared his life with Christ's, complete with nativity, passion, and ascension; and *War and the World* (1916), in which he envisioned a peaceful planet whereby "Jesus Christ would play checkers with Cain." Several pieces in 1915 were among the best he had written to date. A verse work, entitled *A Cloud in Trousers*, focused on unrequited love, ending in the poet's appeal to a fire brigade to extinguish his blazing heart. Another poem, *The Backbone Flute*, likewise dealt with the pain and madness of passion.

Equally intriguing, many Russian writers of the time were sowing the first seeds of their work. In 1914 Pasternak published his first verse collection, *Twin in the Stormclouds*, while Akhmatova finished her second, *The Rosary*.

For Bunin the years immediately before the Revolution of 1917 were ones of sustained depression, darkness, and paralysis. Unlike many of his contemporaries, Bunin sensed that the war would bring about a more decisive (and destructive) upheaval than the one that had occurred in 1905, and that the world conflict would end life as he knew it. Inside Russia he saw villages breathing their last and peasants meeting their end in war, drunkenness, or despair.

Bunin's comment in 1916 that the war had "snapped him in two" suggests what was going on in his soul. On one hand there was the old Bunin, acrid and dark. But a new Bunin was learning to accept life on its own terms, seeing it not as black or white but in varying shades of grey. It added greatly to Bunin's sense of equanimity that he could now accept the fact that good coexisted with bad, or that life was at once beautiful and insane, or that even the precious "moment" contained both sorrow and joy.

He was also learning how to penetrate life's frenzy and to embrace the inner harmony of his land. His portraits of the Kremlins of Moscow and of Rostov-the-Great shared several features: they were calm, quiet, divorced from modern life, and, like a Russian Eden, host to him alone. Such scenes reinforced his earlier beliefs—that life could be sacred and stable, that his race could create enduring testaments to beauty and love, even that the current struggle among nations might act like a biblical flood, washing away sin and sorrow and bringing about a new world filled with brotherhood and peace.

It was not mere chance that Bunin chose precisely this time to talk at length about Chekhov. In telling Chekhov's story Bunin was also telling his own. Specifically, he sought to construct an *apologia pro sua vita*, a defense of his thoughts and deeds, past, present, and future. While he was alive, Chekhov had been Bunin's mentor and friend; now he was an alter ego, a man who had suffered greatly in life but who had triumphed in the end. Between 1914 and 1916 Bunin used Chekhov to assure himself and others that what he was doing was worthwhile, that he would rise to the challenge of the "last nobleman" in literature, and that he would willingly suffer everything that writers before him had endured.

Gorky's 1916 description of Bunin as a "taut spring" aptly describes his inner life: tense, stretched to the limit, yet refusing to break. Many of Bunin's works in the last three years of imperial Russia were among his best—"Brothers" (1914), "The Gentleman from San Francisco" (1915), and "Chang's Dreams" (1916). Interestingly, the focus of these pieces is not Russia but Ceylon, Italy, and the Red Sea. Collectively they give eloquent witness to Bunin's philosophical growth and his concern not only for homeland but for the world.

✳ 1914 ✳

June 1914
Ivan Bunin, from his notebook

"Do you know what happened to me once?" Chekhov said to me.

And, looking at me through his pince-nez, he began to chuckle: "A gentleman was standing with his back to me; he was holding a lesser-known writer by the buttons of his coat and insisting, 'Don't you understand? You are the premier writer in Russia!' Suddenly the gentleman saw my reflection in the mirror. He turned red and added quickly, pointing to me over his shoulder: 'And him, too.'"...

Chekhov did not like actors and actresses. He said about them that "they are vulgar, arch-narcissists."...

Chekhov often said, "In nature the loathsome caterpillar becomes a splendid butterfly, but it is just the opposite with people: the splendid butterfly becomes a loathsome caterpillar...."

"It is terrible to have lunch every day with someone who stammers and says stupid things...."

"When a talentless actress eats a partridge, you feel sorry for the partridge because it was a hundred times more intelligent and talented than the actress."...

Sometimes Chekhov would say, "A writer must be poor. He must be in a situation in which he knows he will die from hunger if he does not write.... Writers should be arrested and forced to write in cells; they should be beaten and flogged.... How grateful I am that I was so poor as a youth!"

But sometimes Chekhov would say just the opposite.

"A writer must be fabulously wealthy, so wealthy that, at any moment, he could travel around the world in his own yacht, so

wealthy that he could outfit an expedition to . . . the Nile, the South
Pole, Tibet, and Arabia, or buy all of the Himalayas and the
Caucasus. . . . Tolstoy said that an individual needs only six feet of
land. Rubbish—a dead man needs six feet, but one who is alive needs
the entire world. Writers especially."

Chekhov said about Tolstoy: "Why do I admire Tolstoy, especially since he . . . regarded us writers as complete nothings? . . . Why
should I praise him? Because Tolstoy saw us as children and our
stories and novels as child's play. . . . Even as an adult, Tolstoy was
annoyed that Shakespeare did not write like *he* did." . . .

Once, while reading the newspapers, Chekhov lifted his head
and said unhurriedly, lifelessly, "Always the same thing: Korolenko
and Chekhov, Potapenko and Chekhov, Gorky and Chekhov. . . ."

Times have changed. Now Chekhov stands alone. But he has not
been understood or valued as he should be. . . . I once wrote that
Chekhov was never friendly or close to anyone. . . . Now I have proof:
A striking line . . . from one of his unpublished notebooks. Chekhov
wrote, "I will lie in the grave alone, just as I have lived alone in
life." . . .

In the same notebook Chekhov wrote these thoughts:

"When a respectable individual looks critically at himself and
his life, people say that he is a 'complainer, a loafer, and a boring
person.'"

"How people willingly deceive themselves, how they love
prophets . . . how they love to be one of the herd!"

"To find one bright individual one has to go through a thousand
dumb ones; to find one bright word one has to go through a
thousand dumb ones; how a thousand words can stifle one bright
one."

Chekhov was stifled for a very long time. People acknowledged
him late in his career. Before his story "The Peasants,"[1] far from one
of his best things, the public read him willingly but only as an
entertaining storyteller. . . . I remember how I was laughed at when,
as a youth, I boldly compared Chekhov to Garshin and Korolenko. . . .

Enduring fame came to Chekhov only after his plays were staged
at the Moscow Art Theatre. . . . But he himself did not have a very
high opinion of these pieces. He often said . . . laughing, "I was
recently at Tolstoy's. He was lying in bed after an illness. . . . When I

[1]Chekhov wrote "The Peasants" in 1897.

got up to leave, he took me by the arm and said, 'Kiss me.' And when I went to do so, he whispered into my ear and said . . . 'All the same I cannot stand your plays! Shakespeare was bad enough, but you are even worse!' "

I have long thought that Chekhov should not have written about the nobility and gentry estates—for he did not know them. This holds especially true for his plays—*Uncle Vanya* and *The Cherry Orchard*.[2] The landowners in these works are really bad. The heroine in *The Cherry Orchard* . . . has nothing in common with the gentry. . . . Her sole reason for being in the play was so that Knipper could have a role. The servant Firs[3] is the height of banality. . . . And just where in Russia are those gentry orchards that are so full of cherries? . . . And why did Lopakhin[4] have to chop down this "cherry orchard"? To build a factory in its place? . . .

Chekhov hated "lofty" expressions. . . . "Once," someone recalled, "I complained to Chekhov: 'Anton Pavlovich! What should I do? I am so eaten up with reflection!' 'Drink a little less vodka' was his reply." . . .

The representatives of the "new" art whom Tolstoy rightly called "extreme caricatures of stupidity," Chekhov also found ludicrous and offensive. . . . He often said in a severe and sad tone, "Tolstoy will die, and everything will go to the devil!"

"Literature?"

"Literature, too." . . .

Chekhov once said about . . . the so-called "decadents": "They are the most robust peasants! They should be arrested." . . .

Chekhov did not fear anyone or anything . . . except Tolstoy. . . . He once said, "Just think, it was Tolstoy, Tolstoy who wrote that Anna Karenina could herself feel and see her eyes blazing in the darkness! Seriously, I'm afraid of him," he laughed as if delighted by his fear.

Once Chekhov spent almost an hour trying to decide which pants to wear to visit Tolstoy. He . . . kept coming out of his bedroom, first with one, then with another pair.

"No, these are indecently narrow!" he said. "Tolstoy will think I'm a hack!"

Then he went to put on another pair and came out laughing:

---

[2]Chekhov wrote *Uncle Vanya* in 1897 and *The Cherry Orchard* in 1904.
[3]Firs is the doddering servant in *The Cherry Orchard*.
[4]Lopakhin is the peasant entrepreneur in *The Cherry Orchard*.

"These are as wide as the Black Sea! Tolstoy will think I'm a smart aleck." . . .

One time Chekhov was having breakfast with a small group of friends in a restaurant. . . . Suddenly a gentleman across the way got up with a glass in his hand and said, "Ladies and gentlemen! A toast . . . to Anton Pavlovich Chekhov, the pride of our literature, the singer of twilight moods!"

Chekhov turned pale, got up, and walked out of the room. With indignation he told me this story many times. . . .

Whenever I was in Yalta for a long time, I spent almost all my days with Chekhov. I often left his home late at night, and he would say, "Come tomorrow a little earlier."

Chekhov often talked without expression, dryly, as if he were mumbling. Sometimes I wondered if he was being sincere. For a while I would refuse to come and visit. But when I did, he would take off his pince-nez, put his hands on his heart, and with a barely noticeable smile on his pale lips he would repeat in a distinct manner:

"Sir Deputy Bouquichonne,[5] I ask you in a most convincing way that if you are bored with this 'old, forgotten writer,' then go sit with [my sister] Masha, or with Mama who is in love with you, or with my wife, Knipshits the Hungarian. . . . Otherwise we will talk about literature."

I loved him very much, and I found such insistence pleasant. When I did come . . . we would go and sit in his study. We would quietly look through the newspapers all morning. Chekhov would say, "Let's read the papers and dig up some themes for dramas and vaudevilles." Every now and then there would be an article about me . . . one that was not very intelligent. I would get upset, and Chekhov would hasten to calm me down.

"They used to write even more stupid and mean things about me, but now they pass over me in complete silence. . . ."

Moreover, the critics would find a "Chekhovian mood" in my writing. Chekhov would come alive, even get upset. He would exclaim with muffled fervor:

"Oh, this is so stupid! . . . They used to find 'Turgenev notes' in me! You and I are about as much alike as a borzoi and a hound. You

---

[5]A mock deputy-marquis character from French vaudeville, and Chekhov's affectionate nickname for Bunin.

are much sharper than I am. I could not steal a single word from you! You, for instance, write: 'the sea smelled like a watermelon.'[6] . . . That is wonderful, but I would not have said it that way. You are a nobleman, the last of the 'hundred Russian writers'; I am petty bourgeois—and proud of it," he said, smiling. . . .

"Now that girl student," Chekhov said, "that was another thing. . . ."

"What girl student?"

"You remember, the one you and I once thought up for a story: it was hot out, the setting was the steppe . . . and there was a very long mail train going along. . . . You added: a girl student wearing a leather belt was standing by the window of a third-class train car. She was shaking some old tea out of a teapot. The tea splashed the face of a portly gentleman who was looking out from another window. . . ."

It was perhaps artistic details like these that drew us so close together. Chekhov so yearned for these types of details that he would repeat a successful one with excitement for two or three days running. For this alone I will never forget him; I will always feel the pain that he is no longer here. . . .

Sometimes Chekhov would put down the paper suddenly, take off his pince-nez, and start to chuckle quietly.

"Something you read?"

"A merchant from Samara . . . has just bequeathed his entire estate to build a monument to Hegel."

"You've got to be joking!"

"No, I'm not, I swear to God. To Hegel."

Then Chekhov asked suddenly, "What will you write about me in your memoirs?"

"What will you write about me?" I said. "You'll outlive me."

"You're old enough to be my son."

"Just the same. You've got peasant blood in you."

"And you have noble blood in you. Peasants and merchants go downhill quickly and terribly. Read my story "Three Years."[7] You're in good health—only very thin like a prize borzoi. Take some pills for your appetite and you'll live for a hundred years. I'll prescribe some for you; I'm a doctor after all. . . . But in your memoirs don't

---

[6]It will be recalled that the image of the sea as a watermelon was not Bunin's but Tolstaya-Krandievskaya's. See her excerpt in 1903.

[7]Chekhov wrote "Three Years" in 1895.

write that I was a 'likable talent, an individual of crystallike pureness.' "

"People have said as much about me," I replied. . . .

Chekhov fell down laughing, his head on his knees; then he put on his pince-nez and, looking at me brightly and gaily, said, "It's better they said such things about me. . . . It serves us right. . . . I'm the proletariat after all. As a child . . . I sold candles. Oh, how devilishly cold it was! . . . The latrine was in a vacant lot, about a mile behind our home. You'd run out there in the evening, and a thief would be spending the night there. We scared the hell out of each other!"

"But here's my advice to you," Chekhov added suddenly. "Stop being a dilettante; work hard. . . . I had to write for a piece of bread, but . . . it formed me to work. Don't always wait for inspiration." . . .

"It's terrible to recall the things critics wrote about me," Chekhov said. "They said I was cold-blooded—do you remember my story 'Cold Blood'?[8]—and that I didn't care what I portrayed, a dog or a drowned man, a train or first love. . . . My collection 'Gloomy People'[9] saved me—the critics said the stories in there were worthwhile because they supposedly depicted the reaction of the eighties. Then there was my story 'An Attack of Nerves'[1]—here an 'honorable' student goes insane because he thinks about prostitution. But I cannot stand Russian students—they are first-class loafers." . . .

Once, when Chekhov again jokingly pestered me about what I would write about him in my memoirs, I answered:

"First of all, I'll write about how I met you. . . . It was in December '95; I didn't know that you were in Moscow. We were at a literary reading . . . and a poet was reading his verse, and getting more and more carried away. . . . It was getting rather late, but the poet kept on reading even when he was coming down the staircase. Then, still reading his verse, the poet began to look for his coat in the cloakroom. The attendant said to him softly, 'Allow me, sir, to help you. . . .'

"But the poet got nasty: 'Silence, do not disturb me!'

" 'But, sir, this is not your coat. . . .'

" 'What do you mean, you scoundrel? Is this someone else's coat?'

[8]Chekhov wrote "Cold Blood" in 1887.
[9]Chekhov published his collection "Gloomy People" in 1892.
[1]Chekhov wrote "An Attack of Nerves" in 1889.

" 'Exactly so, sir.'

" 'Quiet, you scoundrel, this is my coat!'

" 'No, it's not!'

" 'Then tell me whose coat is it?'

" 'Anton Pavlovich Chekhov's.'

" 'You're lying! For that I'll kill you on the spot!'

" 'Do what you like, but all the same it's Anton Pavlovich Chekhov's coat!'

" 'You mean he's here?'

" 'He's been here all night.' . . ."

"The poet and I both rushed up to meet you, at three in the morning. But fortunately we were held back and came by your place the next day. . . ."

"It's a pity you didn't stop by that night," Chekhov said. "I love to go off suddenly into the night. I love restaurants." . . .

I also remember how Chekhov laughed when I told him the story of how our village deacon ate up two pounds of caviar. . . during my father's nameday. He even began his story "In the Ravine"[2] with my tale. . . .

Chekhov loved to repeat that if an individual did not work, that if he did not always live in the artistic sphere which opens the eyes of an artist, then, even if he be Solomon the Wise, he would always feel empty, without talent.

Sometimes Chekhov would take his notebook from the table . . . wave it in the air, and say, "There are exactly one hundred plots in here! Yes, sir! Would you like a couple of them, young man? . . . Would you like to buy some?" . . .

Chekhov would sometimes . . . go out on evening walks. Once he returned home very late. He was very tired; he had really overdone it—his handkerchief had been wet with blood for the past few days. Suddenly Chekhov opened his eyes and said in a very loud voice, "Did you hear the news? A terrible thing has happened! Bunin has been murdered! At the home of a Tatar woman!"

I stopped dead in my tracks, but he quickly whispered with happy, shining eyes, "Not a word to anyone! Tomorrow all of Yalta will be talking about Bunin's murder!" . . .

A certain writer once lamented to Chekhov, "I'm embarrassed to tears when I think about how poor and weak my first stories were."

---

[2]Chekhov wrote "In the Ravine" in 1900.

"Oh, what are you complaining about?" Chekhov said. "It's a good thing when one writes poorly at first. Don't you understand that if a writer begins as he should—then he's as good as lost!... What nonsense I started off with, Good God, what nonsense!"...

Many Turks and other peoples from the Caucasus worked on the shores of the Black Sea. Knowing the suspicion and ill will that Russians have for peoples of other nationalities, Chekhov never missed a chance to note how hardworking, honest, and pious these people were....

Chekhov ate and slept little; he greatly loved order. His rooms were surprisingly clean; his bedroom was like a girl's. No matter how weak he was... Chekhov would always dress as if he were going on a visit.

Chekhov's hands were large, dry, and pleasant.

Like almost anyone who thinks a lot, he often forgot what he was talking about....

A winter day in the Crimea, grey, cool, with thick, sleepy clouds.... It is quiet in Chekhov's home; only the even ticking of the clock from his mother's room. Chekhov is without his pince-nez; he is sitting at the desk in his study and writing something, slowly and precisely. He gets up... and goes to check a mousetrap. He returns, holding a mouse by his tail. He goes out onto the porch, walks slowly through the garden... and carefully tosses the mouse there. Looking attentively at the young trees, he heads for the bench in the middle of the garden.... Having sat down, he plays with one of his dogs... and smiles.... Then he looks out onto the distance... and thinks peacefully about something. He sits there for an hour, an hour and a half....

Did Chekhov ever have a romance that was passionate, "romantic," and blind?

I don't think so, but I find this very surprising. Without a doubt, Chekhov yearned for such a love. A woman's heart he knew surprisingly well; he felt the feminine spirit with all its power and preciseness.... He was one of those rare individuals who could talk with women, touch them, and get close to them spiritually....

"Love," Chekhov wrote in his notebook, "is the remains of something that once was a great thing but that has become depraved; or it is an entity that will become a great thing in the future but does not satisfy in the present, since it gives much less than one expects."...

What did Chekhov think about death?

He often told me, painstakingly and firmly, that immortality, that life after death . . . is complete nonsense: "Immortality is superstition. And superstitions are terrible things. Once should think clearly and bravely. Sometime you and I will discuss this thoroughly. I will prove to you that immortality is rubbish as easy as two times two is four."

But then there were times when Chekhov said something completely the opposite: "In no way can we disappear completely. We must live on after death. Immortality is a fact. . . . Someday I will prove this to you."

But he never did. . . .

Late in his life, Chekhov often dreamed aloud: "I would like to become a vagabond, a pilgrim, to visit the holy places, to live in a monastery surrounded by forests, lakes, and to sit on a bench on a summer evening alongside the monastery gates. . . ." . . .

The last letter I received from Chekhov. . . was in mid-July 1904 while I was living in the village. It was very short and, as almost always, lighthearted. Chekhov wrote that he was feeling well, that he had ordered a white suit for himself, that he was disturbed only by Japan, and that this "heavenly country" would, of course, smash and crush Russia. On the 14th of July I went to the post office. . . . It was a hot and sleepy day in the steppe; the sky was overcast and there was a hot southern wind. I opened the newspaper . . . and suddenly it was like an icy razor slashing my heart. . . .

June 19, 1914
Ivan Bunin, from his diary

All around is filth and stench. The peasants have been drinking all day. A ragged youth sings dully:

> A villainous thought has struck me:
> I found an ax in the dark . . .

A monk, thickset, potbellied, yellow-haired, with a fiery red beard and a dirty canvas cassock, looks like Socrates. He was buying rusty-colored fish with golden brown dust in the holes of their rotting eyes.

Circa July 1914
Valentin Kataev, from his memoirs

With Bunin I was afraid to say the blasphemous name of

Mayakovsky. . . . Later I could not say the word Bunin when I was with Mayakovsky. One excluded the other.

July 2, 1914
Ivan Bunin, from an interview with the Odessa News
Did Chekhov influence me as a writer? No. I was engrossed by him; I was enraptured by him; but I never wanted to write like he did. For me, Leo Tolstoy was a god. . . . Chekhov influenced me, of course, but the influence was not direct.

I consider as Chekhov's best works: "Happiness," "The Student," "A Boring Story," "The Murder," "Ward No. 6," and "The Bishop."[3] Like a mirror, these works reflect the mind and soul of Chekhov, his remarkable inventiveness, his observation, his unusually compact ideas.

July 3, 1914
Ivan Bunin, from a letter to a friend
Only God knows how good I feel when I am on the Volga, when I am in its coastal towns . . . when I visit Rostov-the-Great. . . . Here I again feel, with all the force of my being, this very Rus. . . . I again feel how huge, and wild, and empty, and complex, and terrible, and good Rus is.

July 11, 1914
Ivan Bunin, from his diary
In early July 1914 Yuly and I were sailing up the Volga from Saratov. On the 11th we docked at Samara. . . . Suddenly we caught sight of several boys. . . . They held scraps of newspaper in their hands and were crying with frenzied, happy voices, "Extra! Extra! Read all about it: The Austrian heir has been murdered in Serbia."

Yuly grabbed one of the papers, read it several times, and, after some silence, said to me, "Well, this is the end for us! A war between Russia and Serbia, then revolution in Russia! . . . This is the end of our former way of life!"

Circa Fall 1914
Alexei Zolotarev, from his memoirs
"I was at your Rostov-the Great," Bunin told me.

___

[3]Chekhov wrote "Happiness" in 1887, "The Student" in 1894, "A Boring Story" in 1889, "The Murder" in 1895, "Ward No. 6" in 1892, and "The Bishop" in 1902.

"Were you?" I said, expecting that he would say something bright, joyous, and comforting.

"It was in the summer. I arrived in Rostov: it was hot, dusty, stinking, and stuffy. After some time I found a room in a dirty tavern inn. There was some kind of holiday going on. . . . Everyone was drunk, even the waiters and the cabbies. They were playing bawdy, obscene songs."

I became sick at heart. . . . Then Bunin added hurriedly but sincerely, "But the night was quiet and moonlit. The town had fallen asleep. I went out for a walk, got lost . . . and found myself by the lake. I took a boat, headed out for the middle of the river, and looked at the city and its kremlin. . . . How good it was!"

September 11, 1914
Ivan Bunin, from an interview with the Russian Word
To the great shame of humankind, that which the mind and heart has refused to believe for so long has become indisputable: Every new day brings with it new and terrible evidence of German barbarism and cruelty. . . of their unrealistic hope to rule the world by force, to place only the sword on the scales of justice.

German soldiers . . . remind us that the ancient beast is still alive and powerful in humankind; that civilized peoples can easily surrender their freedom to an evil will; and that they can become like their ancestors, half-naked hordes. Fifteen hundred years ago the Germans crushed the heritage of antiquity under the weight of their heel. Now, and as never before, they will destroy churches and libraries, the precious creations of art; they will wipe whole towns and villages off the face of the earth.

October 15, 1914
Ivan Bunin, from a letter to a friend
For the past three months I sit from morning to evening reading the newspapers. Except for the war I have forgotten everything else in the world. I am not exaggerating.

Mid-November 1914
Ivan Kasatkin, from his memoirs
Gorky had just come to Moscow. . . . He began to talk about the war in an excited sort of way, about the swarms of wounded entering the capital. Later came the somewhat dry, dapper. . . Ivan Bunin. Still later came the handsome Fedor Chaliapin with his kingly

gestures. I looked closely at these three very well-known and yet so very different people; I listened carefully to their widely divergent opinions about the tragedy of the war—the fate of the masses running off to the field of war is unclear. The conversation went on till dawn.

December 15, 1914
Ivan Bunin, from a letter to a friend
I am firmly convinced that the upcoming Christmas will not be the last bloody one. I know that humankind still lives by the Old Testament and that people are still beasts—that has been proven without a doubt.

But there are thousands of "buts" that are joyful and comforting, not to mention the voice of the heart. I cannot foretell the fate of the world with a light heart, for over the last hundred years there have been political, social, and scientific catastrophes unrivaled in history. And how can I, who is not an Isaiah, prophesy at a time when all human hearts are undergoing such ebbs and flows, such a succession of hopes and sorrows, such contradictory visions . . . ?

Late December 1914
Kornei Chukovsky, from a critical article
If I read in Bunin that poetic birches cast a shadow on a poetic grave, then I know in advance that pigs will suddenly appear and plow up the burial grounds, and that cattle will strip the leaves bare. If I read in Bunin that someone has used his last rubles to buy horses, then I know right away they will eat up all his grain and straw but will invariably die by spring. If I read in his book that some estate is called . . . 'The Cheerful Stead,'[4] then I know it harbors only depression and despair; if 'Daybreak,'[5] then only death, destruction, and demise. This is Bunin's law, his fate.

✳ 1915 ✳

January 1, 1915
Ivan Bunin, from his diary
The Kremlin. I sat for a long time in the Cathedral of the

[4]Bunin wrote "The Cheerful Stead" in 1911.
[5]"Daybreak" is the estate in Bunin's story "In the Field," written in 1895.

Annunciation. It was overwhelmingly good there. I heard part of the night service in Archangel Cathedral. . . .

At midnight we went to the Cathedral of the Assumption. A black, endless line of people. The policeman would not let you out of the line. He wouldn't even let you go into a side door or look into the windows. "There's nothing to see there!" he said.

At four o'clock I was at Novodevichy Convent. There was frost all around. By sunset the trees seemed as if outlined in gold enamel. How very strange to see the scattered red dotlike lights of icon lamps over the graves in the daylight.

February 22, 1915
Ivan Bunin, from his diary

Our maid Tanya loves to read. When she empties . . . the basket under my desk, she keeps a thing or two . . . and reads them when she has some time—slowly, with effort, but with such a smile of pleasure on her face. She is afraid to ask me for a book of my writing because she is shy. . . .

How cruel we are!

March 7, 1915?
Ivan Bunin, from a letter to a friend

You have reduced me to absolute despair! What barbarian took *The Gentleman from San Francisco* and put semicolons in place of my commas? Is this any way to treat a writer, the music of his style?

March 15, 1915
Ivan Bunin, from a letter to Maxim Gorky

Truly you are one of very few whom I think about in my soul when I write. I value your support so much.

March 29, 1915
Ivan Bunin, from his diary

I heard Rachmaninov's "All-Night Vigil."[6] . . . But I was touched by only two or three canticles. The rest of it seemed to me to be the usual church rhetoric, which is especially intolerable in services to God.

---

[6]Rachmaninov wrote the "All-Night Vigil" in January and February 1915.

April 10, 1915
Ivan Bunin, from his "Autobiographical Note"

The "Book of Heraldic Arms"[7] says . . . "The Bunin clan comes from Simeon Bunkovsky . . . who left Poland in the fifteenth century to serve the Great Prince Vasily Vasilievich. His great-grandson, Alexander Lavrent'ev Bunin, also served . . . and was killed near Kazan.[8] The courtier, Kozma Leont'ev Bunin, was awarded an estate for his service and bravery. Many other Bunins also served . . . in official capacities; they, too, were given villages." . . .

Our family crest is knightly armor, a helmet with ostrich feathers . . . a blue shield, and a ring, "a sign of eternity and fidelity." . . .

I know almost nothing about the Chubarovs. I only know they were ancient noblemen (some say princes) . . . and that they had estates near Orel. . . . Most likely the Chubarovs did not know much more about themselves: Most Russian gentry were extremely careless about . . . such information. The same can be said about me. Almost from adolescence on I have been a "free thinker" who was completely indifferent not only to my "blue" blood but also to the loss of everything tied up with it. . . .

My paternal great-grandfather was wealthy. My grandfather had land in the Orel region . . . but his brothers robbed him of his patrimony. He was not an entirely normal person. My father did not take care of the little he had inherited but was unusually extravagant and carefree. He took part in the Crimean campaign as a volunteer and even outfitted a regiment at his own expense. . . . Father returned to Voronezh in 1870 to attend to the education of my older brothers, Yuly and Evgeny, and brought us to further ruin. I was born in Voronezh and spent the first three years of my life there. . . . A passion for clubs, wine, and cards forced father . . . to return to Elets, to our estate of Butyrka. There . . . I spent my childhood: a poetry that was peculiar and sad.

My father was healthy and strong . . . to the last days of his long life. He became depressed . . . or angry only in the most difficult moments, and then only for a short time. My father did not touch a drop of liquor until he was thirty years old. . . . Then he began to drink terribly, though he was not the typical alcoholic. . . . Some-

[7]*The Common Book of Heraldic Arms of the Nobility of the All-Russian Empire* was published in Saint Petersburg from 1799 to 1840.
[8]The Russians besieged Kazan from 1552 to 1557.

times he would not drink for several years at a stretch. I was born during one of these respites. . . .

Father. . . could not stand to study. But he willingly read a great deal. His mind was alive and sharp—he always spoke in a way that was lively and picturesque, but not always logical. He was contradictory: fitful, decisive, open, and greathearted. His entire being exuded his nobleman origins so greatly that I could not imagine a place where he would be uncomfortable. His peasants said there was "not a person who was kinder and simpler in the whole world." Father also spent what belonged to mother. He even gave away part of it, for he had an overwhelming need to give away things. Constant hunting and a life out in the open air allowed this good, interesting, and very gifted individual to live until his eighties and then to die a peaceful and easy death.

My mother was not at all like my father—except that she, too, was kind and healthy, and that she also lived a long life, despite unending sadness, asthma . . . and the strict fasts that her piety imposed on her. . . . Her father also drank, but in a different way from my father; he was more cultured, if one can put it this way. . . . He stood out among the gentry; his daughter was better educated than my father. Mother was tender—but she was firm when she had to be. She was self-sacrificing and prone to sad premonitions, tears, and grief. She was extremely devoted to her family . . . she gave birth to nine children, but only four survived . . . and separation from her brood was unbearable for her. When I was a child, my brothers lived far away from the estate, and my father. . . was always off hunting and living beyond his means—all suitable reasons for her tears.

My father's continual good spirits . . . countered my mother's influence; but they made their mark on me only much later. . . . I grew up sad and lonely. We had few servants . . . and we had little to do with our relatives and neighbors. I did not have any children my own age . . . and I was extremely impressionable. Everything affected me—a new face, an event, a song in the field, a pilgrim's story, the mysterious hollows behind the estate, the account of a runaway soldier. . . a raven . . . which, mother said, came from the time of Ivan the Terrible,[9] and the twilight sun shining through rooms that looked out onto a cherry orchard. . . . Mother and the servants loved to tell stories; it was from them that I heard songs, stories,

[9]Ivan the Terrible was tsar of Russia from 1530 to 1584.

legends . . . and first learned of our very rich Russian tongue. . . .

Life began when I was about seven years old. . . . Before I entered school I rarely studied; even during vacations I spent my time in the villages . . . and at the homes of landowners and our former peasants . . . with whom I watched the cattle for days on end. . . . My tutor was a very strange individual. He was the son of a marshal of the nobility, a student of . . . Eastern languages, and a former teacher . . . who had broken with his family . . . and wandered through villages and estates. My tutor . . . was taken with me; his attention and countless stories—he had seen quite a bit of the world and was well read and conversant in three languages—caused me to love him dearly. He taught me to read (using Homer's *The Odyssey*); he excited my imagination with . . . Don Quixote—I became a fanatic about knighthood!—and with original, though not always comprehensible, stories about people and life. My tutor played the violin and painted in watercolors. I was sometimes with him for days on end, and I also painted . . . until I became almost sick to death from it. I will always remember the unspeakable happiness I felt when I was given my first painting set. For a long time I dreamed I would be an artist. . . . My tutor also wrote poetry—satirical pieces on current events; I, too, once wrote a poem . . . about ghosts in a moonlit mountain valley at midnight. I was about eight years old, but I can still see that valley as though it were yesterday. . . .

My tutor, though, was very negligent in my studies; it was pretty much catch-as-catch-can. Of all the languages he knew, he taught me only Latin, and I spent many days cramming grammar into my head.

A year or so before I entered school (I was about eight or nine) I was seized by yet another passion—the lives of the saints. I began to fast and pray. . . . It was nice at first; but then the death of my sister, Nadya, turned my piety into a terrible angst that lasted the entire winter and made me constantly wonder about life beyond the grave. Spring cured me of my morbidity, though I still . . . could come under the sway of the sad all-night vigils in the churches at Elets. . . .

As a youth I did not like religious services. (But now I love them—the rites of ancient Russian churches and those of other faiths, Catholic, Moslem, Buddhist—though I do not adhere to any organized creed.)

The school and my life at Elets left me with impressions that were far from joyous. Everyone knows what a Russian school is like...not to mention the joys of a provincial Russian city!...I went from an absolutely carefree existence...to life in the city, to the absurd severities of school, and to the lamentable life-styles of the philistine and merchant homes where I boarded. At first I studied well and took to almost everything easily; but then it got worse...I started to get ill and waste away. I became extremely nervous, and to make matters worse I fell in love. My love affairs, both then and later on in my youth, were always happy and pure. But this one ended once I left school.

I read little as a child. I cannot say I had a passion for books, but probably I read almost everything that we had in the house and that did not get rolled into cigars....I remember I read Gerbel's *English Poets*, *Robinson Crusoe*...and a book with pictures in it entitled *Lands and Peoples*.[1]...I *could see* what I read—often extremely sharply—and that gave me special pleasure.

I did not like many of the things we read in school. . . . I hardly wrote any poetry in school, but I liked the verse of other writers; I could recall by heart almost a whole page of hexameter, even if I had dashed through it once or twice. (I have a very good memory in general—whatever interests me I can remember especially well—but I cannot force myself to do it...or train myself to observe *à la* Gogol.)

I left school after fourth grade and lived in the village of Ozerka, at an estate that had come down to us from my grandmother Chubarova. There I read and filled many pages with my writing. I...developed quickly, joyfully sensing my youth and prowess. There, also, my brother Yuly completed the rest of my education. He had graduated from the university and had spent a year in prison because of political activity. He made me study languages and read to me excerpts from psychology, philosophy, and the social and natural sciences. We also talked incessantly about literature. I remember how enchanting everything seemed at this time: people, nature, the ancient home with its colored windows, the neighboring estates, hunting, and books, the mere sight of which gave me almost physical delight, every color, every smell. . . .

At first, as a youth, I wrote without difficulty, since I imitated first one writer, then another—Lermontov, most of all, and some-

---

[1]*Lands and Peoples* was a geographic encyclopedia published in thirteen volumes in Saint Petersburg between 1876 and 1893.

times Pushkin whose handwriting I even copied. Then I tried to write something that was original—most often something to do with love. This turned out to be more difficult. I read whatever came my way: old and new journals, Lermontov, Zhukovsky. . . Schiller. . . Turgenev. . . Shakespeare, Belinsky. . . . I genuinely loved Pushkin and was taken for a while with Nadson. . . .

I regarded writers as beings of an unusual, most elevated order. (I remember how impressed I was when my tutor told me that he had once seen Gogol—and that when I read Gogol's "The Terrible Vengeance,"[2] I was deeply moved by the rhythms of the piece.) It never occurred to me to be anything less than a Pushkin or a Lermontov—not because I had that high an opinion of myself but because I felt it could not be otherwise. Lermontov's estate. . . was only twenty miles from us, and almost all our great writers were born nearby. . . . This, though, did not prevent me from being passionately interested in lesser writers, like Nazarov. An innkeeper told me that an "author" had appeared in Elets. I set out there right away, and, with delight, I met this Nazarov, a self-educated poet from the middle class (and from whom I partially took the character of Kuzma in *The Village*). . . . Among the new writers of the time, I liked Garshin very much (his suicide distressed me terribly). I also liked Ertel, though even then I could sense his affected manner. . . and his imitation of Turgenev. . . . Several things by Chekhov annoyed me (I did not know his humorous stories at the time), because they were written hastily, weakly. . . .

In April '87 I sent a poem to the Petersburg weekly *Homeland*, which appeared in one of the May issues. I will never forget that morning when I walked home from the post office with the issue in my hands. . . . I kept reading my piece over and over again. I read and wrote a great deal that summer, and so that nothing would keep me from "observing the mysteries of night life" I . . . slept only in the afternoon.

In September 1888 my verse appeared in *Book Week*. . . which often published pieces by Shchedrin, Gl. Uspensky, and L. Tolstoy. . . . The editor took me under his wing. . . but he would not let me publish in other periodicals.

Meanwhile, our family circumstances again took a turn for the worse, courtesy of my father. Yuly moved to Kharkov; in spring '89 I

[2]Gogol wrote "The Terrible Vengeance" in 1832.

also set out there and moved about among revolutionaries . . . the most narrow-minded "radicals," as they were called then. Later on . . . I moved to the Crimea. . . . It was splendid there. I could walk for miles, get a tan from the sun and wind, and become very light-hearted from hunger and youth. . . . In the Crimea I worked for the *Orel Herald* . . . as a proofreader, translator, and theater critic, none of which, fortunately, I liked. There also, to my great misfortune, I got involved in a long love affair.[3]

I returned to more regular literary and educational pursuits only after about two years, when I moved to Poltava, where Yuly ran the bureau of statistics for the local *zemstvo*. In Poltava I worked as a librarian . . . a statistician, and a newspaper correspondent. I studied and wrote diligently. I also traveled all over the Ukraine . . . and became attracted to Tolstoy's teachings. I started meeting with the "brothers" who lived around Poltava . . . took up barrel-making, and sold publications for the Mediator.[4] It was Tolstoy himself, though . . . who disinclined me to the "simple life." . . . At this time, also, I was taken by Flaubert, *The Lay of the Host of Igor*,[5] Ukrainian folk ballads—often so very majestic and solemn—and Mickiewicz,[6] especially his Crimean sonnets, ballads, and . . . "Pan Tadeusz."[7] Because of Mickiewicz I even studied Polish.

After my time at the *Orel Herald* I wrote in fits and starts, writing for various journals and publishing a first book of verse which was extremely juvenile and excessively intimate. One reviewer . . . reproached me for imitating Fet and told me I would be better off writing prose. The others were sympathetic. It was in Poltava, though, that I first began to write more or less serious stories. I sent my first piece (untitled) to *Russian Wealth*. . . . The editor Mikhailovsky wrote that I would become a "great writer"; the story, now with the terrible title "A Village Sketch," was published in April '94. At the same time the poet A. M. Zhemchuzhnikov, took a special interest in me . . . and introduced me to *Herald of Europe*. . . .

In January '95 . . . I visited Petersburg for the first time and met

---

[3]His relationship with Varvara Pashchenko, 1894–1898.

[4]The Mediator was a publishing house founded by Leo Tolstoy and Vladimir Grigorievich Chertkov in 1884 to print inexpensive books and distribute them among the masses. The Mediator ceased operations in 1935.

[5]*The Lay of the Host of Igor*, written in the twelfth century, is Russia's most famous medieval epic.

[6]Adam Mickiewicz (1798–1855) was a leading Polish poet whose *Ballads and Romances* (1822) initiated the Polish Romantic movement.

[7]Mickiewicz wrote "Pan Tadeusz" in 1834.

several well-known writers . . . Chekhov, Balmont, Ertel, and Bryusov, who was still a student then. . . . I also saw a certain poet who
was famous throughout Moscow for a book which he had dedicated to
"himself and the Egyptian queen Cleopatra"; and who . . . would go
about town in a Caucasian fur cap, felt cloak, underdrawers, and nails
attached to his fingers. This poet caused revolutions in poetic form,
but he was also the first to quit being "daring" and "reappraising
values." He was not included in the history of "new Russian
literature," even though phrases like "close your pale legs" were long
ascribed to him.[8]

In October '95 my story "To the Edge of the World" was
published and was very well received. . . . An edition of my stories
appeared in January '97 and received almost unanimous applause
(which I find very strange now). . . . I suddenly left Petersburg for a
long period of time and did not write for several years. During this
time I lived an especially nomadic and colorful life—first in the Orel
region, then in the Ukraine. I went back to the Crimea, spent time
in Moscow, met with old and young writers more and more often,
and called at the Mediator, which Tolstoy also visited. . . . Since I was
very much aware of my artistic growth, and by virtue of my many
spiritual crises, I destroyed the little prose I wrote then. I published
some verse (the least intimate ones, mostly pictures of nature); but I
translated a great deal—I found it easier to deal with something that
was not mine. It was precisely about this time that I began my adult
life, a period which was so . . . intimate and complex . . . that to talk
about it in detail would be a long and difficult task. . . .

In '98 I married (A. N. Tsakni, a Greek woman, the daughter
of the emigré revolutionary N. P. Tsakni). After that I lived in
Odessa. I then got separated and resumed my wanderings. My travels
did keep me from working but actually brought a large measure of
order into my life: winters—the capitals and villages, and then travel
abroad, springtime—the south of Russia, and summers—the village, most of all. . . . Since '07 I have shared my life with V. N.
Muromtseva. Since then, also, I have been seized by a yearning to
travel and work. Over the past eight years I have written two-thirds
of all I have published. I have also seen a great deal. . . . Turkey, Little
Asia, Greece, Egypt . . . Syria, Palestine . . . Algeria, Tunisia, and the
Sahara. I have sailed to Ceylon, and have been all over Europe. . . .

[8]Bunin is referring to an obscure writer, Alexander Nikolaevich Emelyanov-
Kokhansky, who published his work "Cleopatra" in 1897.

But as [the poet] Boratynsky would say, "I would always return to you, my native steppe, my first love"—then "I would wander the world anew and observe the human tribe. . . ."

My literary career. . . is well known. At the end of 1898 my translation of [Longfellow's] "Song of Hiawatha" gave several critics the chance to repeat their usual hasty conclusions . . . that I was an "idyllicist," a "passive observer" of life. In 1900 I published a book of my verse with Scorpion,[9] but I quickly parted company with the people there since I did not wish to play argonauts, demons, and magicians with my new coworkers, nor could I bear their high-blown nonsense.

At this time, also, several critics began talking about my "attraction to the Decadents" . . . while others applauded the fact that I was holding fast to . . . "tradition," though I believe that to love talent, independence, intelligence, and taste in art does not at all mean to uphold "tradition." In '02 I collaborated closely with Knowledge[1] (but I also found the writers there alien to my spirit). . . . I was awarded Pushkin Prizes by the Academy of Sciences; chosen to an "honored Academician" in 1909; and in 1912 became an honored member of the Society of the Lovers of Russian Literature. . . . I also note that this year. . . I am publishing a collection of my works in which I include *everything* I consider worthy of print.

Generally speaking, I have had a rather unusual life; but I have been represented falsely. . . . The majority of my critics not only rushed to establish the parameters of my talent once and for all, but they also sought to analyze my personality. . . . In their view there was no calmer writer than I (I was "the bard of fall, of sadness, and of gentlemen's nests"); there was no one who was more set in his ways and more reconciled with life. But . . . the truth was that I was far from calm or fully formed. Just the opposite . . . I was leading a life that was sharper and more complex than anything I had expressed in the little I wrote then.

With time, several critics abandoned their early labels, but they then gave labels that were diametrically opposed—a "decadent," a "Parnassian," and a "cold master"—while others affirmed that I was

---

[9]Scorpion was a publishing house founded in Moscow in 1900 to further Russian Symbolism. It ceased operations in 1916.

[1]Knowledge was a publishing association founded in Saint Petersburg in 1898. Knowledge was joined by Gorky in 1900 and published literary almanacs and works of Critical Realism.

"the singer of autumn" who possessed a graceful talent, wrote in splendid Russian, and loved nature and humankind. The critics also said there was "something Turgenevian and Chekhovian in my works" (though there is absolutely nothing of either writer in my fiction).

Everyone knows my most recent literary work. . . . About *The Village* . . . and *Dry Valley* . . . what didn't I hear! Some critics were so low as to say that I was a landowner who was frightened by the Revolution of 1905 (though I never owned any land). They took me to task for my origins, saying I was the first and only "nobleman" in Russian literature. They posited that I was an "intellectual" and a recent arrival to the village. They poked fun at my "trips to India," though I profited greatly from such travels. . . . Several critics added that my works on the people were "false," though they never proved it. . . . None of this, of course, is new in Russian literature. Critics cried that [Gogol's] "Inspector General" and his *Dead Souls*[2] were "not true but slander." Goncharov had to hear that he "did not understand or know the Russian people." *Crime and Punishment*[3] was called "rubbish," a "slur on the younger generation," a "stupid and shameful fabrication," and "a most pitiful piece." . . .

But things have gotten much worse. Our literature has been torn to pieces, our criticism has fallen apart; there exists a huge gap between the city and the village. Our urban intellectual knows the gentry only through books, and the peasants only through cabbies and janitors. . . . Our intellectuals do not know how to speak to the people but portray a tinsellike Russia, since they sit behind old books and write in a Russian that never existed and that is exaggerated, repulsive, tasteless, dishonest, and unreadable. . . . I have often thought: How will the history of this period be written? Wouldn't it be awful if . . . we resigned ourselves to these innovations . . . and that, after a few years, they were acknowledged as "classical" and became the subject matter for teachers of literature?

April 27, 1915
Sergei Rachmaninov, from a letter to Ivan Bunin
I love you very much, and I often recall our get-togethers of long ago. How sad that they cannot be repeated.

---

[2]Gogol wrote "The Inspector General" in 1836.
[3]Dostoevsky wrote *Crime and Punishment* in 1866.

June 28, 1915
Ivan Bunin, from a letter to Maxim Gorky

As you see, we are again in the village. . . . I am deeply struck by the absence of adolescents and middle-age people—everyone here is very young or very old.

July 1, 1915
Ivan Bunin, from his diary

The weather is wonderful. In general, the summer has been marvelous.

I should collect all the human cruelties from history.

August 7, 1915
Ivan Bunin, from his diary

A quiet, warm day. I try to sit down and write, but my heart and head are so quiet, empty, and dead. For a while there is complete despair. Is this really my end as a writer? I only feel like writing about Ceylon.

August 21, 1915
Ivan Bunin, from his diary

I have not written anything for two weeks. Time flies by so quickly that it is horrifying. . . . My soul is dull in general; this I do not like. I do not feel the poetry of the village, and it is very rare when I do.

Three or four boys up for military duty stroll around. They are going to their death, but their only amusement is to howl on the accordion. . . .

Yesterday they took Tikhon Ilyich into the army. "Nikolai Alexeevich should go into the army," he said. "After all, if they kill him, he has no children." There is an absolutely obtuse attitude toward death around here. He who does not value life is an animal. . . .

September 12, 1915
Ivan Bunin, from a letter to a friend

Thank you for Sologub's poetry. I will add it to my collection of other incredibly stupid things.

You keep telling me that there are no good topics for articles. Here's a marvelous one: "About Stupidity in Contemporary Russian

Literature!" I am absolutely serious. One could write and prove that stupidity has invaded a countless number of works in our literature . . . a stupidity that is weightless like air, hard to convey, and thus all the more dangerous.

September 15, 1915
Ivan Bunin, from his diary
I have never had such dullness and spiritual depression as I do now. . . .

The villages are so deserted that it is terrifying. . . . The war wearies me; it worries and torments me. . . . My "briefcase" is empty.

October 10, 1915
Ivan Bunin, from a letter to Maxim Gorky
I cannot recall a year like this one. I have never been so spiritually dark for so long.

✳ 1916 ✳

Circa *1916*
Ivan Bunin, from his story "Chang's Dreams"
Does it matter whom we discuss? Everyone who has lived on this earth deserves to be the subject of a story. . . .

At one time the Captain had two alternate truths . . . the first was that life is unutterably beautiful; the second, that life is meaningful only for the insane. . . . "It's terrifying to live in the world," the Captain said, ". . . especially for one such as I! For I very much yearn for happiness, and all too often I lose my way. . . . But how magnificent life is, my God, how magnificent!"

Circa *1916*
Ivan Bunin, from an early version of his story "Chang's Dreams"
The Captain . . . will sit for a very long time—till late at night. . . . until everyone gets drunk, and then he will utter many evil and bitter truths. "Ha!" he will say. "People! Look around and recall those you've seen in beer halls, in coffee houses! What animallike faces, what vile interests and tastes . . . ! Slavery, wars,

murders, executions; an almost prehistoric poverty of the downtrodden, the beaten, the disfranchised, of those who will be shot by the thousands for just one cry for an extra piece of bread; vulgar, absurd luxury. . . . the darkness of the city. . . standing on giant cesspools, amidst smoke and endless din. . . . I've been all over the world, my friend, and that's the way it is everywhere!"

Circa *1916*
Nikolai Pusheshnikov, from his memoirs
Bunin said, "The war has changed everything. Something has snapped in me; something in me has broken in two. . . ."

Circa *1916*
Vsevelod Rozhdestvensky, from his memoirs
I recall one argument in which Gorky hotly defended Ivan Bunin from accusations that he was a cold and impassive writer.
"Bunin is not a cold writer at all. He is like a taut string, his restraint gives witness to great internal strength. . . . Bunin is cruel and strong. . . . But he attains a merciless grace. What talent! What language! Perhaps the best writer in contemporary prose."

February 23, 1916
Ivan Bunin, from his diary
The diary is one of the most splendid of literary forms. I think this form will force out all others in the not so distant future.

March 7, 1916
Ivan Bunin, from a letter to a friend
We live in a truly contemptible time, from which there is no escape. . . . I am hellishly gloomy. I write but little, and when I do, it is not with my usual thoughts.

Circa *Mid-March 1916*
Nikolai Pusheshnikov, from his memoirs
Bunin said, "I am a writer, but what significance does my voice have? . . . Millions of people are being rushed to their slaughter; we can only become indignant, no more. . . ."

March 17, 1916
Ivan Bunin, from his diary
Today is father's nameday. He has been in the grave for ten

years—alone, forgotten, in a peasant cemetery, long trampled down by cattle. How unspeakably terrible is life! . . .

Pushkin . . . had a morally harmful . . . frivolous, and shameless stance toward life. Only Tolstoy was a teacher in everything.

March 21, 1916
Ivan Bunin, from his diary

All the newspapers put forth one and the same lie: They extol the prowess of the Russian people, their talent for organization. . . . "The people, the people!" The newspapers do not understand nor do they want to understand the people. And what have they done for the people, this truly unhappy people?

March 22, 1916
Ivan Bunin, from his diary

All these Russian intellectuals! How I hate them as a type! . . . These defenders of the people whom they do not understand and about whom they cannot say a single word.

And this idiotic division of the people into two parts. On one side there are plunderers, robbers . . . people without any honor or conscience; on the other the genuine folk, the peasants, the "pure, holy, chosen people, toilers and religious who have taken a vow of silence." . . .

All the stationmasters, telegraphists, and merchants who rob and plunder so shamelessly, who are they? Are they not also the people? Is the folk made up of peasants alone? No.

The people themselves create the government. Not for nothing do they keep flocking to autocracy. Apparently this is the best form of government for the Russian people; not for nothing has it lasted for three hundred years!

Then there are the newspapers! They have become hardened, inveterate liars to Russian society. All this is the doing of the Russian intelligentsia. . . . of their platitudes: "peaceful foundations," "collective beginnings," . . . "a Rus strong in its roots," and so forth. All these vile phrases! And . . . the absolutely erroneous idea that the Russian people are capable of organizing themselves. . . .

There is no other country like ours on the planet! Everyone for himself. If he is a writer, he knows nothing but his writing; he understands neither an ear nor a snout about anything else. If he is an actor, he is only interested in the stage. A landowner? . . . A big head and absolutely unable to do anything. . . . A potbellied policeman with oily eyes—this is "the ruling class."

March 24, 1916
Ivan Bunin, from his diary
    After lunch we went shooting for jackdaws. . . . A repulsive idea. We are still beasts.
    A red-haired kid looks out . . . gloomily indifferent. He intends to volunteer for the army. Why? An entire story in this! "What if you get killed?" "Who cares? It's all the same to me."

March 25, 1916
Ivan Bunin, from his diary
    My God! My God! Why have you abandoned Russia! . . .
    I reread Chekhov's *Uncle Vanya.* Generally speaking, it is a poor piece. The reader should spit on the tragedy of this uncle.

March 27, 1916
Ivan Bunin, from his diary
    How literature influences us! How many people now have two souls—their own and the other formed by books! Many live all their lives reading about life.

March 30, 1916
Ivan Bunin, from his diary
    I was on the porch of a peasant. . . . He himself does not want serfdom, but he says it was better to live "in a fortress": "When there was no bread, you went to the master's yard. . . . And took all you wanted!"

April 1916
Konstantin Paustovsky, from his memoirs
    My first time to Efremov was to visit a relative . . . a teacher. Like all teachers, she suffered angina and would treat herself with anything, including "Bunin's witch doctor method."
    "Which Bunin?" I asked her in surprise.
    "Evgeny Alexeevich. The brother of the writer. . . . He discovered a way to cure angina. He rubs your neck with sandpaper, and the angina goes away immediately. Only it didn't help me. Evgeny Bunin is a no-nonsense, rather unpleasant person. But they say his brother is a splendid individual. He comes here sometimes." . . .

Efremov suddenly took on a new light. Generally speaking, it was a rather dreary city. But now it seemed to personify provincial Russian comfort.

Almost all our provincial cities are alike. In Chekhov's words, they are all Efremovs—abandoned monasteries, earthy saints' faces over church stone gates, the resonant bells of the police chief's troika, the stockade on the commons, the *zemstvo* assembly hall . . . noisy jackdaws on cemetery busts, and deep ravines. In summer thick nettles stand like walls; in winter the snow is grey from ashes . . . and blue-grey smoke.

There, in Efremov, Bunin's Russia entered and took hold of me for a long time.

Elets was close by. I decided to see this Bunin town. . . . The train that took me there was called the "Maxim Gorky."

A cold dawn greeted me that morning. . . . One often feels like escaping this Russia without so much as a backward glance. But a mother loves the beggar woman even in her bitter distress. . . .

It was a grey, sublime day. It began to snow unexpectedly. The wind blew the snow from the roads and exposed the stone white slabs that had been worn down by horses.

The town was all in stone. It was like a fortress. One could feel it in the empty streets, the silence. I had heard that Elets was a noisy commercial town; I was surprised that the city was so quiet until I realized that this was because of the war. . . .

I stood for a long time near the boys' high school and its stone courtyard. Bunin had studied here. It was quiet inside; classes were going on behind the windows.

I then went to the market square; I was amazed by the wealth of smells. . . . dill, horse manure, old herring barrels, incense from an old church, in which a requiem was being sung. . . . and dead, fermented leaves. . . .

On the outskirts of the city . . . black smithies smoked and rang out blows on horseshoes. The sky was white. . . .

I entered the cemetery. Broken china roses and iron rusty leaves rattled and whistled. Here and there stood iron crosses with ornate flourishes and peeling oil paint, and brown photographs in metallic frames blurred by the rain.

I arrived at the station by evening. I have often been alone in my life, but rarely have I experienced such a bitter feeling of hopelessness as that night in Elets. . . .

April 1, 1916
Ivan Bunin, from his diary

A sick old man warms himself in the sun next to his hut. He sighs. He does not believe in our victory. "Where are we going?" he asks. . . .

And they want wisdom, patriotism, messianism from the people! Scoundrels, villains!

April 2, 1916
Ivan Bunin, from his diary

Sologub's feuilleton: "The Transformation of Life."[4] Life should be transformed: poets should be the ones to do it. And since Sologub considers himself a poet, he transforms when he writes. But he always writes about vileness, about nasty little boys, about lusting after them. Oh, these sons of bitches, these transformers of life.

April 8, 1916
Ivan Bunin, from his diary

There has never been anything like it in Russian literature. It used to be that all the journals would catch one mistake, one false note. Never before has the Russian public looked upon their fiction with such indifferent eyes. With absolute equality they praise Fra Beato and Angelico and [the poet] Gorodetsky.

April 14, 1916
Ivan Bunin, from an interview with the Exchange News

For the past year I have worked much less than before. Great events . . . keep turning over all our ideas on life. I am convinced that we will go to our graves with completely different emotions than we do now. . . .

Stories about the war that are written by people who have not visited the front, or who have not actively taken part in events, seem to me frivolous and not at all artistic.

I understand that one could become so saturated with terrible images that he would want to tell them all, but the result would be a cry from the soul and not an artistic piece. . . .

Stories from the home front also demand great care. In the very beginning of the war everyone . . . was excited. They were suddenly

---

[4]Bunin most likely means Sologub's piece "Transformation," written in 1904, or "The Resurrection of the Living," published in 1905.

awakened by a deafening explosion; they could hardly express their emotions accurately. . . . I dare say with certainty that the events which are occurring now will sober people up and change much in their lives for the better. . . .

I find it extremely unpleasant . . . to read for literary evenings. The public expects "lofty" words, declamations; all this is so alien to my character. It seems to me that when I read in public I cannot establish a tie between myself and the audience. I can read with pleasure for an intimate circle of friends, but I do not like to appear on stage. . . .

With great pleasure I recall the love and devotion that the Italians have for Gorky. He is always remembered both in the northern and southern parts of Italy with great enthusiasm.

April 26, 1916
Ivan Bunin, from an interview with the Odessa News

What new literary movements do we have now? . . . Since the beginning of the war everyone has taken up military themes. . . . Literature about the war is now in demand; but it is hackwork done by drones. . . .

The war oppresses me. You live from morning to morning, newspaper to newspaper. You wait for something to happen all the time. Something horrible has occurred like in the first page of the Bible, when the spirit of God hovered over the land, but the land was empty and desolate. . . .

Circa May 1916
Nikolai Pusheshnikov, from his memoirs

We arrived at a peasant hut. The air was warm and fetid. There were two pigs that were already quite big. A girl was sitting by the window in a woolen shawl. An old woman gave us a letter to read; it was from her son who had been captured by the Germans. Ivan Alexeevich said that one had to preserve this hut . . . for posterity, because a hundred years from now no one would be able to imagine how a Russian peasant lived in the twentieth century.

May 23, 1916
Ivan Bunin, from his diary

This is our Rus: The thirst for self-destruction, atavism.

August 29, 1916
Maxim Gorky, from a letter to Ivan Bunin

I so want to see you. . . . But my impressions are repulsive, and my thoughts are sad. I do not like to complain, but for a while now I find it so burdensome to live that I even feel unwell physically, as if I have been poisoned.

What will happen to us, to Russia?

I'm ready to roar like a bear.

October 27, 1916
Ivan Bunin, from his diary

The spiritual and mental dullness, the languor, the literary sterility continues. I have long been a great martyr. . . a man who has gone crazy from impotence. I am mortally tired. This, too, has been going for quite some time; but I do not give up. The war has played a great role; what great spiritual disenchantment it has brought me! . . .

I continue to read Sologub's *The Petty Demon*.[5] . . . *I do not recall* a more boring, monotonous book. . . . And he once was a talented poet.

[5]Sologub wrote *The Petty Demon* in 1907.

PART SIX

In the Eye of the Hurricane
1917–1918

BUNIN, 1917

In November 1917 Russia moved from "imperial" to "soviet," an event that would haunt the world for almost seventy-five years. From the very beginning Russia's dream of a brave new world was a nightmare. Revolution and civil war; the intervention of foreign powers, including the United States; and the contraction of the Russian Empire to a Bolshevik island roughly the size of medieval Muscovy—these were the elements of a national inferno that forged the iron of the new Soviet state.

It is one of the key ironies in modern Russian history that the intelligentsia, the staunchest proponents of reform, paid the highest price in the Revolution. It was as if the folk took revenge for a century of promises that were easily made but never kept. To Trotsky the intelligentsia were the chaff for history's "iron broom"; whatever, they quickly found their niche: the bottom. For many Russian intellectuals, rights and privileges were out, rebuke and suspicion were in. As "enemies of the people" they spent their days not in cerebral or cultural pursuits but merely surviving, in a daily search for food, fuel, and clothing. Everything the intelligentsia had cherished in life was being disparaged or destroyed. Refinement and sophistication, liberalism and compromise, gentleness and compassion, beauty and nobility— these values were suddenly declared antiquated and useless in the first years of bolshevism.

Not surprisingly, many intellectuals joined the "Whites," counterrevolutionaries made up of former tsarist officials, army officers, nobles, liberals, and socialists of all kinds. They also welcomed the interventionists, for example the Germans who established a puppet government in the Ukraine and the French who seized control of Odessa. Both groups, they hoped, would restore the law and order of the *ancien regime*, and in it, of course, the role of the intelligentsia.

Among the Russian intellectuals, writers suffered most. The revolution and civil war had thinned the ranks of literary and artistic groups. Many newspapers and magazines were banned or ceased publication; printing presses were confiscated as state property. Some publishers led a precarious existence, surviving by their wits; others closed their doors forever.

Russian writers saw that was happening in their homeland did not correspond to the prophesies of the Modernist mystics who promised a new world order headed by Christ, Sophia, or the Holy Spirit. Instead they saw a Russia in agony and a life filled with sickness, terror, and death. They were utterly unable to cope with the situation. Many older writers (Realist as well as Modernist) fell silent in the first years after 1917. Those who did not used their literary talents either to attack the communists or to celebrate a requiem for their land. A large number of them sided with the Whites and eventually settled abroad.

Only a few writers, such as the Symbolist Bryusov, joined the new regime early on. Quickly, however, the younger literary generation realized that its time had come and that the energy of its creative endeavors had spilled out into life. The writers who accepted 1917 relished the fact that they were living life on the edge and that existence was at once cruel and heroic, fantastic and thrilling, destructive and untamed. They initiated a new chapter in the history of Russian literature. The Symbolists were the first to join the Revolution. Bely in "Christ Is Risen" and Blok in "The Twelve" and "The Scythians" (all written in 1918) proclaimed Russia as the savior of humanity and its citizens as the builders of a new society. Such poems ushered the "cabaret" period into Soviet fiction. The scarcity of paper, ink, and printing facilities compelled writers to address their audiences directly, in halls and taverns, nightclubs and cafés. The Symbolists shared these environs with (and eventually ceded them to) the Futurists. Their leader, Mayakovsky, was up to the challenge, demanding, first, that Pushkin face the firing squad along with the Whites. The Futurists placed themselves at the service of the communist regime but demanded a privileged position in Soviet arts and letters. As they saw it, they were the vanguard of communist culture, the exclusive interpreters of the revolutionary spirit. For the next decade they were firmly entrenched in literature, theater, and the graphic arts.

The Bolsheviks, however, had other, more utilitarian plans for literature. Specifically they wished to promote fiction as a tool for mass education and revolutionary ideology. To this end they founded the Proletkult (Proletarian Cultural and Educational Organization) to awaken the talents of the people. Young workers and artisans (only men and women of proletarian origins were admitted) met in "worker's clubs" throughout Russia. They were instructed by established writers (for example, Gorky, Blok, and Bryusov) and encouraged to write poems, stories, and plays. The Proletkult was a failure (it disappeared in 1932), but in the early years of the Revolution it vied with the Symbolists and Futurists for cultural leadership in the new Soviet world.

For Bunin the years immediately following the Revolution were *déjà vu*. He had, after all, been predicting catastrophe all along. Yet even he was unprepared for the events of 1917 and its aftermath, and his response was typical of his generation and class: anger, shock, and despair; the feeling that he was in a hell from which there was no escape; and, most painful, the inability or unwillingness to articulate in print all that was going on in his soul. Revolution was Bunin's nemesis, but he could do little other than count his blessings and lament his losses.

The losses were considerable. He had fled his native village in October 1917, Moscow (and Soviet rule) seven months later. Sensing he would never see these places again, he summoned Memory to freeze the "moment" when he walked a final time through the graves of his ancestors or the churches of the Kremlin. Bunin also gazed in horror at "Scythians" and "Tartars" destroying his land: Lenin and his party politically; Blok, Mayakovsky, and other "cabaret" writers culturally; the folk nationally. The folk disturbed him most, for they were now exhibiting what he had always known existed inside them; they were chaotic, atavistic, deranged. They also loved a good show. It seemed Bunin's particular lot in the years 1918 and 1919 to preside at "spectacles" that buried the old or hailed the new. If he was not witness to processions of sobbing citizens singing Orthodox hymns, carrying icons and candles, and begging God for their rescue, he was party to parades of joyous revolutionaries, shouting the "Marseillaise," carrying weapons and banners, and praising the party for their redemption.

Bunin fought desperately to check modernity, to uphold the

old ways, and to maintain a semblance of order and stability in
his life. He upheld the gentry image by dressing tastefully and
maintaining elegant surroundings. Gradually he retreated from
day-to-day happenings and gained a sobering perspective on events.
The Revolution, he came to see, was not the single greatest
catastrophe in history; it was merely the latest episode in the
history of human perfidy, yet another variation on the theme of
humankind's abandoning God and setting idols in His place. In
this sense, Adam Sokolovich, the hero of Bunin's story "Nooselike
Ears," assumes particular importance. Upon first glance Sokolovich
is a "wanderer," a sailor. Close inspection, however, reveals that he
is also akin to a modern-day *raisonneur*, the character from French
classical drama who tells the moral of the tale. Unlike other
raisonneurs, however, Sokolovich does not instruct his listeners in
civic and moral duties; rather, he tells them only of the enduring
evil in the world. He is as good as his word. Amidst the
terrifying gloom of Saint Petersburg, he kills a prostitute without
remorse. Like Dostoevsky's Raskolnikov, he commits a crime
against God and humanity; but unlike the earlier hero he suffers
no punishment for his wrongdoing. He is the "extraordinary
man," the Napoleon that Raskolnikov wanted so desperately to be.

Bunin was one of the few writers in these years who could
transcend the fury of life and discern the inner voices of existence,
the immutable laws of life. He looked within to find happiness
and peace. His ability to feel, to remember, to hope against hope,
and to wait for happiness was for him sufficient proof that life was
worth living, that people were good, that he still was in control,
and, most important, that his name would survive not only in this
life but in the memory of poets and readers.

✳ 1917 ✳

January 1917
Ivan Bunin, from a critical article

The artist must proceed not from the surface phenomena of existence but from the depths, the soil of life. He must listen not to the noise of party affiliations and quarrels but to the inner voices of living life that tell him of the strata of existence . . . and that have come into being despite all desire, and according to the immutable laws of life itself.

February 1917
Maxim Gorky, from a letter to Ivan Bunin

Last night I dreamed I was a magician. I was standing on the stage of a splendid theatre, in front of a splendid audience, and in white tights. I was assuring the spectators:

"Ladies and gentlemen! You see that I'm not wearing coat-tails. . . ."

"We see that," the public roared.

"And I have nowhere to hide things. . . ."

"Nowhere," the public yelled.

I waved my wand, and a lion suddenly appeared on stage! Alive and roaring!

Everyone became frightened. Me, too. I waved my wand again—and the lion became a samovar! It boiled and even whistled—oo-oo-oo!

I laughed with delight and woke up.

What does my dream mean? Please don't say anything to Leonid Andreev, or else he'll give me a scolding!

February 23, 1917
Maxim Gorky, from a letter to Ivan Bunin

I have been informed that you are interested in our undertaking—a series of biographies for children, and that you would be willing to write a life of Cervantes.

If only you would do it!

People have agreed to do biographies of Columbus, Beethoven, Socrates, Joan of Arc, and Edison.

We need Darwin, Francis of Assisi . . . Garibaldi, and a whole list of others.

May 27, 1917
Ivan Bunin, from a letter to a friend

It is now repulsive to live in the village. The peasants are complete children and supremely loathsome to boot. We have full-blown "anarchy" in our region: wilfulness and confusion. . . .

Our intelligentsia is a repulsive tribe. They have . . . lied through their hats about a people whom they do not know. How they'll now pay attention to *The Village* and works like it.

It is not safe to live here now. Three nights ago our barn caught fire. . . .

Our neighbor's barn . . . also went up in flames right in the middle of the day. It turns out that the culprit was a peasant . . . but the peasants arrested the owner of the barn instead. "He himself set his property on fire," they said. They beat him unmercifully and brought him in a cart to the town hall.

I tried to reason with them, to prove to them that it was absurd for the owner to burn his own building . . . but they yelled at me and said I was for the "old regime." An old lady kept crying that we were sons of bitches, and that we should be thrown into the fire. . . .

June 11, 1917
Ivan Bunin, from his diary

There is "revolutionary order" at the station. . . . A military inspection unit . . . asks me my age, if I am a deserter. A feeling of terrible indignation. There are no laws. Everyone has power except us, of course. In "free" Russia only soldiers, peasants, and workers have a voice. Why are there no soviets for the gentry or the intelligentsia?

July 1917
Ivan Bunin, from his story "Nooselike Ears"

On that dark and cold day an unusually tall man appeared at various spots along Nevsky Prospect. He said that his name was Adam Sokolovich, and that he had formerly been a sailor. . . . With an expression that was strangely serious, he gazed at the statue of Alexander III,[1] at the row of streetcars that had formed a circle in the square, at the dark figures of people, at the cab drivers and horses moving toward the station, at the huge mail car that had come from under the station's arch, and at a hearse, which carried . . . a lone, shabby, bright yellow coffin. Standing on Anichkov Bridge he looked gloomily at the dark water and at the barges that had turned grey from the dirty snow. Wandering along Nevsky he attentively studied the goods in the store windows. One could not help but notice and remember him, and anyone who fell his way felt a vague unpleasantness, a kind of anxiety, and turned away thinking:

"What a terrible man!" . . .

Sokolovich . . . spoke slowly, in a muffled voice, addressing no one in particular:

"Why do people collect all sorts of nonsense and not copies of advertisements, that is, those historical documents that show precisely what people live by. . . . After all, aren't dandies really the ones who express the hopes of 90 percent of all humankind?"

"You're the son of a Polak," one of the sailors said hostilely.

"I'm a son of the human race," Sokolovich said with a strange solemnity that could have bordered on irony. "I may be Polish, but it hasn't kept me from seeing the world and all its gods. . . . But my taste for things has become dull. I'm a so-called degenerate. Understand?" . . .

"But how can I recognize a so-called degenerate if he's healthy as a boar?" a sailor asked mockingly.

"By the ears, for example," answered Sokolovich, half serious, half joking. "Degenerates, geniuses, tramps, and murderers have ears . . . that look like a noose—the very thing that strangles them. . . . I suspect though . . . that such ears do not belong to so-called degenerates alone. As you know, the wish to kill . . . the relish for all types of cruelty, is in everyone's soul . . . the reason being atavism or a hatred for humankind that has secretly grown within them. Such

---

[1]Alexander III was tsar of Russia from 1881 to 1894.

people feel nothing when they kill. . . . Not only are they not tormented, as people would like to think, but, just the opposite, they return to normal and feel a sense of relief. . . .

It is high time to abandon this fairy tale about the pangs of conscience, the horrors that murderers reportedly experience. People have lied enough, lying about how they supposedly shudder at the sight of blood. Enough of novels about crime and punishment; it's time to write about crime without any punishment at all. . . . Do those who accept brotherly revenge, duels, war, revolution, and executions really feel so tormented and horrified?" . . .

"I've read Dostoevsky's *Crime and Punishment*," a sailor remarked pretentiously.

"Really?" Sokolovich said, looking at him with a heavy air, "And have you also read about Deibler the executioner?[2] He recently died at his villa near Paris at the age of eighty, after a lifetime of having chopped off exactly five hundred heads by order of his highly civilized government. Criminal records are full of jottings about the cruelest poise, about the cynicism and moral postulating of the bloodiest criminals. But this concerns not only degenerates, hangmen, or convicts. All the books of human civilization—all those myths, sagas, folk epics, histories, dramas, novels—they all contain the very same jottings, and who shudders? Every little boy is thrilled by Cooper, where all they do is take scalps; every high school student learns that the Assyrian rulers covered the walls of their cities with the skins of their prisoners; every pastor knows that in the Bible the word 'killed' is used more than a thousand times and, for the most part, with the greatest boasting and gratitude to the Creator for what they have done."

"That's why it's called the Old Testament; it's ancient history," objected the sailor.

---

[2]Louis Anatole Stanislas Deibler (1823–1903) came from a family of executioners; he was appointed official executioner for France and Algeria in 1879, a post he held until 1898, when he abdicated in favor of his son, Anatole.

Bunin was wrong about several facts of Deibler's life. For instance, Deibler executed more than one thousand criminals, not five hundred. Moreover, he had such a pathological aversion to blood that he wore a shield during executions. Finally, Deibler was deeply troubled by his job. He is said to have wandered about like Lady Macbeth, rubbing his hands and seeking reassurances from family and friends that he was free of blood. Deibler also had nightmares in which he saw the guillotine infinitely duplicated and stretching toward the horizon. For more on Deibler, see Barbara Levy, *Legacy of Death* (Englewood Cliffs, N.J., 1973), and Alister Kershaw, *A History of the Guillotine* (London, 1958).

"And the New Testament is such," Sokolovich said, "that a gorilla's hair would rise straight up if the gorilla knew how to read." . . . "No," Sokolovich said, knitting his brow and looking askance. . . . "Gorillas have yet to have Assyrian rulers, or Caesars, or inquisitions, or the discovery of America, or kings who sign death warrants with cigars in their mouths, or inventors of submarines that immediately send several thousand men to the bottom of the sea, or Robespierres, or Jack the Rippers. . . .

"What do you think . . . ?" Sokolovich asked, once again fixing his stern gaze on the sailors: "Did all those gentlemen suffer the torments of Cain or Raskolnikov?[3] Did all the assassins of tyrants and oppressors—figures whose names appear in golden letters in the so-called annals of history—were they tormented by what they did? Are you tormented when you read that the Turks have murdered another hundred thousand Armenians, that the Germans are poisoning wells with plague-inducing microbes, that the trenches are filled with rotting corpses, that army aviators are dropping bombs on Nazareth? Is some Paris or London bothered by the fact that it has been built on human bones or that it has flourished on the most vicious but everyday cruelty toward one's so-called fellow man? To tell the truth, only Raskolnikov was tormented, and even then only because he was thin-blooded, and by virtue of the fact that his vicious creator shoved Christ into all his cheap novels." . . .

Sokolovich was silent for a moment; then, having spat between his knees, he added calmly, "Tens of millions of people are now taking part in wars. Soon all of Europe will be an entire kingdom of murderers. But we all know perfectly well that this world won't be bothered a bit by it. . . . But I'd like to know who would want to . . . travel through Europe in a year or two, once this war is over." . . .

Sokolovich remarked with gloomy pensiveness, "Generally speaking, people are much more prone to murder a woman than a man. Our sensory perceptions are never so aroused by the body of a man as they are by the body of a woman, that base creature who gives birth to us all and who is truly sensual only when she surrenders to males of the species who are coarse and strong." . . .

Nevsky Prospect is terrifying in the fog of night. Desolate, dead, the mist that envelops it seems to be part of the very arctic

[3]Raskolnikov is the hero of *Crime and Punishment*.

gloom that comes from the end of the world, from that something called the North Pole, a place beyond human comprehension. The center of this misty stream is still illumined from above by the whitish glow of electric globes. But on the sidewalks, alongside the black store windows and the locked gates, it is darker. . . . Women wander along at a leisurely pace, their cheap finery at odds with their surroundings . . . Chilled to the bone by the icy dampness . . . their faces express such emptiness that you find it horrifying, as if you have stumbled across a creature of some unknown species. . . .

Sokolovich . . . latched onto one of these women . . . one Korolkova. . . . Her hat . . . was made of black velvet and decorated with a cluster of glass cherries. Her small, wide-cheekboned face and her black, deeply sunken, beady eyes made her look like a bat. . . . One hand held up her skirt; the other, hidden in a large flat muff made of shiny black fur, covered her mouth. She had suddenly blocked the way for the round-shouldered, shuffling Sokolovich. He gave her a sharp look . . . and shouted for a night cab in his hollow voice. . . . The couple rolled away, first along Nevsky, then through the square, past the lighted clock on Nikolaevsky Station, which was now dark, having sent all its trains into the depths of snowy Russia, past the horrible huge horse that eternally bows its large head, in sleet or in fog, begging its portly rider for free rein[4] . . . through foggy streets and alleyways, and into the mysterious wastelands of the capital's night outskirts. . . .

It was still completely dark and quiet, but one could sense . . . that morning was close . . . the muffled, far-off moan of mills and factories, summoning the countless working masses from all their beggarly haunts, from all their hovels and lairs. . . . A streetlight lit up part of the sidewalk and street. The fog had dissipated, a light snow was falling in the night . . . a mass of lumber planks looked funereally white against the blackness of night. Sokolovich turned to the right and vanished in the distance. . . .

The night watchman suddenly noticed that the door of Number 8 was open and that the light was on. He jumped up and rushed to the room; inside it was strangely quiet . . . sputtering candles crackled in split rosettes, shadows darted in the darkness, and on the bed, protruding from under a blanket, were the short bare legs of a woman. . . . Her head was weighed down by two pillows.

[4]A reference to the famous statue of the "Bronze Horseman" in Saint Petersburg—Peter the Great astride a rebellious horse.

July 27, 1917
Ivan Bunin, from his diary

The village home where I am spending the summer is a century and a half old. I always find it pleasant to recall and feel its ancientness. The old, simple life to which I am tied gives me peace. It gives me rest amidst my continual wanderings.

I think about all the people who were once here . . . people who were born here, grew up here, loved here, married here, became old here, and died here . . . special people of antiquity, of the past. They are completely unknown to me. They are only vague images, only the stuff of my imagination; but they are always with me, close and dear to me, exciting me with the charm of the past.

August 3, 1917
Ivan Bunin, from his diary

I keep on reading Maupassant. He is superb in places. He is the only one who has dared to say repeatedly that women control life.

August 4, 1917
Ivan Bunin, from his diary

If a person does not lose his capacity to wait for happiness—then he is happy. For happiness exists!

August 10, 1917
Ivan Bunin, from a letter to Maxim Gorky

I live poorly. I receive about a thousand newspapers a day; I read them all day long. . . . From what I read and from what I see all around me, I know that . . . everything I have long thought about holy Russia is being affirmed and coming true.

August 11, 1917
Ivan Bunin, from his diary

I've tried to write something for about ten days now, but I just couldn't do it. I find writing so burdensome these days.

August 13, 1917
Ivan Bunin, from his diary

It seems that Kerensky is one of the most harmful figures around. He first goes to the right, then to the left. And he is regarded as a hero.

August 20, 1917
Ivan Bunin, from his diary
How do I live? I keep remembering and remembering. . . .

August 22, 1917
Ivan Bunin, from his diary
"Learning is remembering"—Socrates. . . .
No, people have much that is splendid in them!

August 23, 1917
Ivan Bunin, from his diary
I am reading Gippius's poetry. She's not that bright, and she's completely off her rocker; but she's more decent and intelligent than other so-called "new" poets. But all her thoughts and feelings are dead. . . .

August 25, 1917
Ivan Bunin, from his diary
I have finished reading Gippius. She is such an unusually repulsive soul, not a single living word or clear thought in her vapid verse. Gippius does not have an iota of poetic talent.

September 16, 1917
Ivan Bunin, from his diary
I am finishing up *Anna Karenina*.[5] The last part is weak, even somewhat unpleasant, and unconvincing. I recall that I thought as much earlier.

September 17, 1917
Ivan Bunin, from his diary
I have finished *Anna Karenina*. The ending is splendidly written. Perhaps I was wrong about this part. Perhaps it is especially good because it is so simple?

October 6, 1917
Ivan Bunin, from his diary
I have become dull, without talent. How do I live? Why do I live? What garbage!

[5]Tolstoy wrote *Anna Karenina* in 1875–1877.

October 8, 1917
Ivan Bunin, from his diary

I have been thinking about *The Village.* How true it all is. . . . I have been reading [Dostoevsky's] *The Village of Stepanchikovo.*[6] . . . It's a monstrous thing! There's nothing at all in the first thirty pages, everybody keeps saying the same thing! Sheer chatter, pulp fiction! . . .

October 13, 1917
Ivan Bunin, from his diary

I am reading Merezhkovsky's *Leonardo da Vinci.*[7] . . . The conversations in it are terrible. Long, deadly, and bookish. It's all right in spots, but why do I think that Merezhkovsky stole it from somewhere? What Merezhkovsky says about the character Leonardo is intolerably boring and repulsively sentimental. . . . Also intolerable is the way he keeps harping on his idea of Christ and Antichrist. . . .

The Russian people call upon God only when they are greatly aggrieved. Now they are happy—so where is their religiosity?

October 16, 1917
Ivan Bunin, from a letter to a friend

To Odessa for the winter? Can you be serious? Where will we live, what will we eat? (I do not know where we will live and what we will eat now—a *tragic* situation!)

It is unbearable and very terrifying in the village.

October 17, 1917
Ivan Bunin, from his diary

I have finished reading Leskov's "To the Edge of the World."[8] It is terribly long and verbose, but the main point of the story is very good! Leskov is a powerful, original individual!

October 20, 1917
Ivan Bunin, from his diary

My soul has become completely empty and dull. There is nothing to say; I have written nothing—my craft is even pitiful, dead. . . .

[6]Dostoevsky wrote *The Village of Stepanchikovo* in 1859.
[7]Merezhkovsky published *Leonardo da Vinci, or the Gods Reborn* in 1901.
[8]Leskov wrote "To the Edge of the World" in 1875.

Two peasants: one is red-haired, with a potatolike nose, softly radiant—a professor type. The other comes from the sixteenth century. A real Boris Godunov[9] with a large nose and lips, flared nostrils, an almost severely coarse profile, and coarse black hair streaked with silver. Even people of ancient times did not look like this. . . . The way they talked, it is clear they understand the new order only vaguely. But where would they find out about it? They have lived all their lives in a backwater. How can the people rule when they do not know their government, how it works, the Russian land, but only their little plots?

Our people do everything in excess. They chop down all the orchards. . . . They gorge themselves when they eat and drink. . . . They cannot bear authority or constraints. . . .

October 21, 1917
Ivan Bunin, from his diary

I am reading excerpts from Nietzsche—how Andreev, Balmont, and others stole from him!

October 23, 1917
Vera Muromtseva-Bunina, from her diary

Flight in a foggy dawn. We are captives. For the last time we look at Glotovo, Ozerka. . . .

A mad journey. The wheels gave out; we had to walk seven miles . . . to Elets. There is not a single room in any hotel.

October 23, 1917
Nikolai Pusheshnikov, from his diary

At four o'clock in the morning, we . . . set out in a complete and frosty darkness. The village was still asleep. There was nobody or nothing around, not even a single light. . . . The road was dark and slick. After we got past Ozerka, we set out on a large road. Soldiers began to appear and looked at us suspiciously. When we approached the village of Stansovo we came upon some peasant women, young

---

[9]Boris Godunov, of Mongol extraction, was tsar of Russia from 1598 to 1605. His troubled reign was the first phase of the so-called Time of Troubles (1598–1613), a period of political and social chaos in Russia. Traditionally Boris has been seen as a usurper of the throne and specifically as the murderer of Prince Dmitri, brother of Ivan the Terrible and the only remaining male member of the ruling family. Historians, though, have long discounted this view.

and old . . . about twenty in all. . . . They began screaming and hiss-
ing at us:

"Who are you? You aren't one of us!" they said, laughing at Ivan
Alexeevich who was sitting in a sheepskin coat and a hat with
earmuffs. They crowded around us . . . and wouldn't let us pass. Ivan
Alexeevich went wild. The horses stopped.

"We should get the soldiers," said a snub-nosed woman.

"Get out of our way!" Ivan Alexeevich replied and pulled out
his Browning. "You'd better listen. . . . or else I'll shoot you all!"

The women were stunned. But the snub-nosed one said, "He
wants to shoot us. Mashka, go get help. . . ."

"I'm not putting up with this rot," Ivan Alexeevich said to me.
He grabbed the reins, took out his whip, and beat the horses with all
his might. The horses took off. The women got out of the way. . . .

November 4, 1917
Ivan Bunin, from his diary
I could not write yesterday, for it was one of the most horrible
days of my entire life. . . . Young soldiers rushed into the vestibule
where we were living and demanded weapons from us.

November 21, 1917
Ivan Bunin, from his diary
I am sitting alone and am slightly tipsy. The wine has brought
back my daring, the sweet, murky dream of life, feelings, the
sensation of smells and the like—it is not so simple, for these
emotions are the essence of earthly existence.

Late November 1917
Vera Muromtseva-Bunina, from her diary
The beginning of the Bolshevik revolt. Ian will not call Gorky.

December 28, 1917
Ivan Bunin, from a letter to a friend
I am afraid I cannot give you anything for your alamanac. . . . I
have written nothing summer or fall. My whole head has gone grey
from freedom, equality, and brotherhood.

✳ 1918 ✳

January 14, 1918
Ivan Bunin, from his diary The Cursed Days

This damn year is over. But what will be next? Perhaps it will get worse. And that seems likely.

But, remarkably, almost everyone is unusually happy; no matter whom you meet on the street, you see a radiant face.

"Enough sadness, old sir... in two or three weeks you'll be ashamed of how you're feeling...."...

An old lady stops, her shaking hands leaning on a crutch. She bursts out crying: "Sir, tell me what's going on? Where are we headed? They say that Russia... has vanished!"

February 18, 1918
Ivan Bunin, from his diary The Cursed Days

At a meeting yesterday.... Mayakovsky... acted like a lout, strutting about and shooting off his mouth. He was wearing a shirt without a tie. The collar of his jacket was raised up for some reason, just like those poorly shaven people who... use the latrines in the mornings.

February 21, 1918
Ivan Bunin, from his diary The Cursed Days

Andrei, brother Yuly's servant, is acting more and more insane. It is horrifying to watch.

Andrei... has always been simple, kind, reasonable, polite, and devoted. Now he has gone completely crazy. He still does his job carefully, but... he does not look at us and shies away from our conversations. His whole body shakes from anger; when he can keep silent no longer, he lets loose with wild nonsense.

For instance, this morning at Yuly's a friend said... that everything has perished, and that Russia was flying into an abyss. Andrei was setting the table for tea.... He suddenly began waving his arms, his face aflame:

"Yes, Russia's flying into an abyss, all right! But, who's to

blame, who? The bourgeoisie! You'll see how they'll be cut to pieces!
Just you wait!..."

Yuly asked, "Andrei... why do you hate us?"

Not looking at us, he whispered, "I have nothing to say.... You
yourselves can understand."

February 23, 1918
Ivan Bunin, from his diary The Cursed Days

"Dishonest ones live among My people.... They move close to
the ground and set traps for my flock. But My people love this.
Listen, O Earth: I will bring the people to their destruction, the fruit
of their thoughts."

This is from Jeremiah. I have been reading the Bible all
morning. It is amazing. Especially the words: "But My people love
this...I will bring the people to their destruction, *the fruit of their
thoughts*."...

"The time is not yet right to understand the Russian Revolution
impartially, objectively...." This you hear every minute. Impartially!
There will never be any genuine impartiality.... But our "partiality"
will be very, very valuable for the future historian. Are the "passions"
of "revolutionaries" the only important ones? Are we not also the
people?

February 27, 1918
Ivan Bunin, from his diary The Cursed Days

Everyone is certain the Germans have begun to occupy Russia.
People keep saying, "The Germans are coming; they will bring
order."...

A cabby... says laughingly, "Let the Germans come. So what?
They've ruled us before.... We're a dark people. Tell one 'get
moving' and the rest follow."

February 28, 1918
Ivan Bunin, from his diary The Cursed Days

High school students are being called up for the Red Guard, "to
fight Hindenburg."... I see them going about covered with snow—
all beauty and joy. One of the girls is especially beautiful, with
charming blue eyes that peek out from under a raised fur collar....
What lies ahead for these youth?

March 5, 1918
Ivan Bunin, from his diary The Cursed Days

In the bluish distance are . . . the gold domes of churches. Oh, Moscow! . . . Is this really the end?

Soldiers . . . carry all kinds of weapons. One has a saber; another, a rifle: still another, a huge revolver in his belt. . . . These are now the masters, the inheritors of a colossal legacy. . . .

A friend says . . . they will blow up the Kremlin if the Germans come.

I see the astonishingly green sky over the Kremlin, the ancient gold of the cupolas. . . . The Great Princes . . . Archangel Cathedral—all so native and intimate; only now do I feel and understand them as I should! Blow it up? . . . Anything is possible now.

March 7, 1918
Ivan Bunin, from his diary The Cursed Days

This morning, a sad job: We are going through our books, deciding which to keep, and which to sell (I am getting money together for our departure). . . .

It is terrifying to drive about. The streets are without lights, gravelike and dark. . . . There are few passersby; everyone goes off at a trot.

It's like the Middle Ages! At least then, everyone was armed, and homes were almost impregnable. . . .

March 9, 1918
Ivan Bunin, from his diary The Cursed Days

The other day I bought a pound of tobacco; I hung it on a rope so that it would not dry out. . . . Today about six, something went flying through the glass. . . . I found a rock on the floor. The glass was broken; the tobacco was gone; and someone was running away from the window. Robbers everywhere! . . .

A prayer service is going on in the house across from us. People have brought icons . . . priests are singing. All this seems very strange now. And very touching. Many people are crying.

March 10, 1918
Ivan Bunin, from his diary The Cursed Days

Again street demonstrations, banners, posters, music, and a company singing out of tune: "Stand up, rise up, working people!"

The voices are hollow, primitive. . . . All of the men have criminal faces; some look like they're straight out of jail. . . .

The Romans used to brand the faces of their prisoners with the words: "Cave furem."[1] These Russian faces need nothing; they show it all without any branding.

The Marseillaise, the national hymn of the French, they have changed in the most vulgar way!

March 12, 1918
Ivan Bunin, from his diary The Cursed Days

Another holiday: the anniversary of the revolution. But there are no people on the streets, and not because there are winter and storms. Everybody is just tired of it all.

What savage, horrible nonsense: The phone keeps ringing all day long, pouring out burning news. . . .

An article by Lenin. What a trivial, dishonest piece—first the international, then the "Russian national surge."

March 14, 1918
Ivan Bunin, from his diary The Cursed Days

A friend has news from Rostov: the Kornilov[2] movement is weak. Another friend protests that, just the opposite, it is strong and growing. The former adds, "The Bolsheviks are committing horrible atrocities in Rostov." . . . Still another friend says the Germans will take Moscow on the 17th of March. . . .

A cook told me . . . "A landowner sent his peasants a telegram telling them to burn the house, kill the cattle, and cut down the forests. He also told them to leave one birch tree standing so that he would have rods to beat them as well as something to hang them on."

March 15, 1918
Ivan Bunin, from his diary The Cursed Days

It seems that the new literary decline . . . cannot go any lower. "A Musical Snuffbox" has opened in a most vile tavern. Speculators, cardsharps, and prostitutes sit, gobble up meat pies . . . drink vodka from teacups, while poets and writers (Alyoshka Tolstoy, Bryusov, and

---

[1]That is, "Beware the Madman."
[2]Lavr Georgievich Kornilov (1870–1918) was commander of the anti-Bolshevik Volunteer army in the Don region.

others) read their own pieces and those of others, choosing the most vile ones. Bryusov, they say, has read Pushkin's "Gavriliada,"[3] filling in the blanks with words. Alyoshka had the nerve to suggest that I read there—we'll give you a big fee, he said. . . .

I read in a newspaper about corpses at the bottom of the sea: murdered, drowned officers. And then they go put on "A Musical Snuffbox."

March 22, 1918
Ivan Bunin, from his diary The Cursed Days
I find the following absolutely repugnant to hear or read: "Russia was destroyed by a sluggish, self-interested power that did not heed the wishes of the people, their hopes, their dreams. . . . The revolution was inevitable."

My answer to this: "The people did not start the revolution. . . . The people spat on everything we wanted, on all we were dissatisfied with. . . . They threw away everything that generations of the best Russians had died for. . . ."

March 23, 1918
Ivan Bunin, from his diary The Cursed Days
Tolstoy once said about himself, "All my troubles come from the fact that I have an imagination that is a little more active than others. . . ."

All my troubles, too. . . .

I have to leave. I cannot physically endure this life. . . .

How spiteful, how uncooperative the doorman has become! Everyone, absolutely everyone has an absolutely hateful attitude to any kind of work.

March 24, 1918
Ivan Bunin, from his diary The Cursed Days
A friend said, "I avoid going out as much as possible. Not because I fear someone will mug me, but because I simply cannot look at the people out there."

I understand him as never before. I feel the same thing, perhaps even more sharply than he.

---

[3]The "Gavriliada," a parody of the Virgin Mary's Immaculate Conception, was written by Pushkin in 1821.

March 28, 1918
Ivan Bunin, from his diary The Cursed Days
Always the same freezing weather. There is no heat anywhere; the cold in the apartments is terrible. . . .

"The Commissar for Publications" has shut down a newspaper for "inciting panic and anxiety among the people." Such concern for a people who are being robbed and murdered every minute!

April 4, 1918
Ivan Bunin, from his diary The Cursed Days
This past year will cut no less than ten years from my life!

April 5, 1918
Ivan Bunin, from his diary The Cursed Days
Asia, Asia—soldiers, boys, people selling gingerbread, halvah . . . cigarettes. Eastern cries and speech . . . all those loathsome faces, their yellow and mouselike hair. . . . Soldiers and workers on thundering trucks with triumphant mugs. . . .

April 6, 1918
Ivan Bunin, from his diary The Cursed Days
People say that the ruble will be worth absolutely nothing; that flour will cost a thousand rubles a pound; and that people should stock up. We say we can do nothing; we'll buy two pounds and stay calm. . . .

The end of old Moscow forever. . . .

I bought a book about the Bolsheviks. . . . A real gallery of convicts. Lunacharsky has a neck more than a foot long.

May 19, 1918
Ivan Bunin, from his diary
I tried to find out about passports to go abroad. But the office was closed. . . . At first I behaved formally . . . to hide my distress. Then I conducted myself more simply. I began to smile and to speak more bravely. I promised them all kinds of help. I thought I might go to Japan or . . . through Finland or Germany.

May 23, 1918
Vera Muromtseva-Bunina, from her diary
The 1st of May new style fell on Holy Wednesday. The

Bolsheviks spent a lot of money on their holiday. . . . The usual red, the processions, music, and the singing of the "International." Men and women workers danced about and . . . yelled "Forward, forward, forward!" Moscow, long accustomed to darkness after sunset, was aglow with very expensive lights almost until dawn. . . .

But on this Holy night the new masters decided to end an age-old custom: They would not allow people to enter the Kremlin to hear the moving pealing of the bells. . . . They would also not allow the streets to be lit.

All of us groped through the darkness . . . to our churches, stumbling and falling every minute. The yardkeepers, now called the "watchmen of the courts," did nothing. The ice was not chopped away but lay about in uneven lumps.

Ian and I attended services . . . in a small, comfortable, ancient church that was filled with people. . . . The words "persecutors" and "tormentors" echoed in our hearts in a completely new way. The mood was not Easter-like; many people were crying. For the first time in my life the greeting "Christ Has Risen" did not evoke any holiday joy. . . . For the first time, also, we genuinely understood that we could not breathe the same air as the Bolsheviks. . . .

The noisy streets have taken on a garish look. . . . You think about former times and you sense vaguely that the old world . . . its beauty and charm, are vanishing forever!

I think little about leaving the country. On one hand I suppress the unpleasant thought of parting with close ones; on the other hand I have grown accustomed to the wandering life. . . . I look upon departure with the simple reassurance that I will soon return. . . .

Ian is still firmly convinced that we will have to leave as soon as possible. He wants to go to the south where . . . the Hetman has chased out the Bolsheviks.[4] . . . He has a genuine sense of the bolshevism that is spreading throughout Russia, a sense of terror and abyss.

As regards the arrangements for our departure, I was of little help. Ian did it all.

May 26, 1918
Vera Muromtseva-Bunina, from her diary
   We are in "German" Orsha—abroad.[5] With tears in his eyes,

[4]On April 29, 1918, a German-supported coup d'état named Pavel Skoropadsky "Hetman of the Ukraine."
[5]Orsha is a small town directly southwest of Smolensk.

Ian said, "Never have I crossed into a country with such a feeling of the border. I am shaking all over! Can it be that I am finally safe from the power of the people, from those pigs!"

He was deliriously happy when a German punched a Bolshevik in the face. . . .

Circa *Summer 1918*
Valentin Kataev, from his memoirs
He stood before me as he did earlier, pinched, bilious, cosmopolitan, inaccessible, the same Ivan Bunin about whom I have never stopped thinking all these years—even when I was at an artillery observation post—and who had become the ongoing focus of my artistic consciousness. Taking a step back, Bunin examined me silently, taking in every detail, as if he intended to describe me right then and there.

"Don't you recognize me?" I said.

He did not answer—perhaps he had not heard my question— and continued to look me over. . . as if he were reading me, even at times making mental notes in the margins. . . .

Then he offered me his so familiar dry hand, the palm frank, open, and friendly. "Hello, Valya," he said, seeming to admire me. "The young poet, Valentin Kataev!"

"Have you been in Odessa long?"

I asked the question out of embarrassment, since I already knew of his flight from Bolshevik Moscow to Odessa, where he had recently published several new poems. . . .

"Where are you now?" Bunin wrote. "Do you marvel at the waves of the green Biscay Bay amidst white dresses and panama hats?"

And another: "Give my respects to the Prince and Princess. I kiss your childlike hand with the love that I can now no longer hide." . . .

This was to me a new and frightening Bunin, almost an emigré, or perhaps already a full-blown one, who sensed completely and from the bottom of his soul the collapse, the death of old Russia, and the end of all former ties. Only an individual who understood fully that life was finished could have declared in print his secret, tender, and perhaps even criminal love which "I can no longer hide."

Why now? Why could he not hide it?

Because . . . it was all over. He had stayed in a Russia gripped by a terrible and, for him, merciless revolution. She—a princess—was somewhere far away in France, on the shores of "green Biscay Bay amidst white dresses and panama hats." . . .

"Give my respects to the Prince and Princess."

I felt something tragic in these lines. Despair. Horror. Resignation. Such lines could be written the night before an execution. . . .

How strange it was for me, a Russian officer. . . to walk about a Russian town occupied by the enemy,[6] and alongside a Russian academician, a famous writer, who had of his own free will fled here from Soviet Russia, yielding to the general panic and seeking refuge from no-one-knew-what to the occupied south, to a Ukrainian state created by the Germans. . . .

"When did we last see each other?" Bunin asked.

"In July of '14."

"July of '14," he said thoughtfully. "Four years. War. Revolution. An eternity."

"I had come to your dacha, but I didn't find you there."

"Yes, I left for Moscow the day after the declaration of war. I managed to escape with the greatest difficulty. Troop trains were all over the place. . . ." . . .

Thus began my two years' relationship with Bunin, which continued right up to the day when he finally and forever left the land of his birth.

Vera Nikolaevna Muromtseva was a beautiful young woman— not a society lady but most definitely a woman—tall, with a face like a cameo, her blond hair combed back smoothly and tied in a knot that fell on the back of her neck, with light blue eyes, and dressed like a high school student—a typical Moscow beauty from intellectual, academic circles. . . .

Vera Nikolaevna was beautiful, but she was not my type—she had large feet in button-down shoes and the longish nose of a classical goddess—Demeter, for instance. She was virtuous, but above all she was Bunin's wife, though she had not married him in church but in the liberal Moscow style, at a civil office. . . . Now Bunin and his wife, having fled the Bolsheviks . . . were waiting . . . together with other refugees from Moscow, for the day when Soviet rule would finally collapse and they could return home.

I became such a frequent guest at their house that Bunin seemed

[6]Odessa was occupied by Austrian and German military forces between March and November 1918.

to forget I was there and would sometimes argue with his wife in the Moscow style.

"Vera, you're an absolute idiot!" he would shout irritably.

But she would gaze at her lord and master with her submissively loving, angel-blue eyes and murmur, "Ian, I beg you not to be so unbearably rude." She would wring her long bluish fingers and continue, "Do stop raving! What will this young poet think of us? It will seem to him that you don't respect me."

I recall that I was extremely surprised when she called Bunin by the pretentious "Ian." But I soon realized that this was quite the style in the Moscow of those days. . . . It could also have been an allusion to Ioann [Ivan] the Terrible with his pinched, bilious face, his short beard, his seven wives, and his royally narrow, hawklike eyes. . . .

I kept bringing my Teacher more and more of my new poems and stories.

"Pay attention, Vera," Bunin would say, holding my compositions in his hand and nodding at me. "Like all beginners, he fancies that writing will bring him fame, money, and luxury. Confess, my good sir," he said . . . "that you dream of seeing your picture in journals and newspapers, of applause from the press. You have visions of your own dacha in Finland, a current account with the Credit Lyonnaise, a beautiful wife, a car! Look how he blushes, Vera! Now he'll lie to us and say he wants none of these things . . . only pure art.

"Let me tell you something, sir. Don't think all famous writers are always rich. Before they could enjoy even a modest existence— and very modest at that!—almost all of them knew terrible poverty, they were almost beggars." . . .

In his early days Bunin was still held captive by traditional, populist ideas of his country as a land that was poor, submissive, and wretched.

"I do not love you, Rus, your thousand years of timid, servile poverty. But this cross, this white ladle—these are features native and meek." . . .

But now, in Bunin's latest book of verse . . . I read a poem, "The Archistrategus,"[7] in which he pictures Russia quite differently:

"The Archistrategus of the Middle Ages, painted long ago on a one-dome church, was thin-legged, all in steel and winged. . . . Who knew him? Only recently has he been discovered, the caprice of

---

[7]The Archistrategus corresponds to an archangel or a militant angel.

cosmopolitan fashion—he appears as a marvel in a lavish journal, a subject for mystics, aesthetes, God-seekers, maidens, and poets. Their swollen, prattling lips hail Russia the Archistrategus, blaspheme the rags of Christ, and are moved by books that tell how meek and simple is Rus."

Bunin wrote this poem, it seems, in 1916, with a prophetic sense of the coming revolution that he feared so much, and to which he would never be reconciled, even at his death. . . .

I saw a new Bunin, an emigré from another time and place, from the world of ancient Russia, cruel, fantastic, unlike anything else, and yet profoundly intimate and national—the world of our ancestors who created Rus in their own image and likeness, with all its monstrous mixture of pagan and Christian, old Slavic and Ugro-Finnic, Varangian, Tatar—cruel, bloody, brilliantly original!—a realm that in no way resembled the "ancient Rus" we had come to imagine from the wretched, thin textbook of Russian history we used in grade school.

It is enough to list the titles of Bunin's poems of this period: "The Horde," "The Six-Winged," "The Buffoons," and "The Execution"[8] . . . in order to understand what was going on in Bunin's soul at that time.

"You glowed red in Batu's[9] flames, and your gaze became terrified and dark. You spread your red-gold wings in holy fear. You saw the worn monk's cowl of the Terrible Fool-in-Christ—and you froze your great-eyed face in the vaults of heaven."

His baffling lines of that period still disturb me deeply:

"May this winter be fiercer than all others. . . ." "His taut face creased with laughter, and his mouth turned black from rotting teeth. . . ." "The morning is misty, misty red. . . . Sharpen the knife and soak the whip in brine! . . . Let me wash my face . . . then stab me right away—otherwise beware! My teeth shall rip you apart!" "Prince Vyacheslav[1] in irons chained. . . ." "My cave is cool and dark. . . . My clothes are rags. . . . I sleep in a coffin. . . . Oh, Lord! Revive my faith and brace me for the struggle!" . . .

The soul of my Bunin . . . was writhing in the flames of hell,

[8]Bunin wrote "The Buffoons," "The Execution," and "The Six-Winged" in 1915, and "The Horde" in 1916.

[9]Batu Khan (1208?–1255), Mongol conqueror of northeast and south Russia (1237–1241), and founder of the Golden Horde.

[1]Vyacheslav Vladimirovich (1083–1154), a prince of Kievan Russia.

and if he did not groan it was only because he still hoped the Revolution was coming to an end. . . .

Bunin looked like . . . a vacationer from the capital, intellectual and refined, in expensive summer sandals, foreign-made socks, and an ample, well-ironed, canvaslike shirt . . . girdled with a simple but evidently rather expensive leather belt, behind which he sometimes tucked his hands à la Tolstoy; he did not wear a hat, but if it grew very hot he would suddenly don a splendid genuine panama, which he had brought back from some distant land, or a linen peaked cap like those that Fet, Polonsky, or perhaps even Tolstoy himself used to wear.

I see a large group on the veranda. . . . All these people are refugees from Soviet Russia: famous lawyers, doctors, writers, even academician Ovsyaniko-Kulikovsky himself, the famous author of *The Psychology of Creativity* and of articles on Turgenev, the editor of that outstanding and respected journal *The Herald of Europe*. . . . Never before had Odessa attracted such brilliant society. . . .

Bunin is in a splendid, rather sarcastic mood. He glances sideways at a powerful lady, as if listening to the silky rustle of her corset. It occurs to me that he is about to describe her right then and there. . . . Right away I can see him searching for that one, perfectly accurate word. He is secretly giving me a lesson in writing.

I can tell from his face that he has found precisely what he wants and that his find is unique and precious. He makes a delicate gesture, as if, from afar, to enclose the stout lady's face in a magical, musical oval.

Everyone quiets down to hear what he will say.

"Yes, indeed," he says, his forefinger sketching two commas upwards, one left, one right, into the oval that he has just drawn. "All you need, Elena Vasilyevna, is a little black moustache and you would look like . . . Peter the Great."

And suddenly we all saw Peter's face.

The lady blushes crimson, not knowing how to take the comparison. On the one hand something regal has been discovered in her face, and that's good, particularly in these troubled revolutionary times; on the other hand there's also something mannish there, and that's bad. The main thing, though, is that she has been "described" by the famous Bunin . . . and this resolves all doubts.

She smiles at Bunin both graciously and regally, but, in any event, she also wags her finger at him.

"Oh, Ivan Alexeevich, why do you pay me such compliments in public!" . . .

Bunin could be sad, very lonely, easily wounded, independent, fearless, and yet surprisingly tender. . . .

I was struck that this Bunin, this lucky man and favorite of fortune—as he then seemed to me—was so deeply dissatisfied with his position in literature, or, more to the truth, his position among other contemporary writers.

In truth, for the wider public Bunin was lost in the noisy mob—in the "literary bazaar," as he so bitterly called it. He was overshadowed by first-class stars whose names were on everyone's lips: Korolenko, Kuprin, Gorky, Leonid Andreev, Merezhkovsky, Fyodor Sologub, and many other "trend-setters."

Bunin was not a trend-setter.

Poetry was ruled by Alexander Blok, Balmont, Bryusov, Zinaida Gippius, Gumilyov, Akhmatova, and finally—whether they wanted it or not—by Igor Severyanin, whose name was known not only to young officers and every student from grade school to college but also to many shop assistants, doctors' assistants, traveling salesmen, commercial travelers, and cadets who had no idea that such a Russian writer as Ivan Bunin existed.

Bunin was known and valued—and then only quite recently—by an extremely few genuine connoisseurs and devotees of Russian literature who grasped that he was writing much better than all his contemporaries. The critics—particularly in the beginning of his career—wrote little and rarely about Bunin because his work offered no material for "problem" articles or occasions for literary scandals. For the same reason his name did not appear on notices for public lectures and debates, where the sordid Artsybashev and his sex problems reigned supreme.

Bunin did not tell me all this directly, but such thoughts slipped through in his sporadic remarks about contemporary literature, which were full of venom and sarcasm.

One could conclude that out of all contemporary Russian literature, Bunin unconditionally acknowledged only Leo Tolstoy as his superior. Chekhov he considered a writer of his own level, so to speak, perhaps a little higher—but not that much higher. As for the rest . . . Kuprin was talented, very talented . . . but often slipshod. Of Leonid Andreev, Tolstoy had rightly said, "Andreev tries to scare, but I am not frightened." Gorky and Korolenko were not really artists but publicists, which in no way took away from their ample giftedness. . . . Real poetry had degenerated. Balmont, Bryusov, Bely were nothing more than home-grown Muscovite decadents, a mixture of French and Nizhny-Novgorod[2] slang. "Oh, cover your pale legs," "I want to be brash, I want to be bold, I want to tear off your clothes," "He laughed in a vulgar bass and hurled pineapples into space," and other nonsense; Akhmatova was a provincial lass who wound up in the big city; Alexander Blok wrote false, bookish German poetry; the servile "ditties" of Igor Severyanin—how could anyone think up such a revolting word!—were not worth talking about; and the Futurists were simply "criminal types, runaway convicts. . . ." . . .

Bunin was somehow unusually quiet, pensive, inwardly stern but at the same time sadly tender, like a lone person experiencing an irreparable spiritual loss.

He was like a man who had lost a great deal of blood. . . .

I believe it was the feeling of losing his country. . . .

Dinner time came, Vera Nikolaevna had still not returned. Like a conspirator, Bunin waved me over with his finger, tiptoed furtively through the entire summer house into the kitchen, and, after banging around pots and pans, soon returned with some cold cabbage rolls in a frying pan, a saucepan of stewed fruit, and with a big piece of unleavened bread under his arm. He put it all out on the dinner table and ordered me to sit down.

I had never before eaten at the Bunins'. They were not known for their hospitality; in fact, they were somewhat stingy. I think they had no cook but ate at the neighbors'. Sometimes they dragged me there for company, and to have tea or supper with a large gathering of Moscow refugees, where I met many famous people. There Bunin would boldly heap my plate with all kinds of food.

"Don't be shy," he would say. "I know you have a wolfish appetite. Eat, eat. Your young body needs a lot of food. Poetry and the young ladies exhaust your resources every day. Don't deny it. I was young myself—I know!"

If there was wine on the table . . . Bunin would help himself to a bottle of red while the others had to make do with the rest. . . . Bunin would appoint me, the youngest, as chairman of the table and

[2]Nizhny-Novgorod (renamed Gorky in Soviet times) is a city 265 miles northeast of Moscow.

wine-pourer, so that before I made friends with Alexei Tolstoy, for
instance, I had poured him more than one glass of wine.

But let us return to the stuffed cabbage.

There were four cabbage rolls in the frying pan—golden,
slightly burned, and encased in fat—and Bunin, having put on his
pince-nez, divided them in half. Looking at me askance, he placed
the two larger ones on his own plate, leaving the two smaller ones for
me.

"Eat, don't be shy. I know you eat like the devil, especially
when you're out with guests."

"What will Vera Nikolaevna say!" I exclaimed.

"She shouldn't be late. Anyway, we'll knock this off like two
bachelors, take the dishes back to the kitchen—and no one will
know." . . .

While Bunin ate, his beard moved sensually, and faint tremors
of pleasure ran down his shriveled neck, as if to accompany each bite
of cabbage to its proper place.

When we came to the stewed fruit, he said, licking his
moustache, "We won't dirty any more plates. We'll just help ourselves. . . ."

We quickly ate the fruit right from the saucepan. Bunin first
divided the thick, swollen concoction strictly in half . . . then he
sternly demanded that I not cross the dividing line. . . . We began
eating the fruit, chasing each other with our spoons in a friendly sort
of way; then, for a long time, we dipped pieces of bread into the
thick liquid and emptied the pot of its heavenly sweet and sour
remains. . . .

I don't know why, but it was precisely that saucepan of stewed
fruit that somehow brought us together in a very special way. . . .

Suddenly Bunin began to examine me.

"Before us is the night. How would you describe it in a few
words so that it is precisely this night and no other? You see how
many things there are around us . . . but you must choose only that
which is essential, as they say, the typical. Well?" . . .

We sat on the bench, and while I struggled to select the most
essential features of the night, Bunin suddenly began to murmur
some lines of Fet:

". . . the gleam of the frozen distance, the smell of night
violets. . . ."

He sighed deeply, sorrowful and submissive, as though cocking his ear and trying to grasp the meaning of these lines. He murmured anew:

"... first a windmill, then a nightingale."

He turned his narrow face toward me, lifted it to the sky, and I saw the rapture that was written upon it.

"First a windmill, then a nightingale," he repeated. "Do you realize how splendid that is? There's no way to say it better. He sits there alone in the night, his soul possessed by love that is unique, inimitable ... he sits surrounded by scents, sounds, ill-defined visual images, and his mind cannot focus on one thing. Now he is completely overwhelmed by the gleam of the frozen distance; now he can sense nothing but the scent of night violets; now he hears a windmill drowning out the nightingales; now he hears the nightingales drowning out the windmill; and all this becomes a single, all-consuming love. 'My angel, my distant angel, why do I love you so?'" Bunin murmured the final line of the poem hoarsely, almost in desperation. . . .

Then, without pause, Bunin began to float into the distance his own ... songs, entirely new ones, which I had not yet heard, if only because he had, perhaps, written some of them that very day:

"... The eternal change in this brief life shall be my eternal consolation—this early sun, the smoke over the village, the leaf-fall in the scarlet park, you, old bench, old friend. To future poets unbeknown to me, God will give a secret—the memory of me; I shall be their dreams, a spirit free from flesh, free from death, in this scarlet park, in its silence. . . ."

"... A star trembles in the sky. . . . Whose wondrous hands carry this vessel, overflowing with precious dew? Burning star, chalice of earthly woes, heavenly tears—why, Lord, did you raise my being over the world?"

Bunin spoke mysteriously, as though he wished to instill in me some magnificent sweet truth which only that very moment had been revealed to him:

"In a garden chair," he whispered cryptically, "on a balcony at night. . . . The sea's lullaby murmur. . . . Be trusting, meek, and calm; rest from your thoughts. The breezes come and go, breathing of the endless sea. . . . Does anyone guard this sleeping villa's peace? Does anyone assign our knowledge, our fate, our years? If the heart

wishes it, if it believes it, then so it is. What's in us—that must be.
You doze off, and a soft gentle wind caresses your eyes—how can
there be no Love?"

And then again, without pause:

"The dacha is quiet, the night is dark, the stars are misty blue.
Sighing, the wave unfurls, the blind flowers sway—and, often with
the wind, a new wave appears, like a spirit clad in flesh, and makes
its way to the bench, sighing in its sleep."

There were moments when it seemed to me that all these poems
were being created right then and there, in my presence, and that
every line, the "wave sighing in its sleep," the "soft wind," and
especially the brilliant "blind flowers" (the white tobacco and four
o'clocks) had, by themselves, imperceptibly. . . become elements of
the purest poetry. . . .

My father suddenly appeared at the bathroom door, and from
the expression on his face I knew that something extraordinary had
happened.

"Come here. Someone is here to see you. I don't know who he
is. I think it's . . . Bunin."

I hurried to get dressed. Without having dried myself fully, and
with my hair still wet . . . I ran into the room . . . it was indeed
Bunin. Sitting on a chair, with one leg crossed over the other, he was
conversing urbanely with father. . . . Bunin looked like a young
Chekhov, and father an older one.

I had told Bunin that we rented out rooms; and he had
come . . . to find accommodations for friends of his, Moscow refugees,
who had no place to live. Later I learned that these refugees were
Alexei Tolstoy and his family.

With his sharp eyes Bunin had already managed to look over our
home and most likely had a clear idea of how we lived. . . . He saw a
pitiful place; and he understood right away, of course, that Alexei
Tolstoy, with his lordly ways, would not be at all comfortable in our
rooms with the single sagging couch. . . .

Bunin sat there, like an official visitor, for about twenty
minutes. After talking about Zhukovsky and Turgenev, and after he
and father condemned the Modernists, Bunin got up, said goodbye,
and shook hands politely and briefly.

"Glad to have met you."

"And how do you find my Valya's work?" my father asked
almost plaintively, having overcome his lack of nerve.

"And how do you find it?" Bunin returned the question.

"As his father, I find it difficult to judge. His poems seem all right for rhyme and measure. The stories, I think, are like feuilletons, shallow and superficial. Don't you think so?"

"That's a long and difficult question."

"What do you think—will he make something of himself?"

"That is hard to say in a few words," Bunin replied seriously. "Time will tell."

And he left without allowing me to see him off.

Blushing to the roots of my hair, I stood at the half-open door and listened to the sound of his sprightly, firm footsteps as he ran downstairs from the third floor, filling the staircase with booming and clanking.

Only some time later, when I knew Bunin better, did I realize the true purpose behind his visit. The rooms to let were only an excuse. In reality—and I'm deeply convinced of this—Bunin had simply wanted to catch me unawares and to see how I lived, what kind of place we had, and what my father was like. Bunin was incredibly curious, and he always had to know everything, in all its details, about life about him, to see everything with his mercilessly sharp eyes.

June 5, 1918
Vera Muromtseva-Bunina, from her diary

Ian is coming to himself little by little. He talks little about politics.

July 18, 1918
Vera Muromtseva-Bunina, from her diary

Yesterday evening I overhead Ian saying, "Not long ago I recalled my youth, and I pictured it all so vividly that I burst into tears. . . ."

He also said, "I consider only as genuine writers those who write what they see. Those who do not are not writers. Sometimes they are clever, but they are not artists. Andreev, for example."

July 21, 1918
Vera Muromtseva-Bunina, from her diary

Ian is irritated mornings, but then he goes out. He sits in his study for hours, but he does not say what he does there. It is very difficult. I do not know what is going on in his soul.

News that Nicholas II has been shot has had a depressing effect: extreme lawlessness. . . .

I cannot sleep at night; I am seized with horror. But . . . we can still eat, drink, get dressed up, and enjoy nature.

July 25, 1918
Vera Muromtseva-Bunina, from her diary
Ian praised [Goethe's] *Werther*[3] and said . . . he wanted to dethrone love.

"All those Werthers," he said, "all those sexually crazed creatures who are mesmerized by one woman. I have read many criminal novels and dramas; I even recall a thing or two from my own life when I, too, was an erotomaniac. . . . But, I never idolized *her*, nor did I consider her a summit of perfection; rather, I was filled with a feeling of love for her, the way I would be for a cloud or the horizon. . . . Someday I will describe it in greater detail."[4]

July 27, 1918
Vera Muromtseva-Bunina, from her diary
Ian said that "the Russian people make unhappiness a religion."

August 18, 1918
Vera Muromtseva-Bunina, from a letter to a friend
Ian has gotten back into the swing of work. . . . He has changed a great deal. He has become as before, happy. He has stopped "living for politics." Now we again have conversations about literature. Sometimes we have arguments about politics, but we do not continue them for long.

August 24, 1918
Vera Muromtseva-Bunina, from her diary
A friend told us about the many horrible things going on in Moscow. . . . What will our relatives do there? . . . She told me she saw Ian's brother, Yuly Alexeevich, from afar. . . . I feel so sorry for him, that lonely old man. We tried to take him with us, but to no avail; he will perish there! But he did not have the energy to leave. Here, at least, he could have been better situated. There is no courage, only a fear for life!

[3]Goethe wrote *The Trials of Young Werther* in 1774.
[4]Bunin is referring to his affair with Varvara Pashchenko, which he later recalled in *Mitia's Love*, written in 1924.

August 31, 1918
Vera Muromtseva-Bunina, from her diary
 Explosions began at four o'clock in the afternoon. I do not know where they are coming from, but I could see what was going on from the west room above. . . . Ian told me to write it all down. There would first appear a light, sometimes a small one, sometimes a fiery sphere. One gave off golden sparks; then smoke rose up in a puff. Sometimes they looked like a cauliflower; other times they looked like a tree with a crown of fir. . . .
 The people are in a panic. . . . They say. . . all of Odessa is burning, and there are human sacrifices.

September 7, 1918
Vera Muromtseva-Bunina, from her diary
 The newspaper brings us terrible news. . . . The Great Princes have been shot; a genuine terror has begun. I cannot imagine what people are going through in Moscow, Petrograd, and other cities. Sometimes, though, I think it is better to be there and not here.

September 14, 1918
Vera Muromtseva-Bunina, from her diary
 Yesterday we finally decided and rented two rooms. . . . The apartment is very nice, tastefully furnished, with many antiques. . . . The money we brought from Moscow is gone. . . . Ian got a loan from the bank, about ten thousand rubles. . . . He is very troubled, animated one moment but sad the next. He is not writing. . . . For some reason he has begun looking worse. He is probably worried about the coming winter and about the health of his brother. . . .

September 20, 1918
Vera Muromtseva-Bunina, from her diary
 Ian asked a friend, "Have you heard that . . . Gorky has become a friend of the Minister of People's Education?"
 "That's good. Now we can hang him," the friend replied with malicious delight.

September 20, 1918
Ivan Bunin, from a letter to a friend
 We are living poorly. . . . Inflation, unending pain, horror, and anger upon reading the newspapers; endless worry about loved ones from whom we have heard nothing, and especially since Yuly

Alexeevich has again fallen seriously ill . . . the coming of winter when we, literally speaking, do not have a shred of anything warm, the onslaught of hellish cold—and so on, and so on. . . .

Now about your anthology. Alas, I have nothing except for two or three poems. I would be genuinely happy to fulfill your request— but I cannot. I have not written anything all summer. I am not myself—I am weak in body and heavy in soul—you yourself know what kind of winter we had.

October 7, 1918
Vera Muromtseva-Bunina, from her diary
   The rooms we were renting have been confiscated.

October 20, 1918
Vera Muromtseva-Bunina, from her diary
   Yuly Alexeevich has been in bed for a rather long time. We are forbidden to send a letter to him; we cannot get permission for him to leave Moscow. [A friend] writes about him: "Yuly has gotten thin and pinched-looking; his eyes are sunken; he has become extremely nervous. . . ."
   Ian says he will never forgive Gorky for being in the government. "There will come a day," he said, "when I will rise up against Gorky openly, not only as a man but also as an artist. It is time to tell the truth about Gorky. . . . He once had talent, but now he has drowned it in lies and falsehood."
   I was sad to hear this, since I loved Gorky. I remember that at Capri, after the singing, the mandolins, the tarantellas, and the wine, Ian wrote Gorky this inscription in his book: "Dear Alexei Maximovich, No matter what happens, I will always love you." Did Ian know then that there would be a parting of the ways?

October 28, 1918
Vera Muromtseva-Bunina, from her diary
   Ian cannot restrain himself when he is with "idiots" who tell him that . . . there will be a "genuine paradise," that "no one will take bribes," that "the trains will run smoothly," and so on, and so on. . . .

Late Autumn 1918
Valentin Kataev, from his memoirs
   It was late autumn, and Bunin's returning to Moscow was out of the question. Soviet rule, which everyone had predicted would

quickly fold, had not only not folded but had even—from all signs—grown stronger.

Revolution had come to Germany. The Kaiser had been deposed, the German Army had surrendered, and the Germans and Austrians were quickly abandoning the Ukraine . . . the obscene Treat of Brest-Litovsk[5]—which had been the chief indictment against the Bolsheviks—now had no practical significance: Lenin appeared to have been right.

In Odessa the Germans had now been replaced by their conquerors, the so-called "allies";[6] and in the south of Russia there now began a period of almost two years in which power changed hands six times, if not more, until Soviet rule was established once and for all.[7]

Bunin lived through this uniquely stormy period . . . in the house of his friend, the artist Bukovetsky, who gave him the entire lower floor, three rooms in all, where I would visit Bunin, always experiencing unbelievable excitement before I rang at the back door.

Usually the door was opened by a very elegantly dressed maid in French heels, a starched cap, and a small cambric apron with doll-like pockets. She had been placed at Bunin's disposal along with the rooms, a striking contrast to the situation in the town, in Russia, and in the world.

Bunin's life in these lordly rooms, with their massive shining doors, the exquisitely polished parquet, the Venetian windows with their warm marble sills and brightly gleaming iron latches, the high clean ceilings . . . the small quantity of the most essential but very good furniture—none of those petty bourgeois bookcases, bedside tables, knickknacks, doilies, throw rugs, and pillow covers—corresponded totally to my conception of an aristocrat, a long-established nobleman, a Russian academician, a man of impeccable taste.

---

[5]The Soviet-German Treaty of Brest-Litovsk was signed on March 3, 1918; its stipulations were disastrous for Russia. The Ukraine, Poland, Finland, Lithuania, Estonia, and Latvia received their independence. Russia lost 26 percent of its population, 27 percent of its arable land, 32 percent of its average crops, 26 percent of its railway system, 33 percent of its manufacturing industries, 73 percent of its iron industries, and 75 percent of its coal fields. Moreover, Russia had to pay a huge war indemnity. See Nicholas Riasonovsky, A History of Russia (Oxford, 1984), 477–478.

[6]Austrian and German military forces left Odessa in November 1918. They were replaced by English and French forces which had intervened in the Russian civil war and which remained in Odessa from December 1918 to April 1919.

[7]Soviet armed forces first captured Odessa on April 6, 1919, lost the city to the Whites in August of that year, and then retook Odessa on February 7, 1920, when they consolidated Soviet authority once and for all. For a detailed treatment of Odessa during the Russian civil war, see George A. Brinkley, Allied Intervention in South Russia, 1917–1921 (Notre Dame, 1966).

Here I saw not a summer visitor but a genuinely cosmopolitan individual, perhaps even an involuntary political recluse, who lived by a most exacting schedule.

Bunin worked a great deal. I had the impression that he worked incessantly. No matter when I called I always saw... Bunin—without a jacket, in a fresh shirt with sleeves rolled up to the elbow, exposing his smooth, muscular arms—wearing round glasses that made him look like an owl, and writing rapidly, covering small narrow sheets of writing paper in his characteristically small cuneiform handwriting....

On hearing my steps he would usually say, without turning around, "Go see Vera Nikolaevna. I'll finish up right away."

I would make my way... to their drawing room, where I would be met by Vera Nikolaevna, who, observing duties as mistress of the house, would engage me in light conversation....

Herself a woman of lively intelligence, and with a purely Bunin-like curiosity, she would... soon turn the conversation to more personal matters:

"And how are you getting on with the charming Natasha N.?... a real Natasha Rostova[8]... So it's all over between you and Iren A.? How fickle you are—a real Bunin pupil," she sighed sadly....

She was aware of all my affairs... causing me to see her not as the dour wife of an academician but rather as an elder sister or even a married cousin.

"Ian," she said to Bunin as he entered the room. "He's head over heels in love with Natasha!"

"So it seems," Bunin replied. "Look at him—his cheeks are sunken, there are dark circles under his eyes. You can see right away that instead of working you've been God-knows-where, doing nothing the whole night long. I suppose you stand under her window till dawn, waiting for her to open it and let you in.... I know all about those full-mouthed long-legged schoolgirls!"...

Bunin taught me there are no forbidden topics in literature....
I immediately adopted several of Bunin's recommendations: tact, precision, brevity, and... the simplicity that results from earnest effort on a phrase or a particular word—about an absolutely autonomous vision of surroundings, apart from imitating anyone, even Tolstoy or Pushkin, about the ability to see phenomena and subjects

[8]The heroine of Tolstoy's *War and Peace*.

in an entirely independent way and to write about them in an absolutely individual way, free of any literary influences or reminiscences.

Bunin warned me particularly against literary clichés—"the slanting rays of the setting sun," "the frost got harder," "silence reigned," "rain began drumming on the window," and the like, of which Chekhov had spoken even before Bunin.

Among the minor literary clichés Bunin also included, for example, the custom of literary hacks in those days of invariably portraying a hero as a "first-year student" . . . "Ivanov, a first-year student, came out of the gate and walked down the street," "Sidorov, a first-year student, lit a cigarette," "Nikanorov, a first-year student, was unhappy."

"I'm sick to death of all these literary first-year students," Bunin would say. . . .

I had spread out the manuscript of my new story before me. Coughing from excitement, I anticipated with pleasure Bunin's approval that my young hero was not a first-year student nor even a second lieutenant but—just imagine!—a scene painter: It was splendid and very true to life.

I read my story very hurriedly, fervently. I remember that in it I described the young scene painter's experiences with love, his first meeting, the breakup with his loved one, a night of drunkenness, some sniffing of cocaine in some rather suspect company, and, finally, an early, bright, and bitterly cold morning on Nikolaevsky Boulevard with large rosy pigeons going about on the granite steps of the famous staircase.

I described all this in a grand, lavish way. From time to time I cast furtive looks at Bunin, as if to read in his face what impressions my prose—which I deemed exceptionally exquisite—was making on him.

At first Bunin's taciturn face expressed his usual professional attentiveness. I even noticed that he exchanged a meaningful glance with Vera Nikolaevna. I had finally got to the old man! But then he became noticeably gloomy. He sat up erect, and by the end of the story—and to my horror—he was not hiding his irritation and was even beginning to tap his heel rather loudly on the parquet floor. . . . Bunin was silent for a while. Then he turned toward me. His face was angry; his eyes were terrible and severely questioning. His voice was icy.

"Is that all?"

"Yes," I said.

"You've really done it this time!" Bunin shouted suddenly, banging his fist on the table with such force that the ashtray bounced. "Why the devil have you been leading us on for the last forty-five minutes or more? Vera and I have been sitting on pins and needles, expecting that your scene painter would start painting some scenery . . . but all we get is rosy pigeons—the end!" . . .

Bunin's power as a writer arose from his amazingly rapid, almost instantaneous reaction to outward stimuli and his ability to find an absolutely precise word for them.

He told me he never used a typewriter but always wrote with a pen.

"And I advise you not to use one either. After your piece is in manuscript form you can make a typed copy of it. . . . The creative process is rooted in . . . the mysterious tie that links head, paper, and pen. . . . When you compose on the typewriter, each word you tap out has its individual identity, it becomes depersonalized; whereas when you write it down on paper it becomes, as it were, a material, visible trace of your thought, its pattern. The word has not yet lost its secret connection with your soul . . . your organism. So if the word is false per se, if it is out of place, tactless, then you will not only sense this inwardly but also your eyes will notice this falseness right away, a certain slowing down or speeding up in the tempo of your writing, or even a change in your handwriting itself. In other words, your handwriting—a unique, inimitable part of your soul—will signal to you that something is 'not right!' " . . .

It may seem strange, almost incredible, that at a time when civil war raged all around . . . there continued in Bunin's house, behind the mirrorlike windows, a life more imagined than real, a life in which a quite small circle of people discussed questions of literature, poetry, criticism, the reading of the Goncourt Brothers in the original . . . the eternal Moscow arguments about Tolstoy and Dostoevsky. . . .

Almost every day, in any weather, Bunin would walk about town for several hours. He did not stroll but walked with a light, brisk step . . . with a walking stick and a professorial skullcap instead of a hat—swift, raptly attentive, gaunt. . . .

I observed Bunin at a soldiers' street market where he stood in a crowd, notebook in hand, calmly and unhurriedly writing down . . .

the ditties that two brothers of the Black Sea fleet were reciting as they did a lively dance, their arms on each other's shoulders, swinging their wide bell-bottoms. . . .

I remember that I almost fainted with the sickening smells of sesame oil, garlic, and pungent human sweat.

But Bunin paid no attention to this whatsoever and worked calmly, covering page after page with notes.

What was most amazing, no one paid any attention to Bunin, despite his professorial appearance. . . . Who knows what people took him for? It occurred to me that some might see this gaunt, bony gentleman in his whimsical skullcap . . . as a fairground graphologist, a juggler, a magician, or a fortune-teller who sold horoscopes—which would have been quite in keeping with the spirit of the time. No one would have been surprised if they had seen a parrot or a monkey in a calico skirt suddenly appear on his shoulder. . . .

One day some of Bunin's acquaintances, wishing to give him the chance to earn some money, persuaded him to give a reading of his new piece, "Chang's Dreams."[9] . . . Bunin had been refusing for quite some time, insisting that absolutely no one would be interested, that no one would come, that the broad public did not know him at all, and that to tie up a whole evening with one story would simply be foolish. He kept saying that the public wouldn't put up with it, and that the entire undertaking would turn out to be a loss to its organizers. In the end, though, he consented, but he warned his friends that he wanted a fee—"for the disgrace," as he expressed it—regardless of the revenues, even if the hall were absolutely empty.

"I'm not that rich, gentlemen, that I can disgrace myself in public—and for nothing to boot," Bunin said with grim humor.

Posters were put up throughout the town, slender programs were printed, and precisely at the designated hour in the artists' room of the Odessa School of Music . . . Bunin appeared. He was pale, and exquisitely dressed. . . .

Crackling his starched cuffs, Bunin silently shook hands with all who were present and sat down on a small sofa at the side of the room. Alongside him he had a quite small briefcase, more like a woman's than a man's, made of excellent English tan leather, which contained the manuscript of the story.

[9]Bunin wrote "Chang's Dreams" in 1916.

It was quite clear that the evening was already a failure: the public had not come.

"Night duty at the undertaker's," Bunin said after a short silence, looking up at the shabby, moldy ceiling. "I warned you, gentlemen," he added with a somewhat bitter smile, in which it was not hard to read a nagging concern about his fate as a writer.

(The place would be packed, of course, if Igor Severyanin or Vertinsky were reading! Leonid Andreev, too, not to mention Maxim Gorky. But what can you do—they know how to please the crowd. But who will come to hear me? Only the real connoisseurs. . . .)

"Well, my dear sirs, shall we begin or shall we quietly go home?" Bunin asked.

"People are drifting in," someone suggested uncertainly. "Let's wait another fifteen minutes and then start."

"This is really getting awkward," Bunin muttered. "There's no one here. I warned you no one would come to hear me."

"For God sakes, Ivan Alexeevich! If they won't come for you, then whom will they come for?" one of the organizers exclaimed in a false tone. "The posters were put up late, there weren't enough announcements in the newspapers . . . and people were expecting an armed uprising of the counterrevolutionaries. . . . Surely you can understand. . . ."

"You don't have to console me," Bunin said firmly, and then he held up one of the posters . . . with an idiotic and typically provincial misprint—"The Dreams of Fang"—in huge letters. . . .

Bunin's face contorted as though he had suddenly been hit hard. He even gasped in pain; but immediately he got a grip on himself and wearily waved his hand.

"Oh, the devil with it!" . . .

Someone muttered something about Blok's poem "The Twelve"[1] . . . which had sent young people into raves. . . . "I do not understand what good people see in this "Twelve" thing, or how a poet could sink so low as to cook up these vulgar, stupid ditties," Bunin burst out, shrugging his shoulders. " 'Vanka and Katka drinking booze. /She got Kerensky bucks in her shoes. . . .' Russian literature has never hit such a low point. . . . This man was once a poet . . . who wrote verse about the Madonna, the Beautiful Lady 'aglow from red icon lamps. . . .' But now he's got Jesus Christ surrounded by a white

---

[1]Blok wrote "The Twelve" in 1918.

halo of roses? Maybe he meant to say a wreath of roses? . . . And not even a rudimentary sense for the Russian language. The most typical modernism!"

As he said this Bunin looked me straight in the face with eyes that were not angry so much as truly hate-filled. His cheeks had become sunken and even bonier than before.

"You are most likely tickled to death with it? Of course! You probably think 'The Scythians'[2] is a great prophetic work. . . . Why not? 'We are the shield between two hostile races—the Mongols and Europe.' And what kind of steel machine has integral parts that breathe? Tell me, how can an integral part breathe? And not just any integral part, but precisely those in steel machines! This is crazy! Decadent garbage!" . . .

Alas, no matter how painful it is for me to say so, I came to see quite clearly that Bunin was afraid of the Revolution . . . and that this fear was his main tragedy in these years. . . .

"You, of course, do not agree with me about 'The Scythians' and 'The Twelve'?" Bunin said sharply. "I am afraid that you, and many young people of your age and position, your friends, have set out on a false and slippery path that will lead you to an abyss. . . ." He again looked at me sharply and smiled. "Well, gentlemen, if we're going to begin, then let's begin." And with these words he walked out the side door, up to the steps on to the stage, bowed curtly to the light applause, sat down at the rickety table, pulled a magazine offprint of "Chang's Dreams" out of his briefcase, glanced at his watch, and, never looking again at the half-empty, lighted hall, read his splendid ("symphonic") story with excellent diction and in a clear and resonant voice. Those splendid first phrases resounded like somber musical chords:

"Does it matter whom we discuss? Everyone who has lived on this earth deserves to be the subject of a story. One day Chang discovered the world and the captain, his master, with whom his earthly existence had been united. And since that time an entire six years had passed, trickled away, like sand in a ship's hourglass. Again it is night—dream or reality—and again morning has come—reality or dream?"

Could it have mattered to all those people caught in the height of revolution, in a besieged city, sitting in a cold, half-empty, poorly

[2]Blok wrote "The Scythians" in 1918.

lit hall, what happened to a wasted drunkard captain and his dog Chang who had been purchased on a "cold and dusty day on a broad Chinese river" and had then been brought on a ship to Odessa?

But they sat without moving for the entire forty-five minutes of the reading, bewitched by the music of this scenic symphonic prose with its changes of rhythm, phrasing, like somber chords played by a great organist. . . .

Only once, for a moment, were the listeners distracted from "Chang's Dreams," when beyond the windows, in the dark abyss of the besieged city, a short burst of machine-gun fire was heard, followed by the explosion of a hand grenade, and then by a voice that said softly in the middle of the hall, "Gentlemen, I think they're shooting on Malaya Arnautskaya Street. . . ."

That night I walked with Bunin through the dark, ominously quiet city. He seemed darkly silent. Wishing to distract him from the oppression, I kept trying to say something pleasant to him.

"Ivan Alexeevich, surely much of your work has been translated into other languages?"

"No, I'm very little known abroad . . . or in Russia too, it seems," he added bitterly. . . .

Bunin once told me that if he were very rich he would never live in one place. . . . but would rather travel all over the world, staying at good, comfortable hotels and living there as long as he wished; and as soon as he grew tired of the place, he would move somewhere else with one or two suitcases filled with bare necessities. Nothing superfluous. Never send a dirty shirt to the laundry, just throw it out because it would be much more interesting and easier to buy a new one. The same with suits and shoes. The suitcase would have only notebooks, paper, and the various odds and ends he had grown used to. . . .

I had the impression that the Bunins always seemed to be camping out, using other people's furniture, apartments, curtains, dishes, and lamps. They had only their clothes, their bedding, and a pair of slim English leather suitcases plastered with foreign labels. . . .

Speaking of labels.

I once asked Bunin what literary trend he subscribed to.

"Oh, all these trends are such garbage! What haven't the critics called me: a Decadent, a Symbolist, a mystic, a realist, a Neo-Realist, a God-seeker, a naturalist. They have stuck so many labels on me that I look like a suitcase that has traveled all around the world—all covered with colorful, gaudy labels. But does this explain my essence as an artist in the least? No way! I am myself, unique and inimitable, like everyone else on this earth, and that is the heart of the matter."

November 24, 1918
Vera Muromtseva-Bunina, from her diary
   Ian said, "How is one supposed to make sense of this? The revolutionaries are for freedom, but as soon as they get power, right away. . . they close all the newspapers except their own. The revolutionaries battle against force, but as soon they get power, executions immediately begin."

December 6, 1918
Vera Muromtseva-Bunina, from her diary
   The rumor is that Gorky has said that "it is time to finish off the enemies of Soviet power." And this is the same Gorky who wrote against Soviet power all last winter.

December 13, 1918
Vera Muromtseva-Bunina, from her diary
   The life we had in Moscow is beginning all over again. We stay at home. There is shooting in the streets; people are being stripped of their things. It seems there is a state of siege going on; we can't go out after nine o'clock. . . . they set free eight hundred criminals. . . . The waiting is awful.
   Ian is depressed. He told me that last night he sat up for three hours, holding his knees in his hands, unable to sleep.
   "How I despise everything!" he said.

December 17, 1918
Vera Muromtseva-Bunina, from her diary
   Ian and I went walking through the town. We saw many Scythians on horseback—absolute twelfth-century types. They were sitting on horses in short sheepskin coats. . . . They sat erect, with rifles. One kept wobbling in his saddle, almost grabbing for his horse's mane.
   "A completely savage beast," Ian said, looking at him attentively.
   "Not a beast, but . . . a house pet," I answered. He agreed.

I love going walking with Ian. He responds to everything in such a lively way. He notices everything . . . as if you were out on an organized tour.

December 19, 1918
Vera Muromtseva-Bunina, from her diary

The fighting has gone on all day. Our street was in the battle zone . . . machine-guns, rifles, sometimes gunfire. An hour break, then it started up again; but it soon quieted down. . . .

The weather is rainy. Ian has been on his feet . . . almost the entire day. Every minute he runs out into the yard to talk with the other tenants of our building. This democracy can be a malicious thing.

December 20, 1918
Vera Muromtseva-Bunina, from her diary

The laundress is in a rage. She runs around crying that the counterrevolutionaries have won. She is certain they will bring back serfdom.

December 24, 1918
Vera Muromtseva-Bunina, from her diary

It is raining. Today it is Christmas Eve in the West. We remembered Christmas at Capri, the early morning, the sounds of the musicians. How great it was. The boys lit firecrackers all day long. In Italy, Christmas is a day for children; no one can get angry at their pranks. In the evening there is a procession: Christ is carried in a manger; there is a Joseph and God's Mother. The procession goes all over Capri. . . . Alexei Maximovich was delighted by it all. He was excited, moved. I am sorry I knew him. It is difficult for the heart to reject someone with whom you have spent so many genuinely splendid days, days which are so rare in life.

PART SEVEN

Tidal Wave

1919–1920

SEATED FROM LEFT: ANDREEV, CHALIAPIN,
BUNIN. STANDING, SECOND FROM LEFT:
GORKY. 1902

The only sign of life in Russia was battle. All else had come to a standstill or was being systematically destroyed. Civil war was devastating two-thirds of the country. Foreign powers had accelerated their intervention by blockading Russia for four months beginning in October 1919. The following year Poland declared war on the Bolsheviks in order to seize White Russia and much of western Ukraine. Even God seemed to have entered the struggle against the new Soviet state: a drought in 1920 destroyed what little hope there was for food.

What the civil war left standing, "war communism" finished off. Workers, certain of pay, ceased to work; peasants, doubtful of pay, ceased to plant. All productive effort ceased and the economy ground to a halt. Transportation broke down, foreign trade stopped, domestic business collapsed. Agricultural production in 1920 was half of what it had been before the war. Cultivated land fell by almost 40 percent, harvests by nearly 60 percent. In industry the situation was even worse. Heavy output was only 13 percent of what it had been before 1914. Cotton production declined to 5 percent of its prewar level, iron to 2 percent. Almost a hundred times as much money was in circulation in 1920 as in 1917. If a dollar equaled two rubles in 1914, it was worth 2,420 rubles by 1920, an increase of more than 1,200 percent.

Human suffering was staggering. War, epidemics, migrations, starvation, executions, and exhaustion eventually claimed the lives of twenty million people. A million more, many of these educated and skilled, left Russia. The population in Saint Petersburg dropped from 2.3 million in 1917 to 700,000 in 1919.

Russian literature was similarly decimated. Many writers were physically and spiritually debilitated. Material hardships, social

281

dislocation, and personal fear, coupled with a scarcity of paper, a lack of printing facilities, and the deterioration of means of communication not only doomed creative effort but reduced the number and circulation of publications, Red and White alike. The annual output of books fell to 3,269 titles, compared with some 20,000 in 1919; the few writings that saw the light of day in this period stressed politics and propaganda over imagination and art.

Broadly speaking, writers in these years fell into two groups: those who accepted the Revolution and those who did not. Evgeny Zamyatin wrote his famous novel *We*, warning against the "brave new world" of the socialist state. (The novel was published in Russia only in 1989.) Other writers, many of them flowers of the culturally experimental Silver Age, emigrated—Balmont, Gippius, Merezhkovsky, Kuprin, Andreev, Remizov, Khodasevich, Nabokov, Severyanin, Tsvetaeva, Vyacheslav Ivanov, and Alexei Tolstoy. (Tolstoy returned in 1923; Kurpin returned in 1937 and died a year later; Tsvetaeva returned in 1939 and committed suicide in 1941.)

Still others joined the Bolsheviks, singing their praises. Bryusov became a party member in 1920. Mayakovsky spent much of his time creating avant-garde posters supporting the Revolution and writing such pieces as his poem "150,000,000," an epic struggle between Wilson, the defender of world capitalism, and Ivan, a thoroughly Russian champion of the downtrodden. (Ivan wins, of course.) It was Gorky himself, however, whose Bolshevik career made the epic Ivan pale in comparison. At the beginning of the Revolution Gorky had attacked the communists because he was shocked by the terror and violence of the upheaval, and because he feared (rightfully) both the loss of personal freedoms and the decline of moral and cultural values. Two years later, though, he supported the Bolsheviks, seeking to defend the Revolution from its enemies. In 1919 he published *Follow Us*, an appeal to Russian intellectuals to set aside their mistrust of the communists and to form a united front against the counterrevolutionaries.

Although Gorky's change of heart greatly distressed Bunin and others, it was not entirely regrettable. Indeed, Gorky is often credited with saving Russian culture from extinction and the intelligentsia from starvation, humiliation, and death. He was able to establish International Literature, a huge publishing enterprise supported by the state and employing hundreds of writers, artists, and scholars as translators, researchers, and editors. He also founded the House of Art and the House of the Scholar, similar state-run firms which gave additional shelter and work to hundreds of intellectuals in Petrograd. By 1920 Gorky was not a man so much as an institution, an industry. He was nonetheless hated by many because he continued to champion the Revolution even though he vacillated between the regime and its opponents.

Beyond his famed diary *The Cursed Days*, Bunin wrote little in his last thirteen months in Russia. The dominant impression he conveyed was one of spiritual paralysis. Not only his creativity but also his will to live was eroding. He regularly complained of torpor, frustration, and grief; he feared for himself and his loved ones; he lived from day to day, rumor to rumor, hoping for the best but enduring the worst. Poignantly, he was taking grim stock of his life, his "tragic fate." Mercilessly he berated himself for his inability to leave the Old World and accommodate the New, and for his failure to rescue his country, its culture, and its people.

The boundaries of Bunin's life in Russia were rapidly closing in on him. His land was rejecting him, his writings, and his values; its people were telling him to love Russia or leave it. Not surprisingly, the Revolution and its aftermath resurrected in Bunin his youthful impulse to suicide. At times he seemed poised for the executioner's block, tugging at an imaginary noose which he felt tightening around his neck; other times he was like a mad dog, growling, foaming at the mouth, ready to pounce on anyone who crossed his path.

Such impressions tell only half the story of Bunin's last months in Russia. The other half casts him as a vital and courageous individual, a prophet-pilgrim standing against the events overwhelming his land. Bunin was going down, but he was going down fighting. Revolution in any form—past or present, French or Russian, political or cultural—roused him from his lethargy and energized him for battle. A committee of one, he challenged the regime at every turn, raising more scandals than the Modernists. He took on the mob; he used his poems to welcome the allied interventionists; he attacked the Bolsheviks in lectures and articles. He was even more engaging in his private world, in the thoughts and ideas that he wrote surreptitiously, often slightly tipsy and late at night, abandoning caution and trying to make sense of his world.

Bunin's insights were frequently penetrating and prophetic. He accurately predicted the rise of Russia, Germany, and Japan to world power a generation before the fact; he also foretold the failure of socialism and the resurgence of individualism and faith that would take hold in his country some seventy years later. His observations on the Russian Revolution were also borne out by history. In his view the character of the upheaval—the cry for freedom, equality, and brotherhood—was merely a ruse by which tyrants seized power for themselves. The form of Russia's revolt was equally suspect: a sham spectacle in which posters and parades sapped the energy of the folk and masked the evil underneath.

For Bunin, Russians had no one to blame but themselves for their ills. As was so often the case in their tragic history, they had mistaken freedom for license, giving full vent to the "dark side" of their soul. Bunin believed that Russians suffered from a key flaw: they loved ideals and abstractions, emotions and grand gestures, but they hated reality and the discipline and work needed to realize their dreams. Russians, he observed, also had little genuine or stable sense of self. They were Europeans in times of law and order, Scythians in times of chaos; they eagerly embraced any idea or hero presented to them by their intellectuals and writers.

Bunin realized, though, that many things about his homeland insured its greatness in both bad and good times. He also knew that if he gave full vent to his anger and revulsion, he would destroy his soul along with his body. So he repeatedly sought reconciliation: trying again with Russia, reasoning with its people, showing them their cultural and spiritual riches. He failed completely. It was Bunin's fate to deal with loss in life and specifically to see the collapse of "patriarchal" Russia and everything it entailed.

Ever the fighter, ever the pilgrim, Bunin never relinquished the history of his homeland. His mission, divinely ordained as he saw it, was to take the best of his land with him abroad. There he would keep Russia safe, preserving its values and elaborating on its traditions, until his country returned to its senses, admitted the errors of its ways, and rediscovered the riches of its past.

✳ 1919 ✳

January 3, 1919
Vera Muromtseva-Bunina, from her diary
   Socialists always come to some arrangement with the rich. . . .
They go about at night, never fearing that someone will swipe their
coats or money. . . . They are so accustomed to being taken care
of . . . that they do not worry.

January 12, 1919
Vera Muromtseva-Bunina, from her diary
   [A friend] told us: "You know, Ivan Alexeevich, how I hated you
earlier. I could not bear to hear your name because of the way you
depicted the peasants in your novels. . . . Now here I am, a peasant,
who did not see what you, a *barin*, saw. You alone were right.

January 15, 1919
Vera Muromtseva-Bunina, from her diary
   Today Ian read [Gogol's stories] "The Carriage" and "Rome";[1] he
was enraptured by them. "An entire literature has come from 'The
Carriage' alone," he said, "and half of Chekhov has come from it!"

January 17, 1919
Vera Muromtseva-Bunina, from her diary
   The holidays go on like they did in the old days, but I feel
nothing. It seems as if there have been absolutely no holidays at all.

---

[1]Gogol wrote "The Carriage" in 1836 and "Rome" in 1842.

January 28, 1919
Vera Muromtseva-Bunina, from her diary

The conversation turned to politics. Ian predicted that in twenty-five years . . . the future will belong to the Japanese, the Russians, and the Germans. . . .

Ian also predicted a powerful surge of religious feeling in Russia, and the failure of socialism and a passion for individualism.

He believes that socialism is completely unsuited to the human soul, that it contradicts it. . . .

February 13, 1919
Vera Muromtseva-Bunina, from her diary

It is cold inside and out. Most people have no wood. There is also no bread.

February 20, 1919
Vera Muromtseva-Bunina, from her diary

They again want to confiscate our rooms.

February 26, 1919
Vera Muromtseva-Bunina, from her diary

Ian has reread Tolstoy's *Family Happiness*;[2] he is again enthralled by it. He says that we cannot imagine the revolution that Lev Nikolaevich brought about in literature. . . .

" 'The carts were going along the road; and feet were shaking,' " Ian read. "This was very modern for its time; but how good it is! I see the picture clearly."

Ian reads a great deal in Russian and French. Politics fills up his time less and less. . . . For this I am glad. . . .

Circa *March 1919*
Ivan Bunin, from an interview with the Southern Word

I wrote "Nooselike Ears" toward the end of 1916. But I am reprinting it here . . . because the story's gruesome hero, set against the backdrop of ghastly noctural Petersburg, has so terribly justified my vague premonition of all that has happened in Russia.

---

[2]Tolstoy wrote *Family Happiness* in 1859.

Circa *March 1919*
Konstantin Paustovsky, from his memoirs

"The world has become very bleak," Bunin said. "Even the sea smells like rusty iron."

Spring 1919
Valentin Kataev, from his memoirs

Bunin had many opportunities to leave Odessa, where he was in danger, and to go abroad, especially since, as I have already said, he traveled light and loved to wander towns and countries. But Bunin was stuck in Odessa: he did not want to become an emigré, cut off from his country; he stubbornly hoped for a miracle—for the end of the Bolsheviks, for the overthrow of Soviet rule, and for his return to Moscow amidst the triumphant ringing of the Kremlin bells. But to what kind of Moscow? He hardly had any idea. To the old, familiar Moscow? Perhaps this is why Bunin remained in Odessa in the spring of 1919 when it was occupied by the Red Army and under Soviet rule for several months.[3]

By this time Bunin was so deeply compromised by his counter-revolutionary views, which incidentally he did not hide, that he could have been shot right then and there. Bunin probably would have been shot had it not been for his old friend, the Odessa artist Nilus, who lived in the same house as the Bunins. . . .

If Nilus had not moved quickly—he had telegraphed Lunacharsky in Moscow and almost was on his knees before the chairman of the Odessa Revolutionary Committee—anything could have happened.

Nilus obtained a special "safe conduct" pass for the life and property of academician Bunin, a personal immunity which was pinned to the rich varnished door of the house on Knyazheskaya Street. . . .

A detachment of armed soldiers and sailors of the Special Department went up to the front door of the house. Vera Nikolaevna . . . fainted and fell noiselessly to the floor. Bunin, though, stomped loudly on the parquet floor, went to the door, stood firmly on the threshold, raised his hands backward, and clenched his fists

---

[3]The Soviets captured Odessa on April 6, 1919, but lost the city to the Whites in August of that year.

with all his might. His pale face was convulsed in shudders; his beard trembled, his eyes were terrible.

"If anyone dares to cross my doorstep. . . ."

He did not shout these words so much as he spit them out, grinding the muscles of his jaw and baring his strong yellowish teeth. "I'll bite the first man's throat, and then you can kill me! I don't want to live any more!"

I immediately recalled Bunin's verse: ". . . stab me right away— if you don't, then beware! My teeth will tear you apart!"

I was horrified.

But it all turned out well. The men read the safe-conduct order with its Soviet stamp and signature. They were very surprised, and someone even swore quietly at the Revolutionary Committee. . . . They left quietly. . . .

The Bolshevik government allowed everyone who had remained in the city the right to assemble and to discuss how to organize their lives. In the large and, so it seemed to me at the time, elegant hall of the so-called "Literaturka," where not so long ago servants in frock coats catered to aesthetes in velvet jackets and actresses with made-up eyes, there now were many upset, uprooted people, mostly refugees from the north, sitting on everyday chairs taken from the janitor's room. They now had to define their stance toward Soviet rule, which had finally overtaken them on the shores of the Black Sea.

Bunin sat in the corner, his chin leaning on the knob of a thick walking stick. He was yellow, angry, and wrinkled. His thin neck stuck out like a tight spring from the collar of his starched shirt. His eyes were puffy, as if he had been crying; they looked sharp and fierce. His entire body twitched, and he kept twisting his neck as if his collar was suffocating him. He was uncompromising. Several times he jumped up from his place and banged his stick angrily on the floor.

Yury Olesha had pretty much the same impression.

"While at the meeting of the artists, writers, and poets," Olesha wrote, "Bunin banged the floor with his stick at us young people. . . . He was only forty-two. But he truly was a . . . a mean, bony old man—a real gramps."

Though Olesha was wrong about Bunin's age (he was then almost fifty) . . . he concurs with my impression. Bunin then was truly a mean old man. . . .

I continued to visit Bunin, although it was clear that our paths were moving farther and farther apart. I continued to love him passionately, but not only as an artist. I loved him fully as a person, as an individual. I did not feel any noticeable cooling in Bunin's attitude toward me, though I did notice that he would scrutinize me more and more often, as if trying to understand something that was unclear to him: the soul of a young man infected by the Revolution, to read his deepest thoughts.

Bunin sometimes even became critical over the smallest things. For example, he once noticed that I had begun wearing a gold chain as a bracelet with a kind of pendant on it.

He frowned.

"Aren't we the dandy? You're not a girl; you shouldn't be wearing a gold bracelet."

"It's not completely gold," I said. "It's gilded, hollow copper."

"All the worse. Real gold is neither here nor there. But hollow or fake gold—that's bad. Remember this: a man should use and adorn himself—if he has decided to adorn himself at all!—only with that which is real, genuine. . . . No imitation, no fakes! What is that dangling from it?"

"It's a splinter from a shell they took out of my upper thigh," I said not without boasting, though I blushed to the roots of my hair.

Bunin . . . examined the splinter from all sides. . . .

"Then why don't you wear it on a plain steel chain? That would be much better. Hollow American gold is not worthy of your real splinter," he stressed the last word. "It only demeans it. . . . Wear it for good luck, if you want to appear richer than you really are," Bunin said after a little thought. . . .

In autumn, power changed hands again. This time Denikin[4] occupied the town. On one of the city's dark wet mornings—a real Paris morning!—I read Bunin my latest story . . . about a student who, like Pushkin's Herman,[5] was a maniacal gambler . . . and an actor . . . who envied this student and even wanted to kill him. . . . All this, of course, was made more complicated by the presence of a captivating ballerina and the background of the final days of a doomed and decaying bourgeois city under siege by the Red Army. . . .

Bunin listened in silence, his elbow leaning on the polished table, and fearfully I watched his face for signs of irritation or perhaps

[4]Anton Ivanovich Denikin (1872–1947) was general of the anti-Bolshevik forces in southern Russia during the Russian civil war.
[5]Herman is the hero in Pushkin's story "Queen of Spades," written in 1834.

even outright anger. But his eyes were tired and stared into the distance, as though he could really see the bloody revolutionary dawn over the . . . black factory chimneys. His entire figure . . . expressed deep distress, almost unconcealed pain. . . .

He looked at me and said bitterly, as though answering his own thoughts, "Well, I should have expected it. I no longer see myself there. You are leaving me for Leonid Andreev. But tell me this. Could you, like your hero, kill a person to get his wallet?"

"I couldn't, but my character. . . ."

"Not true!" Bunin said sharply, almost shouting. . . . "Every character is the author himself."

"But what about Raskolnikov. . . ."

"Aha! I knew you were going to say this! A starving young man with an ax under his jacket. Who knows what Dostoevsky was going through while he was creating this Raskolnikov of his. . . . In those moments Dostoevsky was himself Raskolnikov. I hate your Dostoevsky," Bunin burst out passionately. "A loathsome writer with all his plots and subplots, his terribly slovenly and contrived language which no one ever spoke or speaks, and with all those importunate, wearisome repetitions, those garbled prolixities. . . .

"Dostoevsky keeps grabbing you by the ears and he pushes, and pushes, and pushes your nose into this impossible abomination, this mess he has invented, into a kind of spiritual vomit. Moreover, it is also so mannered, artificial, and unnatural. The legend of the Grand Inquisitor!"[6] Bunin exclaimed with an expression of disgust, and burst out laughing. "That's where everything that has happened to Russia has come from: decadence, modernism, revolution, young people like yourself, infected to the bone with Dostoevskyism—aimless, lost, spiritually and physically crippled by the war, not knowing what to do with their energy, capabilities, their often outstanding, even enormous talents. . . . But why talk about it!" Bunin waved his hand in despair.

Perhaps Bunin was the first person in the world to speak of a lost generation.

March 8, 1919
Vera Muromtseva-Bunina, from her diary

The conversation turned to Gorky. . . . [A friend] said that once

---

[6]The Grand Inquisitor is a character in Book Five of *The Brothers Karamazov*.

the Bolsheviks are defeated, Gorky should be chased out of all societies. . . .

March 9, 1919
Vera Muromtseva-Bunina, from her diary
   [A friend] spoke a great deal about Gorky. Gorky's entry into the ranks of government has been very important. It has made it possible for intellectuals who were otherwise dying of hunger to be won over and to work for the Bolsheviks who, in their turn, need intelligent people in their ranks. . . .
   Gorky has 250 million rubles at his disposal. The bribery of the intelligentsia has gone on like mad; the more counterrevolutionary a person is, the more he is valued.

March 12, 1919
Vera Muromtseva-Bunina, from her diary
   Two years, two nightmarish years. How many expectations, how many hopes have been buried in this time. How much blood has been spilt, how much has been destroyed, almost all of Russia has been turned upside down.

March 13, 1919
Vera Muromtseva-Bunina, from her diary
   Ian is very upset. There are rumors that the French are leaving Odessa.[7]

March 18, 1919
Vera Muromtseva-Bunina, from her diary
   I sat with Ian for a long time. He was upset. He drank a bit and became more open. He kept saying there was once a Russian history, a Russian state, and now they are no more. The Kostomarovs, the Klyuchevskys, the Karamzins wrote history, but now there is no history. . . . "My ancestors took Kazan,[8] they built the Russian state, and now it is all being destroyed before my eyes—but who is responsible? The Sverdlovs of this world? The blood of my ancestors bursts forth in me; I feel that I should not have been a writer but that I should have taken part in the government."

   [7]The French left Odessa in April 1919.
   [8]A reference to the successful Russian offensive against the Tartars in Kazan in the reign of Ivan the Terrible in the mid-sixteenth century.

Ian sat in his yellow robe. . . . He suddenly looked like a boyar.[9]

"I keep thinking more and more," he continued, "that I should enter the Volunteer army[1] and take part in the government. I find it tormenting to sit in one spot and read the newspapers; you cannot imagine how I am suffering."

March 30, 1919
Vera Muromtseva-Bunina, from her diary

Ian says that he alone is genuinely suffering and that everyone else is a robot.

April 1, 1919
Vera Muromtseva-Bunina, from her diary

Ian has become calmer. These days he cuts out articles from the newspapers. Most likely he is gathering materials for future articles. Will they be as good as his artistic works? But I am glad he has come out of his isolation and gloom. . . . For some reason Ian keeps talking about his tragic fate. By birth he belonged to one class, and then, by virtue of his poverty and fate, he grew up in another world where he could not live as he should, since so much repulsed him from early youth on. That is why he has found it very difficult to write what he feels.

April 3, 1919
Vera Muromtseva-Bunina, from her diary

The radio: Clemenceau has fallen. The French army is being called back in twenty-four hours. The Bolsheviks will be here in three days! . . .

My peaceful existence is coming to an end. My wandering life is beginning; we have no ties to the cities we will visit.

April 5, 1919
Vera Muromtseva-Bunina, from her diary

I ask for advice: should we leave? People convince me to stay, telling me that life will go on as before. I do not argue. But I know that we will suffer morally under the Bolsheviks, and that it will be difficult for Ian, especially since . . . he has openly declared himself in

---

[9]Boyars were members of the old Russian aristocracy before the time of Peter the Great.

[1]The Volunteers were part of the anti-Bolshevik forces.

favor of the Volunteers. But where should we go? To the Don? But it is terrible there—typhus has broken out! Abroad?—we do not have money for that; besides, it would be difficult to tear ourselves away from Russia. . . .

The streets are unusually animated, almost panic-stricken. People are running about with frightened faces. They crowd in groups on the sidewalks, talk loudly, and wave their hands. Those who are leaving are just as upset as those who are staying. The banks are under siege. The franc, which used to cost a ruble, has reached ten to twelve rubles; the pound now costs two hundred rubles. . . .

[A friend] again convinces us to leave. She tells us that the Tolstoys are leaving. She offers us money and . . . passports. Ian does not refuse the money, but we do not decide to leave. She gives us ten thousand rubles. . . .

We go to see off . . . political and social figures who are leaving Russia. . . . All have anxious looks on their faces. We bid farewell to the Tolstoys who have decided to . . . go to Paris. . . . [2]

Masses of automobiles, trucks, people, carts, soldiers, cabbies with passengers, suitcases, loaded-up donkeys, Frenchmen, Greeks, Volunteers—in a word, all of international Odessa is up and bustling about. . . .

A cabby carries off a murdered man. His cap is on his rump, his shoes are gone, and his foot bindings stick out. "What nerve, what a callous heart must one have to take the shoes off a dead man," Ian said. . . .

People are dancing on our street. . . . From time to time bombs and shells tear through, shots ring out. . . .

"Dance, dance, soon you'll cry," Ian says with a sad grin.

April 6, 1919
Vera Muromtseva-Bunina, from her diary
The first Bolshevik troops have entered the city, fifteen hundred soldiers in all! . . . Odessa is a Bolshevik city. . . .

April 7, 1919
Vera Muromtseva-Bunina, from her diary
I have been lying down for two days. The Feast of the Annunciation. The weather is splendid, with sun and a blue sky. I look at the flowering tree in front of my window. It is so good, and so sad!

[2]Alexei Tolstoy returned to the Soviet Union in 1923.

A dead man was carried past us in an open coffin. He . . . had a priest there. But in front of him were red banners with the inscription: "Workers of the world, unite!" . . .

Although I do not go out, I already feel that "airlessness" which always attends the Bolsheviks. I felt it during the five months we were in Moscow, when they were still not as savage and bloodthirsty as they were after our departure, but even then I could not breathe. I remember, when we rushed out of their sweet paradise, the great gladness, the joy of light breathing that seized us right away. . . . The Bolsheviks bring with them something new, something unbearable for human nature. I find it terrible to come across people who truly believe that the Bolsheviks will bring them something positive, a new "system of life." . . .

I am terribly afraid for Ian who began publishing a newspaper three days before the allies left! As if on purpose everyone spoke his mind. Only one of the group has left; the rest have remained.

April 8, 1919
Vera Muromtseva-Bunina, from her diary
There is nothing to buy at the market. Where has it all disappeared to? . . . I run into Ian. . . . He says excitedly: "It's the same thing everywhere: 'Hang him, kill him.' For two years I have heard only baseness, absurdities, and spite; not once have I heard a kind word. . . . I have a terrible feeling—that the final tie with the cultural world is being broken."

April 10, 1919
Vera Muromtseva-Bunina, from her diary
We see troops, tired and looking like peasants. A peasant woman rides a horse amidst them.

"Is this not the seventeenth century!" Ian exclaimed gloomily. "How well the International suits them!"

April 12, 1919
Vera Muromtseva-Bunina, from her diary
Vulgarity is the distinguishing mark of the Bolshevik revolution. People have become very coarse.

Yesterday there was a meeting of the union of writers. There were many people there. They asked Ian to preside. He refused. . . . Kataev, Olesha, Bagritsky, and others behaved like regular scoundrels. They cried out that they were ready to die for the Soviet platform, that it was necessary to screen the meeting and to silence bourgeois, decrepit writers. . . . After they raised a ruckus, they left. Voloshin ran after them and talked to them for some time. They told him the real reason for their actions: first, they were afraid for their own skins, since almost all of them had been Volunteers; second, someone is giving them money for an almanac, and they were afraid they would get too little. . . .

Our apartment will not be confiscated. . . . Voloshin moves about very easily, freely, and unselfishly. Apparently he is a very easygoing and pleasantly simple person. He visited us this afternoon to tell us about our apartment, then he happily began drawing a sign: "The Artistic Neo-Realist School" of Bukovetsky, Nilus, and Voloshin. We divided up the tasks. . . . The pupils will be the children of friends and acquaintances.

Voloshin believes that anyone can write.

"You only have to teach someone how to look at the object. If you can teach him to see, then it's easy to teach him to write."

"Well, then that means I do not know how to see," I said, laughing, "because I cannot write about the simplest things." . . .

At dinner [a friend] talked about a meeting of artists during which some sculptors . . . were treated with great deference. A discussion began about how the sculptor and artist are almost one and the same thing. Medieval workshops were cited as evidence. We proposed to return to this topic. . . .

Ian and Bukovetsky rushed at Nilus because he saw the Bolsheviks as defenders of art.

"You've got to understand," they told him, "that the Bolsheviks are making indulgences only so they can bring intellectuals over to their side, shut their mouths, and make even shorter work of counterrevolutionaries."

April 13, 1919
Vera Muromtseva-Bunina, from her diary

Today we saw civil funerals. They really know how to stage funerals in Russia—no matter what the regime. Are they not symbols of our land? . . . Bolshevik funerals are pompous. Masses of red banners with inscriptions. Some were black with savage sayings— "Death to the bourgeois," "One of ours, ten of theirs." . . . The orchestra plays a march by Chopin. The dead are carried in open coffins. I saw several faces. For some reason they were very dark, but only one was bruised. . . . Several had very peaceful expressions which means they had an easy death and not at all the "sacrifices of Volunteer torments" that the illiterate newspapers said they were. Instead of a *venchik*,[3] a piece of red material surrounded the head. The procession was very long. I stood for about an hour. . . and saw Chinese going along with very serious faces: Their attitude toward death is different, somehow ancient; looking at them, I feel a terrible awe. In front of the coffins were various delegations with crowns made of red ribbons. Masses of young ladies, students, and workers. The order was exemplary. The public stood on the sidewalks like soldiers on parade.

April 14, 1919
Vera Muromtseva-Bunina, from her diary

[A friend] has been very worried about Ian. . . .

"Aren't you afraid," she asks Ian, "after the article you wrote?"

"What can I tell you. For some reason I really haven't thought about it. Perhaps it was stupid that I stayed behind, but then, too, they wouldn't dare touch me. . . ." . . .

Ian treated us to wine and brisket. Voloshin ate very well—he is always starving. He even ate up our rationed pealike bread which we cannot swallow.

The poets asked each other to read their verse. Ian again refused. Voloshin read his poetry. He knows and feels precisely. . . . But much of his verse is bombastic, rhetorical, and empty.

Voloshin . . . is interested in no one, he loves monologues, he often repeats himself, and if something interests his listener he goes on willingly. . . .

April 15, 1919
Vera Muromtseva-Bunina, from her diary

Nilus started talking about the fact that artists have been invited to decorate the city for the 1st of May.

"I have a sketch on how the city should be decorated."

"Are you really going to take part in this?" Ian asked.

"Why not? I believe that one cannot escape from life. And since the Bolsheviks acknowledge science and art, one must take advantage

---

[3]A *venchik* is a paper band placed on the forehead of a dead person.

of this because science and art are the most important things in life," he said with a sweet smile.

"Then that means," I remarked, "that we should not be angry with Gorky?"

"Of course," Voloshin chimed in, "I have never been angry with him. . . ." Then he launched into his theory. Voloshin believes that people are actually angels who take on a devil's form on earth, and that a crucified Seraphim lives in each and every person, even in murderers and idiots. Thus one cannot turn his back on anyone but must accept all. The world has everything except love. Humankind brought love. Hate is the first step to love.

Ian could hardly restrain himself. He asked that "all these Seraphims be left in peace." Voloshin hurriedly changed the topic to how to decorate the city.

Ian, getting himself under control, said, "I do not understand how at a time when people are almost dying from hunger, when they go about ragged from lack of essentials, when scoundrels rule the land—you quietly discuss how best to decorate the city, to adorn the executioner's block? That means to help the very enemy we hate and wish to destroy; to talk about art, science, and the government when people are dying of hunger. . . this I cannot bear!"

April 18, 1919
Vera Muromtseva-Bunina, from her diary

Yesterday at twilight Ian stopped by the church . . . where he married A. S. Tsakni.[4] Returning from there he said: "It was no more than twenty years ago that I walked out of that church! I asked myself, why did I rush and marry the Greek girl? Then I thought: How frivolously we act in life which is so short!" . . .

At tea, Voloshin developed his theory of motherhood.

"If a woman has loved without love in return, then in the next incarnation she will give birth to a son whose soul will be entered by the one whom she has loved. . . . Hence the relationship between mother and son is first love, then crucifixion. . . ."

Voloshin has theories that reconcile one with everything. He is probably one of the happiest people on earth. No matter what happens, with the ease of a juggler he will throw a thing upward and it will fly to its place. . . .

[4]Bunin married Tsakni on September 23, 1898.

Already many homes are without water; many people must carry buckets for several blocks.

Ian reads the newspapers avidly. He lives and breathes current events almost the entire day; only in the evenings, when one cannot go out, is he able to read a French novel. I do just the opposite. I devote less time to contemporary affairs; I escape from them at the first opportunity. I immerse myself in a book, a translation, or a conversation with the children of our school.

Many people are preoccupied and keep busy mostly with getting food. . . . We are already beginning to live on the edge of malnutrition.

Many people are also beginning to take their books to the city library . . . to preserve them from today's barbarians.

We carry cards that label us professional people; but we do not feel particularly safe if, strictly speaking, we suddenly find ourselves outside the law.

Rumors keep on growing. Where do they come from? What force brings them into being? Why does everyone find them so necessary? Maybe it is because our salvation is in them? It is strange how avidly we get hold of them and pass them on to our friends, even though we do not fully believe them, but find them consoling. . . .

It is interesting to note how everyone finds a place in the "communist paradise." Nilus, for example, keeps wishing to see something positive in the Bolsheviks. But he is like that: he always finds the good in someone. He is innately alien to all that is base. . . .

April 21, 1919
Vera Muromtseva-Bunina, from her diary

Easter. The weather is splendid. It is sunny out. There is a blue sky. The trees are beginning to blossom. But there is sadness in my soul.

I have not been to church in a week. Ian and I went . . . only on Holy Saturday. The archbishop said the mass. There were few people there. One male high school student, several female high school students, two or three elderly clerks, several old men and ladies. The archbishop, a thin man with a pleasant Russian peasant face, celebrated the service very well, somewhere between simple and majestic. . . . How strange that the church was so empty on such a day.

In church you feel sharply how the heavy hand of bolshevism weighs down upon you. With the wonderful words and hymns, you first forget; but then you wake up and recall that your life is finished, that you have fallen captive to monsters, that there is no longer truth, beauty, poetry, goodness, but only a cynical forgery of everything, a license for all kinds of boorishness . . . and cynicism. What is unique, our spiritual riches, they cannot take from you—but they can, of course, weaken you with hunger, cold, and all kinds of torture. Here in church I understand suddenly the direction I must pursue so as to preserve myself, my ego. . . .

On the way home we read a new decree on the wall: all bourgeois, forty years old or younger, must work tomorrow on Easter Day—and clean the streets! At the gates to our house we ran into Thomas, our caretaker. We are friends with him—he is from my uncle's village. We see each other as fellow countrymen, and we poke fun at everything that has to do with southern Russia. I told him about the decree. He laughed, and he was even stung by the lack of respect for his work.

"They think anyone can sweep the street," he said impressively. "You'll only make more dirt. You have to know how to do it. But don't you worry. I'll do it all. All you have to do is hold the broom in your hands."

Ian and I went to the morning service. The streets were empty; sometimes we met one or two passersby. When we approached the church we ran up against hooligans who were laughing loudly. . . . Our mood fell. Ian felt faint; we returned home and lay down to sleep. . . . He said he had gone to church earlier . . . but there was no one there. He stood there like a stone . . . and did not know what to do. A priest passed him by and looked at him. Ian then went out, sat on the church porch, and . . . fell into despair. . . .

The icon of Saint Casper was found at the marketplace, all stripped away and scratched. The archbishop said a prayer service over it; the crowd cried. People crowded around the cathedral the entire day; they even had to be chased away. Women fell and writhed in hysterics. . . .

We told [a friend of ours] of how Kataev acted at a meeting. He laughed and recalled how Kataev hid at his house during the first days of bolshevism:

"It is a pity I wasn't at the meeting," he said. "I would have said to Kataev in front of everyone . . . that I allowed him to hide at my place. . . ."

"These sons of bitches are really something," Ian said. . . .

April 23, 1919
Vera Muromtseva-Bunina, from her diary

It is twelve years today that Ian and I have set out on our way!

Odessa has turned into an Eastern city in which important trading takes place on the street. Socks, oranges, string, candles; the traders sit along the walls; beggars and the less fortunate sing, play, and beg. Several of them simply sit with signs on their chests.

Odessa has changed greatly. Instead of a sea of soldiers—Frenchmen, Poles, Volunteers, Greeks, and colored warriors—the streets are filled with Red Army soldiers with huge bows on their hats. The public has become greylike. . . . Everyone is dressed more simply. . . . The majority of faces are repulsive. Ian looks about attentively and exclaims from time to time: "What a bunch! Just look at their faces! Take a good look at them! They were different before! How can you explain what has happened!" This time I became upset because Ian was perturbed and was speaking loudly. I asked him to be more careful. But he paid no attention to what I was saying. . . .

My head started spinning from all this; I wanted to get home as quickly as possible.

The arrests continue.

April 24, 1919
Vera Muromtseva-Bunina, from her diary

Yesterday evening Voloshin came to see us. . . . At tea we began to talk a great deal about Nicholas II.[5] Voloshin told us many interesting things: the accounts of eyewitnesses . . . friends in the Crimea who had held high positions in the government. Unfortunately it is dangerous to write down anything. He did, though, tell us that the Empress said, "You cannot betray the homeland twice!" . . . when it was suggested to Nicholas that he conclude peace with Germany. She hated Wilhelm.

April 25, 1919
Vera Muromtseva-Bunina, from her diary

Izvestia reported that Voloshin has been dismissed from the Commission for the First of May. . . . Not long ago he had called the people "bastards" in his verse.

This morning Voloshin came to us. He had written an answer to

[5]Nicholas II, the last of the Romanovs, was tsar of Russia from 1894 to 1917, and was murdered by the Bolsheviks in 1918.

the commission; he wanted to read it to Ian. The contents of his letter were roughly the following: There is a difference when an individual offers his services and when people come to him for help. In this case people came to him as an authority on Russian poetry. He agreed to serve; suddenly he is discredited.

Ian smirked, "Splendid, but they won't publish your answer." Voloshin was surprised: "What do you mean? I was promised. I was already at the editorial office." "Go ahead and try," Ian said. "But I doubt if anything will happen."

Ian is in a depressed state: "Everything has been taken from us—the press, the means to live. How many more months will this half-starving state continue, and for what? I cannot go and work for these pigs. . . . I cannot be in the same room with them. How can I associate with them? I cannot repress my disgust. . . . Many have had to come up with theories from hunger, from need. I am glad that Voloshin fell, and with his crucified seraphims to boot. . . . Kataev is coming today, and I will curse him out so he will remember. Not so very long ago he strolled about as a Volunteer."

Rumors, the most improbable things: 1) Kolchak[6] has joined Denikin. 2) Hindenburg is coming to Russia. 3) Odessa will be a free city. 4) Lenin and Trotsky are delivering very anxious speeches. 5) Kiev has been taken by the Poles. 6) Petersburg has been taken, but by whom?

They've begun destroying Ian in *Izvestia*. They write, for instance, that the "lower part of his face looks like something from a Gogolian Christmas Eve."[7] What that means we do not understand. I even went through Gogol's works, but Gogol did not help.

We go along the street, and as always we feel loathing. But suddenly there is this marvelous singing. What is it?

"It's from the synagogue," Ian said. "Let's drop in."

We went in. I very much liked the singing. There was a lot of light but few people. . . . I felt a religious trembling. Religion is the best thing humankind has created.

April 25, 1919
Ivan Bunin, from his diary The Cursed Days
Almost three weeks have passed already since our ruin.

---

[6]Alexander Vasilyevich Kolchak (1874–1920) was recognized as "supreme ruler" of Russia by the anti-Bolsheviks. He was later executed by the Soviets.
[7]Most likely a reference to the character of the devil in Gogol's story "The Night Before Christmas," published in 1832.

I very much regret I did not write anything down. I should have taken note of every minute. But I had absolutely no strength to do so. We had absolutely no idea of what was going to happen on April 3!

On noon of that day our maid Anyuta called me to the phone. . . . I picked up the receiver. "Who is it?" I asked. "Valentine Kataev. I'm rushing to tell you some unbelievable news: the French are leaving." "How can this be, when?" "This very minute." "Have you gone out of your mind?" "I swear to you, it's true. They're fleeing in panic!"

I ran out of the house, grabbed a cab, and did not believe my eyes. Donkeys loaded with goods, French and Greek soldiers in field dress, gigs with all kinds of military property, all were racing at a trot. . . . A telegram in the editorial office: "Clemenceau's ministry is falling apart. Revolution and barricades in Paris."

On this very day twelve years ago Vera and I came to Odessa en route to Palestine. What fantastic changes have occurred since that time! A dead, empty port; a dead, burned-out town. . . . Our children and grandchildren will not be able even to imagine the Russia in which we once lived, which we ourselves did not value or understand—all its might, complexity, richness, and happiness. . . .

I very often now see death in my dreams: one of my close friends or relatives, and especially often my brother Yuly. I find it quite terrible even to think about him: how and on what is he living, or even if he is alive? The last news I had about him was on November 23 of last year. . . .

The Satan of Cain's anger, of bloodlust, of the most savage cruelty wafted over Russia while its people were extolling brotherhood, equality, and freedom. Suddenly everyone became crazy, deranged. Everyone yelled at everyone else . . . : "I'm arresting you, you son of a bitch!"

In mid-March of '17 a soldier almost killed me on the Arbat—I had allowed myself a certain "freedom of speech" and cursed the newspaper *Social Democrat* because one of its vendors had thrust himself upon me. That scoundrel of a soldier knew perfectly well that he could do with me whatever he liked, and absolutely without recrimination. The crowd that surrounded us suddenly turned out to be on his side: "Really, old boy, are you so repulsed by a newspaper that is for the working masses? Does this mean you are a counter-revolutionary?"

How all these revolutions are the same! During the French Revolution a plethora of new administrative institutions suddenly appeared. A whole flood of decrees, instructions sprang forth. The number of commissars . . . and all kinds of authorities in general went on without end; committees, unions, and parties grew like mushrooms; and everyone "started devouring everyone else." A completely new and special language came into being: "bombast mixed up with the coarsest abuse and targeted at the *vulgar remains of a dying tyranny. . . .*"

One of the most distinguishing features of a revolution is the ravenous hunger for play, dissembling, posturing, and puppet show. The ape has awakened in man.

Oh, these dreams about death! What a huge place death occupies in our short lives! . . . Day and night we live in an orgy of death. They say a "bright future" will issue forth from this satanic gloom. Already there have appeared on this earth an entire legion of specialists and contractors to fashion human well-being. . . . They always say, "This will be the last and decisive battle!" The eternal fairy tale. . . .

The tree in our yard has burst into flower. Some damned spring this has been! . . . I do not *feel* spring at all. What is spring *now*?

Rumors and more rumors. . . . This waiting around for something to come and resolve it all, always in vain. But we will not pass through unscathed; our souls will be maimed even if we do survive. But what would life be like if we did not have these expectations, these hopes?

Dear God, what a time you have ordered me to be born!

April 29, 1919
Ivan Bunin, from his diary The Cursed Days

I cannot describe the heaviness in my soul. The crowd in the street is physically repulsive. I am sick to death of these animals. If only I could find some respite, to hide somewhere, perhaps go to Australia! But all roads out have long been closed. . . . You can't leave without permission, otherwise they'll kill you like a dog. . . .

"Blok hears 'Russia' and 'revolution' like the wind. . . ." Rivers of blood, a sea of tears, but these do not phase him. . . .

I often recall the outrage with which critics greeted my supposedly all-black portraits of the Russian people. Now who is outraged? . . . The "priest," the "philistine," the bureaucrat, the policeman, the landowner, the prosperous peasant, in a word, everyone except the "people"—the "poor ones," of course. . . .

April 29, 1919
Vera Muromtseva-Bunina, from her diary
Yesterday Ian was in a very poor frame of mind. He is suffering terribly: "I'm not living now," he said to me. "I don't care if I live or die. Life is unbearable for me now."

April 30, 1919
Ivan Bunin, from his diary The Cursed Days
I lie in bed with closed eyes. I am reading a book . . . simply for something to do. I am completely indifferent to everything; my only feeling now is that this is *not life*. Then, I repeat, there is this exhausting waiting around. It simply cannot continue like this; someone or something will save us—tomorrow, the day after tomorrow, perhaps, even this evening! . . .

I've gone out twice to look at the crowds celebrating the First of May. I had to force myself; such spectacles literally make me sick to my stomach. "I feel people physically," Tolstoy once wrote about himself. Me, too. People did not understand this about Tolstoy, nor do they understand it about me. . . . Until now most people have seen the "people" and the "proletariat" only as words, but for me they have always had eyes, mouths, voices. . . .

There was a fair number of people at Cathedral Square, but they were standing about senselessly, looking at the whole show in an unusually dull manner. There were, of course, the processions with red and black banners, the "chariots" decked out in paper flowers, ribbons, and flags. Actors and actresses dressed in opera folk costumes stood, sang, and comforted the "proletariat." There were "living *tableaux*" depicting the "might and beauty of the worker's world," of "brother"-communists with arms embraced, of "docile *paysants*," and of "grim-faced" workers in leather aprons. . . . When will the Bolsheviks end this most base mockery of the mob, this repulsive buying of their souls and bellies? . . .

This evening I was at Catherine Square. It was gloomy and damp. Catherine's monument was wrapped and bandaged with dirty wet rags; it was entwined and pasted over with red wooden stars. Across from the monument . . . red flags, filthy and droopy from the rain, cast thin and bloodlike reflections on the wet asphalt.

I recall an old worker . . . the first day the Bolsheviks took

control. Suddenly a crowd of boys jumped up from behind the gates
with piles of fresh *Izvestias*, crying, "The bourgeois in Odessa must
contribute 500 million rubles!" The worker began to wheeze, choking with anger and malicious joy: "That's too little! Way too little!"
Of course, the Bolsheviks were to him the genuine "worker-peasant
force." They "were realizing the most cherished hopes of the people."
It is well known what kinds of hopes these "people" have: they have
been called upon to rule the world and to take charge of all culture,
law, honor, consciousness, religion, and art.

"Without any annexations and contributions to Germany!"
"That's the way it should be!" "Five hundred billion to Russia!"
"That's too little, Way too little!" . . .

The "left-wing," all the "excesses" of the revolution are blaming
the old regime. The Black Hundreds are pointing the finger at the
Jews. But the people are not guilty! Soon they will blame everything
on someone else—their neighbor and the Jew. . . . "The Jews are
always starting something. . . ."

May 1, 1919
Vera Muromtseva-Bunina, from her diary
A decree forbids everyone to use electricity, except for the
communists. . . .

A friend and I decided to go out around twilight and take a look
at how our new masters tried to decorate the city. The overall
impression: tasteless, undistinguished, spiteful, and monotonous.

When I returned, Ian was already at home. He and his friends
had already walked about town. I asked him for his impressions. He
said, "A dirty, repulsive, mournful picture!" . . .

For the most part the streets this evening were host to high
school students, maids, and individual regiments of soldiers. Middle-
aged people were almost nowhere to be seen. Many people flashed red
badges.

The worker's holiday. After breakfast I went out to wander the
city alone. All the homes had red flags and rugs on the balconies—by
order of the new masters. Most likely they want to know who has
rugs so they can confiscate them.

A poster on Cathedral Square: On the left a fat bourgeois stands,
holding a worker by the collar; under it is written the year "1918."
On the right a worker stands and a bourgeois is sweeping the street.
Under it is written "1919."

Other posters show the same thing: the difference between 1918 and 1919. Pictures of 1918: a bourgeois and a German have a worker underneath them. Pictures of 1919: a worker and a soldier stand on a bourgeois who has a fiery tongue sticking out of his mouth. . . . A worker, a soldier, and a sailor press the huge stomach of a bourgeois, and money pours out of his mouth. The people stop, look silently, and move on further. . . . The statue of Catherine the Great is covered with a great overcoat. Behind her is a huge poster done in the Cubic style. Someone with an artificially large nose stands on steps topped by a throne; the inscription:

> The thrones are covered with the people's blood.
> We will cover our enemies with blood.

In most cases the authors of these posters are very young artists. Among them are children of rich bourgeois, who are poorly versed in politics and who do not understand what they are doing.

An illuminated sign has been erected over the home of the former governor general: *"Vive la révolution mondiale."* It was done for the crews aboard the French ship which, alas, and as if on purpose, has left port. So it was for nothing.

Over the London Hotel: "Peace to the huts; war on the palaces." I go along the avenue . . . and come across chariots slowly returning from the parade. In them are young actors and actresses in various national costumes. Everyone has tired and frightened faces. . . .

On the way home we wonder why there was no joy in the festivities. We conclude that the bloody posters have made even the sympathizers despondent and oppressed.

May 2, 1919
Ivan Bunin, from his diary The Cursed Days

I went out . . . looking for food. They say everything will be closed, and there will be nothing. Sure enough, there is almost nothing in the stores that are still open. Sure enough, it has all vanished somewhere. . . .

[A friend] cannot rent out his small dacha because it is now "the property of the people." . . . You could hang yourself from outrage!

All day there has been a persistent rumor about . . . "the fall of Petersburg." Oh, how everybody really wants that! But, of course, it's all nonsense.

In the evening I was at a synagogue. It has been so terrifying and repulsive of late that one is drawn to churches, the only havens still untouched by cruelty and dirt. . . .

Now all the homes are dark. The entire city is in darkness except for the thieves' dens. There one can hear balalaikas and see shining chandeliers and walls decorated with black banners with white skulls and the inscription: "Death, death to the bourgeois!"

I am writing by the light of a stinking kitchen lamp, using up the last of the kerosine. How sick, how outrageous. My Capri friends, the Lunacharskys and the Gorkys, the guardians of Russian culture and art, express righteous anger when they warn a journal about abetting "tsarist sympathizers." What would they do with me if they caught me writing this criminal tract or trying to hide it in the crack of the ledge? . . .

First it was the Mensheviks and the trucks, then the Bolsheviks and the armored cars. . . .

The truck: what a terrible symbol it has become for us. How many trucks have there been in our most difficult and terrible memories! From the very first day the revolution has been tied to this roaring and stinking animal. . . . All the vulgarity of contemporary culture, its "social pathos," is embodied in the truck. . . .

From Tatishchev's *History of Russia*:

"Brother against brother, sons against fathers, slaves against masters; each one trying to kill the other from motives of self-interest, lust, power; each one trying to rob the other of dignity. . . . each one wanting what the other has and crying over what they have not. . . ."

Now these idiots are convinced that a great "shift" has taken place in Russian history, and that this "shift" will lead to something completely new and unprecedented!

Russian history has always been a terrible tragedy, but no one has the slightest genuine understanding of it.

May 2, 1919
Vera Muromtseva-Bunina, from her diary
In the newspapers—lists of people who have been shot. The tone is immeasurably coarse. The orders that concern the bourgeois are rendered in the most insulting tones: "Bourgeois, surrender your mattresses." In the newspapers there is, generally speaking, the most

extensive abuse. The word "bastard" has become a technical word . . . "the money-chasing bastard," "the Denikin-loving bastard," the "White-Guard bastard."

About town, posters show a similarly disturbing content, so much so that Ian said, "My fists clench and my head swirls from such helpless rage."

May 3, 1919
Ivan Bunin, from his diary The Cursed Days

There is so much lying going around that you could scream. All our friends, all our acquaintances . . . are lying at every turn. They cannot help but lie; they cannot help but add to *their own lies, their own* flourishes to well-known falsehoods. . . . They rave on like they have a fever; and when you hear their ravings you take them in greedily, you become infected by them. Otherwise it seems you will not survive the week.

This self-inflicted torpor gains such force that by evening you go to bed as if in a drunken haze, almost certain that something will happen during the night. You cross yourself firmly, furiously. You pray with such force that your body hurts. It seems that God, or a miracle, or the heavenly powers cannot but help you. You fall asleep, exhausted from the unbelievable tension. . . . In the middle of the night you jump up with a wildly beating heart: Somewhere you hear rat-a-tat-tat. Sometimes it is very close by, like a hail of stones on the roof. Here it is, you think, something has happened; someone has attacked the city—finally the end of this cursed life.

The next morning you sober up with a heavy hangover. You rush to the newspapers; no, nothing has happened. Again the same cries, the new "victories." . . . People are standing in lines at the stores. . . . Again the same dullness and hopelessness, again the empty long day lies before you; not one day, but days, long, empty, and useless to all! Why bother living? For what? Why do anything? In this world, in their world, the world of colossal boars and beasts, I need nothing. . . .

It is night. I am writing this in a slightly tipsy frame of mind. A friend stopped by in the evening. Just like a conspirator, he . . . insisted that everything people were saying during the day was the honest truth. . . . My nerves were so shot that I got tipsy on two glasses of wine. I know all these rumors are nonsense—but I believe them nonetheless; I am writing with cold and shaking hands. . . .

"Oh, revenge, revenge!"—Batyushkov wrote after the fire of Moscow in 1812. . . .

There are two types of people in our country. Ancient Rus presides in one, wild tribes in the other. Both are terribly capricious; "unstable," as they said in the old days. The folk have said about themselves: "We are like the tree—from it comes the icon or the club, depending on who treats the wood: Sergei Radonezhsky or Emelyan Pugachev."

If I did not love, if I did not know this "icon," this Rus, then why have I gone insane all these years, why have I suffered so incessantly, so cruelly for my homeland? People say I only hate. But who are these people? They are those who would readily spit on the folk—if the folk were not an impetus for their splendid feelings about life. . . . They are those who know "folk" and "humanity" only as words . . . and for whom the famous expression "feed the hungry" . . . sprang from a desire to kick the government for the umpteenth time, to undermine it again.

It is a terrible thing to say, but it is the truth: if it were not for the misfortunes of the folk, thousands of our intellectuals would be profoundly unhappy people. How else could they have sat around and protested; about what could they have cried and written? Without the folk, life would not have been life for them.

The same thing happened during the war. . . . the most cruel indifference to the people. The "soldiers" were an object of ridicule. How the people poked fun at their speech in the hospitals, how they indulged them with candy, rolls, even ballet dances! The soldiers themselves went along and pretended to be terribly noble, meek and resigned. "What can you do, little sister, all is God's will!" they said, agreeing with the nurses, the ladies with the candy, the reporters. They lied when they said how much they enjoyed the dances. (When I asked a soldier. . . what he thought was going on, he said, "They're playing the devil. . . . dressing up like goats. . . .")

People were terribly indifferent to the folk during the war. They lied like criminals about the folk's patriotism, even when a child could see that the war repelled them. Where did this indifference come from? From our terribly typical carelessness, our frivolity, our unwillingness . . . to be serious in serious moments. Just think how carelessly. . . how gaily all Russia looked upon the . . . the revolution, the greatest event in all of history. . . and during the greatest war in the world!

Yes, before the Revolution we all lived (the peasants included) extremely freely, with rustic carefreeness; we all lived on what seemed to be a very rich estate . . . because our needs were so elementary and limited.

We studied a little here and there. And that we did only because we had to. . . . We cared little for long daily routines. We shirked work terribly. And from this came our idealism, a very gentrylike idealism, our eternal opposition, our criticism of everyone and everything: after all, to criticize is much easier than to work.

"Oh, how I am suffocating under Tsar Nicholas.[8] I cannot be a bureaucrat and sit next to Akaky Akakyevich[9]—a carriage, get me a carriage!"

Hence the Herzens, the Chatskys.[1] . . . What an old Russian disease is all this languishing, this boredom, this babbling—this eternal hope that a frog with a magic ring will come and do it all for you. . . .

"I never did anything because I always wanted to do something special."

This is Herzen's confession.

I recall other remarkable lines of his: "We are sobering up humanity. We are its hangover. . . . We canonized humanity. . . . We canonized revolution. . . . We are delivering coming generations from sorrow by our disenchantment, our suffering. . . ."

No, we are still a long way from sobering up humanity.

May 4, 1919
Ivan Bunin, from his diary The Cursed Days
Passively I read about the shooting of twenty-six people.

I am in a stupor. Twenty-six people, not sometime but yesterday, here, right next to me. How can I forget, how can I forgive the Russian people? But everything will be forgiven; everything will be forgotten. I *only try* to be horrified; for, to tell the truth, I am shocked by nothing any more. This is the hellish secret of the Bolsheviks—to kill all sensitivity. . . .

It is like the price of bread, of beef. "What? Three rubles a pound?" Then it goes up to a thousand—shock, stupor, screams,

[8]Nicholas I was tsar of Russia from 1825 to 1855.
[9]Akaky Akakyevich is the hapless hero in Gogol's story "The Overcoat," written in 1842.
[1]Chatsky is the hero of the play *Woe from Wit*, written by Alexander Sergeevich Griboyedov in 1822–1824.

passivity. "What? Seven were hanged?!" "No, my dear, not seven, but seven hundred!" Already you are shocked beyond measure—you can still imagine seven being hanged, but try to imagine seven hundred, even seventy!...

I recall a gloomy evening on the First of May. People were getting married in a cathedral; a woman's choir sang. I entered; as always, this churchly beauty, this island of the "old" world amidst a sea of the dirt, vileness, and baseness of the "new," touched me in a most unusual way.

How the evening sky shone through the windows!... They were purplish blue—my favorite color. The dear faces of the choir girls, the white veils on their heads, the gold crosses on their foreheads, the music in their hands, the golden lights of their small candles—this was so charming that... I cried quite a bit. I went home with such a feeling of lightness, of youth. And along with this—such sadness, such pain!...

For the last month our cook Marusya hid and fed my bread to a Bolshevik, her lover. I knew, I knew. So much for my bloodthirstiness ... but we cannot be like them. And once we are like them, this is the end for us!...

We should have hanged ourselves a long time ago.

May 5, 1919
Ivan Bunin, from his diary The Cursed Days
At a funeral procession an old woman ... cried so bitterly that I stopped and began to console her. I muttered, "What will be, will be. God be with you!" I asked her, "Was the dead person a relative of yours?" The old lady paused for breath and dried her tears. Finally she said with difficulty, "No.... I don't know him.... *I envy him...*." ...

I find respite from my insanity (which began with the war) by reading the newspapers. Why am I so brutal with myself? Why do I tear my heart to shreds by reading them?...

I find this Bolshevik jargon intolerable. What kind of language does our left speak? "Cynicism, bordering on gracefulness... Now a brunette, today a blond ... Reading in a fit of temper... To conduct an interrogation with passion ... Either-or: there is no in-between ... To make the proper conclusions ... To whom it is necessary to inform ... To stew in one's own juice ... The dexterity of hands ... New-era lads ..."

Then they attempt to use high style with supposed bitter irony (though it is not clear who or what is the target). . . . It is not a horse but a Russian High-Stepper; it is not "I sat down to write" but "I mounted my Pegasus"; they are not policemen but "uniforms of a heavenly blue color." . . .

It is terrifyingly mystical in the evenings. . . . The fountains are not lit, but all the "government" buildings, the police headquarters, the theaters and clubs bearing the names of Trotsky, Sverdlov, and Lenin blaze forth brightly, like medusas or rosy glass stars.

People rush along. . . . They are the red aristocracy: sailors with huge revolvers in their belts, pickpockets, criminal villains, and shaved dandies . . . all with gold teeth and with big, dark, cocainelike eyes. . . .

But it is terrifying also in the afternoon. This whole huge town does not live; it stays home and goes out but little. It feels it has been conquered by an allegedly special type of people . . . more terrible . . . than our ancestors, the Pechenegi.[2] But the conquerors reel, trade at hawker's stands, spit sunflower seeds, and swear in the foulest language. . . .

Generally speaking, the minute a city becomes "red" the mob changes suddenly and sharply. . . . There is a new assortment of faces; the street becomes transformed.

How those faces affected me in Moscow! It was because of them that I left there.

Now it is the same thing in Odessa. . . . These faces lack ordinariness, simplicity. Almost all of them are so utterly repulsive, so frightening in their evil dullness, in their gloomy and lackeylike challenge to everyone and everything.

This is already the third year of this monstrous thing. A third year of only baseness, only dirt, only brutality. If only for a laugh, if only for fun, you wish for something . . . that is simply ordinary, simply different! . . .

"No wholesale making fun of the people!"

"The Whites,"[3] of course, are open fire!

The people, the revolution are always being forgiven "excesses."

But for the Whites, from whom everything has been taken away, who have been profaned, assaulted, and murdered—the homeland, the native cradles and graves, mothers, fathers, sisters—there cannot be, of course, any "excesses." . . .

---

[2] The Pechenegi were Turkic nomads who continually assaulted the Kievan state in the second half of the twelfth century.

[3] The "Whites" were the anti-Bolshevik forces.

"Revolution is an elemental force. . . ."

Earthquake, plague, cholera are also elemental forces. No one extols them, though; no one canonizes them; no one struggles with them. And the revolution is always "deepening."

"The people who gave us Pushkin, Tolstoy."

The Whites are not the people. . . .

But the Decembrists,[4] the famous Moscow University of the '30s and '40s,[5] the conquerors and colonizers of the Caucasus, the Westerners and Slavophiles,[6] the agents of the "era of the great reforms,"[7] the "repentant noblemen," the first members of "The People's Will,"[8] the government duma?[9] What about the editors of the well-known journals? And the entire cast of Russian literature? And its heroes? No other country in the world can lay claim to such nobility.

"The decay of the Whites. . . ."

What monstrous nerve to talk like this after the unheard-of "decay" in the world which marked the appearance of the "Reds." . . .

But many things arise from stupidity. Tolstoy said that nine-tenths of human folly can be explained exclusively by stupidity.

"In my youth," he would say, "we had a friend, a poor fellow, who with his last pennies suddenly bought a wind-up metal canary. We cracked our heads trying to explain this stupid act, until we remembered that our friend was simply very stupid."

May 6, 1919
Ivan Bunin, from his diary The Cursed Days
I make an effort every morning to get dressed quietly, to overcome my impatience with the newspapers—and all in vain. In vain I try to do so today. Cold and rain, but I again run out into the

---

[4]The Decembrists were a group of Russian noblemen who staged an unsuccessful revolt against autocracy in 1825.

[5]Moscow University in the 1830s and 1840s was a center of Western idealist and rationalist thought in Russia.

[6]The Westerners and Slavophiles were two opposing groups in the mid-nineteenth century who argued over whether Russian society should follow European or indigenous patterns of thought, culture, and government.

[7]The Great Reforms took place in the reign of Alexander II; they began with the emancipation of the serfs in 1861 and included changes in local government, the courts, and the military.

[8]The People's Will protested the highly centralized nature of the Russian state and were ultimately responsible for the death of Tsar Alexander II.

[9]The four dumas (1906, 1907, 1907–1912, and 1912–1917) were nationally elected assemblies and attempted parliamentary government in Russia.

slime and waste my money on them. What is going on in Petersburg? . . . Not a word, of course, about anything important. . . .

Voloshin says that. . . . what is going on is the uniting and building of Russia. . . .

Over the past few decades Russian literature has become extremely depraved. The street, the mob have begun to play a very great role in it. . . . Russian literature now has only "geniuses." An amazing harvest! The genius Bryusov, the genius Gorky, the genius Igor Severyanin, Blok, Bely. . . . How can one stay calm when one becomes a genius so quickly, so easily? Anyone can fight his way through, stun the mob, and call attention to himself.

Take Voloshin. The day before yesterday he called Russia the "Angel of Revenge" who had to stab a maiden's heart with the ecstasy of murder, to pierce a child's soul with bloody dreams. Yesterday he was a member of the White Guard, but today he is ready to sing of the Bolsheviks. He tried to drum the following into my head: The worse it gets, the better it will be; nine seraphims are descending upon earth and are dwelling among us in order to reconcile us with crucifixion and burning, and to turn us into new, tempered, enlightened beings. I told him to choose someone a bit more stupid for such conversations.

A. K. Tolstoy once wrote, "When I recall the beauty of our history before the cursed Mongols, I want to throw myself on the ground and roll about in despair." Yesterday Russian literature had Pushkins and Tolstoys, now it has only "cursed Mongols." . . .

The last time I was in Petersburg was in late March, '17. . . . Meetings and mass gatherings were going on nonstop: appeals and decrees were being published one after another. . . . Along Nevsky there rushed government cars with red flags . . . trucks filled to overflowing . . . and detachments with red banners marching to music and in an excessively lively and precise manner. . . .

Nevsky was being trampled underfoot by a grey mob, soldiers with overcoats thrown over their shoulders, unemployed workers . . . drunkards of all kinds, trading cigarettes, red ribbons, obscene cards, sweets, and anything else you might want. The sidewalks were filled with litter and piles of sunflowers; the streets had manure, humps, and holes. . . .

I went to the Field of Mars.[1] People had just finished celebrat-

---

[1] In pre-Revolutionary times, the Field of Mars was a place for folk festivals and military parades.

ing a . . . sacrifice to the revolution: a comedy funeral for alleged heroes who had fallen for freedom. . . . It was a mockery of the dead: the deceased were deprived of an honest Christian burial; they were boarded up in red coffins and buried in the very center of town right among the living! . . . From one end to the other, the great square was dug up and trampled underfoot; it was disfigured with mounds, pierced with tall, bare poles with very long, thin black rags on them, and closed off by fences that were hastily joined together. . . .

I attended . . . a celebration honoring some Finns. . . . The poet Mayakovsky reigned over all. I sat with Gorky and the Finnish artist Gallen.[2] Mayakovsky came over to us without any invitation. He shoved a chair between us and began to eat from our dishes and to drink from our glasses. Gallen's eyes popped out of his head. . . . Gorky just tittered. I moved aside. Mayakovsky noticed this.

"Do you really hate me that much?" he asked me gaily.

I said "no" quite freely: that would be too much of an honor for him. He was about to open his troughlike mouth and ask me something else, but at that moment the minister for foreign affairs got up to give the official toast. Mayakovsky rushed over to him. He jumped on a chair and began to yell something so obscene that the minister was frozen to the spot. The minister quickly got hold of himself and again proclaimed, "Ladies and gentlemen!" But Mayakovsky yelled something even fouler than before. The minister . . . shrugged his shoulders and sat down.

Then the French ambassador got up. Apparently he was certain that the Russian hooligan would back off in confusion. Was he wrong! Mayakovsky drowned him out in a still more shrill voice. Moreover, and to the ambassador's extreme amazement, the entire hall suddenly erupted into a savage and senseless frenzy. Infected by Mayakovsky, everyone began to shout for no reason at all. They began to bang their shoes on the floor and to beat their fists on the table. They laughed, howled, yelped, grunted; they even shut off the electricity. . . .

There was still another celebration then in Leningrad—the arrival of Lenin. "We bid you welcome!" Gorky wrote to him in his newspaper. . . . Lenin was met at the station with an honor guard and music, and was whisked off to one of the best homes in Petersburg which, of course, did not belong to him. . . .

[2] Axel Gallen-Kallela (1865–1931) was a Finnish painter and advocate of Expressionism in art.

We had one banquet after another, and the only sober ones were the Lenins and the Mayakovskys.

One-eyed Polyphemus[3] . . . wished to devour Odysseus. Lenin and Mayakovsky (whom high school students prophetically called Idiot Polyphemovich) were also rather gluttonous and extremely powerful in their one-eyedness. At one time both seemed to be little more than street clowns. Not for nothing was Mayakovsky called a Futurist, a man of the future; the polyphemiclike future of Russia undoubtedly belonged to the Mayakovskys, the Lenins. . . .

Before I left Petersburg I was in the Peter-Paul Cathedral. Everything was wide open—the fortress gates, the cathedral doors. Idle people were roaming everywhere, looking around and spitting out sunflower seeds. I walked around the cathedral, looked at the grave sites of the tsars, and, with a bow to the ground, I begged their forgiveness. . . .

I stood for a long time in a state of shock: The entire endless universe of Russia was becoming unraveled before my very eyes. Spring, the Easter chimes called forth feelings of joy and resurrection. But an immense grave yawned in the world. Death was in this spring, the final kiss. . . .

"The world did not know disappointment," Herzen said, "until the great French Revolution; skepticism arrived together with the Republic of 1792."

As far as we are concerned, we will carry to the grave the greatest disappointment in the world.

May 6, 1919
Vera Muromtseva-Bunina, from her diary

It is evening. We are sitting with lamps. We have four of them in all! Voloshin is reading his translations of Verhaeren.[4]

I sit on an oilskin couch; under Voloshin's rhythmic reading I am carried away by thoughts into distant, happy times, still before the war. It is winter. A brightly lit hall. . . . Verhaeren is giving a lecture about his dear, heroic land. There are a great many people there, listening attentively. Verhaeren immediately conquers the hall. I especially like his unusually pleasant face. On stage, as always, sits the director of the club and writers. Hidden from public view,

[3]Polyphemus was the Cyclops in Book Nine of *The Odyssey*.
[4]Emile Verhaeren (1855–1916) was a prominent Belgian poet whose works have been compared with those of Victor Hugo and Walt Whitman.

Bryusov peeks out. He has only just survived a tragic story: the poetess L'vova[5] has shot herself because of him. She asked him to come and visit her. He refused and she—bang! So not her but Mamontov gives the welcoming address to the guest. Bryusov did not stay for dinner. . . . I sat next to Verhaeren. He told me about his country, about his life there and in France. . . . We touched upon poetry. He, of course, paid his compliments to Russian verse. . . . Verhaeren was enraptured by Moscow, the Kremlin. For the first time in my life I asked for an autograph. . . .

Several years have passed since that time, but it seems that it was so endlessly long ago. Verhaeren died a senseless death. . . . our Russia is also dying.

May 7, 1919
Ivan Bunin, from his diary The Cursed Days
Yesterday evening I decided to hide these notes so well that not even the devil could find them. . . . All the same, these notes can be found; that will be my ruin. *Izvestia* wrote about me: "It is long overdue to pay attention to this academician with the face of a Gogolian Christmas Eve, to remember how he extolled the arrival of the French in Odessa!". . . .

Just think: I *still must explain* first to one, then to another, why I will not go and work for Proletkult.[6] I still must *prove* I cannot sit down right next to the police, where almost every hour they are breaking someone's head, and enlighten some idiot who sticks his hands in his mouth and teach him about "the latest achievements in the instrumentation of verse"!. . .

It would be a thousand times better to die from hunger than to teach iambic verse and trochees to such an idiot so that he can sing while his colleagues rob, beat, and rape!. . .

Tolstoy once told [a friend]: "Schoolgirls who read Gorky and Andreev sincerely believe they cannot penetrate the depths of their writing. . . . This is complete nonsense. . . . What is going on in their heads, all these Bryusovs and Belys?"

Chekhov also did not understand them. In front of people he would say they were "marvelous" writers, but at home he would laugh loudly: "What characters! They should be arrested!" And about

[5]Nadezhda Grigor'evna L'vova actually shot herself on December 7, 1913.
[6]The Proletkult (1917–1932) was an early Soviet project to develop a distinctly proletarian literature and art.

Andreev: "I will read two pages, then I need two hours of fresh air!"

Tolstoy said, "Today literary success is only stupidity and insolence."

He forgot that the critics were helping.

Who are they, these critics?

People turn to doctors for medical advice, lawyers for legal affairs, engineers to construct a bridge, architects to build a home. But when it comes to art, anyone who wants to can be a critic, often people who by nature are completely alien to art. These are the only ones people listen to. . . .

Even when you give up hope completely you harbor a secret dream that there will come a day of revenge, the day for a universal damnation of these days. One cannot live without this hope. But what can one believe now, when such an unbelievably terrible truth has been revealed about man?

Everything will be forgotten and even extolled! . . . *Literature will help.* It will soundly distort everything, just like it did with the French Revolution, when poets, the most noxious tribe on earth . . . stepped forth by the thousands as verse-idlers, degenerates, and charlatans.

We complicate, we philosophize over everything, even over the unspeakable things that are now going on about us. . . . Right now, for example, we have been arguing about Blok: about his drunkards who first kill a street girl and who then become Christ's apostles.[7] . . .

Generally speaking, we have been poisoned by the literary approach to life. Look at what we have done to the great . . . last century in Russia. We have smashed it and broken it up into decades—the twenties, the thirties, the forties, the sixties—each decade defined by *literary heroes*: Chatsky, Onegin, Pechorin, Bazarov. . . . It would make a cat laugh, especially when you recall that these heroes were eighteen, nineteen, or, at the most, twenty years old! . . .

The journals are calling for a crusade to Europe. I remember the fall of '14, a meeting of intellectuals. Gorky, green from excitement, said in a speech, "I'm afraid of a Russian victory, that savage Russia will fall with its hundred-million-man belly on Europe!"

Now the belly is a Bolshevik one, but Gorky is not afraid of it.

In the newspapers a "warning": ". . . There will soon be no electricity." In one month they have screwed up everything: no

---

[7] A reference to Blok's poem "The Twelve," written in 1918.

factories, no railroads, no buses, no water, no bread, no clothes—no nothing!

Yes, yes—"Seven thin cows will devour seven fat ones, but they themselves will not become fat."

Now (it is eleven o'clock at night) I opened the window and looked out onto the street. . . . There is not a soul in sight. It is so quiet that one can hear, somewhere beyond the road, a dog gnawing on a bone. Just where did it get a bone? Look at what we have come to!

May 8, 1919
Ivan Bunin, from his diary The Cursed Days

Late yesterday night some people, together with the "commissar" of our home, came to measure the width, length, and height of all our rooms "to consolidate the proletariat." . . . These damned monkeys made me furious! I did not say a word. I silently lay on the couch while they measured all around me, but I got so upset . . . that my heart started to flutter and my veins pulsed on my forehead. . . .

The "commissar" of our house . . . accepted his office out of fear; he is modest, shy, and now shakes at the words "revolutionary tribunal." He runs through the building, begging us to fulfill the decrees. . . .

I get a sharp pain next to my left nipple when I hear words like "revolutionary tribunal." Why "commissar," why "tribunal," why not simply "court"? All because when the Bolsheviks take cover under sacred revolutionary words, they can bravely step in blood up to their knees. Thanks to such words they . . . can become indignant over everyday pillaging, robbery, and murder. They know perfectly well they must tie up and drag a tramp into the police station because he has mugged a passerby by the throat *in ordinary daylight*; but they choke from ecstasy . . . if this tramp does the same thing in "revolutionary" times because he has the fullest right to express "the anger of the lower classes, the sacrifices of social injustice." . . .

There was a knock at the front door; I immediately became rabid. I opened the door—and again the commissar with a mob of his friends and members of the Red Army. With hurried vulgarity they asked that I give them any extra mattresses. I said I had no extra ones. They came in, looked around, and left. Again the stiffness of the head, the heart beating, the arms and legs shaking from outrage, from insult. . . .

In the courtyard . . . cooks scream (about us): "Let them sleep on shingles, on boards!"

Kataev was here. The cynicism of today's young people is unbelievable. He said, "For a hundred thousand, I'll kill anyone. I want to eat well, I want to have a nice hat, excellent shoes. . . ." . . .

I again take a long look at the pulp fiction before me: "Library of the Working People. The Songs of Folk Anger. Odessa, 1917." . . .

There is "The Worker's Marseillaise," "The Warsaw Hymn," "The International," "The Hymn of the People's Will," "The Red Banner." . . . It is all malicious, bloody to the extreme, deceitful ad nauseam, flat, and incredibly wretched:

We'll hurl our curses at all villains,
We'll call all warriors to battle,
Hostile whirlwinds waft over us
But we'll rise proudly and brave
The banner of struggle for the worker's cause.
We'll reforge the sword into plowshares
And we'll begin a new life.

Good God, how it all sounds alike! What a terrible, unnatural thing has happened to entire generations of boys and girls. . . . every minute fanning hatred for the landowner, the factory owner, the philistine, all "bloodsuckers, spiders, obscurants, and knights of darkness and violence!" . . .

An official gave a speech before some peasant "deputies": "Friends, the power of the soviets will soon be throughout the whole world!"

Suddenly a voice from the crowd: "Not a chance!" The official angrily: "And why not?"

"Because you haven't got all the Jews yet!"

May 8, 1919
Vera Muromtseva-Bunina, from her diary
They came for the mattresses. The Red Army soldiers were polite, but I experienced an unpleasant feeling when they barged in to take what you sleep on. They took nothing from us, though Ian and I have two mattresses apiece. But I used a bit of psychology on them. I told them we had only one apiece; and, having made a gesture with my hand, I bid them: "If you like, go behind the screens and look for yourselves."

They hemmed and hawed for a while, then they left. A nice home still embarrasses them; they are more boorish in poorer apartments. They have been at this a whole week, collecting mattresses which will probably rot somewhere else. . . .

"The French," Ian said after a reading, "are different from the Russians in poetry. Whereas Russians leave much of the work to the reader, the French keep trying to convince you of something." . . .

It's nine o'clock. . . . Suddenly I heard a knock on the door. I rushed to the door; I saw two peasant figures with long sticks.

"What is it?" I asked, opening the door and feeling my heart beating strongly.

"Excuse me, I am the house commissar; I have been ordered to take the measurements of all the rooms."

May 9, 1919
Ivan Bunin, from his diary The Cursed Days
I woke up at six from palpitations of the heart.

Going for the newspapers, I heard the curses of a peasant woman. She has a small fish in her basket—eighty rubles! . . .

Izvestia has been answering letters from its readers:

"Dear Citizen Guberman. So you think the war with those bastards Kolchak and Denikin is fratricide?"

"Dear Comrade A. Praises to Russia, even if they be to Soviet Russia, have nothing to do with the Marxist approach to the question."

"Dear Citizeness Glikman. Have you still not understood that a life that revolves about money is gone forever?"

May 9, 1919
Vera Muromtseva-Bunina, from her diary
[A friend tells us about] the day of "world insurrection." . . . Such an absurd combination of words—"world insurrection"! . . . They say that everything will be taken and that people can keep only very small amounts of essentials. Somehow I cannot believe it. They will only . . . rouse the entire population against them.

At home . . . we spite the Bolsheviks by drinking good wine.

May 10, 1919
Vera Muromtseva-Bunina, from her diary
Voloshin has gotten passage out of the country. . . .
The final evening with him. . . . We sat . . . in half darkness. It

was sad. Pitiful refreshments on the table. Over the past few months we have gotten accustomed to Voloshin. He is a man of good cheer. He accepts everything. He bears no malice against bolshevism, but he does not defend it. He forgives people not only for their inadequacies but also for their vices. Perhaps this bespeaks a great indifference to the world—but then this is not a virtue. But such calmness is pleasant amidst universal excitement, irritation, and bitterness.

May 12, 1919
Vera Muromtseva-Bunina, from her diary
It is getting more and more difficult to make breakfast and lunch. Meanwhile, I go to the library and read from the famous physiologist Bunge:[8] "... Food should bring a person joy, every meal should be a holiday for him. ..." What will happen to Russia ... when there is nothing to eat! ... Already people are starving.

May 13, 1919
Ivan Bunin, from his diary The Cursed Days
Two soldiers. ... One is big and bent over. ... He gobbles up a sausage, tearing off pieces with his teeth and ... slapping himself below the stomach: "Here's my commune! ... your Jerusalem excellency, it's hanging right below my stomach. ..."

May 14, 1919
Ivan Bunin, from his diary The Cursed Days
The "commissar" of our building came to verify how old I was; they want to recruit all the bourgeois into a "rear-guard militia."

May 15, 1919
Ivan Bunin, from his diary The Cursed Days
A pogrom ... under the auspices of the Odessa Red Army. ...
About thirty Jews were killed. ... Many stores were destroyed. Soldiers tore through at night, dragged them from their beds, and killed whomever they got. People ran into the steppe; they rushed to the sea. They were chased after and fired upon—a genuine hunt. [Our friend] saved himself by accident. He had spent the night not in

[8]Gustav von Bunge (1844–1920) was a Swiss physiologist and an expert in nutrition.

his home but at a sanitorium. . . . At dawn a detachment of Red Army soldiers suddenly appeared. "Are there any Jews here?" they asked the watchman. "No, no Jews here." "Swear!" The watchman swore, and they went on. . . .

I went along and thought. More accurately, I felt: if only I could get out of here and go to Italy or France. . . . Life has forced us to feel so sharply, so attentively. . . Our eyes—even mine!—saw so little earlier.

May 16, 1919
Ivan Bunin, from his diary The Cursed Days

You fight the tension, you try to come out from under it, this intolerable waiting for something to happen . . . all in vain. It is especially horrible when you yearn for time to fly by as quickly as possible.

May 18, 1919
Ivan Bunin, from his diary The Cursed Days

I had a dream about the sea, milky white in the light blue night. I saw the pale rose lights of a ship; I said to myself that I had to remember that the lights were pale rose. What does this all mean?

A notice from the *Voice of the Red Army*:

"Death to people who take part in pogroms! The enemies of the people wish to drown the revolution in Jewish blood; they want the masters to live in storybook mansions, the peasants to go back to the fields . . . with the cows, and to bend their backs for parasites and lazy bones. . . ."

An article in Kiev's *Izvestia*. . . . "Unfortunately the Ukrainian village is like what it was in Gogol's day: ignorant, anti-Semitic, illiterate. . . . Commissars bribe, extort, get drunk, and violate the law at every step. . . . Soviet workers win and lose thousands at cards, distilleries support the drunkenness." . . .

I am not a strong believer in their "ideology". . . . Communism, socialism for the peasants, is like a saddle for the cow: it will bring them to frenzy. The "cause" is becoming the "den of thieves" so cherished by Rus from time immemorial, a search for the pirates' free way of life so beloved by people who stray from the herd, who are not used to home and work, and who are corrupt in every way.

Almost ten years ago I wrote an epigraph to my stories about the people, about its soul, using the words of Ivan Aksakov: "Ancient

Rus still has not passed by!" I was correct to do so. Klyuchevsky notes the extreme "repetitiveness" of Russian history. To our supreme misfortune, no one has paid attention to this "repetitiveness." The "freedom movement" came into being with lighthearted amazement, with indispensable, obligatory optimism . . . "warriors" and realistic literature on one hand . . . some kind of mysticism on the other. Everyone "put laurel wreaths on lice-ridden heads," to use Dostoevsky's phrase. Herzen was a thousand times right when he said, "We have divorced ourselves profoundly from existence. . . . We became capricious, we did not want to know reality, we continually excited ourselves with dreams. . . ."

Don't the people know that revolution is only a bloody game to change places, and that it always ends with . . . the folk going . . . from the frying pan into the fire? The leaders are wise and sly. They know fully well what they are doing; they unveil the mocking sign: "Freedom, brotherhood, equality, socialism, communism!" And the sign will hang for a long time—so long as it does not bear down too heavily on people's necks. . . .

Dostoevsky said, ". . . We have been taken not by socialism but by the emotional side of socialism. . . ." But this is the underground after all, and in the underground one knows exactly where he must direct his steps and which qualities of the Russian people are extremely useful to him. . . .

"A people—young, unbalanced, perpetually dissatisfied, and spiritually dark—readily ceded to disturbances, waverings, instability. . . . The spirit of materialism, of unrestrained will, of coarse self-interest wafted destructively over Rus. . . . The hands of the righteous were paralyzed; those of evil men were untied. . . . Crowds of outcasts, the scum of society devastated their home under the banners of . . . guides, impostors, hypocrites, degenerates, criminals, and ambitious people. . . ."

This is from Solovyov, about the Time of Troubles. Here is an excerpt from Kostomarov, about Stenka Razin:

"The people followed Stenka, but they were deceived. . . . There were promises, bribes, lures, and . . . traps. . . . All types of Asians and pagans rose up . . . they rioted and slashed, not knowing why. . . . There were Stenka's 'charming letters'—'I will be just to the boyars, officials, and other powers-to-be; I want equality. . . .' But full-scale pillaging went on. . . . Stenka, his associates, his armies were drunk from wine and blood. . . . They hated laws, society, religion, everything that checked personal incentive. . . . They breathed vengeance and envy. . . . They were fugitives, idlers, and thieves. . . . Stenka promised the bastards freedom in everything, but in reality he made them . . . complete slaves. He tortured and executed them for the slightest disobedience; he called everyone 'brother,' but they all fell prostrate before him. . . ."

Don't think the Lenins of this world did not know and count on all this!

May 19, 1919
Ivan Bunin, from his diary The Cursed Days

How terrible are the old Russian chronicles: endless sedition, insatiable self-interest, ferocious struggles for power, deceptive kissings of the cross, flights to Lithuania, to the Crimea "for the rising up of non-Christians for their own native ancestral homes," the slavish missives to one another ("I bow to the earth, as your faithful slave") only to fool someone . . . evil and shameless reproaches from one brother to another. . . . "Shame and disgrace to you: You wish to abandon your father's blessings, your native graves, your sacred fatherland, your Orthodox faith in our Lord, Jesus Christ!"

May 20, 1919
Vera Muromtseva-Bunina, from her diary

I leave for the library with the joyous feeling that the Bolsheviks still have not forced me to do any dirty work, and that I can sit quietly here as long as I want, isolated from everything—it is genuine rest! But sadness has taken hold of me. I cannot read—instead I write my thoughts into my notebook. I have my own bookshelf. Sometimes my notebook lies there . . . among my other books; but sometimes I'm afraid there will be a search, and so I take it home.

May 22, 1919
Ivan Bunin, from his diary The Cursed Days

At night anxious dreams about trains and seas and very pretty landscapes which . . . leave me morbid and sad—with the tense expectation of something. . . .

A new list of those who have been shot . . . then an article:

"A happy, joyous time at Club Trotsky. . . . People first sang the 'International.' Then one comrade delighted the audience by imitating a barking dog, a chirping chick, a singing nightingale . . . and a notorious pig. . . ."

Why were the pigs the only "notorious" ones; why was the "International" performed right before someone imitated them? . . .

Our literature now has such an incredible number of self-assured, impudent fellows who pass themselves off as connoisseurs of the word! How many champions do we have of the ancient ("fresh and juicy") folk tongue, individuals who never say a simple word but who exhaust themselves with their arch-Russianness!

After all their international "searchings," that is, after their Young Turk imitations of all Western models. . . . many writers of poetry and prose are creating a nauseating Russian language. They are taking the most precious folk legends, fairy tales, and "golden words," and they are shamelessly passing them off as their own. . . . They defile these with their own additions, rooting about in regional dictionaries and compiling the most obscene arch-Russianness, which no one ever spoke in old Russia, and which is impossible to read! How our Moscow and Petersburg salons are host to all the Klyuevs and Esenins who dress like pilgrims . . . and who sing through their nose about "dear little candles," "sweet little rivers" . . . and "their bold little heads"!

The Russian language is becoming fractured, it is failing the people.

May 23, 1919
Ivan Bunin, from his diary The Cursed Days

From the newspapers: "Kolchak . . . is flogging the peasants to death. . . . Mikhail Romanov is riding with him. . . . They are traveling on an old troika: autocracy, orthodoxy, nationality. . . . They bear Jewish pogroms, vodka. . . . Kolchak has entered into the service of international predators . . . the cold-blooded, *fat* hand of Lloyd-George will bring an exhausted country into shudders. . . . Kolchak waits to drink the blood of the workers." . . .

It rains almost the entire day, charming, with a marvelous springlike sky among the clouds. But I almost fainted twice. I have to stop writing these notes. Jotting them down I irritate my heart even more.

Again rumors—ten transports are coming to rescue us.

May 23, 1919
Vera Muromtseva-Bunina, from her diary

Our school keeps growing and growing. I find it so pleasant to be with children. But I notice that the artists do not feel this way. Apparently it is not for them. They only fulfill their duty and that's all. . . .

May 24, 1919
Ivan Bunin, from his diary The Cursed Days

Slogans in the classic Russian style:
"Forward, native sons, do not count *the corpses!*" . . .

I am reading . . . Saint-Just,[9] Robespierre, Couthon[1] . . . Lenin, Trotsky, Dzerzhinsky. . . . Who is the most base, bloodthirsty, and vile? . . .

May 25, 1919
Ivan Bunin, from his diary The Cursed Days

They carry a corpse past us (the deceased was not a Bolshevik). "Bless him, O Lord, he whom you have chosen and taken onto Yourself. . . ."

Truly, the dead are blessed.

May 25, 1919
Vera Muromtseva-Bunina, from her diary

All the posters are now being drawn in absolutely realistic tones—just like pictures from tobacco or cigarette boxes. This is what the public wants. The citizens still have not taken to Cubist art. The inscriptions under these pictures are milder in tone. . . . The posters keep showing Red soldiers beating up fat generals. . . .

A huge poster in the middle of the square: A five-headed snake, two heads have been chopped off . . . and a knife hangs over a third.

"Take a look at that," a woman in a kerchief says to her husband, nudging him with her elbow. "I have never seen a snake with five heads. . . ."

The hydra of the counterrevolution!

[9]Louis-Antoine-Leon de Saint-Just (1767–1794) was a Jacobin, famous for his energy, oratorical ability, military leadership, and political role in the French Terror.
[1]Georges-Auguste Couthon (1755–1794) was a member of the Committee of Public Safety.

May 27, 1919
Ivan Bunin, from his diary The Cursed Days

I looked through my "briefcase," and I quickly tore up several poems and stories I never finished. Now I regret what I have done. All this from grief, a sense of hopelessness. . . .

Oh, these nightly furtive hidings and rehidings of papers, money! Millions of Russians have endured this corruption, this degradation over these years. How many treasures will people now find! Our entire time will become a fairy tale, a legend. . . .

May 28, 1919
Ivan Bunin, from his diary The Cursed Days

I go and listen carefully on the streets, around the gates, in the bazaar. The air is filled with pervasive spite toward the "communes" and the Jews. The most vicious anti-Semites are the workers. . . . What scoundrels! . . . Three-quarters of the people are like that: if they're allowed to pillage, rob, for crumbs, they will give up their conscience, soul, God. . . .

May 28, 1919
Vera Muromtseva-Bunina, from her diary

[A friend] came to convince Ian to work for Agit-Prop. He tried to prove to him that education under any form of government is good. Ian only shrugged his shoulders. Our friend kept insisting, saying that Ian could be accused of sabotage. Ian exclaimed, "Saboteurs are those who serve and ruin things. I have not served, and no one can make me do so." "But you will die of hunger," our friend said. "It is better to stand with an uplifted fist on Cathedral Square than go work for them. Let this fact be recorded in history. . . ."

Both men began to scream at each other; they were both very upset. Our friend asked Ian to give him an answer tomorrow. "Think it over," he said. . . .

May 29, 1919
Ivan Bunin, from his diary The Cursed Days

As far as I can make out, the Bolsheviks are doing poorly on the Don and beyond the Volga. God help us!

I have read a biography of the poet Polezhaev. . . . It is painful and sad and sweet. Not Polezhaev. . . but the fact that I am the last who feels his past, the time of our fathers and grandfathers. . . .

The rain shower has passed. A cloud is high in the sky, the sun peeks out, the birds chirp sweetly outside in bright yellow-green acacia trees. Fragments of thoughts, of memories which truly will never return. . . . I recall the woods of the village—the backwoods, the birch grove, the grass, the waist-high flowers—I recall how a similar rain shower once sped by it, and how I breathed in the sweetness of birch trees, the fields, and the rye, of everything, of all the charm of Russia. . . .

They chased [a friend of mine] from his estate (near Odessa). Then they began to chase him from his apartment in the city. He went to church and prayed up a storm—it was the feast day of his Guardian Angel. Then he went to the Bolsheviks about his apartment—and died suddenly. It was decided to bury him at his estate. Now he lies in eternal rest in his native nest, next to his loved ones. A hundred years will pass by—will there be anyone then who, when by his grave, will feel his time? No, never, no one. My time as well. But what if I will not lie next to my loved ones . . . ?

May 31, 1919
Vera Muromtseva-Bunina, from her diary
The repertoire in the theaters: Chekhov, Tolstoy, Gogol, and others. I am always impatient about the reviews. . . . But it so happens they are not well received. Yesterday [our maid] Anyuta saw [Tolstoy's] *The Power of Darkness.*[2] Today I asked her for her impressions of it: "It was surprising that the characters all ate out of one bowl. . . . We never did that. . . ."

I did not get any more out of her.

June 5, 1919
Vera Muromtseva-Bunina, from a letter to Yuly Bunin
It is even strange that I have not been in Moscow for a whole year and have not seen you. I have been terribly bored. Ian, too. We often talk about a trip to Moscow, but we have no idea how to go about this. We have permission to enter the city, but we also need permission to leave Odessa—and this seems rather difficult to do—it would mean a lot of effort. This is only part of the problem. To live in Moscow we would most likely need about ten thousand rubles—or else we would face a slow death, at least for me, since all the

[2]Tolstoy wrote *The Power of Darkness* in 1888.

doctors . . . have told me there is almost no medicine there. . . . It is becoming more difficult to live here with each passing day—the prices keep rising. . . . I have been offered a position for twelve hundred to fifteen hundred rubles a month, but Ian still will not agree to let me work.

June 6, 1919
Ivan Bunin, from his diary The Cursed Days
I am going through and tearing up some papers, cuttings from old newspapers. Here is some very sweet poetry that the *Southern Worker* (a Menshevik newspaper before the arrival of the Bolsheviks) addressed to me:

> Frightened, you suddenly bowed
> Slavishly, with hurried praise
> Before the Varangian. . . .

This had to do with some verse I published in the *Odessa Leaflet* the day the French departed Odessa.

How these internationalists can turn into nationalists, patriots when it suits them! How arrogantly they make fun of "frightened intellectuals"—as if there were no reasons to be frightened—and of "frightened philistines," as if the Bolsheviks have some great advantage over them. Just who are these philistines, these "well-off petty bourgeois" . . . ?

You suddenly attack any old house where a large family has lived for decades; you kill or take captive the masters, stewards, servants; you seize the family archives; you start to go through them and investigate the life of the family, this house—how much that is dark, sinful, unjust will be uncovered, what a terrible picture can be drawn, and especially when . . . people wish desperately to find something shameful, no matter what . . . !

Suddenly, completely suddenly the old Russian home is seized. Precisely what has been uncovered? Truly one has to marvel at the trifles that have been discovered! . . . It is amazing: absolutely nothing!

June 8, 1919
Ivan Bunin, from his diary The Cursed Days
Dostoevsky said, "Give teachers full opportunity to destroy the old society and to build a new one, and there will be such darkness,

such chaos, such unheard-of coarseness, blindness, and inhumanity that the entire new structure will collapse and be cursed by all humankind, before it is completed. . . ."

Such lines now seem weak.

June 9, 1919
Ivan Bunin, from his diary The Cursed Days

Pentecost. . . . The dead railway station with its broken windows, the train rails red from rust, a huge dirty wasteland next to the station where there are people, screaming, laughter, swings, and carousels. . . . And all the time fear. . . .

News: "The Bolsheviks are leaving! An English ultimatum— clear out of the city!"

[A friend] said that the people are filled with spite toward us, and that "we ourselves have instilled it in them for a hundred years. . . ." Rumors: "Suitcases, trunks, and baskets are being confiscated; they are on the run. . . . Communications with Kiev have completely broken down. . . . Proskurov, Zhmerinka, Slavyansk have been taken. . . ." Who has taken them? No one can tell me.

I have smoked almost a hundred cigarettes. My head burns, my hands are ice.

June 15, 1919
Ivan Bunin, from his diary The Cursed Days

[A friend] keeps asking me to write a mystery play where she will have the role of the Mother of God "or something saintly, something that would call people to Christianity." I ask her, "Call whom? These animals?" "Yes, why not? Not long ago I saw a sailor, a real big guy, who was crying. . . ." Crocodiles also cry, I said.

We went out after dinner. As always, my soul is terribly heavy. Again the glassy rose stars in the evening sky. . . . Again a terrible poster—the head of Our Lord, dead, blue, mournful, wearing a crown that is shoved to one side by a peasant's club.

June 22, 1919
Ivan Bunin, from his diary The Cursed Days

A most ancient belief of savages: "The brilliance of the star to which our soul passes after death comes from the brilliance of the eyes which we have eaten in life. . . ."

Now that does not sound so archaic. . . .

A biblical citation: "Honor will decline, baseness will grow. . . . Social assemblies will turn into houses of ill repute. . . . The face of a generation will become doglike. . . ."

Still one more, well known to all: "Taste—and you will become like the gods. . . ."

People have often tasted—but it has been in vain.

"The French attempt to restore the sacred rights of the people, to win freedom for all, has only revealed full human impotence. . . . Coarse anarchistic instincts . . . have broken all social ties with animal-like self-satisfaction. . . . But a powerful individual will check anarchy, and his fists will firmly grab the reins of government!"

What is most surprising is that these words—justifying Napoleon—belong to the singer of The Bell.[3]

But Napoleon himself said, "What has made a revolution? Ambition. What has put an end to it? Also ambition. What splendid pretext to fool the mob . . . freedom for all!"

June 23, 1919
Ivan Bunin, from his diary The Cursed Days

What vileness! . . . "Citizens" carry water from morning to night because the plumbing has not been working for a long time. From morning to night people talk only about getting food. Science, art, technology, all kinds of human work or creative life—all this has perished. They have devoured Pharaoh's fat cows; they have not only grown fat, but they themselves are dying!

Now village mothers are scaring their children: "Quiet down! Or else I'll give you to the Odessa commune!" . . .

The Red officer: a boy about twenty years old, his face is all bare, shaven, his cheeks are hollow, his pupils are dark and wide: He does not have lips but a loathsome sphinxlike stance. His teeth are almost all gold. A high school girl hangs on his chickenlike body. . . . She wears an absurdly huge pistol on her skeletonlike legs. . . .

Everything in the university is in the hands of seven freshmen and sophomores. The main commissar, a student from the Kiev veterinary school . . . bangs his fist on the table and puts his feet up on it. . . . The commissar of the polytechnic institute always carries a loaded revolver in his hand. . . .

Everyone is preparing to flee. The pillaging is terrible. The most faithful "communists" are given anything that falls into their

---

[3]*The Bell* was published by Alexander Herzen from 1857 to 1867, in London and Geneva.

hands: tea, coffee, tobacco, wine. Rumors have it that . . . the sailors especially like cognac. Now we must prove that these convict gorillas are dying not for the revolution but for cognac.

June 24, 1919
Ivan Bunin, from his diary The Cursed Days
Having awakened, I understand with horror, so especially clearly and soberly, that I am simply dying from this way of life, physically and spiritually. . . .

God marks the scoundrel. Even in ancient times there was a universal hatred for people with red hair and high cheekbones. Socrates could not bear pale-faced individuals. Now there is a modern-day anthropology for the criminal type . . . pale faces, big cheekbones, a coarse lower jaw, and deeply shining eyes.

How can one not recall this after Lenin and the thousands of others like him? (Incidentally, criminal anthropology makes note of a special type among innate criminals and especially women criminals: the doll-like, "angelic" face, like Kollontai once had, for example.)

How many pale faces, high cheekbones, and striking asymmetric features mark the soldiers of the Russian army and the common Russian people—how many of them . . . have Mongolian atavism in their blood. . . . It is precisely these individuals, these very Russians who, from time immemorial, were known for their *antisocialness* and who gave us so many "daring pirates," so many vagabonds, runners, scoundrels, tramps, wanderers—it is precisely these people whom we have recruited for the glory, pride, and hope of the Russian *social* revolution. So why should we be surprised at the results?

Turgenev once reproached Herzen: "You bow before the sheepskin coat; you see in it some great grace and novelty, the originality of future forms." Novelty of form! The fact of the matter is that any Russian revolt (and especially the current one) first of all shows to what extent everything is *old* in Russia, and how much it yearns first of all for *formlessness*. From time immemorial there have been "pirates" . . . loafers, rebels against everyone and everything, drunkards, tavern riffraff, hypocrites, sowers of all types of lies, unrealizable dreams, and the like. Classical Rus is a country of brawlers. It has the saint and also the builder, tall but cruelly firm. But what a long and incessant struggle these two have waged with the brawler, the destroyer, with all kinds of sedition, dissension, and bloody "disorder and absurdities"!

Criminal anthropology makes special note of occasional criminals: people "who are alien to antisocial instincts" and who commit crime every now and then. But it also tells us there is another group, "instinctive criminals." They always act like children, like animals; their most distinguishing feature, their innate symptom, is the thirst for destruction, for *antisociality.*

Take a woman criminal, a girl. As a child she is stubborn, fickle. From adolescence on she displays highly destructive behavior: she tears up books, breaks dishes, burns her clothes. She avidly reads a great deal; her favorite reading is passionate, involved novels, dangerous adventure stories, heartless and daring feats. She falls in love with the first fellow she meets; she is ruled by her sexual drives. She is always extremely logical in her discourse; she deftly blames others for her actions; she lies so brazenly, assuredly, and to such an extreme that she paralyzes anyone whom she lies to.

Take a male criminal, a youth. He is a guest at his family's dacha. He rips down trees, tears off the wallpaper, breaks glass, makes fun of religious symbols, and draws all kinds of vulgar things everywhere. "Typically antisocial . . ." There are thousands of such examples.

In peaceful times these degenerate types sit in prisons and asylums. But then there comes a time when "the supreme people" triumph. The doors of the prisons and the asylums fling open, the archives of criminal investigative units are burned—the orgy begins. But the present orgy has exceeded everything that has gone before it—it has even astounded and grieved those who have for many years called for Stenka Razin and what he thought. A strange wonder! Stenka could not think about anything social, he was a "born" criminal—from exactly the same villainous tribe that perhaps augured this new *many-yeared* struggle.

You remembered the summer of '17 as the beginning of some terrible illness, when you already felt sick. Your head burned, your thoughts became confused, everything around you took on a terrifying air; but you still managed to stay on your legs and wait for something with the feverous tension of all your last physical and spiritual powers.

But at the end of this summer, when you opened the morning newspaper, always with shaking hands, you suddenly felt you were getting pale, that the top of your head was being drained, like right before you faint: Big letters hit you in the eyes with an hysterical cry—"Everyone, everyone, everyone!"—a cry that Kornilov is a "rebel, a traitor of the revolution and the homeland. . . ."

And then there was November 16.

The Cain of Russia, with a joyously mad frenzy, giving his soul to be trampled on by the devil for thirty pieces of silver, triumphed in full splendor.

Moscow, being defended for a whole week by a handful of a cadets, burned for a week and shook from the cannonade, then surrendered and resigned itself.

Everything quieted down, all the barriers, all the divine and human gates fell—-the conquerors freely took control of it, each of its streets, each of its dwellings. They quickly hoisted their banner over its stronghold and sacred place, over the Kremlin. There has never been a day in my entire life more terrible than that one—God be my witness, it is true!

After a week of being cooped up, surrounded by four walls, without air, sleep, or food, and with barricaded windows and walls, I walked out of the house on unsteady feet. No sooner had I flung open the door when a gang of "warriors for a bright future" rushed in no less than three times. Looking for enemies and weapons, they were completely crazed by victory, booze, and the most animallike hatred. They had parched lips and savage looks; ever faithful to the traditions of all "great revolutions," they carried all kinds of weapons with an almost carnivallike grotesquerie.

Ravens cried hoarsely in the evening of that dark, short, icy, and rainy day of late autumn. Moscow, pitiful, dirty, disgraced, riddled with bullets, and even submissive, took on a humdrum look.

Cabbies made their way; the triumphant Moscow mob poured through the streets. A filthy old woman with spitefully green eyes and raised veins on her neck stood and cried for the whole street to hear: "Comrades, dear ones! Beat them, punish them, burn them!"

I stood for a while, looked around—and wandered home. But at night, being alone, and by nature extremely disinclined to tears, I suddenly burst out crying with such terrible and copious tears even beyond my imagination.

I also cried during Holy Week, this time not alone but with the many, many others who had gathered in the dark evenings, in dark churches dimly lit with the red lights of candles, amidst dark Moscow with its hermetically sealed Kremlin, and who cried when they sang the terrible hymn: "By a sea wave . . . of the persecutor, the tormentor hidden under the wave. . . ."

How many people were there then in these churches who had never before been in them, who had never cried as they did now!

But then I cried tears of cruel grief and sickly delight when I left Russia and my entire former life behind, when I crossed the new Russian border, the border at Orsha; when I raced from that boiling sea of screaming savages who were terrible and unhappy; who screamed with violence and passion; who were devoid of any vestige of humanity; and who had set to the torch all the stations, beginning from Moscow itself and right up to Orsha, where all the platforms and paths were literally covered with vomit and defecation. . . .

June 24, 1919
Vera Muromtseva-Bunina, from her diary
Yesterday I did laundry all day long; today I rinsed clothes and hung them out to dry. I found the physical work pleasant, but I was very annoyed that I was so tired out that I did not have strength for intellectual pursuits.

June 25, 1919
Vera Muromtseva-Bunina, from her diary
I ironed all day long. I grew even more tired than when I washed clothes. I never suspected that ironing was such difficult work. My fingers look like those of a laundress: they are all peeled. But I had a pleasant feeling of accomplishment. I did what seemed to be impossible.

June 26, 1919
Ivan Bunin, from his diary The Cursed Days
Yes, peace has been signed. Now will they really not think about Russia? How true the words: "Fight, those of you who believe in God!" Tens of millions of Russian souls cry out in a frenzy for help. Will they really not interfere in our "internal affairs"? Will they finally not rush into our unhappy home where a ravenous gorilla has literally been swallowing our blood?

June 26, 1919
Vera Muromtseva-Bunina, from her diary
I went out walking after dinner and suddenly ran into [our former maid] Anyuta. How happy I was! Proudly I showed her my peeled hands.

June 30, 1919
Ivan Bunin, from his diary The Cursed Days

A new poster. . . pulp-art of a peasant and a worker with axes who are angrily bashing away at the bald head of an extremely bowlegged general, stuck through with the bayonet of a Red Army soldier; under it the inscription: "Beat them, lads, good and hard!". . .

I walked home like I was drunk. . . .

A story: Last year, when the Germans came to Odessa, "friends" asked them for permission to have a ball that would last until morning. The German commandant shrugged his shoulders with contempt: "Russia is such a surprising country! Why is everyone so eager to have a good time!"

July 1, 1919
Ivan Bunin, from his diary The Cursed Days

I was just at the market. A vagabond was running along with a newspaper extra: "We have just retaken Belgorod and Kharkov. . . ." It literally got dark before my eyes; I almost fell.

July 1, 1919
Vera Muromtseva-Bunina, from her diary

[A friend] says the Proletkult has an exhibit of books. . . . Its catalog recommended *The Village.*

July 2, 1919
Ivan Bunin, from his diary The Cursed Days

Yesterday, for several minutes at the market, I felt as though I was going to fall. That never happened to me before. Then I felt lethargy, a revulsion for everything, and a complete loss for the taste of life.

July 3, 1919
Ivan Bunin, from his diary The Cursed Days

Our heads spin all the time from malnutrition. There are only piles of rotten vegetables and potatoes at the market. . . . The harvest this year is truly biblical. . . .

We again go to the archbishop's garden. We are often there. It is the only pure and quiet place in town. But the view from there is especially sad—a country that is completely dead. Has not the port

been deprived of its riches and people for a long time? . . . But the
garden is splendid, uninhabited, and silent. We often drop in at the
church, and we are so taken by the singing, the bows of the
celebrants, and the incense that we almost cry. Everything here is
grand and proper, a world that is noble and merciful, and where all
human suffering is comforted with such tenderness. Then you think
that people of the class to which I belong used to come to church
only for funerals! [A friend of mine] once died. . . . I had only one
thought, one dream at his funeral: how I could get out to the porch
and have a smoke. . . .

P.S. My Odessa notes end here. The pages which followed them
I buried in the ground so well before I fled Odessa in January 1920
that I could not find them.

July 3, 1919
Vera Muromtseva-Bunina, from her diary
   [A friend] happily reports: "You can sleep peacefully. There is an
order from Moscow—'Leave writers alone.' "
   We breathed a sigh of relief, for it has already been three weeks
since we have discussed with Ian whether he should spend nights at
home. Many friends have offered to give him cover; but we keep
deciding . . . not to put Ian in an illegal position. He is already so
nervous. Sleep is important for him; he cannot always rest quietly in
these unusual circumstances. We hope he will be warned of any
danger. But this evening passed in a terrifying sort of way.

July 10, 1919
Vera Muromtseva-Bunina, from her diary
   We went along the boulevard. . . . We stopped . . . by the statue
of Richelieu which had been spared by the Bolsheviks. Not far from
us we saw two young and stylishly dressed ladies and a young man.
They all wore a band on their arms with the initials "Che-Ka."[4] They
had lively faces and were laughing at something. I looked at Ian. He
was white as a sheet; his face was distorted. He said, "That's whom
our fate depends on. They should be ashamed to be walking out in
public with such a mark." . . .
   I tried to usher Ian away as quickly as possible, though I felt
like following this threesome. I swore I would not come this way

[4]The first Soviet secret police, from the Russian *Chrezvychaynaya Komissiya.*

again, since Ian is so careless; also I saw that such a sight brings him unbearable suffering. . . .

Ian could not keep calm the whole way back. He even became haggard-looking. He kept repeating, "No, this is a different tribe. In the old days hangmen were ashamed of their craft, they lived by themselves, they avoided people's eyes; but these men are not ashamed to go out into public places and even wear an armband. . . ."

July 12, 1919
Vera Muromtseva-Bunina, from her diary

People tell us there will be searches in our region; they keep looking for people who are avoiding military service. We fly home.

We are in a panic momentarily, hiding our money wherever we can. Then we get hold of ourselves and sit at the table. Ian reads.

July 13, 1919
Vera Muromtseva-Bunina, from her diary

It is difficult to describe what happened yesterday. I have never experienced anything like it.

About ten o'clock . . . we heard voices outside the windows in the yard, the sound of shoes, the clanging of rifles. Anyuta rushed in, pale but calm: "They've come . . . they're in the dining room."

Ian remained at his place behind the desk. . . . I rushed to where they were searching. I tried to be calm. But I was sure it would end in catastrophe. . . . The pantry had . . . a great deal of unwashed underwear that belonged to our boarders. . . . If they looked there, all would be lost. . . . The Red Army soldiers, the most ordinary-looking Russians, stood by, not knowing what to do. I went past them, said "hello," and headed for the dining room where the landlord lived. Near the dining room was a very small room with a chest of drawers. The soldiers began to search the chest. . . .

Ian kept sitting in the same pose he had had half an hour earlier. He was wearing his glasses, a book lay before him, but he was not reading. . . .

The landlord led the soldiers into Ian's room. . . . My heart was beating so hard I could hardly breathe. . . . We had hidden our valuables in a very tall stove—the soldiers would hardly climb up there. They could take only the last of our money. But, worst of all, if they searched through Ian's manuscripts—what would they not stumble upon.

Three more or less intelligent-looking people entered; after them the clang of rifles and several Red Army soldiers, bowlegged with big fat faces. Ian, still wearing his glasses, and with an unusually ferocious look, suddenly announced:

"You do not have the right to search my room. Here is my passport. I have passed the age for conscription."

"Perhaps you have stockpiles of goods," a young man asked politely. . . .

"Unfortunately, I have no stockpiles," Ian replied abruptly and spitefully.

"What about weapons?" the leader of the gang asked even more politely.

"I don't have them, either. But it's your affair, search if you like," and he rushed to turn on the light.

With the light on I was frightened by Ian's pale, stern face. I thought: The soldiers were going to search his room anyway, so why did he irritate them?

But the soldiers began to back off; the young man bowed with these words: "I beg your pardon." Then everyone quietly left, one after the other.

We sat in silence for a long time; we were too stunned to say anything.

July 19, 1919
Vera Muromtseva-Bunina, from her diary

There are many amusing stories going about town. For example, several soldiers went to the store for fruit. One basket had the number 17 on it. The soldiers thought that the fruit cost seventeen kopecks, but it turned out to be seventeen rubles, a hundred times higher!

July 20, 1919
Vera Muromtseva-Bunina, from her diary

From a letter from mother: "I do not even want to remember all the many difficult things which we experienced. I have decided that human beings are such dogs that they will not survive. At present my life seems like a paradise when compared to what went on in winter and spring here in Moscow. . . . I have somehow gotten so used to suffering that I react to everything calmly. . . . I have sold our things and gotten together about five thousand rubles during father's illness, and I have spent it all on him. . . . I have decided I will take half your money and try to keep it for you. I will use it only to keep from starving, as I did this fall. . . . Bread costs forty-five to fifty rubles a pound. . . . Is this not a joyful life?"

From a letter from brother: "Our parents have changed in appearance. They have grown thin and have aged about fifteen years; they have become hunched, bent over, and very nervous. . . . Illness has turned papa into a very old man. But he is not alone. There are many like him. . . . I, too, have become old and worn out. . . ."

Circa *August 1919*
Valentin Kataev, from his memoirs

The last months before Bunin and I parted forever. Here are some of Bunin's thoughts at that time that struck me by their *singularity.*

"For all his genius . . . Leo Tolstoy was not always beyond reproach as an artist. He has much that is raw and overdone in his work. One fine day I would like to take his *Anna Karenina*, for example, and rewrite it . . . to make a clean copy, removing all the long passages, throwing out one or two things, making some of the sentences more precise, graceful, but, of course, not adding a word of my own, leaving everything of Tolstoy's absolutely intact. I would do it, of course, only as an experiment, exclusively for myself, not for print. I am deeply convinced that Tolstoy, edited like that—not by some Strakhov but by a genuine, great artist—would be read with more pleasure and would gain those readers who cannot abide his novels simply because of their stylistic flaws."

One can imagine what a storm of the most contradictory emotions Bunin's thoughts had awakened in my frail young soul. But my teacher had uttered them in a very simple, everyday tone, without any posturing or desire to *épater*,[5] as people liked to say in those days, but with that indestructible force of inner conviction which is more powerful than truth itself. . . .

In answer to my question about Scriabin, about his innovations in music, his attempts to unite sound and light, his strange orchestration and unprecedented counterpoint, Bunin responded with something like this:

"Scriabin? . . . Hm. . . . You want to know what Scriabin is and

[5]From the Futurist slogan *épater les bourgeois* or "to shock the bourgeois."

what his music is all about, for example, his musical poem, *L'Extase?*[6]
I can tell you. Imagine the Large Hall of the Moscow Conservatory.
The luminous chandeliers. The oval portraits of the great composers,
the huge organ with the symphony orchestra before it—violins, the
music stands, the blinding shirt-fronts and white ties of the musicians, each a celebrity in his field. The public is the most refined
audience: great Moscow connoisseurs and music critics, high school
students, professors, actors, rich people, prize beauties, officers, the
cream of Moscow intelligentsia. The suspense is slightly feverish. The
hall is electrified. Impatience rises to the breaking point, but the
conductor sweeps back his coattails and waves his baton—the famous
symphony begins, the last, most revolutionary word in contemporary
modernistic decadent music. Now then ... shall I describe this
symphony so that everyone can understand it? I'll try. Off go the
violins. Some play this way, some play that way. But so far it's still
more or less generally accepted and befitting the famous Moscow
Conservatory. Then all of a sudden a violin squeals in a more
desperate manner, just like a piglet: Ee-e-eekh! Ee-e-eekh!" With this
Bunin made a terrible face and then ... he began squealing all over
the apartment. "And then comes the sickening, nerve-wracking wail
from the trumpet. . . ."

"Ioann, you've gone completely crazy!" Vera Nikolaevna exclaimed in horror, running into the room with her fingers in her ears.

"I'm explaining Scriabin's *L'Extase* so that everyone can understand it," Bunin said drily, sending me a piercing glance. "You, of
course, are enraptured by the 'new music,' as befits a modern young
poet and a fan of Dostoevsky and Leonid Andreev?"

"I've never heard Scriabin's symphonies, but I like his piano
pieces very much," I said, wishing to be independent. (I had
intended to write a story in which the hero played a Scriabin
prelude. . . .)

But, glancing at Bunin, at the venomous expression on his
hemorrhoidal face, I added hesitantly, "But, of course, my hero could
play Grieg."

"Perhaps Tchaikovsky?" Bunin asked in a strange tone.

"Yes, of course, perhaps Tchaikovsky," I said.

"Well, there you are," Bunin exclaimed, somewhat happier.
"Grieg or Tchaikovsky, Levitan's sad nature, Chekhov's gentle humor.

[6]Scriabin wrote *Poeme de l'extase* in 1908.

. . . The heroine, of course, is a former actress. Yellow leaves.
Solitude. Watercolors—"

He said suddenly, "Do you like Andersen?"

"Sort of—yes."

"Just as I thought. Vera, he purports to like Andersen. Andersen is fashionable now. So is Alexander Grin. So, when you write
your story, besides Grieg, Tchaikovsky, Levitan, and Chekhov, don't
forget Andersen; mention the poor toy soldier, the charred paper rose,
or something like that; and, if you can manage it, link it up to one of
Grin's captains complete with pipe and a pint of peach brandy—and
you'll be a hit with middle-aged intellectual ladies from the provinces. Oh no, you're smiling in vain, my dear sir. It's precisely these
ladies, the fans of Grin and Grieg, who make a writer famous, who
establish his reputation as a romantic, almost a classic. Believe a
hunted-down literary wolf. You'll often remember what I'm telling
you." Suddenly Bunin said without any apparent connection, "What's
the point of all this? The main thing is to learn to write simply. . . .
Noun, verb, period, perhaps a subordinate clause when absolutely
necessary, always childishly simple. Like a fable. A prayer. A fairy
tale. . . ."

August 2, 1919
Ivan Bunin, from his diary

We find it terrible to think what will happen to us if the
Bolsheviks stay in power. . . .

I bought—by accident!—eleven eggs for eighty-eight rubles.

August 3, 1919
Ivan Bunin, from his diary

A pound of butter already costs 160 rubles; one gets bread for
90 rubles.

August 4, 1919
Vera Muromtseva-Bunina, from her diary

Rumors come in waves. They first rise and rise; then they fall.
The Bolsheviks calm everyone down, but we get depressed.

A bucket of water costs between five and ten rubles. . . . even
more for those who live farther.

August 7, 1919
Ivan Bunin, from his diary

I feel my head spinning . . . from an empty stomach—from hunger. I drop in at a store—it is completely empty! "There is nothing to eat!"—This is the first time in my life this has happened. . . . I grit my teeth. "Revolutionaries, republicans, you should all go to hell, you damned savages!"

August 8, 1919
Ivan Bunin, from his diary

It is terrible to think we have been here almost four months and we know *precisely* nothing about events in Europe—and at such a time as this—thanks to this hottentot captivity! . . .

It hit me right in the eyes, and I stand as if struck by lightning. Bread is 150 rubles a pound.

August 9, 1919
Vera Muromtseva-Bunina, from her diary

I find it repulsive to go out walking along the streets. . . .

But the other day a very dear woman brought me to the archbishop's garden. . . . There were fruit trees, a shining blue sea behind them, and green grass where you could lie down. . . . How could the Bolsheviks let this heavenly corner slip by them? How come they did not claim it?

August 17, 1919
Ivan Bunin, from his diary

Today was one of those many days on which, over the past months, you felt like spending money on foolishness, and as quickly as possible—on a shave, stuff for the table, French lessons, and the like. Of course, you sit all the time inwardly hoping for something; when a wave of hopelessness and grief overwhelms you, you wait and hope that God will reward you for your pain, but only pain remains. Yesterday Vera and I stopped by at the archbishop's church—again we were delighted by the singing, by the bows of the clergymen, by an entire world which perhaps seems poor and infantile from an elevated point of view, but which is nevertheless splendid in that it separates you from dirty and invariably brutish human life . . . a world which is alien to all human suffering, a world of propriety, purity, and decency. . . .

August 19, 1919
Ivan Bunin, from his diary

I was twice in the archbishop's garden. The view of the port from there continues to stagger me—a dead country—everything in the port is ragged, rusting, peeling. . . . "Democracy!" How shameful! Laziness, sponging. . . . Everyone whom I see hates the Bolsheviks and spends his days yearning for them to leave!

August 22, 1919
Ivan Bunin, from his diary

An intercepted broadcast says the Whites are allegedly thirty to forty miles from Odessa. God grant they finally get here.

The weather is heavenly, with signs of fall. I am getting thin from the poor food; my stomach sticks out. Nights I fall asleep with a beating heart, with fear and anguish.

August 24, 1919
Vera Muromtseva-Bunina, from her diary

This morning I was awakened by cannon fire. It was 6 a.m. Ian was already up; we got dressed right away. When the shelling stopped, Ian disappeared. He went to the cathedral, and while he was there the banner of Saint George was carried out from the altar.

I went to the market. Prices for everything have increased greatly. Then Ian and I . . . met automobiles with Volunteers in them: masses of flowers, unanimous hurrahs, many were crying. The faces of the Volunteers were tired, but good.

August 25, 1919
Vera Muromtseva-Bunina, from her diary

We have decided to leave Odessa at the first opportunity, but we still do not know where we will go. The Volunteers have still not consolidated their grip. We have to wait and see. It is terrible to go somewhere now, but we cannot spend a second winter in this dear city.

August 30, 1919
Vera Muromtseva-Bunina, from her diary

There was a . . . prayer service in the cathedral and a parade on the square.

Ian finds it pleasant to see such order. . . . I never would have thought that Ian could be so patriotic. He literally glows.

We often talk about the future. We cannot decide whether we should head for the Crimea, go abroad, or stay here. We are fed up with this place, but can we get along in the Crimea?

August 31, 1919
Vera Muromtseva-Bunina, from her diary

I have lost all hope to visit Moscow this fall. How my heart aches for those who have been left behind there. I do not have the strength or resources to help them. Is it possible that I will never see them again?

September 6, 1919
Vera Muromtseva-Bunina, from her diary

Yesterday Valya Kataev was here. He read his poetry; it was a great success. Nonetheless his opinion of himself is many times greater than his talent. Ian talked with him for a long time . . . scolding him, advising him, and insisting that he change his life, that he raise his moral outlook. But it seemed to me that Valya did not take any of this to heart. I remembered that a poetess told me that Kataev was made of horseflesh. Perhaps he will grow up and catch on. Right now, though, he is not ashamed of what he is doing. Ian told him, "You are mean, envious, and ambitious." He told him to change the city, society, and take up self-education. Valya was not offended by these words, but I did not feel he had internalized them. I am surprised he responds to Ian so calmly. He lacks youthful emotion. He says he values only Ian's opinion, but if this is so, I find his calmness strange. Ian said to him, "After all my talking to you, if you do something with your life, then that means I have done you *some good*. . . . Once you become a poet, you still must be very strict with yourself." Ian reproached him also for his wordy verse: "You are so much like all those philologists that it is simply horrible."

Valya lashed out at Voloshin. For some reason he can't stand him. Ian defended Voloshin, saying that though his verse is also wordy, something genuine and personal shines forth from it. "There are too few Voloshins around for you to be negative toward him. How well Voloshin has sung of his country. How very good are his portraits."

September 18, 1919
Vera Muromtseva-Bunina, from her diary

A knock at the door. There is noise. I go to the door, open it, and see a soldier. I hear him asking [our maid] Lyudmilla, "Does the academician Bunin live here?" I go into the foyer and say hello.

I: "I am very pleased to meet you. Ivan Alexeevich will probably be home soon."

He: "Someone told me that Ivan Alexeevich would like to meet me."

I: "Yes, and he will really feel bad if you don't wait for him."

He: "I can't. Give Ivan Alexeevich the program for our party. I hope he will go along with us. Our party has two platforms—a constitutional monarchy and opposition to the Jews."

I: "Ivan Alexeevich is not an anti-Semite. Also, he is not a party person."

He: "Everyone must be a party person now."

I: "Yes, you are right. But Ivan Alexeevich is a poet. And a poet cannot be a party person."

He: "I am also a poet, but at the same time I will do everything the party wants, even go to the moon for them."

September 20, 1919
Vera Muromtseva-Bunina, from her diary

We have decided not to go to the Crimea. . . .
Ian has been writing a lecture, "The Great Narcotic."[7]

September 21, 1919
Vera Muromtseva-Bunina, from her diary

Ian became completely hoarse after the lecture. He never imagined how hard it would be to read it through twice. Also, he got so carried away that he forgot to take a break. He held the public's attention for three hours; not one person left the hall. When he finished, everyone rose and applauded him for a long time. Everyone was very excited. . . . One said, "Ivan Alexeevich is the greatest of all writers—what courage, what truth! It is remarkable! What an historic day!" He had tears in his eyes, and I was deeply touched. . . . Now Ian wants to read it somewhere else.

[7]Bunin's lecture "The Great Narcotic" has not been preserved.

October 7, 1919
Vera Muromtseva-Bunina, from her diary

Ian read his "The Great Narcotic" a second time. Even more people turned out to hear him. Not everyone got in to hear him. Again they listened very well. Ian read better than he did the last time, with greater feeling. The end was especially good. But I did not agree with certain details. I would have liked it if it had been less personal. . . .

I very much like to go to the library in the evenings when no one else is there. I am reading [Herzen's] *My Past and Thoughts.* How good it is!

October 20, 1919
Vera Muromtseva-Bunina, from her diary

Ian went to work for the first time. He likes to go there by the car with the national flag on it. A Volunteer attends him, a very dear man . . . who says with every word, "So it is, your Excellency." These days Ian is alive, excited, and active. The inertia which he experienced under the Bolsheviks was, undoubtedly, very bad for his nerves and soul. There were minutes when I feared for his psychological health. I do not know how it all will end. . . . Rarely has anyone suffered as much as Ian has. He positively cannot stand the Bolsheviks. . . .

November 3, 1919
Ivan Bunin, from an article in Southern Word

Again Jewish pogroms. Before the revolution they were rare, unusual events. For the past two years, though, they have become an . . . everyday phenomenon. This is intolerable. To live forever dependent on the mercy or wrath of some unbridled man-beast, to live in perpetual fear for your home, your honor, your personal life, for the honor and life of your family and close ones, to live in an atmosphere of impending catastrophe, bloody atrocity, pillage and looting, to perish . . . at the whim of a scoundrel, a brigrand—this is an unspeakable horror that we who have suffered in this third year of the "great Russian revolution" understand all too well. It is our constant duty, though, to rise up against this, to tell . . . people what is going on. . . . For it is simply unbearable to live like this. It is time for everyone to take stock of what they are doing, people who instigate killings on the right and the left, Russian and Jewish revolutionaries, everyone who for so long . . . have called for hostilities and malice . . . who welcome "struggles for one's rights," who openly scream "death, death" on street corners, and who forever arouse the beast in the folk, who pit one against another, class against class, who hoist red banners and black pennants with pictures of white skulls. . . . One cannot live without divine or human laws, without order and restraints. Leo Tolstoy said, "It is a terrible thing to say, but most people are animals." One must rise up and restrain the animal in man—this is the duty of every individual, near and far, Russian and Jew, French and Japanese. . . .

The pogroms are not the government's fault. The fault lies with . . . the Russian people, still inflamed by. . . fratricidal differences and brutality. . . .

The pogroms have been going on for quite some time. One only has to recall what the unfortunate Jewish population suffered not only in the Ukraine but also . . . in Poland . . . last year. Streams of Jewish blood mix with the rivers of blood that flow on all fronts from this terribly absurd civil war. The people's fury, aroused so savagely in the years of the great Russian revolt, rages on with barbaric force. . . .

One must suppress those who take part in pogroms, people who set themselves up as the law; they must be suppressed in word and deed. I repeat that one must restrain the beast in man. . . . Of this revolutionaries of all persuasions must be reminded.

Everyone is justifiably angered by the pogroms, by the Russians' extermination of the Jews. Everyone fervently swears to send protests "to all peoples of the world." And they agree that not only the Russian Volunteer but also the French, English, and Japanese punish mercilessly . . . those who take part in Russian, Ukrainian, Polish, Austrian, and Hungarian pogroms. . . . But, good God, how frequently and cruelly these same people will throw spears at me when I talk about the dark and animallike aspects of our people, when I extend this darkness and savagery . . . to all villainy that bears the name of revolution, when I wait for Europe to interfere in the fierce and absurd villainy that has gone on for two and a half years already, in a Christian country, in the twentieth century!

In December of last year, in days which . . . were so very bitter but which promised to return us to some minimal standard of humanity, when Odessa was hailing the arrival of the French, I wrote:

Let there be pain and shame—and joy.
Hail to you, Varangians!
In the name of God and his subjects,
Stop the bloody carnage,
Tear down the insolent banner,
Subdue the pig,
Dethrone the demagogue!

How did the revolutionaries respond to me? *Odessa News* said that my politics were "wretched." . . . *Southern Worker* had me in mind when they wrote:

Frightened, you, with chaotic praise,
Bowed like a slave before the Varangian. . . .

Others wrote, "Bunin's opinions about the revolution are withered and bilious." . . . Still others wrote, "Deeply respected academician Bunin, one cannot approach the revolution . . . like a crime reporter." . . . "Hegel said that reality is reasonable . . . thus the Russian Revolution has its own reason, its own logic." . . . Oh, my extremely wise Hegelian, the cruellest autocracy, plague, and cholera can fit marvelously into Hegel's ideas. After all, Hegel asserted that there is reason and logic when landowners, merchants, and officers get their heads smashed. With that type of logic, one can come to God knows what kinds of conclusions. . . .

November 7, 1919
Ivan Bunin, from an article in Southern Word
    October 25, 1917, marked the fall of the Winter Palace, the headquarters of the so-called Provisional Government, a group of doctors, lawyers, and journalists, who would sometimes down a few beers and sing songs about . . . Stenka Razin. What is so important about this day? What so special happened on this day? Only what . . . was already going on for six months in Russia under the great leadership of a second-rate lawyer [Kerensky] who . . . could not live for an hour without cocaine.
    The defenders of the . . . "the great Russian uprising" say that this time is identical to that of the great French Revolution. . . . Yes, it certainly is the same. First there are idealists and dreamers torn from life . . . fickle, shortsighted, possessed by noble goals, perhaps, but not thinking things out clearly; then there are phrasemongers and ambitious types. Authority grows weaker and more confused.

What next? The people become more crazed and animallike. They scream in the name of the scum in their ranks, innate murderers, robbers, scoundrels . . . gangs of the most select bums and beasts, genuine fomentors of all kinds of revolution, villains who are frenzied, pompous, theatrical, people who scream "in the name of the people," "freedom, brotherhood, and equality," and who prepare for a bloody carnival.

One must always keep in mind that a repulsive theatricality is one of the most important features of any revolution.

These villains are acting out such a base and ferocious comedy that it will take a hundred years for the world to recover. . . . Yes, the French Revolution was monstrously loathsome and bloody. But how can one justify the baseness and blood of one upheaval with the baseness and blood of another? One should be truly grateful to the revolutionaries for such a comparison—for it argues *against* revolution. . . . The "great Russian Revolution" differs from the French only in that its baseness, absurdity, villainy, destruction, shame, cold, hunger, and death are greater in number and senselessness; and, of course, its boorishness, dirt, and stupidity are a thousand times greater. . . .

October 25, 1917, was the beginning of a folk spectacle. Before that day the violins were only tuning up, so to speak, though Russia was finished—disgraced, debased not only by Kerenskys of all shapes and colors but also by the brutality of the folk. *Tens of thousands* of the most bloody, absurd, and mob-inspired laws came on the books . . . put forth by the Provisional Government.

I know well that this day will someday be cursed by . . . the Russian press, in places where the White Army . . . is gradually destroying the blood-soaked stagings of this spectacle. But I also know that people will continue to cry out joyously: "Long live . . . !"—even though they do not understand or want to understand that "the drum thunders only when it is beaten." The Odessa press will be particularly zealous in this regard. After all, was it that long ago that almost a third of Odessa's population . . . was seized by panic . . . when the "people's revolutionary army" entered the city— just as our ancestors panicked when the Polovetsian hordes came into their towns? Was it that long ago that revolutionary bows and ribbons glowed like fire on Odessa "supporters," even on carriage horses—red calico whose very color makes the heart sick and nauseated? Was it that long ago that red flags and glassy rose stars hung like medusas over the streets, the police stations, the theatres, and the clubs named for Trotsky, Sverdlov, and Lenin, their reflections flowing like blood on the asphalt . . . when all the "warriors for socialism" . . . all the sailors with their huge guns and lacquered shoes, pickpockets, criminals, and shaven dandies . . . all so full of hatred for the "old regime" . . . tore through the . . . streets, attended by prostitutes, to go to their own theatres, to see their own peasant actors?

Was it that long ago that trucks banged and boomed all night long . . . or that they would be cranked up next to police stations so that no one could hear the shots from rifles and the cries of those being killed and tortured? . . . Was it that long ago that . . . there flowered all kinds of "proletkults," or that young villains by the name of Futurists, i.e., people of the future, were drawing savagely boorish posters, or that artists were bustling about with ideas on how to paint Japanese lanterns for this godforsaken city . . . this lavish place of execution—to decorate for the joyous May 1st . . . for the "revolutionary proletariat" who will come and look, spit out sunflower seeds, and cover their socialist legs with the pants of murdered and robbed "counterrevolutionaries"?

Was it that long ago that these very same democrats who . . . protested so fearlessly when the volunteers were here, taking them to task for the "repression of the free word," "the interference with the democratic congress," and the "arbitrary execution" of dozens of scoundrels, were so quiet and took cover when the "workers and peasants" returned and immediately snuffed out any humane word, when they screamed . . . "Death, death!" . . . when they began "arbitrarily" to execute and torture hundreds and thousands? . . .

Bolshevism is a revolution, all right, the very same revolution which forever gladdens those who do not have a present, who have a past that is always "cursed" and a future that is always "bright." . . . "Seven lean cows will devour seven fat ones—but they themselves will not become fat." . . . "Darkness will cover the earth and gloom, its peoples." . . . "Baseness will grow and honor will decline." . . . "Houses of ill repute will become social assemblies." . . . "And the face of a generation will be like a dog's." . . .

November 10, 1919
Vera Muromtseva-Bunina, from her diary
    Yesterday [Chekhov's widow] Olga Leonardovna Knipper visited us. She made a strange impression. She was very sweet and friendly; she spoke intelligently, but I got the idea that she had nothing in her

soul, that she was like a house without a foundation . . . without a cellar stocked with provisions and good wine.

The Bolsheviks have been very courteous to her, so she does not see them as we do. . . . They have saved the apartment of [Chekhov's sister] Maria Pavlovna. Chaliapin is on familiar terms with Trotsky and Lenin. . . .

[Gorky's wife] Ek. Pavl. Peshkova is a completely dried-up woman.

November 13, 1919
Vera Muromtseva-Bunina, from her diary
Ian said with great sadness, "Our poor loved ones, will they survive the winter? Could it be that we will never see them again? I cannot believe this."

November 21, 1919
Ivan Bunin, from an article in Southern Word
I am neither for the left or the right. I have been and will be an unbending enemy of all that is stupid, estranged form life, evil, false, dishonorable, harmful, no matter where it comes from. I am not a Russophobe, though I have dared to utter bitter words about my people, but in a terrible way reality has justified all that I have said. Reality has justified even L. N. Tolstoy who . . . said in 1909, "If I had to find something particularly attractive about Russian peasants, then, sorry to say, I could not."

I am not afraid of Germans, Englishmen, Rumanians, and Jews—and it is stupid to label me for wicked political ends. But I recognize rather keenly . . . regrettable features in various nationalities; and, generally speaking, I do not have a high opinion of people, especially now, after all that God has caused me to see in recent years.

I believe less in people than I did earlier. . . . Please do not roll your eyes or tell me that "you're not afraid"—I am not like our Odessa journalists who think that the things that please Englishmen, with their constitutional monarchies, would satisfy our bunglers who lose their way in broad daylight and who . . . goad each other with toasts to Satan for their joy and amusement.

I sometimes now think: "There is something marvelous in this ideal . . . democracy," but, as I am not a child, I also speak openly and without fear . . . that this Russian "democracy" will give birth to the most vile and bloody nonsense, for we have seen and continue to see how this "democracy" has manifested itself!

I choke from shame and pain at the thought of this "democracy," of the days of the Provisional Government, of "Worker-Peasant Power." But for a while at least I do not believe in anything different or better. . . . Try and persuade me—I will be only too happy to listen.

I have one more thing to say. . . . I have a truly savage contempt for revolutionaries, for how can I not have these feelings . . . when I must have a stone-cold heart . . . when I am in the midst of fratricidal slaughter . . . in shackles, standing at the edge of a hellish abyss to which my homeland is rushing, where hundreds of thousands . . . are perishing in tears, grief, darkness, cold, amid torture, firing, bloody indignities, eternal insult and outrage, and under the heel of triumphant scoundrels, monsters, and boors!

This is it. This is how I feel and think now. I don't know about tomorrow. I'll be the first one to smile if life diminishes my pessimism. But as long as I am speaking, I will say, "I suggest nothing, I propose nothing—I'm only telling the truth."

December 15, 1919
Vera Muromtseva-Bunina, from her diary
It is December already. The rooms are cold. We are again on pins and needles. Any minute, perhaps, we will have to rush out of here. But where should we run to? We find it difficult even to imagine. . . . To tell the truth, we now find it difficult to be frightened by anything anymore—we know what cold is, what hunger is, but it is easier to endure everything at home.

December 20, 1919
Vera Muromtseva-Bunina, from her diary
The Bolsheviks are coming, like Atilla, like clouds of locusts. They are destroying everything in their path. . . .
We got visas for Constantinople. . . .
We must leave here, but only God knows when and where. . . .
One idea is to go to France. . . .
We have no hopes left.

December 24, 1919
Vera Muromtseva-Bunina, from her diary
Ian was all over the city today. Panic everywhere! . . .
The rumor is that Odessa will be taken on January 3.

December 26, 1919
Vera Muromtseva-Bunina, from her diary

We went to the Serbian consulate. . . . The consul said it is very crowded in Belgrade but probably we could settle there. . . .

Yesterday we had some wine. Ian came alive. He talked about how he could not live in the new world and that he belonged to . . . the world of Goncharov, Tolstoy, Moscow, and Petersburg. . . . His eyes glistened with tears. He cannot accept socialism nor the collective; he is alien to all of it. He can relate only to an individual perception of the world. . . . He said, "There is nothing now. I will never accept that Russia has been destroyed. . . . I never thought I could feel the loss so sharply." . . .

I almost turned down the idea of going to Paris. Paris is cold, starving, and most likely we will be treated arrogantly. The Balkans are better.

December 31, 1919
Vera Muromtseva-Bunina, from her diary

Ian was at the English consulate who received him very kindly. . . . He promised to help us depart.

✳ 1920 ✳

January 5, 1920
Vera Muromtseva-Bunina, from her diary

Ian is suffering greatly these days. He wakes up at night; he does not sleep from six in the morning on. . . . He cannot understand how it all fell apart so quickly, or the reasons why. He is outraged by the attitude toward him of those in power. . . .

We have visas to France. . . . My inner voice tells me we should go there. The Balkans scare me. There it will be crowded, confused, and pretentious, and that is worse than cold and hunger. There is disease there, too.

January 13, 1920
Vera Muromtseva-Bunina, from her diary

We are on the eve of leaving our homeland, perhaps, for a long time. . . . It will be very difficult to wander without a goal, without

ties. . . . Our loved ones are in a worse situation than we, and we do
not have the resources to help them.

January 14, 1920
Vera Muromtseva-Bunina, from her diary
[A friend] found a five-kopeck piece baked in a piece of
gingerbread. He gave it to me; people say it will lead to wealth.

January 16, 1920
Vera Muromtseva-Bunina, from her diary
A friend said, "Well, Ivan Alexeevich, you were again right in
your judgments of the Russian people: their confusion, their weak
will, their disorder, their inability to finish anything, the eternal
hostility toward others . . . their Asiatic intrigue."
"Yes," Ian answered, "Trotsky may rule Russia, but so what?
The people are unwilling or unable to remove the yoke. For two
hundred years they were under the Tatars, now they have submitted
to the Soviets."

January 19, 1920
Vera Muromtseva-Bunina, from her diary
Ian: "The tsar most likely will be considered a martyr and will
be made a saint. How could he not flee? Perhaps he didn't want to at
first, but then—how could he have stayed among such scoundrels,
and with his daughters to boot?"
I: "Gorky tried to save the Great Princes, but he was too late."
Ian: "Yes, what a shame. Could it be that I'll see him some-
time?"
I: "And what if you do meet him?" . . .
Ian: "First, I'll spit at him. Then, anything I can get my hands
on, I'll throw at his head."
I: "Really?"
Ian: "How can I forgive him that . . . he first brought Russia to
such a disaster, and that now he remains with the Bolsheviks? No, for
such a person there can be no forgiveness!"

January 20, 1920
Vera Muromtseva-Bunina, from her diary
[A friend] said it well when he said we . . . should carry Russia
away from Russia and try to preserve it abroad until we return.

January 31, 1920
Vera Muromtseva-Bunina, from her diary

Ian returned home very upset. . . . We have no details as to our departure. We still have not received passes. . . . The ships have no coal. Even foreign nationals cannot leave. . . .

Perhaps we will have to leave Odessa on foot. I keep wondering what to take with me. Where should I leave my things? . . .

I very much regret we did not leave earlier. . . . Our room is so cold I am wearing three coats . . . and my feet are like ice. What must it be like in Moscow, in Petersburg?

February 2, 1920
Vera Muromtseva-Bunina, from her diary

Yesterday we were told that perhaps we could board the ship *Ksenya.* . . .

My heart is very heavy. Soon we will be emigrés. And for how many years? All our hopes have been dashed, even our hopes to see our loved ones. How everything has gone to pieces. . . .

February 3, 1920
Vera Muromtseva-Bunina, from her diary

We cannot get on the *Ksenya.* But we were promised we could board the *Dmitry* . . . on Thursday.

Yesterday I ran all over the city looking for wood. Friends gave me six logs. . . . so that I could dry out underwear in case we have to leave.

There is such stealing going on inside the port that, packing things, you look at each thing and think, "Well, perhaps, this is the last time I'll see this." You feel such hopelessness in your heart. . . .

It is impossible to buy anything, rubles or foreign currency. . . .

God knows what is going on . . . A panic has begun. . . . Our chances are slim that we will get away alive and unharmed. We cannot buy bread. . . . Ian bought five pounds of lard for fifteen hundred rubles. . . .

The *Dmitry* can leave only after February 8.

February 4, 1920
Vera Muromtseva-Bunina, from her diary

Tomorrow, perhaps, will be my last day on Russian soil. I never thought I would have to drag out my life as an emigré. . . . I still

cannot believe this is happening. It still seems possible that something will happen and that I will return to Moscow. . . .

No matter whom we meet, everyone tells us, "Ivan Alexeevich,
get out of here!"

[A friend] said to Ian yesterday, "I would give my life for you if
I had to." He had tears in his eyes. He thanked Ian for being the one
bright spot . . . in Odessa.

Ian got tickets for *third class* on the *Dmitry.*

"I wonder who's in first class," a friend said. . . .

We will receive passes tomorrow.

February 5, 1920
Vera Muromtseva-Bunina, from her diary

The day is overcast. We got up early. We finally decide: We will
get on board tomorrow. This is the last day we will be here on
Knyazheskaya Street where, despite all our misfortunes, we have been
relatively happy for a year and a half. . . .

Our rooms have already been rented.

Ian was . . . promised by soldiers to help bring things to the
ship.

February 6, 1920
Vera Muromtseva-Bunina, from her diary

At 4 p.m. we're on our way. Having said farewell to our
landlord . . . we go out through front doors that have not been open
for some time. We load our things on a small cart driven by a very
old and tipsy man.

It is a miracle that I got him for five hundred rubles! In the
morning I had set out . . . to get the soldier who was to escort us to
the dock. But when I got there I understood that the enemy was very
close by and that I had to think about . . . how to get to the ship as
quickly as possible. . . .

We finally board the *Dmitry.* . . .

We heard firing from cannons. . . . Was it really the Bolsheviks? . . . Thank God we got on ship today. We don't know what
would have happened if we had waited another day. . . .

We have no hope left.

February 7, 1920
Vera Muromtseva-Bunina, from her diary

We have survived the most difficult morning of our lives. We kept hearing shelling from the city. People without things and with frightened faces are running and jumping on board. Some have tickets. Some do not. . . .

Finally the ship is filled to overflowing; they have to say "No more." A terrible moment. . . .

There is shelling all around us. . . . The public has been chased off the ship's deck. . . .

Endless conversations, opinions, convictions. One thing is clear: many people have fallen into the trap.[8]

February 8, 1920
Vera Muromtseva-Bunina, from her diary
Our third day on ship. I sleep with Ian in one berth; we are like sardines. . . . But for a while I am happy in my soul.

Our boat is on the outside berth. The Bolsheviks cannot get to us even if they wanted to. But you constantly worry about loved ones who remain in Odessa. What awaits them—cold, hunger, death?

We begin to make our way among those people who are in first class. . . .

February 9, 1920
Vera Muromtseva-Bunina, from her diary
Our fourth day on the ship. This is the last time I will see the Russian shore; I burst out crying. . . .

We are on the open sea. How this trip differs from earlier ones. Before us are darkness and terror. Behind us—horror and hopelessness. I continue to worry about those who have been left behind—did they manage to save themselves?

Ivan Bunin spent the remaining thirty-three years of his life in exile from Russia, briefly in the Balkans and then in France.

[8]The Bolsheviks in fact entered Odessa on February 7, 1920.

INDEX OF PROMINENT RUSSIANS
MENTIONED IN THE TEXT

Nadson, Semyon Yakolevich (1862–1887), populist poet of the 1880s.

Nazarov, Egor Ivanovich (1849?–1900), self-educated poet about whom Bunin wrote his first critical article in 1888.

Nemirovich-Danchenko, Vladimir Ivanovich (1858–1943), dramatist, director, and co-founder of the Moscow Art Theatre in 1898.

Nilus, Petr Alexandrovich (1869–?), artist and fellow traveler of the Itinerants. See Levitan.

Olesha, Yuri Karlovich (1899–1960), Soviet writer of the late 1920s and early 1930s.

Ovsyaniko-Kulikovsky, Dmitri Nikolaevich (1853–1920), literary scholar, linguist, and historian of culture.

Pashchenko, Varvara Vladimirovna (1870–1918), wife (most likely common-law) of Ivan Bunin, 1891–1894.

Paustovsky, Konstantin Georgievich (1892–1968), Soviet prose writer and editor.

Peshkova, Ekaterina Pavlovna (1876–1965), wife of Maxim Gorky.

Pisarev, Dmitri Ivanovich (1840–1868), political thinker and radical critic of the 1860s.

Polezhaev, Alexander Ivanovich (1805–1838), poet of the 1820s and 1830s.

Polonsky, Yakov Petrovich (1819–1898), poet of the mid-nineteenth century.

Potapenko, Ignaty Nikolaevich (1856–1929), writer of Russian peasant life.

Pugachev, Emelyan Ivanovich (1742?–1775), leader of the massive uprising that threatened the government of Catherine the Great in 1773–1775.

Pusheshnikov, Nikolai Alexeevich (1882–1939), Bunin's nephew, and a translator of Kipling, Galsworthy, and Jack London.

Pushkin, Alexander Sergeevich (1799–1837), writer and poet.

Rachmaninoff, Sergei Vasilievich (1872–1943), composer, pianist, and conductor.

Radonezhsky, Sergei (1321?–1392), leading participant in the monastic revival of the fourteenth century, founder of the Trinity Monastery at present-day Zagorsk, and important political and diplomatic figure.

Razin, Stepan (Stenka) Timofeevich (1630?–1671), Cossack leader of the massive popular uprising in 1667–1671.

Rozhdestvensky, Vsevelod Alexandrovich (1895–1977), Soviet poet.

Ryleev, Kondraty Fyodorovich (1795–1826), poet and one of the principal leaders of the Decembrist uprising of 1825.

Saltykov-Shchedrin, Mikhail Yevgrafovich (1826–1889), satirist of the second half of the nineteenth century.

Scriabin, Alexander Nikolaevich (1871–1915), composer.

Severyanin, Igor Vasilievich (pseudonym of Lotaryov, Igor Vasilievich) (1887–1941), poet of the early twentieth century.

Skoropadsky, Pavel Petrovich (1873–1945), officer in the Imperial Russian army and, for a brief period of time, hetman of the Ukraine.

BIBLIOGRAPHY

SELECTED TRANSLATIONS OF BUNIN'S WORKS

Robert Bowie, *Ivan Bunin. In a Far Distant Land: Selected Stories* (Hermitage, 1983).
John Cournos, *Grammar of Love and Other Stories* (Westport, Conn., 1977).
Bernard Guerney, *The Elagin Affair and Other Stories* (New York, 1968); *The Gentleman from San Francisco and Other Stories by Ivan Bunin* (New York, 1964).
Isabel Hapgood, *The Village* (New York, 1923 and 1933).
Richard Hare, *Dark Avenues and Other Stories by Ivan Bunin* (London, 1984).
David Richards, *The Gentleman from San Francisco and Other Stories* (Penguin, 1987).
William Sansom, *The Gentleman from San Francisco and Other Stories* (London, 1975).
Mark Scott, *Wolves and other Stories* (Capra, 1989).
Olga Shartse, *Ivan Bunin. Shadowed Paths* (Moscow, 195- and 1979); *Light Breathing and Other Stories* (Moscow, 1988).

CRITICAL WORKS ON BUNIN

Julian Connolly, *Ivan Bunin* (Boston, 1982).
Serge Kryzytski, *The Works of Ivan Bunin* (The Hague, 1971).
James Woodward, *Ivan Bunin: A Study of His Fiction* (Chapel Hill, 1980).

SOURCE NOTES

[1885]

December 29, 1885. M. Grin., ed., *Ustami Buninykh. Dnevniki Ivana Alexeevicha i Very Nikolaevny i drugie arkhivnye materialy*, vol. 1 (Possev-Verlag, 1977), 21–22.

[1886]

December 20, 1886. Grin, 23.

[1887]

Circa 1887. S. Gol'din, "O literaturnoi deiatel'nosti I. A. Bunina kontsa vos'-midesiatykh—nachala devianostykh go-dov," *Uchenye zapiski Orekhovo-Zuevskogo pedagogicheskogo instituta*, vol. 9, no. 3 (1958), 4.

[1888]

June 12, 1888. I. Bunin, "Poet-samouch-ka. Po povodu stikhotvoreniia E. I. Na-zarova," in V. Shcherbina, et al., eds., *Literaturnoe nasledstvo. Ivan Bunin. Kniga pervaia* (Moscow, 1973), 290.
Late July 1888. I. Bunin, "Nedostatki sovremennoi poezii," in I. Bunin, *Sobranie sochinenii v deviati tomakh*, vol. 9 (Moscow, 1967), 489, 490, 492.

December 26, 1888. A. Baboreko, *I. A. Bunin. Materialy dlia biografii* (Moscow, 1967), 17–18.

[1890]

June 12, 1890. A. Baboreko, "Iz perepiski I. A. Bunina," *Novyi mir*, no. 10 (1956), 197–198.
July 22, 1890. A. Baboreko, "Pis'ma I. A. Bunina," *Literaturnyi Smolensk. Al'-manakh*, no. 15 (Smolensk, 1956), 288–289.
July 27, 1890. Baboreko, *I. A. Bunin. Materialy*, 22.

[1891]

Circa 1891. Baboreko, "Pis'ma I. A. Bunina," 313.
January 1891. Baboreko, "Iz perepiski," 199.
January 17, 1891. Baboreko, "Pis'ma I. A. Bunina," 292.
January 30, 1891. A. Chekhov, *Polnoe sobranie sochinenii v tridtsati tomakh*, vol. 4 (Moscow, 1976), 171–172.
March–October 1891. A. Baboreko, "Neopublikovannye pis'ma I. A. Bunina," *Vesna prishla* (Smolensk, 1959), 219–220.
May 14, 1891, Baboreko, "Pis'ma I. A. Bunina," 295–296.

May 29, 1891. Baboreko, *I. A. Bunin. Materialy*, 29–30.

Circa Summer 1891. T. Bonami, *Khudozhestvennaia proza I. A. Bunina (1887–1904)* (Vladimir, 1962), 13.

July 1, 1891. Baboreko, "Pis'ma I. A. Bunina," 297.

August 10, 1891. Baboreko, "Neopublikovannye pis'ma I. A. Bunina," 220–221.

August 14, 1891. N. Bazhanov, "Rasskaz I. A. Bunina 'Antonovskie iabloki'," *Voprosy russkoi literatury*, no. 2 (1970), 23.

August 15, 1891. A. Baboreko, "Iunosheskii roman I. A. Bunina (Po neopublikovannym pis'mam)," *Literaturnyi Smolensk*, 258.

October 31, 1891. Baboreko, "Pis'ma I. A. Bunina," 308.

November 12, 1891. Baboreko, "Iz perepiski," 206.

November 17, 1891. Baboreko, I. A. Bunin. Materialy, 33–34.

December 13, 1891. N. Kucherovskii, "'Mundir' Tolstovstva (Molodoi I. A. Bunin i tolstovstvo)," *Iz istorii russkoi literatury XIX veka* (Kaluga, 1966), 114.

[1892]

Circa 1892. Baboreko, "Neopublikovannye pis'ma I. A. Bunina," 223.

March 19, 1892. Baboreko, "Iunosheskii roman I. A. Bunina," 282.

May 14, 1892. *Ibid.*, 283.

Circa June 12, 1892. Baboreko, "Pis'ma I. A. Bunina," 321.

July 8, 1892. Baboreko, "Iunosheskii roman I. A. Bunina," 280.

[1893]

February 7, 1893. Baboreko, "Iz perepiski," 198.

February 20, 1893. L. Tolstoy, "Pis'ma," *Polnoe sobranie sochinenii v devianosta tomakh*, vol. 66 (Moscow, 1953), 297.

April 28, 1893. Baboreko. *I. A. Bunin. Materialy*, 43.

July 15, 1893. Baboreko, "Iz perepiski," 198.

[1894]

January 30, 1894. Tolstoy, "Pis'ma," vol. 67 (Moscow, 1955), 49.

February 15, 1894. Baboreko, "Iz perepiski," 199.

February 23, 1894. Tolstoy, 48.

Mid-March 1894. I. Bunin, "Pamiati sil'nogo cheloveka," 506.

May 19, 1894. Grin, 25.

[1895]

Circa March 1895. *Ibid.*, 26.

April 3, 1895. Baboreko, "Neopublikovannye pis'ma I. A. Bunina," 229.

May 1895. I. Bunin, "Na khutore," vol. 2 (Moscow, 1965), 34.

October 14, 1895. I. Gazer, "Neopublikovannye pis'ma Bunina," *Problemy realizma khudozhestvennoi pravdy* (L'vov, 1961), 167.

November 18, 1895. Baboreko, "Iunosheskii roman I. A. Bunina," 275–276.

Winter 1895. Grin, 27.

[1896]

January 21, 1896. A. Baboreko, "Neopublikovannye pis'ma I. A. Bunina," *Russkaia literatura*, no. 2 (1963), 178.

March 21, 1896. Baboreko, *I. A. Bunin. Materialy*, 55–57.

October 10, 1896. Baboreko, "Neopublikovannye pis'ma I. A. Bunina" (1959), 232.

October 25, 1896. Baboreko, *I. A. Bunin. Materialy*, 59.

[1897]

March 15, 1897. *Ibid.*, 60.

Circa April 1897. *Ibid.*, 61.

[1898]

Early 1898. Bonami, 24.

January 27, 1898. A. Baboreko, "Bunin i Ertel'," *Russkaia literatura*, no. 4 (1961), 150–51.

[1899]

January 1899. Baboreko, *I. A. Bunin. Materialy*, 73.
April 1899. I. Bunin, "Bez rodu-plemeni," 169, 171, 174.
April 14, 1899. A. Ninov, *M. Gor'kii i Iv. Bunin* (Moscow, 1984), 24–25.
April 26, 1899. Baboreko, *I. A. Bunin. Materialy*, 74.
May 1899. *Ibid.*, 75.
June 18, 1899. Bazhanov, "Rasskaz I. A. Bunina 'Antonovskie iabloki,' " 22.
August 7, 1899. A. Dubovikova, "Perepiski s N. D. Teleshovym, 1897–1947," in Shcherbina, 495.
November 14, 1899. Gazer, "Neopublikovannye pis'ma," 169.

[1900]

Circa 1900. Baboreko, *I. A. Bunin. Materialy*, 80.
Late January 1900. V. Bryusov, *Dnevniki, 1891–1910* (Moscow, 1927), 80.
February 1900. Baboreko, *I. A. Bunin. Materialy*, 78.
March 1900. I. Bunin, "Poet-gumanist. Po povodu piatidesiatiletnego iubeliia literaturnoi deiatel'nosti A. M. Zhemchuzhnikova," *Vestnik vospitaniia*, no. 3 (1900), 77, 84, 86–87, 89–90, 92.
April 18, 1900. A. Baboreko, "Chekhov v perepiske i zapiskakh Bunina," *A. P. Chekhov. Sbornik statei i materialy* (Simferopol', 1962), 22–23.
May 28, 1900. A. Baboreko, "Chekhov i Bunin," *Literaturnoe nasledstvo. Anton Chekhov* (V. Vinogradov, et al., eds.), vol. 68 (Moscow, 1960), 395.
June 1900. I. Bunin, "E. A. Baratynskii," vol. 9, 508, 509, 512, 523.
July 16, 1900. Dubovikova, 514.
Early September 1900. A. Ninov, "Bunin i Gor'kii, 1899–1918 gg.," in V. Shcherbina, et al., eds., *Literaturnoe nasledstvo.*

Ivan Bunin. Kniga vtoraia (Moscow, 1973), 12.
October 1900. I. Bunin, "Antonovskie iabloki," vol. 2, 179–193; as translated by O. Shartse, *Ivan Bunin. Shadowed Paths* (Moscow, 195-), 7–37, with editorial changes.
November 18, 1900. Baboreko, "Iz perepiski," 207–209.
Circa November 25, 1900. B. Mikhailovskii, ed., *Gor'kovskie chteniia, 1958–1959* (Moscow, 1961), 16.

[1901]

January 13, 1901. Baboreko, "Iz perepiski I. A. Bunina," 200.
February 5, 1901. V. Desnitskii, et al., eds., *Literaturnyi arkhiv. M. Gor'kii. Materialy i issledovaniia*, vol. 2 (Moscow, 1936), 388.
February 15, 1901. Grin, 37.
Mid-February 1901. Baboreko, "Chekhov i Bunin," 396.
February 18, 1901. *Ibid.*, 396.
February 22, 1901. A. Baboreko, "Pis'ma I. A. Bunina," *Na rodnoi zemle* (Orel, 1956), 305.
Spring 1901. *Ibid.*
March 8, 1901. Baboreko, "Iz neopublikovannoi perepiski Bunina," *Vremia* (Smolensk, 1962), 93–94.
April 1901. As quoted in I. Bunin, "Novaia doroga," 229; Bez podpisi, "Ivan Bunin. Rasskazy. Tom pervyi," *Russkaia mysl'*, no. 2 (1903), 54; and, Iu. Alexandrovich, *Posle Chekhova. Ocherk molodoi literatury poslednego desiatiletiia, 1898–1908* (Moscow, 1908), 51, 55.
April 1901. I. Bunin, "Tuman," 232–234.
April 30, 1901. Baboreko, "Chekhov i Bunin," 411.
June 1, 1901. K. Muratova, "I. A. Bunin. Pis'ma k V. S. Miroliubovu (1899–1904)," *Literaturnyi arkhiv*, no. 5 (1960), 132.
June 6, 1901. Baboreko, "Chekhov i Bunin," 398–399.
July 1901. I. Bunin, "Tishina," 239.

August 1901. I. Bunin, "Pereval," 7–9.
August 1901. I. Bunin, "Epitafiia," 197–198.
Mid-October 1901. *Arkhiv Gor'kogo. Pis'-ma k K. P. Piatnitskomu*, vol. 4 (Moscow, 1954), 42.
Mid-November 1901. *Ibid.*, 53.

[1902]

January 15, 1902. A. Chekhov, *Sobranie sochinenii v dvednatsati tomakh*, vol. 12 (Moscow, 1964), 428–429.
July 2–3, 1902. *Arkhiv Gor'kogo*, 92.
August 2, 1902. M. Chekhova, *Iz dalekogo proshlogo* (Moscow, 1960), 240.
December 28, 1902. G. Adamovich, "Bunin," *Odinochestvo i svoboda* (New York, 1955), 94–95; and Shcherbina, *Kniga pervaia*, 360.
December 29, 1902. A. Baboreko, "Chekhov i Bunin," 406.

[1903]

Circa 1903. N. Tolstaia-Krandievskaia, "Konets Georga Vendelia. Glava iz vospominanii," *Leningrad*, nos. 15–16 (1945), 9–10.
Circa March–April 1903. Andrei Bely, *Nachalo veka* (Chicago, 1966), 221.
April 27, 1903. '. Gazer, "Pis'ma L. Andreeva i I. Bunina," *Voprosy literatury*, no. 7 (1969), 178.

[1904]

January 1904. I. Bunin, "Zolotoe dno," 283.
Circa July 1904. A. Izmailov, "Rannaia osen'," *Pestrye znamena* (Moscow, 1913), 201.
July 9, 1904. Baboreko, "Chekhov i Bunin," 400–401.
September 1904. Ivan Bunin, "Chekhov," *Polnoe sobranie sochinenii v piati tomakh*, vol. 5 (Moscow, 1915), 292–302; and *Sobranie sochinenii v piati tomakh*, vol. 5 (Moscow, 1956), 265–270.

[1905]

October 18, 1905. I. Bunin, "K moim vospominaniiam," *Novoe russkoe slovo* (May 17, 1953), 4; and Grin, 45–47.
October 19, 1905. Grin, 47–49.
October 20, 1905. *Ibid.*, 49.
October 22, 1905. *Ibid.*, 50–52.

[1906]

May 19, 1906. Baboreko, "Iz neopublikovannoi perepiski Bunina," 99.
June 14, 1906. *Ibid.*, 101–102.
June 25, 1906. *Ibid.*, 102.
August 19, 1906. *Ibid.*
November 4, 1906. Grin, 53–54.

[1907]

February 1907. V. Muromtseva-Bunina, "Beseda s pamiat'iu," *Novyi zhurnal*, no. 59 (1960), 149.
March 1907. Grin, 55.
Circa March 1907. *Arkhiv A. M. Gor'kogo*, vol. 7 (Moscow, 1959), 58.
Circa May 1907. I. Bunin, "Ten' ptitsy," *Sobranie sochinenii*, vol. 3 (Moscow, 1965), 314, 428.
May 4, 1907. Baboreko, "Neopublikovannye pis'ma I. A. Bunina," 212.
May 5, 1907. Baboreko, "Pis'ma I. A. Bunina," *Na rodnoi zemle*, 306.
May 9, 1907. Grin, 62.
May 10, 1907. *Ibid.*, 64.
Mid-May 1907. Baboreko, *I. A. Bunin, Materialy*, 110.
Circa May 17, 1907. *Ibid.*, 111.
June 6, 1907. Grin, 69; and V. Muromtseva-Bunina, "Pervye vpechatleniia o Vasil'evskom," *Novoe russkoe slovo* (August 7, 1955), 2.
Late June 1907. Grin, 69–71.
Late November 1907. *Ibid.*, 75.

[1908]

Circa 1908. A. Kuprin, *Polnoe sobranie sochinenii v deviati tomakh*, vol. 7 (Moscow, 1912), 5–6.

February 1908?, Grin, 76.
November 5, 1908. Baboreko, "Pis'ma I.
A. Bunina," *Na rodnoi zemle*, 306.

[1909]

Circa 1909. V. Kataev, *Sviatoi kolodets.
Trava zabven'ia.* (Moscow, 1969), 138–
140.
March 16, 1909. *Arkhiv A. M. Gor'kogo*,
vol. 9 (Moscow, 1966), 64.
March 26, 1909. Grin, 80.
April 9, 1909. *Ibid.*, 80–81.
May 26, 1909. *Ibid.*, 83–84.
August 26, 1909. Mikhailovskii, 42.
September 22, 1909. Desnitskii, 414.

[1910]

Circa 1910. Kataev, 126–128, 132, 142–
144, 146–147, 152–153.
January 13, 1910. Baboreko, "Neopubli-
kovannye pis'ma I. A. Bunina," 213–
214.
January 17, 1910. Baboreko, "Chekhov i
Bunin," 401.
February 5, 1910. Baboreko, "Iz perepiski
Bunina," 210.
February 11, 1910. Mikhailovskii, 45.
March 1910. I. Bunin, "Derevnia," 12–
14, 17–18, 20, 24–26, 28–35, 37–40,
44, 50–51, 53–54, 57–58, 64–65.
March 2, 1910. Shcherbina, 362.
March 12, 1910. A. Ninov, "K avtobio-
grafii I. Bunina," *Novyi mir*, no. 10,
224.
March 21, 1910. Baboreko, *I. A. Bunin.
Materialy*, 143.
May 16, 1910. I. Bunin, "Interv'iu," vol.
9, 533.
June 10, 1910. Grin, 92.
June 15, 1910. Desnitskii, 415–416.
July 7, 1910. Baboreko, "Iz neopubli-
kovannoi perepiski Bunina," 105.
August 1, 1910. *Ibid.*, 105.
August 3, 1910. Grin, 93.
August 20, 1910. Desnitskii, 419.
October 1910. Bunin, "Derevnia," vol. 3,
65–68, 70–72, 84, 90.

October 13, 1910. Bunin, "Interv'iu,"
vol. 9, 534–535.
November 1910. Bunin, "Derevnia," vol.
3, 92–93, 111–113, 130–132.
November 9, 1910. Mikhailovskii, 49–50.
November 13, 1910. *Ibid.*, 51.
November 26, 1910. Baboreko, *I. A. Bu-
nin. Materialy*, 150–151.
Mid-December 1910. Mikhailovskii, 52–
53.
December 15, 1910. Shcherbina, 364–
366.
December 16, 1910. *Ibid.*, 368.
December 17, 1910. Desnitskii, 422.

[1911]

Circa 1911. Baboreko, "Neopublikovan-
nye pis'ma I. A. Bunina" (1963), 180.
January 20, 1911. Desnitskii, 423–424.
February 1911. E. Koltonovskaia, "Ivan
Bunin. 'Derevnia,'" *Vestnik Evropy*, no.
2 (1911), 396.
February 12, 1911. Grin, 95–96.
February 13, 1911. Baboreko, "Neopub-
likovannye pis'ma I. A. Bunina,"
(1959), 215.
February 13, 1911. Grin, 96–97.
February 15, 1911. *Ibid.*, 97.
February 16, 1911. *Ibid.*, 97–98.
February 18, 1911. Baboreko, "Neopub-
likovannye pis'ma I. A. Bunina," 236.
February 19, 1911. Grin, 98.
February 20, 1911. *Ibid.*, 98–99.
February 20, 1911. Baboreko, "Iz neopub-
likovannoi perepiski Bunina," 102.
February 25, 1911. Grin, 99–100.
February 28, 1911. *Ibid.*, 100.
March 1, 1911. *Ibid.*
March 19, 1911. *Ibid.*, 101–102.
April 20, 1911. Desnitskii, 425–426.
May 10, 1911. N. Gitovich, "I. A. Bu-
nin. Iz nezakonchennoi knigi o Chek-
hove," in *Chekhov*, 640.
May 20, 1911. Grin, 105–106.
June 5, 1911. *Ibid.*, 107.
June 8, 1911. *Ibid.*, 108.
July 3, 1911. *Ibid.*, 109.
Circa mid-July 1911. G. Mezinova, "Na-

Circa mid-July 1911 (*cont'd.*)
rodnoe slovo v kratkikh rasskazakh I.
A. Bunina," *Russkaia rech'*, no. 3
(1987), 103.

July 15, 1911. Grin, 110–111.

July 20, 1911. Gazer, "Pis'ma L. Andreeva i I. Bunina," 179.

July 29, 1911. Grin, 113.

July 30, 1911. *Ibid.*, 114.

August 7, 1911. E. Koltonovskaia, "Intelligent i derevnia (O 'Derevne' Bunina)," *Rech'* (August 7, 1911), 3.

August 12, 1911. Mikhailovskii, 62.

August 14–15, 1911. A. Baboreko, "Tipy i prototipy," *Voprosy literatury*, no. 6 (1960), 254.

September 8, 1911. Shcherbina, 369–370.

September 12, 1911. Ninov, 225.

October 19, 1911. A. Baboreko, "I. A. Bunin na Kapri (Po neopublikovannym materialam)," *V bol'shoi sem'e* (Smolensk, 1960), 239–240.

October 21, 1911. *Ibid.*, 240–241.

October 26, 1911. *Ibid.*, 242.

November 21, 1911. *Arkhiv Gor'kogo*, vol. 13 (Moscow, 1971), 193.

November 25, 1911. Z. Karasik, "A. M. Gor'kii v perepiske sovremennikov," *Voprosy literatury*, no. 3 (1968), 96.

December 1911. A. Grigor'eva, et al., *Mariia Fedorovna Andreeva* (Moscow, 1961), 177.

Circa December 1911. Baboreko, "I. A. Bunin na Kapri," 242–243, 245–246.

December 8, 1911. Karasik, 97.

December 19, 1911. Baboreko, *I. A. Bunin. Materialy*, 168.

Circa December 28, 1911. *Arkhiv A. M. Gor'kogo*, vol. 7, 103.

[1912]

Circa 1912. A. Zolotarev, "Bunin i Gor'kii," *Nash sovremennik*, no. 7 (July 1965), 103–104.

Circa 1912. E. Viktorova, "Gor'kii na Kapri," *O Gor'kom—Sovremenniki. Sbornik vospominanii i statei* (Moscow, 1928), 172–174, 176–177.

January 30, 1912. *Arkhiv A. M. Gor'kogo*, vol. 9, 135.

February 1912. A. Baboreko, "Bunin o Tolstom," *Iasnopolianskii sbornik. Stat'i i materialy. God 1960-i* (Tula, 1960), 131–132; and "I. A. Bunin na Kapri," 246–249.

March 1, 1912. Bunin, "Interv'iu," vol. 9, 542–543.

April 1912. I. Bunin, "Sukhodol," vol. 3, 133–140, 146–150, 158–164, 170–171, 174–176, 178–181, 183–187; as translated by Shartse, 38–154, with editorial changes.

May 14, 1912. E. Koltonovskaia, "Kto my? Ivan Bunin. Sukhodol," *Rech'* (May 14, 1912), 2.

May 19, 1912. Grin 118–119.

May 21, 1912. Baboreko, *I. A. Bunin. Materialy*, 174.

May 25, 1912. N. Korobka, "Literaturnoe obozrenie. 'Dvorianskie gnezda' v izobrazhenii sovremennoi belletristiki," *Zaprosy zhizni*, no. 21 (1912), 1263–1264.

May 28, 1912. Grin, 123–124.

May 30, 1912. Baboreko, "Iunosheshkii roman," 278.

May 31, 1912. Grin, 124.

June 16, 1912. *Ibid.*, 125.

July 6, 1912. Desnitskii, 430–431.

July 23, 1912. Shcherbina, 372.

August 12, 1912. Desnitskii, 433.

September 6, 1912. Shcherbina, 373.

September 9, 1912. A. Baboreko, "V. N. Muromtseva-Bunina," *Pod"em*, no. 3 (1974), 115.

October 22, 1912. Ninov, 226–227.

October 24, 1912. Bunin, "Interv'iu," vol. 9, 540–541.

October 31, 1912. Mikhailovskii, 69–70.

Circa November 1912. Shcherbina, 374–375.

[1913]

Circa 1913. V. Desnitskii, ed., *M. Gor'kii. Materialy i issledovaniia*, vol. 1 (Moscow, 1934), 329.

January 11, 1913. Baboreko, *I. A. Bunin. Materialy*, 178–179.

Circa February 1913. *Ibid.*, 183.

February 28, 1913. Baboreko, "I. A. Bunin na Kapri," 251.

March 1913. P. Grigor'ev, "Ivan Bunin. Sukhodol," *Sovremennik*, no. 3 (1913), 342–343.

March 1, 1913. Baboreko, *I. A. Bunin. Materialy*, 183–184.

March 10, 1913. I. Bunin, "Kop'e gospodne," vol. 4 (Moscow, 1965), 121.

March 27, 1913. Shcherbina, *Kniga vtoraia* (Moscow, 1973), 42.

April 14, 1913. Desnitskii, vol. 2, 438.

May 4, 1913. I. Bunin, "Interv'iu," vol. 9, 545–546.

May 14, 1913. Mikhailovskii, 72–73.

May 18, 1913. Baboreko, "Pis'ma I. A. Bunina," 308.

July 26, 1913. Grin, 134.

October 8, 1913. Shcherbina, *Kniga pervaia*, 316–320.

October 8, 1913. "Moskovskaia khronika. Intsident na bankete," *Rech'*, no. 275 (October 8, 1913), 5.

October 13, 1913. "Prav li Bunin? Nasha anketa," *Golos Moskvy*, October 13, 1913, 2.

November 17, 1913. Mikhailovskii, 75.

[1914]

June 1914. I. Bunin, *Polnoe sobranie sochinenii*, vol. 5 (1915), 303–313; and *Sobranie sochinenii*, vol. 5 (1956), 270–281.

June 19, 1914. Grin, 137.

Circa July 1914. Kataev, 157–158.

July 2, 1914. Ninov, 228–230.

July 3, 1914. Baboreko, *I. A. Bunin. Materialy*, 200.

July 11, 1914. Grin, 138.

Circa Fall 1914. A Zolotarev, "Bunin i Gor'kii," *Nash sovremennik*, no. 7 (July 1965), 105.

September 11, 1914. Baboreko, 200–201.

October 15, 1914. *Ibid.*, 201.

Mid-November 1914. Shcherbina, *Kniga vtoraia*, 44.

December 15, 1914. Gazer, "Pis'ma L. Andreeva i I. Bunina," 192.

Late December 1914. K. Chukovskii, "Rannii Bunin," *Voprosy literatury*, no. 5 (1968), 94.

[1915]

January 1, 1915. Grin, 141.

February 22, 1915. *Ibid.*, 143.

March 7, 1915? A. Baboreko, "Novye izdaniia sochinenii Bunina," *Voprosy literatury*, no. 2 (1958), 215.

March 15, 1915. Desnitskii, 447.

March 29, 1915. Grin, 144.

April 10, 1915. I Bunin, "Iz pis'ma k S. A. Vengerov," in I. Bunin, *Sobranie sochinenii I. A. Bunin v odinadtsati tomakh*, vol. 1 (Paris, 1934), 13–23; and "Avtobiograficheskaia zametka," vol. 9 (1965), 253–266.

April 27, 1915. Baboreko, *I. A. Bunin. Materialy*, 201.

June 28, 1915. Desnitskii, 449.

July 1, 1915. Grin, 145.

August 7, 1915. *Ibid.*, 146.

August 21, 1915. *Ibid.*, 147.

September 12, 1915. A. Baboreko, "I. A. Bunin. Pis'ma D. L. Tal'nikovu," *Russkaia literatura*, no. 1 (1974), 175.

September 15, 1915. Grin, 147–148.

October 10, 1915. Desnitskii, 449.

[1916]

Circa 1916. I. Bunin, "Sny Changa," *Sobranie sochinenii*, vol. 4 (Moscow, 1965), 370–371, 377.

Circa 1916. Baboreko, *I. A. Bunin. Materialy*, 208.

Circa 1916. *Ibid.*, 211.

Circa 1916. V. Rozhdestvenskii, "V Petrograde s A. M. Gor'kogo," *M. Gor'kii v vospominaniiakh sovremennikov* (Moscow, 1955), 334.

February 23, 1916. Grin, 149.

March 7, 1916. Baboreko, 206.
Circa mid-March 1916. Ibid., 206.
March 17, 1916. Grin, 149.
March 21, 1916. Ibid., 150.
March 22, 1916. Ibid., 150–151.
March 24, 1916. Ibid., 152.
March 25, 1916. Ibid., 152–153.
March 27, 1916. Ibid., 153.
March 30, 1916. Ibid., 153–154.
April 1916. K. Paustovsky, Sobranie so-
chinenii v vos'mi tomakh, vol. 3 (Moscow,
1967), 465–468.
April 1, 1916. Grin, 154.
April 2, 1916. Ibid., 154.
April 8, 1916. Ibid., 155.
April 14, 1916. Shcherbina, Kniga pervaia,
378–380.
April 26, 1916. Bunin, "Interv'iu," vol.
9, 547–548.
Circa May 1916. Baboreko, 206–207.
May 23, 1916. Grin, 156.
August 29, 1916. Mikhailovskii, 88.
October 27, 1916, Grin, 156–157.

[1917]

January 1917. I. Bunin, "Samo saboi ra-
zumeetsia," Novaia zhizn', no. 1 (1917),
74.
February 1917. Mikhailovskii, 90.
February 23, 1917. Ibid., 91.
May 27, 1917. Grin, 160–161.
June 11, 1917. Ibid., 161–162.
July 1917. I. Bunin, "Petlistye ushi,"
386–391, 393–394, 397.
July 27, 1917. Grin, 163–164.
August 3, 1917. N. Smirnov-Sokol'skii,
"Poslednaia nakhodka," Novyi mir, no.
10 (1956), 216.
August 4, 1917. Ibid., 218.
August 10, 1917. Desnitskii, 457–458.
August 11, 1917. Smirnov-Sokol'skii,
218.
August 13, 1917. Ibid., 219.
August 20, 1917. Ibid., 218.
August 22, 1917. Ibid., 217, 218.
August 23, 1917. Ibid., 217.
August 25, 1917. Ibid.
September 16, 1917. Ibid.
September 17, 1917. Ibid.

October 6, 1917. Ibid., 218.
October 8, 1917. Ibid., 215, 217.
October 13, 1917. Ibid., 217, 220.
October 16, 1917. Grin, 167.
October 17, 1917. Smirnov-Sokol'skii,
217.
October 20, 1917. Ibid., 218, 219.
October 21, 1917. Ibid., 218.
October 23, 1917. Grin, 168.
October 23, 1917. A. Baboreko, I. A.
Bunin. Materialy dlia biografii (Moscow,
1983), 248.
November 4, 1917. Ibid., 250.
November 21, 1917. Ibid.
Late November 1917. Grin, 168.
December 28, 1917. Shcherbina, Kniga
vtoraia, 57.

[1918]

January 14, 1918. I. Bunin, Okaiannye dni
(London, Canada, 1982), 5.
February 18, 1918. Ibid., 6.
February 21, 1918. Ibid., 12–13.
February 23, 1918. Ibid., 14–16.
February 27, 1918. Ibid., 16–17.
February 28, 1918. Ibid., 17–18.
March 5, 1918. Ibid., 24–26.
March 7, 1918. Ibid., 26–27.
March 9, 1918. Ibid., 29.
March 10, 1918. Ibid., 30–31.
March 12, 1918. Ibid., 31.
March 14, 1918. Ibid., 32–33.
March 15, 1918. Ibid., 34–35.
March 22, 1918. Ibid., 37–38.
March 23, 1918. Ibid., 38–39.
March 24, 1918. Ibid., 39.
March 28, 1918. Ibid., 42.
April 4, 1918. Ibid.
April 5, 1918. Ibid., 43.
April 6, 1918. Ibid., 44–45.
May 19, 1918. Baboreko, 251.
May 23, 1918. Grin, 169–171.
May 26, 1918. Ibid., 173.
Circa Summer 1918. Kataev, 153–161,
164–168, 170–180.
June 5, 1918. Grin, 178.
July 18, 1918. Ibid., 180.
July 21, 1918. Ibid., 180–181.
July 25, 1918. Ibid., 181.

July 27, 1918. *Ibid.*, 183.

August 18, 1918. Shcherbina, *Kniga pervaia*, 622.

August 24, 1918. Grin, 185–186.

August 31, 1918. *Ibid.*, 187.

September 7, 1918. *Ibid.*, 188.

September 14, 1918. *Ibid.*, 189.

September 20, 1918. *Ibid.*, 190.

September 20, 1918. Baboreko, 253.

October 7, 1918. Grin, 190.

October 20, 1918. *Ibid.*, 191.

October 28, 1918. *Ibid.*, 192.

Late Autumn 1918. Kataev, 182–185, 187–191, 193, 195–200, 203–206.

November 24, 1918. Grin, 194.

December 6, 1918. *Ibid.*, 197.

December 13, 1918. *Ibid.*, 198.

December 17, 1918. *Ibid.*, 199–200.

December 19, 1918. *Ibid.*, 200–201.

December 20, 1918. *Ibid.*, 201.

December 24, 1918. *Ibid.*

[1919]

January 3, 1919. *Ibid.*, 202.

January 12, 1919. *Ibid.*, 205.

January 15, 1919. *Ibid.*, 206.

January 17, 1919. *Ibid.*

January 28, 1919. *Ibid.*, 207.

February 13, 1919. *Ibid.*, 208.

February 20, 1919. *Ibid.*

February 26, 1919. *Ibid.*, 208–209.

Circa March 1919. N. Kucherovskii, *I. Bunin i ego proza (1887–1917)* (Tula, 1980), 266.

Circa March 1919. Paustovsky, 706.

Spring 1919. Kataev, 206–214.

March 8, 1919. Grin 212.

March 9, 1919. *Ibid.*, 213–214.

March 12, 1919. *Ibid.*, 215.

March 13, 1919. *Ibid.*

March 18, 1919. *Ibid.*, 215–216.

March 30, 1919. *Ibid.*, 219.

April 1, 1919. *Ibid.*, 219–220.

April 3, 1919. *Ibid.*, 220–221.

April 5, 1919. *Ibid.*, 221–224.

April 6, 1919. *Ibid.*, 224.

April 7, 1919. *Ibid.*, 224–226.

April 8, 1919. *Ibid.*, 226.

April 10, 1919. *Ibid.*, 228.

April 12, 1919. *Ibid.*, 229–230.

April 13, 1919. *Ibid.*, 231.

April 14, 1919. *Ibid.*, 231–232.

April 15, 1919. *Ibid.*, 232–233.

April 18, 1919. *Ibid.*, 233–235.

April 21, 1919. *Ibid.*, 235–238.

April 23, 1919. *Ibid.*, 238–239.

April 24, 1919. *Ibid.*, 239.

April 25, 1919. *Ibid.*, 240–241.

April 25, 1919. Bunin, 47–50.

April 29, 1919. *Ibid.*, 52–54.

April 29, 1919. Grin, 242.

April 30, 1919. Bunin, 55–58.

May 1, 1919. Grin, 243–245.

May 2, 1919. Bunin, 58–62.

May 2, 1919. Grin, 245.

May 3, 1919. Bunin, 63–70.

May 4, 1919. *Ibid.*, 71–74.

May 5, 1919. *Ibid.*, 75–80.

May 6, 1919. *Ibid.*, 80–90.

May 6, 1919. Grin, 246–247.

May 7, 1919. Bunin, 91, 94–98.

May 8, 1919. *Ibid.*, 99–101, 104–106.

May 8, 1919. Grin, 247.

May 9, 1919. Bunin, 106–107.

May 9, 1919. Grin, 248–249.

May 10, 1919. *Ibid.*, 249.

May 12, 1919. *Ibid.*, 250.

May 13, 1919. Bunin, 112.

May 14, 1919. *Ibid.*

May 15, 1919. *Ibid.*, 112–114.

May 16, 1919. *Ibid.*, 114.

May 18, 1919. *Ibid.*, 115–116, 118–122.

May 19, 1919. *Ibid.*, 124–125.

May 20, 1919. Grin, 253.

May 22, 1919. Bunin, 126–130.

May 23, 1919. *Ibid.*, 130–131.

May 23, 1919. Grin, 255.

May 24, 1919. Bunin, 131.

May 25, 1919. *Ibid.*, 133.

May 25, 1919. Grin, 255–256.

May 27, 1919. Bunin, 134.

May 28, 1919. *Ibid.*, 138.

May 28, 1919. Grin, 256–257.

May 29, 1919. Bunin, 139–140.

May 31, 1919. Grin, 258.

June 5, 1919. Baboreko, 261.

June 6, 1919. Bunin, 143–144.

June 8, 1919. *Ibid.*, 144–145.

June 9, 1919. *Ibid.*, 145–146.

June 15, 1919. *Ibid.*, 149.
June 22, 1919. *Ibid.*, 152–153.
June 23, 1919. *Ibid.*, 159–162.
June 24, 1919. *Ibid.*, 170–176.
June 24, 1919. Grin, 268.
June 25, 1919. *Ibid.*, 270.
June 26, 1919. Bunin, 176–177.
June 26, 1919. Grin, 270.
June 30, 1919. Bunin, 178–179.
July 1, 1919. *Ibid.*, 179.
July 1, 1919. Grin, 272.
July 2, 1919. Bunin, 179.
July 3, 1919. *Ibid.*, 182–183.
July 3, 1919. Grin, 272–273.
July 10, 1919. *Ibid.*, 274–275.
July 12, 1919. *Ibid.*, 275.
July 13, 1919. *Ibid.*, 275–278.
July 19, 1919. *Ibid.*, 280.
July 20, 1919. *Ibid.*, Grin, 282–283.
Circa August 1919. Kataev, 214–218.
August 2, 1919. Grin, 288–289.
August 3, 1919. *Ibid.*, 289.
August 4, 1919. *Ibid.*, 291.
August 7, 1919. *Ibid.*, 294.
August 8, 1919. *Ibid.*, 295.
August 9, 1919. *Ibid.*, 296.
August 17, 1919. *Ibid.*, 303–304.
August 19, 1919. *Ibid.*, 305.
August 22, 1919. *Ibid.*
August 24, 1919. *Ibid.*, 307.
August 25, 1919. *Ibid.*
August 30, 1919. *Ibid.*, 309–310.
August 31, 1919. *Ibid.*, 310.
September 6, 1919. *Ibid.*, 310–311.
September 18, 1919. *Ibid.*, 313–314.

September 20, 1919. *Ibid.*, 314–315.
September 21, 1919. *Ibid.*, 315.
October 7, 1919. *Ibid.*, 316.
October 20, 1919. *Ibid.*, 318.
November 3, 1919. B. Lipin, "Bunin v 'Iuzhnom slove'," *Literator*, no. 32 (August 1991), 6.
November 7, 1919. *Ibid.*, 6–7.
November 10, 1919. Grin, 319.
November 13, 1919. *Ibid.*
November 21, 1919. Lipin, 7.
December 15, 1919. Grin, 321.
December 20, 1919. *Ibid.*, 322.
December 24, 1919. *Ibid.*, 323.
December 26, 1919. *Ibid.*, 324–325.
December 31, 1919. *Ibid.*, 327.

[1920]

January 5, 1920. *Ibid.*, 328–329.
January 13, 1920. *Ibid.*, 331.
January 14, 1920. *Ibid.*
January 16, 1920. *Ibid.*, 332.
January 19, 1920. *Ibid.*, 333.
January 20, 1920. *Ibid.*
January 31, 1920. *Ibid.*, 335.
February 2, 1920. *Ibid.*, 336.
February 3, 1920. *Ibid.*, 336–338.
February 4, 1920. *Ibid.*, 338–339.
February 5, 1920. *Ibid.*, 339.
February 6, 1920. *Ibid.*, 340–342.
February 7, 1920. *Ibid.*, 342–344.
February 8, 1920. *Ibid.*, 344.
February 9, 1920. *Ibid.*, 344–345.

INDEX

81, excerpt 62–66; "The Archistrategus," 257; biblical images in, 8, "The Brothers," ix, 4; "The Buffoons," 258; "Chang's Dream," 4, 27, 199, 273, 275–276, excerpt 223–224; "The Cheerful Stead," 211; "The Crime," 188; critical articles, 39–40, 50, 59, 60–61, 236; "The Crossing," 27, excerpt 79–81; "The Desert of the Devil," 182; *Dry Valley*, ix, 2, 4, 8, 11, 14, 21, 27, 141, 151, 182, excerpt 161–176; reviews, 176, 178, 185–186, 221; early literary pursuits, 3; "The Epitaph," excerpt 81; "The Execution," 258; *Falling Leaves*, 72–73; "The Fog," 73, excerpt 77–78; *The Gentleman from San Francisco*, ix, 4, 199, 212; "The Golden Bottom," excerpt 85; "The Great Narcotic," 347–348; "The Horde," 258; image of train in his work, 73; "In the Field," 211; international pieces, ix; "Judea," 182; Last Will and Testament, vii; *The Liberation of Tolstoy*, 16; "The Lord's Spear," 13, 187; "The New Road," excerpt 77; "Nooselike Ears," 4, 9, 236, 239, 286, excerpt 239–242; "On the Farm," 14, 51; "Over the Grave of Nadson," 3; "The Pines," 82; "The Rose of Jericho," 16; "The Shadow of a Bird," 10, 106, 182; *Shadowed Paths*, ix; "Silence," excerpt 79; "The Six-Winged," 258; speeches, 189–190; "To the Edge of the World," 3, 52, 219; translations, 219; of Byron, 3; of *Hiawatha*, 73, 220; of Tennyson, 3; *Under the Open Sky*, 3; *The Village*, 4, 7, 8, 11, 14, 27, 101–102, 133, 141, 182, 238, 337, excerpt 118–126, 129–130, 131–133; reviews, 143–144, 147, 150–151, 221; "A Village Sketch," 218; "Without Kith or Kin," 56
Bunin, Nikolai, 3, 6, 73
Bunina, Marina Alexeevna (Masha), 109
Bunina, Nadya, 215
Bunin, Yuly Alexeevich, 2–3, 5, 38, 209, 217, 218, 268; letters from Bunin,

14, 40–48, 51, 55–58, 60, 66, 76, 117; letters from Muromtseva-Bunina, 329; miscellaneous letters to friends, 103–104
Bunina, Anna Petrovna, 182
Bunina, Lyudmilla Alexandrovna, 2, 6, 109, 214
Bunins (family), 1, 2, 107–108, 213
Bunkovsky, Simeon, 213
Bykov, Pyotr, letters from Chekhova, 148

"Cabaret" period, 234
Capri, 101, 126, 157, 160, 185
"The Carriage" (Gogol), 285
Caruso, Enrico, 155
Cathedral of the Annunciation (Russia), 211–212
Censorship, 9
Cervantes Saavedra, Miguel de, 238
Ceylon, Colombo, 147, 199
Chaliapin, Fyodor, 155, 185, 210, 353
"Chang's Dream" (Bunin), 4, 27, 273, 275–276; excerpts, 223–224
Chekhov, Anton Pavlovich, 1, 4, 21, 57, 83, 153, 187; "The Archbishop," 153; "An Attack of Nerves," 205; "The Bishop," 209; "A Boring Story," 209; Bunin's impressions of, 86–91, 117, 199, 200–208, 209; *The Cherry Orchard*, 1, 34, 74, 87, 202; "Cold Blood," 205; and the critics, 204–205; death of, 6, 73, 87, 88; description of his house, 92, 207; *The Duel*, 35; "Gloomy People," 205; "Gusev," 75; "Happiness," 209; on immortality, 208; "In the Ravine," 153, 206; letters from Bunin, 42, 75, 78; letters to Bunin, 81–82; on love, 207; marriage of, 78; "The Murder," 209; as older brother to Bunin, 24; "The Peasants," 201; quote from Bunin, 86; *The Seagull*, 35; sense of details, 204; "The Student," 89–90, 209; *The Three Sisters*, 73, 76; "Three Years," 204; *Uncle Vanya*, 35, 76, 202; "Ward No. 6," 35, 209
Chekhova, Maria Pavlovna, 60, 73, 75, 353; letters from Bunin, 76, 82, 86, 103, 146–147; letters to Bunin, 76, 78; letters to Bykov, 148

A NOTE ON THE EDITOR

Thomas Gaiton Marullo is associate professor of Russian and Russian Literature at the University of Notre Dame. He was born in Brooklyn, New York, and grew up on Long Island. He received a bachelor's degree from the College of the Holy Cross, and M.A. and Ph.D. degrees from Cornell University, and has held fellowships from the Lilly Endowment and the National Endowment for the Humanities. Mr. Marullo's articles on Russian literature, and especially on Ivan Bunin, have appeared in a variety of books and journals. He is currently at work on a critical study of Bunin and on a portrait of Bunin in exile, 1920–1953.